Operating Systems
ADVANCED CONCEPTS

Operating Systems

ADVANCED CONCEPTS

Mamoru Maekawa
University of Tokyo

Arthur E. Oldehoeft
Iowa State University

Rodney R. Oldehoeft
Colorado State University

THE BENJAMIN/CUMMINGS PUBLISHING COMPANY, INC.

Menlo Park, California ● Reading, Massachusetts
Don Mills, Ontario ● Wokingham, U.K. ● Amsterdam
Sydney ● Singapore ● Tokyo ● Madrid ● Bogota
Santiago ● San Juan

Sponsoring Editor: Alan Apt
Production Editors: Laura Kenney, Julie Kranhold
Copyeditor: Carol Dondrea
Illustrator: Lisa Torri
Cover Designer: John Edeen
Compositor: Graphic Typesetting Service

The basic text of this book was designed using the Modular Design System, as developed by Wendy Earl and Design Office Bruce Kortebein.

The programs presented in this book have been included for their instructional value. They have been tested with care but are not guaranteed for any particular purpose. The publisher does not offer any warranties or representations, nor does it accept any liabilities with respect to the programs.

Library of Congress Cataloging-in-Publication Data

Maekawa, M. (Mamoru), 1942-
  Operating systems.

  Includes bibliographies and index.
  1. Operating systems (Computers) I. Oldehoeft, Arthur E. II. Oldehoeft, Rodney R. III. Title.
QA76.76.063M335 1987   005.4′3   86-28419
ISBN 0-8053-7121-4

BCDEFGHIJ-DO-8 987

The Benjamin/Cummings Publishing Company, Inc.
2727 Sand Hill Road
Menlo Park, CA 94025

Preface

The study of computer operating systems has progressed from learning an ad hoc collection of folk wisdom about how systems work to examining a coherent set of topics about which substantial theoretical and practical knowledge has been developed. We have been teaching modern operating systems to undergraduates and graduate students for 10 to 15 years at several universities, and believe that introductory material for the undergraduate student is well agreed upon and adequately exposited in several modern texts.

Unfortunately, at the graduate-student or professional level, no such agreement exists. Worse, to teach advanced material properly we have been forced to rely directly on the current literature. Although reference to the contemporary work of researchers and practitioners is useful at this level, students (and instructors as well) have felt the lack of a centralized source of information upon which to rely for an overall framework and source of direction.

The purpose of this book is to provide that needed resource. We have identified eight major subjects in the design and analysis of modern operating systems and have brought together our work on each topic to give the reader a modern course in the advanced topics of importance. The synthesis of many points of view gives the reader an accurate picture of the current state of each topic. The subjects are enduring ones that are not dependent on a particular vendor's system or on current technology; this material should be useful in design and analysis of future systems as well.

Operating Systems: Advanced Concepts continues to rely on original sources for two reasons. First, to keep the book to a manageable size, some subjects are covered completely at a fundamental level with references to generalizations and special cases that the interested reader may pursue. Second, we believe that at this level the serious student of operating systems must be cognizant of the contemporary literature; we hope this approach will help train the reader in professional reading habits if they are not already established. To make this easy, we have often chosen to refer to the most accessible items of literature (major journal or conference articles) instead of the earliest sources (often internal technical reports). In addition to cited references, we provide an additional bibliography of literature for each topic.

Our appreciation is due to Misses Noriko Shiogama and Nahoko Murao, who entered the first handwritten version of the manuscript. The following reviewers have carefully read and improved the book through several drafts: Imtiaz Ahmad, University of Windsor; Rob Cubert, Sacramento State University; D. M. Etter, University of New Mexico; William Franta, University of Minnesota; Dale Grit, Colorado State University; Teofilo Gonzales, University of Texas at Dallas; Evan Ivie,

Brigham Young University; Roger King, University of Colorado; Marek Rusinkiewicz, University of Houston; and Nish Thakor, Northwestern University. Many students in our operating classes have been exposed to this material and have selflessly pointed out areas for clarification and improvement. All of these people have made this an enjoyable project and, we hope, a valuable product. Finally, we would like to acknowledge our families and friends who have provided support and encouragement over the course of the project.

Mamoru Maekawa
Arthur E. Oldehoeft
Rodney R. Oldehoeft

Acknowledgments

Figure 3.12 is reprinted from *Ada for Experienced Programmers* by A. Nico Habermann and Dwane E. Perry (Addison-Wesley, 1983).

Figures 6.21 and 6.22 and Tables 6.3 and 6.4 are reprinted from Mamoru Maekawa, "A N Algorithm for Mutual Exclusion in Decentralized Systems," in *ACM Transactions on Computer Systems* 3 (May 1985). Reprinted by permission of the Association for Computing Machinery, Inc.

Figure 8.24 is reprinted from Voydock and Kent, "Security Mechanisms in High-Level Network Protocols," in *Computing Surveys* 15 (1983). Reprinted by permission of the Association for Computing Machinery, Inc.

Contents

7 *Distributed Concurrency Control, Deadlock, and Recovery*   *239*

Overview   **1**

1.1   Introduction

The purpose of this book is to serve as a resource in the advanced study of modern computer operating systems. The book can be used in at least three ways. First, it can serve as a textbook in a formal course in advanced operating systems for students who have mastered fundamental material in an undergraduate course. We include here advanced-level material on familiar topics (synchronization, deadlock, virtual memory), as well as material that is not generally covered at an elementary level (security, distributed systems and control, modeling and analysis). There is enough material for a two-quarter sequence, and more than enough for a single semester. There are numerous questions and problems. The former will help students review the chapter; the latter should help them delve more deeply into the material of each chapter. Each chapter also includes a list of important terms to help ensure subject mastery.

Second, the book is useful as an organized course for professionals or for self-study. The chapters are organized so that a brief but adequate review precedes material at an advanced level. This will allow the professional whose background is strong but incomplete to quickly "come up to speed" on a particular subject. Where appropriate, references are given to background material that may be valuable for the reader who is working independently.

Third, the book is a guide to current research and methodology for operating system designers. The individual chapters are independent of each other and well suited for the reader who wants to study a particular subject in depth.

The chapters each center on a major topic in the advanced study of operating systems. The following briefly describes the contents of each chapter. The references in this chapter are the basis on which most significant topics in this book are based.

1.2   Chapter 2: Process Synchronization

In this chapter we cover methods for process management that are more advanced than those found in an introductory course. After a brief review of processes and their synchronization via elementary methods, we describe a model that is valuable for analyzing sets of concurrent processes [Bernstein, 1966]. With this model we can demonstrate safe, deterministic execution while ensuring the maximum potential for parallel processing. Advanced methods of process synchronization are surveyed and exemplified, using the solutions to classical problems. These include sequencers and eventcounts [Reed and Kanodia, 1979] and tagged messages [Maekawa, 1980]. We discuss the rationale for and the implementation of disjunctions and conjunctions of general semaphores, along with their negation. We show how processes may cooperate without mutual exclusion [Lamport, 1977]. Discussion follows on the design issues for interprocess communication. A comprehensive summary of mechanisms concludes the chapter.

Each of the mechanisms is meant for use by an operating system designer or implementor. Their low level and unstructured nature precludes their use by programmers with conventional applications.

1.3   Chapter 3: Language Mechanism for Concurrency

This chapter complements the previous one by describing modern, high-level techniques for parallel programming that offer more safety and structure than low-level operations. We introduce the object model and its incarnation in the monitor [Hoare, 1974]. We present a framework within which mechanisms of this kind can be effectively analyzed [Bloom, 1979]. Next the major approaches to concurrent programming (in addition to monitors) are described, and examples are given of programming languages that use them. These major approaches include serializers [Hewitt and Atkinson, 1979], path expressions [Campbell and Habermann, 1974; Andler, 1979], and communicating sequential processes [Hoare, 1978]. This sets the stage for the final section in which the concurrent programming mechanisms of Ada[†] [U.S. Department of Defense, 1983] are described, exemplified, and analyzed.

1.4   Chapter 4: Deadlock

Deadlock is a serious problem, one that needs to be overcome in the design of multiprogramming and multiprocessing operating systems. Our presentation of the problem and its solutions is based on Holt [1972]. We first define and exemplify deadlock, distinguish between reusable and consumable resources, and identify three policies for handling deadlock: detection and recovery, prevention, and avoidance. In this chapter we use Holt's abstract model, which retains precisely the essential nature of processes and resources for us to discuss the subject accurately. The model is defined in terms of graph theory; the necessary definitions and results are included here. This model allows us to characterize the necessary and sufficient conditions for deadlock, and to show why this is a serious problem: No useful methods for dealing with deadlock are possible in the most general case. Following that, a number of special cases with satisfactory solutions are explained. These include restricting

---

[†]Ada is a trademark of the U. S. Government, Ada Joint Program Office.

processes to requesting single units, working with consumable resources only, and dealing just with reusable resources. In this chapter the operating system designer will find a variety of methods from which to select.

1.5   Chapter 5: Virtual Memory

We begin by reviewing introductory material that may be familiar to some readers. The various policy categories (and their alternatives) that characterize a virtual memory management system are explored. We characterize a class of paged memory replacement policies called stack algorithms [Mattson, et al., 1970] with the property that one can determine the cost of executing the algorithm for a program in all memory sizes of interest very inexpensively. In addition, an analyst can determine the reduced cost of executing in a larger memory without interpretively executing the program to analyze each memory reference. One of the most important topics in the area, working sets [Denning, 1968; Denning, 1970], are covered next. Using working sets allows a link between memory management and process management that prevents thrashing, an overcommitment of memory. Implementation techniques are included. Two models of virtual memory behavior are introduced. We include recent research [Carr, 1984] that demonstrates that simple global memory management policies can be equipped with feedback mechanisms to prevent thrashing and maximize system throughput, as well as more complex local policies. Finally, we introduce the idea of restructuring programs to improve their performance in virtual memory systems [Johnson, 1975].

1.6   Chapter 6: Distributed Systems

In a distributed system (or network), processors do not share a common memory and, as a consequence, they must communicate by means of passing messages. Two basic types of networks are the long-haul network and the local area network (LAN) and, for both, a set of protocols is required to govern the manner in which communication is allowed to take place. At lower levels, protocols are required to effect such functions as efficient routing of messages, congestion control, sender–receiver synchronization, and recovery from transmission errors or lost messages. Some of these functions are also required in an LAN. At the higher level, in both long-haul and local area networks, protocols are required to ensure effective coordination of processes as they cooperate to achieve a common objective or compete to access a resource. The overall framework introduced in this chapter is the seven-layer ISO Reference Model of Open Systems Interconnection. Much of the material is derived from numerous reports by international standards committees and general papers [Myers, 1982; Tanenbaum, 1981; Zimmermann, 1980]. The first half of the chapter deals with the bottom five layers. Since there is a major overlap of this material with that found in conventional textbooks on computer networks, this part of the chapter serves only to summarize the vast amount of information that is available. The last part of the chapter deals with distributed process management at a higher level. A reliable underlying message-passing system is assumed to exist. In this discussion, a formal characterization of a distributed algorithm is presented first [Maekawa, 1986]. Since a temporal ordering of events is natural in our concept of computer systems, a system of distributed clocks is introduced [Lamport, 1978]. Finally, several algorithms are presented for mutual exclusion in a distributed environment [Lamport, 1978; Ricart, 1981; Maekawa, 1986]. These algorithms are classified according to their degree of distribution, and a comparative analysis of their performance is made.

1.7   Chapter 7: Distributed Concurrency Control, Deadlock, and Recovery

This chapter builds on the concepts introduced in Chapters 2, 3, 4, and 6. The first major issue is concerned with maintaining consistency in a distributed database. The fundamental notions of a transaction and consistency are introduced [Eswaren, et al., 1976] and a formal model is presented in order to establish a theoretical framework in which to study the problem [Traiger, et al., 1982]. This theoretical development shows how individual actions of concurrent transactions must be sequenced at each site in order to ensure consistency. The second major problem deals with deadlock detection. The discussion uses the theoretical model of Chapter 4. Several approaches are presented with the focus of attention placed on two algorithms from Maekawa [1983]: periodic deadlock detection and continuous deadlock detection. To further increase the potential for concurrency, an elaborate system of locks and a locking protocol is described [Gray, 1978]. The third major issue deals with recovery of a previous consistent state in the event of transaction or system failure. The recovery schemes are based on the concept of a two-phase commit protocol [Gray, 1978; Kohler, 1981]. Finally, the use of time stamps is presented as an alternative to the use of locks in synchronizing the concurrent transactions. Several variations are presented [Bernstein and Goodman, 1981].

1.8   Chapter 8: Computer Security

This chapter surveys common approaches to implementing computer security. General resources for many of these ideas can be found in Denning and Denning [1981] and Landwehr [1981]. We begin by defining the notions of interface security and internal security. Three general techniques are presented to enforce internal security: access control, information flow control, and encryption. For the first technique, a formal model of access control [Lampson, 1971; Graham and Denning, 1972] is presented to encompass the diverse approaches found in real operating systems. In addition, several implementations are discussed. Access control is based on the concept of trust: If some subject is given access rights to an object, then the subject is trusted not to abuse these rights by leaking the information to other subjects. Some of these leakage problems can be solved by the second technique, which places controls on the flow of information rather than on the right to access information. In order to precisely define the concept of legitimate information flow, this model requires the ability to classify information and to form a mathematical lattice of information classes. Two well-known approaches are described: flow-secure access control [Bell and LaPadula, 1973], which uses flow constraints to implement access control, and pure information flow control [Denning, 1976; Denning, 1977], which is considered an independent adjunct to access control. The third technique, encryption, provides an approach for securing physical channels against illegal wiretaps and for further securing information by rendering it unintelligible to the would-be reader. Two common approaches, conventional cryptosystems and public-key cryptosystems, are presented [Diffie and Hellman, 1979; Popek and Kline, 1979]. The Data Encryption Standard [NBS, 1977] and the RSA algorithm [Rivest, et al., 1978] are presented as the major examples of a conventional cryptosystem and a public-key cryptosystem, respectively. Finally, the use of passwords is discussed as a technique to implement interface security.

1.9   Chapter 9: Queuing Models of Computer Systems

The reader is introduced to mathematical tools that can be valuable in performance analysis and prediction. A careful analysis of the simplest single-queue model is presented to give an understanding of the statistical processes at work. Generalizations and variations of the single-queue model are also given. These include multiple processors, infinite number of processors (no delay before processing), and general probability distributions for describing service times.

An important class of networks of queues is called open networks because jobs arrive from and exit to the outside. Under the proper assumptions, a remarkably simple result [from Jackson, 1957] allows for the analysis of these networks. Networks without exogenous arrivals and departures are called closed networks; they model pure time-sharing systems. The first method of solution, the normalization constant method, relies on an important algorithm first given in Buzen [1972]. Analysis of closed networks is possible with reasonable computational effort. Important generalizations of this approach are found in Baskett, et al. [1975]. Another method that is applicable to closed networks is mean value analysis [Reiser and Lavenberg, 1980]; the need for Buzen's algorithm is eliminated here. Mean value analysis has been generalized to be as applicable as the normalization constant method. Both approaches have complementary advantages and disadvantages.

Finally, a much less mathematical approach that allows quick analysis of observable systems is included [Denning and Buzen, 1978]. Operational analysis does not rely on the statistical assumptions of classical methods, which are often violated in real systems.

References

Andler, S. (1979). "Predicate path expressions." *Sixth Annual ACM Symposium on Principles of Programming Languages,* San Antonio, TX., pp. 226–236.

Baskett, F.; K. Chandy; et al. (April 1975). "Open, closed, and mixed networks of queues with different classes of customers." *Journal of the ACM* 22, 2, pp. 248–260.

Bell, D. E., and L. J. LaPadula. (November 1973). "Secure computer systems: mathematical foundations." *ESD-TR-278* 1, ESD/AFSC, Hanscomm AFB, Bedford, MA.

Bernstein, A. J. (October 1966). "Analysis of programs for parallel processing." *IEEE Transactions on Computers* EC-15, 5, pp. 757–762.

Bernstein, P. A., and N. Goodman. (June 1981). "Concurrency control in distributed database systems." *ACM Computing Surveys* 13, 2, pp. 185–221.

Bloom, T. (1979). "Evaluating synchronization mechanisms." *Proceedings of the Eighth ACM Symposium on Operating System Principles,* pp. 24–31.

Buzen, J. (September 1972). "Computational algorithms for closed queueing networks with exponential servers." *Communications of the ACM* 16, 9, pp. 527–531.

Campbell, R. H., and A. N. Habermann. (1974). "The specification of process synchronization by path expressions." *Lecture Notes in Computer Science* 16, Springer-Verlag, pp. 89–102.

Carr, R. W. 1984. *Virtual Memory Management.* UMI Research Press, Ann Arbor, Mich.

Denning, D. E. (May 1976). "A lattice model of secure information flow." *Communications of the ACM* 19, 5, p. 236.

―――. (July 1977). "Certification of programs for secure information flow." *Communications of the ACM* 20, 7, pp. 504–512.

Denning, D. E., and P. J. Denning. (September 1981). "Data security." *ACM Computing Surveys* 13, 3, pp. 227–249.

Denning, P. J. (May 1968). "The working set model for program behavior." *Communications of the ACM* 11, 5, pp. 323–333.

―――. (September 1970). "Virtual memory." *ACM Computing Surveys* 2, 3, pp. 153–189.

Denning, P., and J. Buzen. (September 1978). "The operational analysis of queueing network models." *ACM Computing Surveys* 10, 3, pp. 225–261.

Diffie, W., and M. E. Hellman. (March 1979). "Privacy and authentication: an introduction to cryptography." *Proceedings of the IEEE,* pp. 397–427.

Eswaran, K. P.; J. N. Gray; et al. (November 1976). "The notions of consistency and predicate locks in a database system." *Communications of the ACM* 19, 11, pp. 624–633.

Graham, G. S., and P. J. Denning. (1972). "Protection: principles and practices." *Proceedings of the AFIPS Spring Joint Computer Conference* 40, pp. 417–429.

Gray, J. N. (1978). "Notes on database operating systems." In *Operating Systems: An Advanced Course, Lecture Notes in Computer Science* 60, Springer-Verlag, pp. 393–481.

Hewitt, C. E., and R. R. Atkinson. (1979). "Specification and proof techniques for serializers." *IEEE Transactions on Software Engineering* SE-5, 1, pp. 10–23.

Hoare, C. A. R. (October 1974). "Monitors: an operating system structuring concept." *Communications of the ACM* 17, 10, pp. 549–557.

————. (August 1978). "Communicating sequential processes." *Communications of the ACM* 21, 8, pp. 666–677.

Holt, R. C. (September 1972). "Some deadlock properties of computer systems." *ACM Computing Surveys* 4, 3, pp. 179–196.

Jackson, J. (1957). "Networks of waiting lines." *Operations Research* 5, pp. 518–521.

Johnson, J. W. (March 1975). "Program restructuring for virtual memory systems." Project MAC TR-148, MIT, Cambridge, MA.

Kohler, W. H. (June 1981). "A survey of techniques for synchronization and recovery in decentralized computer systems." *ACM Computing Surveys* 13, 2, pp. 149–183.

Lamport, L. (November 1977). "Concurrent reading and writing." *Communications of the ACM* 20, 11, pp. 806–811.

————. (July 1978). "Time, clocks and the ordering of events in a distributed system." *Communications of the ACM* 21, 7, pp. 558–564.

Lampson, B. W. (March 1971). "Protection." *Fifth Princeton Conference on Information and Systems Sciences,* pp. 437–443.

Landwehr, C. E. (September 1981). "Formal models for computer security." *Computing Surveys* 13, 3, pp. 247–275.

Maekawa, M. (1980). "A classification of process coordination schemes in descriptive power." *International Journal of Computer and Information Science* 9, 5, pp. 383–406.

————. (1983). "Distributed deadlock detection algorithms without phantom deadlocks." Technical Report 83-11, Department of Information Science, University of Tokyo, Tokyo, Japan.

————. (May 1985). A $\sqrt{}$ algorithm for mutual exclusion in decentralized systems." *ACM Transactions on Computer Systems* 3, 2, pp. 145–159.

Mattson, R. L.; J. Gecsei; et al. (1970). "Evaluation techniques for storage hierarchies." *IBM Systems Journal* 9, 2, pp. 78–117.

Myers, W. (August 1982). "Toward a local network standard." *IEEE MICRO* 2, 3, pp. 28–45.

National Bureau of Standards. (January 1977). *Data Encryption Standard.* Federal Information Processing Standards, Publication 46.

Popek, G. J., and C. S. Kline. (December 1979). "Encryption and secure computer networks." *ACM Computing Surveys* 11, 4, pp. 331–356.

Reed, D. P., and R. K. Kanodia. (February 1979). "Synchronization with eventcounts and sequencers." *Communications of the ACM* 22, 2, pp. 115–123.

Reiser, M., and S. Lavenberg. (April 1980). "Mean value analysis of closed multichain queueing networks." *Journal of the ACM* 27, 2, pp. 313–322.

Ricart, G., and A. K. Agrawala. (January 1981). "An optimal algorithm for mutual exclusion." *Communications of the ACM* 24, 1, pp. 9–17. [Corrigendum: *Communications of the ACM* 24, 9 (September 1981), p. 578.]

Rivest, R. L., A. Shamir, and L. Adleman. (February 1978). "A method for obtaining digital signatures and public key cryptosystems." *Communications of the ACM* 21, 2, pp. 120–126.

Tanenbaum, A. S. (December 1981). "Network protocols." *Computing Surveys* 13, 4, pp. 453–489.

Traiger, I. L.; J. Gray; et al. (September 1982). "Transactions and consistency in distributed database systems." *ACM Transactions on Database Systems* 7, 3, pp. 323–342.

U.S. Department of Defense. (January 1983). *Military Standard Ada Programming Language.* ANSI/MIL-STD-1815A, Washington D.C.

Zimmermann, H. (1980). "OSI reference model—the ISO model of architecture for open system interconnection." *IEEE Transactions on Communications* COM-28, 4, pp. 425–432.

Process Synchronization

2.1 Background and Review

In this chapter we cover low-level mechanisms for process synchronization that are derived from the classic methods discussed in an introductory course. First, we review ideas about processes and examine some elementary methods.

2.1.1 Concept of a Process

The idea of a *process* is fundamental to most of the material in this book, and many authors have tried to define it precisely—with varying degrees of success. In this section we think of a process as a program whose execution has started and not yet terminated. This does not mean that the program is actually executing. A process might be temporarily halted because some resource (processor, input data, main storage, and so on) is not available at the moment, and the operating system has elected to run some other process. At any moment a process is in one of several states. Three of these are:

1. *Running*: The process is using a processor to execute instructions.
2. *Ready*: The process is executable, but other processes are executing and all the processors are currently in use.
3. *Blocked*: The process is waiting for an event to occur.

Other states will be discussed later.

The complete state of a process is reflected by a data structure that describes the status of all the hardware and software entities the process uses; this structure is often called a *process control block* (PCB). Fields that commonly appear in a PCB include the following:

- The name of the process
- The processor state (program counter, register contents, interrupt masks)— valid only when the process is not currently running
- The current process state (e.g., running, ready, blocked)
- The relative priority of the process for acquiring resources such as a processor
- Information about protection state (e.g., main storage access control)
- Virtual memory address translation maps
- Information about other resources (e.g., files, devices) owned by the process

- Accounting information (e.g., processor time used, memory held, I/O volume logged)

A PCB might range from a few hundred to several thousand bytes in size. The collection of all PCBs for extant processes defines for the operating system all current computational activities.

The operating system itself and other processes can perform *operations on processes* that change process status or other information in a PCB. Although systems may have specialized operations, the following are typical in batch, time-sharing, and real-time systems:

Create: Adds a new PCB with appropriate initial information.

Delete: Removes the identified process from the system.

Signal: Indicates that a specific event has occurred.

Wait: Causes execution to cease until a specific event occurrence is signaled.

Schedule: Reassigns runnable processes to the available processors of the system.

Change-priority: Alters the relative priority of a process to influence its future resource acquisition success.

Suspend: Makes a running, ready, or blocked process *suspended-ready* or *suspended-blocked*.

Resume: Changes a suspended-ready or suspended-blocked process back to ready or blocked.

A few words are necessary about these operations. *Process creation* often results in a hierarchical structure of processes, with created processes being descendents of their creator in a tree structure. In most systems processes may *delete* only processes they have created. There are numerous techniques for creating and terminating processes. Several low-level mechanisms have been proposed. In each, the purpose of initiation is to provide the address of executable code to the operating system so that a separate "thread of execution" may be established beginning at that point. *Process termination* is the reverse: A process may request that the operating system terminate its execution, or it may wait for the self-termination of other, identified processes. Each of the forms mentioned here is primitive in the sense that processes are not "first-class" objects in the notation; rather, they come into existence only as a result of initiation operations. These schemes are often used to extend the definition of an extant programming language with process management operations. Mechanisms include the **fork** and **join** operations proposed in [Conway, 1963] and the **cobegin-coend** block-structured statements from [Brinch-Hansen, 1973]. Assuming some techniques exist for process initiation and termination, we focus on process synchronization.

The signal and wait operations are really operations on events. An *event* is a change in the status of any entity that a process uses to execute. Low-level mechanisms are the subject of much of this chapter; high-level language mechanisms are discussed in Chapter 3.

The schedule operation is often performed as a result of a change in system state that may influence which processes should be currently running. An example of such a change is the change-priority operation. This kind of *processor scheduling* is often called *short-term scheduling,* or *dispatching.* It is also performed in most systems as a result of a hardware clock interrupt. By using this operation, the operating system can preserve the illusion that each process has its own *virtual processor* that is slower than the actual hardware processors. This illusion is necessary for the success of a time-sharing system, but the overhead would be unnecessary in a batch-processing system.

The operations that involve suspended processes are necessary for several reasons. A user may wish to suspend temporarily the execution of an interactive process to work with some other process instead. The operating system may need to prevent normal scheduling in order to recover from failure, or it may need to suspend the execution of some processes in order to prevent the overloading of a critical resource (see, for example, Chapter 5).

These states and operations are summarized in Figure 2.1. In this graph the nodes represent all possible process states, and the directed arcs between nodes are labeled with the operations that make such state changes possible.

2.1.2 Concurrent Processes

In this chapter we are concerned with the interactions among processes that communicate or compete for resources. We lay some groundwork for this in this section by discussing the idea of determinacy. First we set up a model and then we define determinacy in terms of the model. Informally, a set of processes is determinate if,

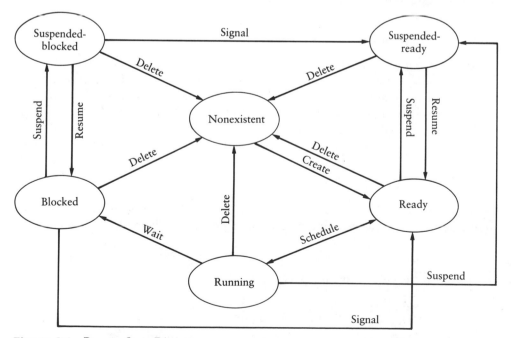

Figure 2.1 Process State Diagram.

given the same input, the same results are produced regardless of the relative speeds of execution of the processes or the legal overlaps in execution. Next, we link determinacy to mutual noninterference; this will give us an effective mechanism for determining whether a system of processes is determinate. We then explore how parallelism can be maximized for a set of processes [Bernstein, 1966]. Finally, we define the fundamental problem of process interaction.

The Model

Let $P = \{P_1, P_2, \ldots, P_n\}$ be a set of processes that comprise some computation. The execution order of the processes is defined by a *precedence relation* "$\Rightarrow$," a set of ordered pairs drawn from $P \times P$:

$$\Rightarrow = \{\, (P_i, P_j) \mid P_i \text{ must complete before } P_j \text{ may start} \,\}$$

If $(P_i, P_j) \in \Rightarrow$, we write $P_i \Rightarrow P_j$, and say that P_i is a *direct predecessor* of P_j (P_j is a *direct successor* of P_i). If there is a sequence $P_i \Rightarrow P_j \Rightarrow \cdots \Rightarrow P_k$, P_i is a *predecessor* of P_k and we write $P_i \overset{*}{\Rightarrow} P_k$. P_k is a *successor* of P_i. Two processes are *independent* if neither is a successor of the other. Observe that only independent processes may execute at the same time. Figure 2.2(a) shows a system of processes and an associated precedence relation.

An acyclic, directed graph can be used to show such a system of processes. The only difference between the two representations is that no *redundant edges* appear in the graph, even though they are members of $\Rightarrow$. A redundant edge (P_i, P_j) is one for which there is a longer path between P_i and P_j. Figure 2.2(b) shows the graph corresponding to the system in Figure 2.2(a).

Determinate Systems of Processes

Processes execute by using input values from a universe of *memory cells* collectively called M, and writing some cells as output. For each process P we have a static *domain* D(P) and *range* R(P) for these two subsets of M. Process P reads its domain D(P) at its initiation, runs without interruption to completion, and writes its range R(P) upon termination. We insist only that $R(P) \neq \phi$; that is, each process must have an effect. One may think of an associated function f_P that maps its set of domain values into its range:

$$f_P : D(P) \rightarrow R(P)$$

By supplying the definition of f_P we are giving an *interpretation*. We will want our results to be independent of interpretations of processes. Figure 2.2(c) shows a pos-

$$P = \{P_1, P_2, P_3, P_4, P_5, P_6, P_7, P_8, P_9\}$$
$$\Rightarrow = \{(1,2), (1,3), (1,4), (2,5), (3,5), (4,6),$$
$$(4,7), (4,8), (5,8), (6,8), (7,9), (8,9)\}$$

Figure 2.2(a)   A Process System with Precedence Relation.

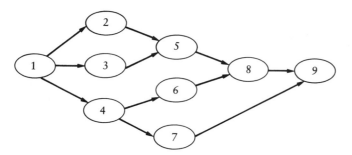

Figure 2.2(b) The Corresponding Process System Graph.

sible set of process domains and ranges for the system of Figure 2.2(a), if memory consists of six cells, $(M_1, \ldots, M_6)$.

In terms of the model, we define a system of processes to be *determinate* if, regardless of the orders and overlaps in execution allowed by $\Rightarrow$, the sequence of values written in each memory cell is the same. Naturally, this implies that the final state of memory is the same for each legal combination of ways to execute processes.

Although this definition is precise, it is not especially helpful when we are faced with a system of processes whose determinacy is to be established. The difficulty lies in the enormous number of different ways that the processes may be executed temporally; each must be tried, and the values stored in memory cells must be the same in each case. This problem is solved in the next section.

Mutually Noninterfering Systems

Two processes, P_i and P_j, are *mutually noninterfering* if $P_i \overset{*}{\Rightarrow} P_j$ or $P_j \overset{*}{\Rightarrow} P_i$ or

$$(R(P_i) \cap R(P_j)) \cup (R(P_i) \cap D(P_j)) \cup (D(P_i) \cap R(P_j)) = \phi$$

A system is mutually noninterfering if this is true for each pair of processes in the system. We refer to these alternatives as the *Bernstein conditions*. Clearly, we can efficiently check that a system is mutually noninterfering. The following two results tie determinacy and mutual noninterference together.

Process	Domain	Range
1	1	2, 3
2	4	4
3	3	2, 3
4	1	1
5	3	3
6	6	6
7	5	5
8	1, 3	4
9	1, 4, 6	2, 3

Figure 2.2(c) Process Domains and Ranges.

THEOREM 2.1

A mutually noninterfering system of processes is determinate.

THEOREM 2.2

Consider a system of processes in which, for each process P, D(P) and R(P) are given but the interpretation f_P is left unspecified. If the system is determinate for all interpretations, then all processes are mutually noninterfering.

Theorem 2.1 means that, if a system satisfies the Bernstein conditions, then it is a determinate system. Theorem 2.2 tells us that the Bernstein conditions are very strong in the sense that, for some interpretations of the processes, the system may be mutually interfering and still determinate. Together they yield an efficient method of checking a system of processes for determinacy by checking for mutual noninterference instead. The reader is invited to check that the system in Figure 2.2 is determinate.

Maximally Parallel Systems

As a complex system of cooperating processes is being designed and constructed, it is possible to incorrectly specify the execution precedence constraints and accidentally build an indeterminate system. This problem was solved in the last section. But it is also possible to be too conservative and overspecify the execution precedence in the interests of safety, thus building a system that takes longer to execute than it should. That is the situation we discuss here.

Given a determinate system of processes, it is a *maximally parallel* system if removal of any pair (P_i, P_j) from $\Rightarrow$ makes the processes P_i and P_j interfering processes. Stated another way, in a maximally parallel system each restriction on overlapped execution in $\Rightarrow$ is actually necessary for correct processing. Such systems have the best potential for execution in the shortest total time. Two systems with the same processes and different precedence relations are *equivalent* if, given the same initial memory state, the processes write the same sequences of values into memory cells and hence produce the same results. The following theorem gives a method for building maximally parallel systems.

THEOREM 2.3

Given a determinate system of processes with precedence relation $\Rightarrow$, construct another system with the same processes and a new precedence relation $\Rightarrow'$ defined by

$$\Rightarrow' = \{(P_i, P_j)\epsilon \, cl(\Rightarrow)|(R(P_i)\cap R(P_j))\cup(R(P_i)\cap D(P_j))\cup(D(P_i)\cap R(P_j)) \neq \phi \}$$

Then the new system is the unique, maximally parallel system equivalent to the original.

Observe that there is only one maximally parallel system. Also, it is not sufficient to use pairs from $\Rightarrow$ when building $\Rightarrow'$; we must use the *transitive closure,* cl $(\Rightarrow)$ of $\Rightarrow$. (P_i, P_k) is a member of $cl(\Rightarrow)$ if (P_i, P_j) and (P_j, P_k) are elements of $\Rightarrow$. Figure

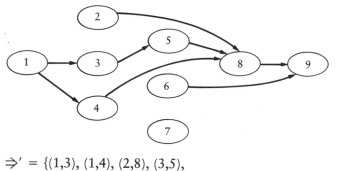

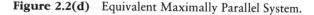

$$\Rightarrow' = \{(1,3), (1,4), (2,8), (3,5),$$
$$(4,8), (5,8), (6,9), (8,9)\}$$

Figure 2.2(d) Equivalent Maximally Parallel System.

2.2(d) shows the maximally parallel process system derived from the system in Figure 2.2(a), along with its graph. It is important to note that the graph of the maximally parallel system does not necessarily have the fewest edges of all graphs of equivalent systems.

2.1.3 Critical Sections

In most computer systems processes *compete* with each other by requesting and holding system resources exclusively. In addition, processes may *cooperate* by planned interactions involving shared data or by message passing. In either case *mutual exclusion* is necessary: We must ensure that only one process at a time holds a resource or modifies shared information. A *critical section* is a code segment in a process in which some shared resource is referenced. During the execution of a critical section, mutual exclusion with respect to certain information or resources must be ensured. Specifically, the following requirements must be satisfied:

1. When no process is in a critical section, any process that requests entry to its critical section must be permitted to enter without delay.

2. When two or more processes compete to enter their respective critical sections, the selection cannot be postponed indefinitely.

3. No process can prevent another process from entering its critical section indefinitely; that is, any process should be given a fair chance to enter its critical section.

2.1.4 Early Mechanisms

The problem of how to implement mutual exclusion has been studied extensively. A solution to this problem for two processes that requires no special hardware (only load and store instructions are indivisible) is credited to the Dutch mathematician T. Dekker. Dijkstra extended this technique to any number of processes [Dijkstra, 1965]. Since that time numerous extensions have been devised to simplify the algorithm or improve fairness [Knuth, 1966; Eisenberg, 1972; Lamport, 1974; Peterson, 1981]. The problem with all the versions of *Dekker's Algorithm* is that they require a process that cannot enter its critical section to execute instructions continually. This *busy waiting* is wasteful of the CPU resource and the memory access bandwidth as well.

In uniprocessor systems it may be sufficient to *disable interrupts* at the start of a critical section. A process is then assured that no input-output completion or timer interrupt can intervene during critical section execution. After the critical section a process *enables interrupts*. In this method critical sections must be short. Otherwise system response can degrade, or important input-output events may be improperly handled. This technique cannot be made available to user programs in most systems.

Interrupt disabling is not sufficient in multiprocessor systems. However, a technique that can be effective in this setting is the special *test-and-set instruction*. When executed, a specified memory cell is tested for a particular value. If a match occurs, the cell is altered; the test section and the set section are all one indivisible operation on that memory cell. This low-level building block can be used to construct busy-waiting solutions to the mutual exclusion problem (simply loop until the cell's value is altered), or it can be incorporated in schemes that relinquish the CPU when the instruction fails. Other versions of this technique include instructions that obtain the value of a memory cell and also increment the value indivisibly.

2.1.5   Semaphores

A conceptually more elegant construction that can be implemented effectively in single processor and multiple processor systems is the semaphore [Dijkstra, 1968]. A *semaphore* is an integer variable S and an associated group of waiting processes upon which only two operations may be performed:

P(S): **if** $S \geq 1$ **then** $S := S - 1$
      else the executing process places itself in S's waiting group and
          relinquishes the CPU by invoking CPU scheduler
      endif

V(S): **if** S's waiting queue is nonempty **then**
      remove one waiting process and make it available for execution (some
      implementations invoke a CPU scheduler)
      else $S := S + 1$
      endif

If the P and V operations are not supplied as indivisible instructions, then techniques discussed earlier can ensure that all P and V operations on a particular semaphore execute in mutual exclusion.

We have described the processes waiting in association with a semaphore as a group. We do this to avoid implying that any queuing mechanism is automatically imposed; that is, a first-come, first-served discipline is not necessarily the only way to organize the waiting group. Subject to the requirements on any solution to the mutual exclusion problem, some uncertainty remains about how processes are selected and made ready for continued execution; this is implementation-dependent.

2.1.6   Common Synchronization Problems

A few common situations reappear often enough so that their names evoke standard solutions in terms of semaphores. We review them here.

The *mutual exclusion problem* was introduced above. To implement critical sections among several processes sharing information, we need only a single semaphore, as seen in Figure 2.3.

The *producer/consumer problem* occurs frequently among cooperating processes. In its general form a set of *producer* processes supplies messages to a set of *consumer* processes. They all share a common pool of spaces into which messages may be placed by producers or removed by consumers. A solution using a circular buffer and semaphores is found in Figure 2.4. Note that "nrfull" and "nrempty" keep track of the number of full and empty buffers, respectively, and also prevent a producer from overwriting a message or a consumer from obtaining an already used message. If only one producer or consumer exists, then the semaphore "mutexP" or "mutexC" is unnecessary. In this version of the problem, any consumer handles any message; later in this chapter special cases will be discussed.

The *reader/writer problem* also occurs frequently. Here, reader processes access shared data but do not alter it, and writer processes change the values of shared information. Any number of readers should be allowed to proceed concurrently in the absence of a writer, but only one writer may execute at a time while readers are excluded. There are several solutions that provide greater or lesser priority to readers or writers. The version in Figure 2.5 is called the *weak reader preference solution;* others will be seen elsewhere in this text.

2.2   Sequencers and Eventcounts

A *sequencer* S is a nondecreasing integer variable, initialized to 0, that can be used to totally order events [Reed, 1979]. The inspiration behind this sequencer is the automatic ticket machine used to control the order of service in bakeries or other

Figure 2.3   The Mutual Exclusion Problem Using Semaphores.

Shared Variable

var S: semaphore : = 1;

Process i	Process j
loop	**loop**
. . .	. . .
P(S);	P(S);
Access shared	Access shared
data safely	data safely
V(S);	V(S);
. . .	. . .
endloop	**endloop**

Figure 2.4   The Producer/Consumer Problem Using Semaphores.

Shared Variables

var nrfull: **semaphore** : = 0;
  nrempty: **semaphore** : = N;
  mutexP: **semaphore** : = 1;
  mutexC: **semaphore** : = 1;
  buffer: **array**[0..N − 1] **of** message;
  in, out: 0..N − 1: = 0, 0;

Producer i	**Consumer j**
loop	**loop**
. . .	. . .
Create a new message m;	. . .
—One producer at a time	—One consumer at a time
P(mutexP);	P(mutexC);
—Await an empty cell	—Await a message
P(nrempty);	P(nrfull);
buffer[in] : = m;	m : = buffer[out];
in : = (in + 1) **mod** N;	out : = (out + 1) **mod** N;
—Signal a full buffer	—Signal an empty buffer
V(nrfull);	V(nrempty);
—Allow other producers	—Allow other consumers
V(mutexP);	V(mutexC);
. . .	Consume message m;
. . .	. . .
endloop	**endloop**

busy stores. A sequencer corresponds to the numbered tags that are obtained by arriving customers. The value of a sequencer is the value of the next numbered tag to be taken. Customers wait for service after they have obtained numbered tags. The server, on the other hand, holds the numbered tags of the customers who have already been serviced; the top of this stack is the numbered tag of the customer being serviced or, if the "system" is idle, the last customer processed. The stack of numbered tags is represented by an *eventcount* E, whose current value is the value of the top numbered tag. Its initial value is 0. To a sequencer only one operation, **ticket**(S), can be applied. It returns as its result the number of executions of the **ticket** operation prior to the current one. A sequence of **ticket** operations yields a non-negative, increasing, contiguous sequence of integers. A **ticket** operation corresponds to a newly arriving customer taking a unique numbered tag. An eventcount has three associated operations: **await**(E, v), **advance**(E), and **read**(E), where E is an eventcount and v is an integer. An **await** corresponds to a customer beginning to wait for service. A sequence

  v : = **ticket**(S);
  await(E, v);

Figure 2.5 A Weak Reader Preference Solution Using Semaphores.

Shared Variables

var wmutex, rmutex: **semaphore** : = 1, 1;
   nreaders: **integer** : = 0;

A Reader	**A Writer**
loop	**loop**
—Readers enter one at a time	—Each writer operates alone
P(rmutex);	P(wmutex);
—First reader waits for reader's turn,	Perform write operations;
—then inhibits other writers	V(wmutex)
if nreaders = 0 **then**	**endloop**
P(wmutex)	
endif;	
nreaders : = nreaders + 1;	
—Allow other reader entries/exits	
V(rmutex);	
Perform read operations;	
—Readers exit one at a time	
P(rmutex);	
nreaders : = nreaders − 1;	
—Last reader allows writers	
if nreaders = 0 **then**	
V(wmutex)	
endif;	
—Allow reader entry/exit	
V(rmutex)	
endloop	

causes the process (customer) to wait until E reaches v. That is, an **await**(E, v) suspends the process if E < v; otherwise, it allows the process to proceed. Usually, these two lines comprise the only use of the integer variable v; it makes sense to write the briefer functional form:

await(E, **ticket**(S))

In any case, **await** is defined as follows:

await(E,v):
   if E < v **then**
      place the executing process in the waiting queue associated with E and
      invoke CPU scheduler
   endif;

An **advance** corresponds to an initiation of service: The eventcount value is incremented and the next customer (process) is admitted for service. The value of this customer's numbered tag becomes the value of the eventcount. An **advance**(E) operation reawakens one or more processes on the waiting queue of an eventcount, and is defined as follows:

> **advance**(E):
>   E := E + 1;
>   Wake up the process(es) waiting for E's value
>   to reach the current value just attained;

A sequence of operations for a process executing a critical section is:

> . . .
> **await**(E, **ticket**(S));
>   —Access the critical resources;
> **advance**(E);
> . . .

A **read** operation is provided for inspecting the current value of an eventcount. It may be useful for a process to check whether its turn will come soon. If it will not, the process may have alternate work to do before blocking via an **await** operation.

Eventcounts, if designed properly, allow for concurrent execution of **advance,** **await,** and **read** on the same eventcount. They can be implemented without using mutual exclusion as an underlying mechanism [Reed, 1979]. Lamport's concurrent reading and writing scheme, discussed later in this chapter, is useful in this regard. Sequencers, on the other hand, must use mutual exclusion: two **ticket** operations on the same sequencer may not be concurrent and will always return different values.

2.2.1   The Producer/Consumer Problem Using Eventcounts

A solution to the multiple producer/consumer problem can be devised using eventcounts; this is shown in Figure 2.6. This solution, like the solution based on semaphores, completely arbitrates producers and consumers, respectively. It allows an enabled consumer process to read a stored value, so that reading a message from a buffer slot can proceed concurrently with storing a message into another slot. The solution shows the broadcast character of **advance.** Each execution of an **advance**(In) or an **advance**(Out) enables two processes (a producer and a consumer), respectively. If concurrent executions of a producer and a consumer are not necessary, we can totally order all the producers and consumers by using just one sequencer, and each process needs to execute only a single **await.**

2.2.2   The Reader/Writer Problem Using Eventcounts

Based on eventcounts and sequencers, a solution similar to that based on semaphores can be easily constructed, as shown in Figure 2.7. This solution again allows a writer to write only when all readers are idle. Note that this solution totally orders the requests to the shared data on a first-come, first-served basis, unlike the solution based on semaphores. Uncertainty occurs only with respect to the access to the sequencer by **ticket** operations.

Figure 2.6 The Producer/Consumer Problem Using
Eventcounts and Sequencers.

Shared Variables

var Pticket, Cticket: **sequencer**;
In, Out: **eventcount**;
buffer: **array**[0..N − 1] **of** message;

Producer i	**Consumer j**
—A variable, t, local	—A variable, u, local
—to each producer	—to each consumer
var t: **integer**;	**var** u: **integer**;
loop	**loop**
. . .	. . .
Create a new message m;	. . .
—One producer at a time	—One consumer at a time
t : = **ticket**(Pticket);	u : = **ticket**(Cticket);
await(In, t);	**await**(Out, u);
—Await an empty cell	—Await a message
await(Out, t − N + 1);	**await**(In, u + 1);
buffer[t **mod** N] : = m;	m : = buffer[u **mod** N];
—Signal a full buffer and	—Signal an empty buffer and
—allow other producers	—allow other consumers
advance(In);	**advance**(Out);
. . .	Consume message m;
. . .	. . .
endloop	**endloop**

2.2.3 Tagged Messages

The solutions given so far for the producer/consumer problem are based on the allocation control of the buffer slots. In this sense, the coordination is competitive although the objective is cooperation. A more natural approach for the producer/ consumer problem is to retain the flavor of cooperation and avoid competition for buffer slots [Maekawa, 1980]. This can be done by treating messages as resources. A producer generates a message which, along with a sequence number, is picked up by a consumer whose ticket matches the message's sequence number. A consumer returns an acknowledgment message with a different sequence number, which is picked up by a producer whose ticket matches the acknowledgment message's sequence number. This whole procedure of *tagged messages,* which consists of sequencers, their operation **ticket** as defined before, and the operation **replace** as defined below, is then repeated.

replace(B,s,M,t):
Search the buffers B for one containing a sequence number s. Exchange the message in that element with the message in parameter M and set the sequence number in this

element to t. If there is no such message in buffer B, place the executing process in the waiting queue; it will be reawakened when the required message is placed into a buffer of B by another **replace** operation.

Parameters s and t are input parameters to **replace**, and M is both used and set. The message with associated sequence number s is swapped with M, and the sequence number becomes t. Note that the sequence number t is always placed into the buffer last in the above data manipulation, and that **replace** operations need not be mutually exclusive. Even a busy-waiting implementation will work properly.

A solution based on this mechanism is shown in Figure 2.8. The type "message" has capacity for both a message and a sequence number. The solution is simple, and, except for the **ticket** operations, no mutual exclusion is required. The processes can operate on each buffer slot concurrently. Furthermore, this approach does not require

Figure 2.7   A Weak Reader Preference Solution Using
Sequencers and Eventcounts.

Shared Variables

var Wticket, Rticket: **sequencer**;
   Win, Rin: **eventcount**;
   nreaders: **integer** : = 0;

A Reader	**A Writer**
loop	**loop**
. . .	. . .
—Readers enter one at a time	—Each writer operates alone
await(Rin, **ticket**(Rticket));	**await**(Win, **ticket**(Wticket));
—First reader waits for reader's turn,	Perform write operations;
—then inhibits other writers	—Allow other writers (or
if nreaders = 0 **then**	—a reader) to lock out
await(Win, **ticket**(Wticket))	**advance**(Win);
endif;	. . .
nreaders : = nreaders + 1;	**endloop**
—Allow other reader entries	
advance(Rin);	
Perform read operations;	
—Readers exit one at a time	
await(Rin, **ticket**(Rticket));	
nreaders : = nreaders − 1;	
—Last reader allows writers	
if nreaders = 0 **then**	
advance(Win)	
endif;	
—Allow reader entry/exit	
advance(Rin);	
. . .	
endloop	

Figure 2.8 Producer/Consumer Problem Using Tagged
Messages.

Shared Variables

var buffer: **array**[0..N − 1] **of** message : = (−1, −2,..., −N);

Producer	Consumer
var T: **sequencer**;	var U: **sequencer**;
t: **integer**;	u: **integer**;
loop	**loop**
...	...
Produce a message A;	u : = **ticket**(U);
t : = **ticket**(T);	**replace**(buffer, u + 1, B, −(u + 1 + N));
replace(buffer, −(t + 1), A, t + 1);	Consume the message B;
...	...
endloop	**endloop**

accessing processes to know the details of buffer management although the total capacity of the buffer (N) must be known. In this sense, this approach is at a higher level than the semaphore solution.

2.3 *OR* Synchronization

In synchronization problems, a process may wait for the occurrence of any one of a collection of events, and take different actions depending on the type of event. In order to do this, the process must know which type of event has occurred. If a message-passing scheme is used, then the message itself can carry the information and tell the process which action to take. The producer/consumer scheme can be used for this purpose. If message passing is not suitable, it is convenient to convey the information as to which event has occurred to the activated process by providing an additional parameter A. This is exemplified by the

wait-or($e_1, e_2, \ldots, e_n$, A)

operation in which each e_i denotes an event and A returns event discrimination information. It is convenient for A to identify *all* the events that have occurred rather than just one because the process is in the better position to decide the order of actions to be taken. For example, in a time-sharing system with many terminals it is easy to associate an input process with each terminal. But this may not be practical since many identical processes exist for the same purpose. An alternative approach is to instantiate a single input process and multiplex its service over all terminals. The process executes **wait-or** to wait for input from any terminal and responds to the first input. Such a process can easily handle all the interactive input from people typing at all the terminals. This scheme may be extended to handle both input and output activities. We assign different *event variables* for different operations, as

Figure 2.9(a)   Two Processes for Two Terminals.

Terminal 1 Process	Terminal 2 Process
loop	**loop**
wait(e1);	wait(e4);
Perform action 1;	Perform action 4;
wait(e2);	wait(e5);
Perform action 2;	Perform action 5;
wait(e3);	wait(e6);
Perform action 3	Perform action 6
endloop	**endloop**

shown in Figure 2.9. The two processes in Figure 2.9(a) are replaced by the process in Figure 2.9(b). Whenever the server must wait for some event, it executes the **wait-or** primitive, receives one of the ready event signals, and processes it. The process will never block if there is always a ready event signal.

The implementation of the above **wait-or** primitive, however, causes a problem. Its implementation requires (1) placing a suspended process in every waiting queue of semaphores $e_1, e_2, \ldots, e_n$, and (2) removing the process from every waiting queue when the process is reawakened. This is complex, however, and causes excessive overhead. Instead of this, then, an OR condition is implemented by combining all the event variables, as well as the parameter A, into a single event variable [Presser, 1975]. The combined event variable e stands for $e_1, e_2, \ldots, e_n$ and A. The modified operations have the form **wait**(e) and **signal**(e). In this way, OR conditions and multiplexing are easily realized. Using this method, Figure 2.9(b) is modified to the mechanism shown in Figure 2.9(c).

2.4   AND Synchronization

In this section we consider process coordination requiring AND conditions. Since an AND condition is one of the simplest approaches for avoiding system deadlocks in

Figure 2.9(b)   One Process for Two Terminals.

```
loop
  wait-or(e1,e2,e3,e4,e5,e6,A);
  case A of
    e1: Perform action 1;
    e2: Perform action 2;
    e3: Perform action 3;
    e4: Perform action 4;
    e5: Perform action 5;
    e6: Perform action 6
  endcase
endloop
```

Figure 2.9(c) Combined Event Variable.

```
loop
  wait(e);
  case e of
    e1: Perform action 1;
    e2: Perform action 2;
    e3: Perform action 3;
    e4: Perform action 4;
    e5: Perform action 5;
    e6: Perform action 6
  endcase
endloop
```

resource allocation, many extensions have been proposed to facilitate their use; Table 2.1 lists some of them. *AND* conditions frequently arise in operating systems. For instance, a process may require access to two files simultaneously to perform its task, or require several I/O devices at the same time. Several shared variables may be needed simultaneously to make some decision. Such *AND* conditions may be implemented sequentially by testing individual conditions. The following sequence, for instance, acquires mutual exclusion of two shared data structures D and E:

P(Dmutex); P(Emutex);

where Dmutex and Emutex are semaphores for exclusive access to D and E, respectively. But suppose that two processes, A and B, both request D and E by the following sequences:

Process A	Process B
P(Dmutex);	P(Emutex);
P(Emutex);	P(Dmutex);

If the two processes execute adjacent lines simultaneously, *deadlock* results. In this particular example, there is a method for avoiding deadlocks: Restrict the order in which requests can be made. However, this is not always possible. If each process requests at once all the resources necessary and acquires either all of them or none, deadlocks are avoided. This is the basic idea behind providing *AND* conditions in the P operation. A P primitive with an *AND* condition is a *simultaneous* P, which is defined as follows:

$SP(S_1, S_2, \ldots, S_n)$:
  if $S_1 \geq 1$ and ... and $S_n \geq 1$ then
    for $i := 1$ to n do
      $S_i := S_i - 1$
    endfor
  else
    Place the process in the waiting queue associated with the first S_i found
    with $S_i < 1$, and set the program counter of this process to the beginning

Table 2.1 A Summary of Process Coordination Mechanisms

Mechanism	Primitives	Predicate	Operation
A. *Mechanisms used in operating system kernels*			
1. Lock/Unlock [Dijkstra, 1968]	**lock** (E)	E = 1	*true* E := 0 *false* repeat
	unlock (E)	*true*	E := 1
B. *Mechanisms that do not require mutual exclusion*			
2. Concurrent Reading and Writing	—	—	—
3. Eventcount [Reed and Kanodia, 1979]	**advance** (E)	*true*	E := E + 1
	read (E)	*true*	w := read (E)
	await (E, v)	E ≥ V	$\begin{cases} true & \text{proceed} \\ false & \text{suspend} \end{cases}$
4. Block/Wakeup [Saltzer, 1966]	**block** (P) (P is a process)	P's WWS = 1	$\begin{cases} true & \text{P's WWS} := 0 \\ false & \text{suspend P} \end{cases}$
	wakeup (P)	*true*	P's WWS := 1
C. *Mechanisms with a single variable using mutual exclusion*			
5. Wait/ Signal	**wait** (E)	E (E: boolean variable)	$\begin{cases} true & \text{E} := false \\ false & \text{suspend} \end{cases}$
	signal (E)	*true*	E := true
6. Wait/Post/ Turnoff	**wait** (E) (E consists of two bits: W and P)	P = 1	$\begin{cases} true & \text{W} := 1 \\ false & \text{W} := 1; \text{suspend} \end{cases}$
	post (E)	*true*	P := 1
	turnoff	*true*	W := 0, P := 0

	Operation	Condition	Action
7. Sequencer [Reed and Kanodia, 1979]	ticket (S)	*true*	$w := \text{ticket}(S)$
8. P/V [Dijkstra, 1968]	$P(S)$	$S > 0$	$\begin{cases} true & S := S - 1 \\ false & \text{suspend} \end{cases}$
	$V(S)$	*true*	$S := S + 1$
9. P/V chunk [Vantigorgh, 1972]	$P(S \mid t)$	$S \geq t$	$\begin{cases} true & S := S - t \\ false & \text{suspend} \end{cases}$
	$V(S \mid t)$	*true*	$S := S + t$
10. P/V two-way bounded [Lipton, 1974]	$P_k(S)$	$S > 0$	$\begin{cases} true & S := S - 1 \\ false & \text{suspend} \end{cases}$
	$V_k(S)$	$S < k$	$\begin{cases} true & S := S + 1 \\ false & \text{suspend} \end{cases}$

D. Mechanisms that allow an OR condition

	Operation	Condition	Action
11. P/V or [Lipton, 1974]	$P_{or}\,(S_1,..., S_n)$	$S_1 > 0 \lor ... \lor S_n > 0$	$\begin{cases} true & S_j := S_j - 1 \\ & (j \text{ is the smallest index with } S_j > 0) \\ false & \text{suspend} \end{cases}$
	$V(S_j)$	*true*	$S_j := S_j + 1$

E. Mechanisms that allow an AND condition

	Operation	Condition	Action
12. P/V multiple [Patil, 1971]	$P(S_1,..., S_n)$	$S_1 > 0 \land ... \land S_n > 0$	$\begin{cases} true & S_1 := S_1 - 1; ...; \\ & S_n := S_n - 1 \\ false & \text{suspend} \end{cases}$
13. P/V general [Lipton 1974]	$P(S_1,t_1;...; S_n,t_n)$	$S_1 \geq t_1 \land ... \land S_n \geq t_n$	$\begin{cases} true & S_1 := S_1 - t_1; ...; \\ & S_n := S_n - t_n \\ false & \text{suspend} \end{cases}$
	$V(S_1,t_1;...;S_n,t_n)$	*true*	$S_1 := S_1 + t_1; ...;$ $S_n := S_n + t_n$

(continued on next page)

Table 2.1 A Summary of Process Coordination Mechanisms (Continued)

Mechanism	Primitives	Predicate	Operation
14. Bilogic [Lipton 1974]	$P_{or}(S_1,..., S_n)$	$S_1 > 0 \lor ... \lor S_n > 0$	*true* $S_j := S_j - 1$ (j is the smallest index with $S_j > 0$); *false* suspend
	$P(S_1,t_1;...; S_n,t_n)$	$S_1 \geq t_1 \land ... \land S_n \geq t_n$	*true* $S_1 := S_1 - t_1;...;$ $S_n := S_n - t_n$; *false* suspend
	$V(S_1,t_n;...;S_n,t_n)$	*true*	$S_1 := S_1 + t_1;...;$ $S_n := S_n + t_n$
F. Mechanisms that allow dynamic creation of a process			
15. Fork/Join [Conway, 1963]	join J	$J - 1 = 0$	*true* $J := J - 1$; *false* $J := J - 1$; suspend
	join J, B	$J - 1 = 0$	*true* $J := J - 1$; *false* branch to B
	fork A	*true*	Initiate process at A
	fork A, J	*true*	$J := J + 1$; initiate process at A
	fork A, J, N	*true*	$J := N$; initiate process at A
G. Mechanisms that allow NOT conditions			
16. P/V parameterized [Presser, 1975]	$P(S_1,t_1,\delta_1;...;$ $S_n,t_n,\delta_n)$	$S_1 \geq t_1 \land ... \land S_n \geq t_n$	*true* $S_1 := S_1 - \delta_1;...;$ $S_n := S_n - \delta_n$; *false* suspend
	$V(S_1,\delta_1;...;$ $S_n,\delta_n)$	*true*	$S_1 := S_1 + \delta_1;...;$ $S_n := S_n + \delta_n$
17. Wait (B)/ Signal (E) [Maekawa, 1980]	wait(B) (B is a boolean expression of boolean variables with operation $\land, \lor, \lnot$)	B	*true* turn off the nonnegated variables in B; *false* suspend

28

signal,$(e_1,e_2,...,e_n)$ (e: boolean variable)	*true*	$e_1 := true;...; e_n := true$
wait(B:C) (B is a boolean expression of semaphores with relational operators; C specifies the actions to be taken when B is true)	B	*true* C (C specifies how semaphores are changed in the form $S := S - C$ where C is a constant) / *false* suspend
18. Wait(B;C) Signal (C) [Maekawa, 1980]		
signal(C)	*true*	C

H. Mechanisms that allow history information

rwait(A;r) (A specifies a finite automation; r specifies a designated state)	A has reached the designated state specified by r	*true* signals are consumed / *false* suspend
19. Rwait (A;r)/ Rsignal (A;E) [Maekawa, 1980]		
rsignal(A;E)	*true*	change the state of A accepting signals on E
20. Supervisory computer [Gaines, 1972]		
block	*true*	suspend
equal(A,B,Mask)	A = B(Masked)	conditional statements
less than (A,B,Mask)	A < B(Masked)	
greater than (A,B,Mask)	A > B(Masked)	

of the **SP** operation so that all conditions are reexamined when the
process is reactivated

endif;

A **V** operation is similarly modified as follows:

SV($S_1, S_2, \ldots, S_n$):
  for i := 1 **to** n **do**
    $S_i := S_i + 1$;
    Remove all the processes waiting in the queue associated with S_i into the
    ready queue
  endfor;
  The process that has requested the **SV** operation continues or is placed in
  the ready queue and control is passed to the CPU scheduler;

These **SP** and **SV** operations remain simple. We illustrate their use with the *dining philosopher problem,* an abstraction of resource competition that frequently arises in operating systems.

2.4.1   Dining Philosopher Problem

The dining philosopher problem is stated as follows [Dijkstra, 1968]. Five philosophers sit around a table. Each philosopher alternates between thinking and eating. In front of each philosopher there is a rice bowl. (The problem was originally defined with a plate of spaghetti.) When a philosopher wishes to eat, he picks up two chopsticks next to his plate. (The original problem was defined with forks, but we state the problem with chopsticks because hardly anyone can eat with just one chopstick.) There are, however, only five chopsticks on the table. So a philosopher can eat only when neither of his neighbors is eating. The problem is to write the algorithm for philosopher i ($0 \le i \le 4$).

It is difficult to construct a deadlock-free solution for this problem based on the simple **P** operation without explicitly constraining concurrency. If shared variables are allowed, the solutions tend to be complex. With an **SP** operation, writing a solution for philosopher i is straightforward. See Figure 2.10.

With eventcounts and sequencers, AND conditions can be enforced by coordinating two (or more) ticket operations, as shown in Figure 2.11 [Reed, 1979]. This **Pboth** procedure is also sufficient to solve the dining philosopher problem without extra variables. As shown in this example, a sequencer and its corresponding eventcount should be associated so that their unmatched use is avoided. The association is the responsibility of programmers: a disadvantage of low-level mechanisms.

2.4.2   Starvation and Efficiency

Solutions for the dining philosopher problem based on semaphores and on eventcounts and sequencers both have some problems. The solution based on semaphores cannot prevent a philosopher (process) from being permanently locked out by two conspiring neighbor processes; this is known as *starvation,* or *indefinite delay.* The

Figure 2.10   The Dining Philosophers Problem Using **SP**.

Shared Variables

var chopstick: **array**[0..4] **of semaphore** : = (1, 1, 1, 1, 1);

Process i
loop
    Think;
    SP(chopstick[(i + 1) **mod** 5], chopstick[i]);
    Eat;
    SV(chopstick[(i + 1) **mod** 5], chopstick[i])
endloop

solution based on eventcounts and sequencers does not have this problem but may keep a process waiting even though all its necessary resources are available. The solution based on eventcounts and sequencers is fairer but less efficient. These problems of *starvation* and *efficiency* are important in operating systems. Neither semaphores nor eventcounts and sequencers are sufficient. More complex scheduling algorithms (such as one that gives a process a higher priority after it has waited for a specified time) require some form of history information.

2.4.3   Cigarette Smoker's Problem

The *cigarette smoker's problem* [Patil, 1971] is as follows. There are three processes, X, Y, and Z, that supply tobacco, matches, and wrappers as follows:

X supplies tobacco and a match.

Y supplies a match and a wrapper.

Z supplies a wrapper and tobacco.

There are three processes (smokers), A, B, and C, that possess tobacco, matches, and wrappers, respectively, but they can smoke only when they possess all three items. We are asked to write processes A, B, and C under the conditions that only one of X, Y, and Z can supply materials at a time and that none of them can proceed until the materials supplied are consumed by a process A, B, or C. Processes X, Y, and Z are easily written using ordinary **P** and **V** operations; see Figure 2.12(a). Semaphores t, w, and m correspond to tobacco, wrapper, and match, respectively. A solution for this problem is straightforward using **SP** operations: see Figure 2.12(b). The **Pboth** procedure from above is *not* sufficient for this problem because it always serves processes on a first-come, first-served basis.

2.5   *NOT* Synchronization

It is sometimes convenient to synchronize processes using the *absence* of a condition instead of its presence. In this section, we show how this can be done with sema-

Figure 2.11   An *AND* Condition with Eventcounts and Sequencers [From Reed, 1979. Copyright © 1979 by Association for Computing Machinery, Inc. Reprinted by permission].

```
var G, R, S: record
              T: sequencer;
              E: eventcount
          end;
procedure Pboth(R, S);
var r, s: integer;
begin
  —First lock the coordinated ticket generator
  await(G.E, ticket(G.T));
  —Get a coordinated set of tickets
  r := ticket(R.T);
  s := ticket(S.T);
  advance(G.E);
  —Now wait for both R and S to happen
  await(R.E, r);
  await(S.E, s)
end Pboth
```

phores extended to an even more general definition, and exemplify the use of this mechanism in two reader/writer algorithms and a general scheme for statically prioritizing processes. In Kosaraju [Kosaraju, 1973] we see that **SP** operations cannot implement static priorities if no shared variables other than semaphores are allowed: *NOT* conditions, therefore, are necessary. Various methods for implementing *NOT* conditions (shown in entries 16–18 of Table 2.1) differ in implementation complexity and ease of use. Queue handling is complex since an arbitrary *NOT* condition

Figure 2.12(a)   Cigarette Smokers Problem—Supplier Processes [Patil, 1970].

Shared Variables
```
var t, w, m: semaphore := 0, 0, 0;
    s: semaphore := 1;
```

Process X	Process Y	Process Z
loop	loop	loop
P(s);	P(s);	P(s);
V(t);	V(m);	V(w);
V(m)	V(w)	V(t)
endloop	endloop	endloop

Figure 2.12(b) Cigarette Smokers Problem—Smoker
Processes [Patil, 1970].

Process A	Process B	Process C
loop	**loop**	**loop**
SP(m, w);	SP(t, w);	SP(t, m);
Smoke;	Smoke;	Smoke;
V(s)	V(s)	V(s)
endloop	**endloop**	**endloop**

requires waiting processes to be activated by both **V** and **P** operations. This makes the *NOT* condition more complex than either the *AND* or *OR* condition. However, an effective method does exist that avoids this complexity. It is an extension of the **SP** operation that admits test and decrement/increment values as parameters.

$$SP(S_1, t_1, d_1; \ldots ; S_n, t_n, d_n):$$
if $S_1 \geq t_1$ **and** ... **and** $S_n \geq t_n$ **then**
    for $i := 1$ **to** n **do** $S_i := S_i - d_i$ **endfor;**
else
    Place the executing process in the waiting queue of the first S_i with $S_i < t_i$
    and set its program counter to the beginning of the **SP** operation so that all
    conditions will be reexamined when the process is reactivated
endif;

We can also extend the **SV** operation to allow an increment argument. The **SP** primitive has the same complexity as the previous version, yet it can implement *NOT* conditions. By initializing semaphore S_i to 1 we indicate *false*. To reverse the condition to *true*, execute **SP**(S_i, 0, 1). This tests for $S_i \geq 0$, which always succeeds, and decrements S_i. The operation **SP**(S_i, 1, 0) tests for $S_i \geq 1$, allows continued execution only if the condition is *false*, but does not alter the condition. This operation blocks if the condition is *true*. Finally, **V**(S_i) resets the condition to *false*. This interpretation is, however, fixed and so restricts ways of stating coordination.

Based on this version of **SP**, Presser [Presser, 1975] presented the solutions for several variations of the reader/writer problem as well as general priority problems. Due to the inflexibility of the interpretation, as stated above, the solutions require knowledge of the number of processes at each priority level. We present the solutions for the strong reader preference case of the reader/writer problem, a writer preference case of the reader/writer problem, and a general priority problem in Figures 2.13, 2.14, and 2.15. If more general *AND* conditions are allowed, solutions are more straightforward and easier to understand. In the solution of the general priority problem shown in Figure 2.15, N processes are prioritized into N classes that compete for a resource. Semaphore r corresponds to the resource and semaphore s_i is used to signal via **SP**(s_i, 1, 1) that process i is requesting the resource. Semaphore s_i is tested by processes $i + 1, \ldots,$ N.

Figure 2.13 A Strong Reader Preference Solution.

Shared Variables

var L: **semaphore** : = number of readers;
   mx: **semaphore** : = 1;

Reader	Writer
loop	**loop**
. . .	. . .
SP(L,1,1);	
SP(mx,1,0);	SP(mx,1,1; L, number of readers, 0);
Perform read;	Perform write;
SV(L,1);	SV(1; mx, 1);
. . .	. . .
endloop	**endloop**

2.6 Cooperation Without Mutual Exclusion

In certain limited cases, processes may cooperate without using mutual exclusion. We describe such cases in this section. By "without using mutual exclusion" we mean that no higher level of mutual exclusion other than exclusive access to memory cells via conventional load and store instructions is assumed. Lamport's solution, presented in this section, is motivated by the need to solve the synchronization problem for processes running on separate processors, all of which share a common memory. Processes run without using mutual exclusion have advantages because they can respond quickly to external signals and do not cause deadlock even if a process fails, since no resource is held exclusively. However, the type of process cooperation scheme explained in this section is applicable only to problems in which a single process has write access to a shared variable. This restricts such schemes

Figure 2.14 A Writer Preference Solution.

Shared Variables

var NW: **semaphore** : = number of writers = W;
   NR: **semaphore** : = number of readers = R;
   mx: **semaphore** : = 1;

Writer	Reader
loop	**loop**
. . .	. . .
SP(NW,1,1); SP(mx,1,1; NR,R,0);	SP(NR,1,1; NW,W,0);
Perform write;	Perform read;
SV(mx,1; NW,1);	SV(NR,1);
. . .	. . .
endloop	**endloop**

Figure 2.15 A Solution for a General Priority Problem.

Shared Variables

var r: **semaphore** := 1;
   s: **array**[1..N] **of semaphore** := (1,1, ..., 1);

Process i

loop

  . . .

  SP(s[i],1,1);
  SP(r,1,1; s[1],1,0; ...; s[i − 1],1,0);
  Use resource;
  SV(r,1; s[i],1);

  . . .

endloop;

only to the very basic level of process coordination. Lamport's concurrent reading and writing theorem is the basis of process *cooperation without mutual exclusion* [Lamport, 1977].

2.6.1 Lamport's Theorem

Let $v = d_1 d_2 \ldots d_m$ be an *m*-digit variable that assumes a sequence of values $v^{[0]}$, $v^{[1]}$, . . . such that $i < j$ implies $v^{[i]} < v^{[j]}$. Since reading may be concurrent with writing, reading v yields $v^{[k,l]} = d^{[i_1]} d^{[i_2]} \ldots d^{[i_m]}$, where $d^{[i_j]}$ comes from the i_j value of v, $k = \min(i_1, i_2, \ldots, i_m)$ and $l = \max(i_1, i_2, \ldots, i_m)$. We first state the following preliminary result.

LEMMA

1. If $k_1 \leq k_2 \leq \ldots \leq k_m \leq k$, then $d^{[k_1]} d^{[k_2]} \ldots d^{[k_m]} \leq v^{[k]}$.
2. If $k_1 \geq k_2 \geq \ldots \geq k_m \geq k$, then $d^{[k_1]} d^{[k_2]} \ldots d^{[k_m]} \geq v^{[k]}$.

The proof of the lemma, along with the following theorem, is left as an exercise (see Question 11).

THEOREM 2.4

All reads and writes of v are assumed to be serial, digit by digit.

1. If v is always written (serially, digit by digit) from *right* to *left*, then a read (serially, digit by digit) from *left* to *right* yields a value $v_1^{[k_1,l_1]} \ldots v_m^{[k_m,l_m]}$ with $k_1 \leq l_1 \leq \ldots \leq k_m \leq l_m$.
2. If v is always written from *right* to *left*, then reading v from *left* to *right* yields a value $v^{[k,l]} \leq v^{[l]}$. In other words, a left-to-right reading of v while v is changing from $v^{[k]}$ to $v^{[l]}$ yields a value that will not exceed $v^{[l]}$. If $k = l$, then v was not changed during the reading process.

3. If v is always written from *left* to *right*, then reading v from *right* to *left* yields a value $v^{[k,l]} \geqslant v^{[k]}$. In this case, we are assured that the value obtained will be at least as large as the stored value at the beginning of the read operation.

For instance, if $v^{[0]} = 0999$, $v^{[1]} = 1000$, and $v^{[2]} = 1001$, reading v in case 2 may produce a value $v^{[0,1]}$, $v^{[0,2]}$, or $v^{[1,2]}$, depending on the relative speed of the read and write operations, and assuming that v actually changes during the reading:

$$v^{[0,1]} = 0^{[0]}9^{[0]}9^{[0]}0^{[1]} \quad \text{or} \quad 0^{[0]}9^{[0]}0^{[1]}0^{[1]} \quad \text{or} \quad 0^{[0]}0^{[1]}0^{[1]}0^{[1]};$$

In any case, $v^{[0,1]} \leqslant v^{[1]} = 1000$.

$$v^{[0,2]} = 0^{[0]}9^{[0]}9^{[0]}1^{[2]} \quad \text{or} \quad 0^{[0]}9^{[0]}0^{[1]}1^{[2]} \quad \text{or} \quad 0^{[0]}0^{[1]}0^{[1]}1^{[2]} \quad \text{or}$$
$$0^{[0]}9^{[0]}0^{[2]}1^{[2]} \quad \text{or} \quad 0^{[0]}0^{[1]}0^{[2]}1^{[2]} \quad \text{or} \quad 0^{[0]}0^{[2]}0^{[2]}1^{[2]};$$

Thus, $v^{[0,2]} \leqslant v^{[2]} = 1001$.

$$v^{[1,2]} = 1^{[1]}0^{[1]}0^{[1]}1^{[2]} \quad \text{or} \quad 1^{[1]}0^{[1]}0^{[2]}1^{[2]} \quad \text{or} \quad 1^{[1]}0^{[2]}0^{[2]}1^{[2]};$$

Thus, $v^{[1,2]} \leqslant v^{[2]} = 1001$.
We will show an application of this result.

2.6.2　Single Writer/Multiple Reader Problem

Lamport's concurrent reading and writing scheme can be used to solve the single writer/multiple reader problem, as seen in Figure 2.16. The solution maintains two version numbers, v1 and v2 (multidigit shared variables; initially v1 = v2), for the shared data. The writer increments v1 before writing the data item and sets v2 equal to v1 after writing. A reader reads v2 before reading the shared data and v1 after reading it; if the reader finds them equal, then it knows that during its read cycle no write operation was performed: It has a consistent copy of the data. If a reader finds v1 $\neq$ v2, it may have read inconsistent data, and it retries the read operation. A problem might arise if a read operation of v1 or v2 is performed concurrently with a write operation of v1 or v2. However, Lamport's theorem ensures that the above condition will be successfully tested even if reading and writing operations to either v1 or v2 are performed concurrently. The solution permits an arbitrary numbers of readers.

We now sketch a proof that a reader will accept only a consistent value of the resource D. Viewing D as a sequence of digits (which may be read in any order), suppose that the reader obtains

$$v2^{[k_1,l_1]} \qquad D^{[k_2,l_2]} \qquad v1^{[k_3,l_3]}$$

We need to show that $v2^{[k_1,l_1]} = v1^{[k_3,l_3]}$ implies that $k_2 = l_2$. Applying Lamport's theorem, we have

(a)　$v2^{[k_1,l_1]} \leqslant v2^{[l_1]}$　　and　　$v1^{[k_3]} \leqslant v1^{[k_3,l_3]}$

Since v2, D, and v1 are read as entities from left to right (independent of the internal order), it follows that

Figure 2.16 Single Writer/Multiple Reader Using
Concurrent Reading and Writing.

Shared Variables

var v1, v2: **multidigitinteger** : = 0, 0;

Writer	Reader
loop	**loop**
. . .	. . .
LR(v1) : = v1 + 1;	**repeat**
Perform write;	temp : = LR(v2);
RL(v2) : = v1;	Perform read
. . .	**until** RL(v1) = temp;
. . .	. . .
endloop	**endloop**

(b) $k_1 \leq l_1 \leq k_2 \leq l_2 \leq k_3 \leq l_3$

Furthermore, since $l_1 \leq k_3$, we have

(c) $v2^{[l_1]} \leq v1^{[k_3]}$ with equality only if $l_1 = k_3$

Combining (c) with (a) yields $v2^{[k_1, l_1]} \leq v2^{[l_1]} \leq v1^{[k_3]} \leq v1^{[k_3, l_3]}$.

If $v2^{[k_1, l_1]} = v1^{[k_3, l_3]}$, then $v2^{[l_1]} = v1^{[k_3]}$ and therefore $l_1 = k_3$. By (b), it follows that $l_2 = k_2$.

Advantages of this solution are that no mutual exclusion is required, priority problems do not arise, and every process proceeds as it wishes. A possible drawback is that a reader may be delayed for some time before obtaining correct data if the writer is rapidly changing the data. Also, the use of busy waiting further limits the applicability of this scheme.

2.7 Interprocess Communication

The correct use of the techniques described in previous sections of this chapter is the responsibility of each individual process. The programmer must be completely aware of the information (such as buffer space, semaphores) shared among processes. The operating system provides its services by simply executing the code for the primitive commands whenever they are invoked. A contrasting approach is to provide the programmer only with commands that implement *message communication*. The operating system hides implementation details and manages underlying storage and communication media. In a network environment, *interprocess communication* is the only technique for communication among remote processes. In many systems, the service is also available for communication among local processes. Some systems provide both shared memory and interprocess communication facilities.

Figure 2.17 depicts a generalized implementation of interprocess communication. Actual communication typically requires two primitives [Brinch-Hansen, 1973]:

send(destination process, message)
receive(source process, message)

A **send**(P_2, M_1) moves message M_1 from the memory space of the sending process to a buffer in operating system space. A **receive**(P_1, M_2) moves a message in the opposite direction. Operating system processes at each site are in charge of transferring messages to/from the buffers from/to the communication medium between the sites. These network services are described in Chapter 6. Some implementations merge the P_i_inbuffer and P_i_outbuffer. The result is contention for the same buffer space by outgoing and incoming messages, and care must be taken to avoid deadlock. If communication is between local processes, then P_i_inbuffer and P_j_outbuffer are identical and the operating system is no longer required to transfer information between buffers. A further optimization might be to pass a message by reference (rather than copy), thereby avoiding the use of any buffer space. Since the receiving process must reference the memory space of the sending process, this technique should be restricted to processes known to be reliable.

The channel through which one process communicates with another process is called a *communication link.* We distinguish between the *physical link* (memory space, bus, twisted pair, coaxial cable, fiber optic line, microwave, TV or radio transmission, satellite, and so on) and the *logical link,* which provides operating system software and logical management of the communication. In this section, we confine our attention to logical links and some of their properties. Several operating system design issues are important in providing appropriate logical communication links:

1. How are links established between processes?
2. What is the capacity of a link?
3. Are messages fixed or variable in length?
4. Are links unidirectional or bidirectional?
5. What parameters are allowed in **send** and **receive** operations?

These issues are discussed in the rest of this section.

2.7.1   Direct and Indirect Communication

In *direct communication,* communicating processes must explicitly name each other, and the operating system automatically establishes a unique bidirectional link between each pair of communicating processes. Figure 2.18 illustrates the use of direct communication to solve the producer/consumer problem using commands previously defined. This allows a consumer to serve all client producers via the established links. An enhancement is

broadcast(message)

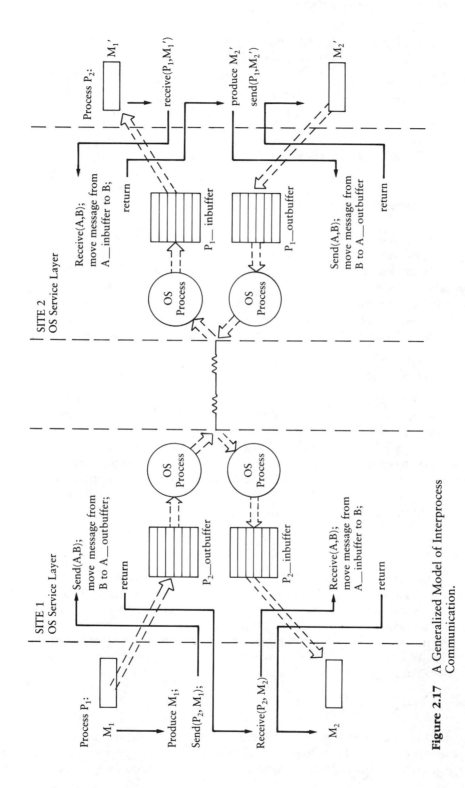

Figure 2.17   A Generalized Model of Interprocess Communication.

39

Figure 2.18   The Producer/Consumer Problem Using Direct
Interprocess Communication.

Producer P_i	Consumer P_j
var m1: **message**;	var m2: **message**;
loop	**loop**
. . .	. . .
Create a new message m1;	**receive**(P_i, m2);
send(P_j, m1);	Use message m2;
. . .	. . .
endloop	**endloop**

which allows a producer to send a message to all other processes with whom links
are established.

In *indirect communication,* processes communicate via an intermediate repo-
sitory for messages (a *mailbox*). The operating system creates this buffering facility
on behalf of some owner. A **create_mailbox** call may also specify protection rights
as to who can receive and send messages. A process may request the creation of a
link to an existing mailbox. Communication is carried out by means of

> **send**(mailbox, message)
> **receive**(mailbox, message)

commands, and it may be useful to have multiple senders (and possibly multiple
receivers). Indirect communication is the preferred way to provide operating system
services (such as remote login or file servers) to the user community. Consider, for
example, a printer service. The name of the service is public knowledge, allowing
any user to send files to be printed. Multiple consumers may be linked to the mailbox
if multiple printers (and corresponding driver processes) are involved. Depending
on the requirements, both unidirectional and bidirectional communication may be
allowed in indirect communication.

2.7.2   Capacity

The capacity of a link is normally limited by the amount of preallocated buffer
space. As a result, a **send** operation may block the invoking process if enough buffer
space is not available; the blocked process is reactivated when the required space
becomes available. If the buffer has zero capacity, that is, does not exist at all, the
sender always blocks until the message receiver accepts the message. An infinite
capacity implies that buffer space is dynamically allocated from a "large" available
pool of storage.

2.7.3   Message Size

The size of the message may be fixed or variable. Implementation of variable-size
messages requires the management of "holes" left by vacated message slots; *external
fragmentation* becomes a problem. If only fixed-size messages are supplied, a sender

must split a variable-length message and send it as separate messages. The receiver must reassemble the components of the message. Since the last component must be padded, *internal fragmentation* is a disadvantage.

2.8 Summary of Mechanisms

Table 2.1 summarizes many low-level process synchronization mechanisms (some have been introduced in this chapter) in increasing order of descriptive power. A predicate is a condition that must be satisfied for a process to complete the execution of a primitive. If the condition is not satisfied, the process is suspended. The kinds of information available and the kinds of operations allowed in stating conditions determine the descriptive power of primitives.

The group (A) mechanism is very basic and equivalent to the test-and-set instruction. It is often a machine instruction used in operating system kernels that perform CPU allocation and implement process synchronization primitives.

Group (B) mechanisms do not require mutual exclusion, an advantage previously discussed. The Block/Wakeup mechanism was proposed for the virtual memory environment of Multics [Saltzer, 1966]. It requires that the processes be cognizant of each other and that a process issuing a wakeup maintain a queue in its own area. The group (B) mechanisms are also primarily used in operating system kernels to implement other primitives.

Group (C) contains the most basic process synchronization mechanisms provided to processes by operating system kernels. (Note that operating system kernels are not processes.) Although the semaphore and sequencer mechanisms are most important, the Wait/Signal and Wait/Post mechanisms are also often used. Wait/Post has enjoyed widespread use thanks to its adoption by IBM. It has been criticized, however, because of its nonassociativity [Dijkstra, 1968]: It requires two separate mechanisms, one for event notification and one for mutual exclusion. An associative mechanism can be used for both event notification and for mutual exclusion.

The Wait/Signal and Wait/Post mechanisms use boolean variables instead of the integer variables used in the semaphore and sequencer mechanisms. This is a disadvantage as well as an advantage. The disadvantage is in the loss of a counting capability; the advantage is in a more precise description of OR conditions.

The group (D) mechanism is discussed in Section 2.3, and group (E) mechanisms are discussed in Section 2.4.

The Fork/Join mechanism of group (F), proposed by Conway [1963] allows for the dynamic creation and deletion of processes and for testing the number currently running. The Fork/Join mechanism and other extensions to high-level languages such as **cobegin-coend** [Brinch-Hansen, 1973] are rarely used in operating systems because of their limited expressive power [Baer, 1973].

Group (G) mechanisms allow priority relations to be stated. The need for them is not as great as for the group (F) mechanism, however.

Finally, group (H) mechanisms allow conditions to be stated based on history information (the order in which events have occurred). They are useful when the need arises.

2.9   Issues of Design and Implementation

Conventional implementations of a centralized CPU dispatcher and of P and V semaphore operations use busy waiting or disable interrupts to achieve mutual exclusion. This is satisfactory in systems with only a few central processors. However, for a large number of processors problems arise because overhead and lock contention become too severe. Real-time applications and fault-tolerant computing cannot be properly handled in conventional ways. For real-time applications a uniprocessor does not work well because the system fails to respond to an external signal quickly if the processor is in the dispatcher or a process synchronization primitive. Fault tolerance is only partly achieved in multiprocessors because, in a shared-memory system, a single copy of the data used to control operating system actions can be lost if a memory module fails. Further, if a processor fails while executing the dispatcher or another primitive, total system failure is likely. We describe solutions to these problems.

2.9.1   Overhead

Performance is degraded because of nonignorable execution times of the dispatcher and process coordination primitives, and memory contention by *lock instructions* for a lock bit (such as when using a test-and-set instruction). The execution time of the dispatcher or primitive varies depending on dispatching discipline, queue maintenance complexity, and the number of processes, as well as on hardware characteristics such as the number of registers and instruction set. The overhead becomes more severe when there are many operating system processes such as spoolers, operator interfaces, and device drivers because they contend for primitives and the dispatcher as well. The only real solution is hardware support [Denning, 1981; Lamport, 1977; Maekawa, 1982].

The overhead also becomes more severe as more user processes compete. The overhead increases not only because only one processor is allowed to execute a primitive at a time but also because acquiring exclusive access to the primitive is delayed due to memory contention for the lock bit associated with the primitive. The latter delay occurs when an unlock instruction cannot perform its operation because other processors are continuously accessing the lock bit with lock instructions. This delay also occurs due to memory contention when both the primitive and the lock bit reside in the same memory bank. This can be mitigated by inserting delay between retrials of lock instructions. The priority system among processors regarding memory access is also important. A higher priority given to an unlock instruction reduces unnecessary delay, but a fixed priority system must be avoided because it may permanently keep a lock bit uncleared and lead to a deadlock.

Firmware Implementations

Firmware implementations provide primitives as machine instructions; the dispatcher is a firmware procedure. Primitives are thus executed as normal machine instructions in which the dispatcher is internally invoked. The resulting speedup varies from computer to computer, but a factor of several is the minimum to be expected. A firmware implementation is the same as one in software with some modifications. First, interrupt enabling and disabling are unnecessary because interrupt signals are not interrogated during the execution of a primitive. This is important because most interrupt inhibitions are for mutual exclusion of primitives. Since nearly all are eliminated, low-level systems programming is greatly simplified. Second, when locking a primitive fails, it is more efficient to expose the processor to a possible interrupt before a retrial. In this case, the microprogram does not advance the instruction counter, and it interrogates interrupt signals at a retrial after a delay.

Private Semaphores

If process synchronization is performed only between a pair of processes, we can simplify primitives and reduce overhead by using *private semaphores* [Denning, 1981]. The only process allowed to wait on a private semaphore is the owner, and only one other process is allowed to signal event completion. So the number of **P** operations cannot differ by more than one from the number of **V** operations on a private semaphore.

A private semaphore has several fields in addition to the *owner* field. The *priority* field contains the priority of the owner; it is used to determine if a signaling process should relinquish the processor. The *waiting bit* indicates whether the owner is waiting on this semaphore and the *signal bit* shows whether a signal has been received or not. The *lock bit* prevents a signaler from interfering with the receiver.

Machine instructions **pwait** and **psignal** receive and send signals via private semaphores. Their microprograms, shown in Figure 2.19, are very similar to **wait** and **post** in Table 2.1. At a **psignal,** the dispatcher is invoked if the waiting bit is on. This keeps the highest priority processes running. A less exact but simpler approach is to compare the priority of the running process (executing **psignal**) with the priority of the process blocked via **pwait.** The process is switched to the newly unblocked process if it has the higher priority. This approach is exact for a uniprocessor.

2.9.2   Real-Time and Fault Tolerance

Since conventional dispatcher and synchronization primitive implementations disable interrupts during their execution, resulting real-time response may be unacceptable. This problem can be mitigated either by reducing the execution times of primitives or by eliminating interrupt inhibition. We have seen that firmware implementations can solve the problem. Here we discuss another approach.

Fault tolerance problems arise when data that controls system execution are centralized. A processor or memory failure will lead to a total system failure because centralized data become inaccessible. By decentralizing control data, these problems are solved. Lamport [Lamport, 1974] has shown a method of obtaining mutual exclusion based on decentralized data. The assumption is that each processor con-

Figure 2.19   Microprograms for **pwait** and **psignal**.

```
pwait(S):
  begin
    while S.lock = 1 do endwhile;
    if S.signal = 1 then
      S.signal : = 0; S.lock : = 0
    else
      S.waiting : = 1; S.lock : = 0;
      Dispatcher
    endif
  end pwait

psignal(S):
  begin
    while S.lock = 1 do endwhile;
    if S.waiting = 0 then
      S.signal : = 1; S.lock : = 0
    else
      S.waiting : = 0; S.lock : = 0;
      Dispatcher
    endif
  end psignal
```

tains its own memory unit but may read from any other processor's memory. The decentralized common data base consists of two arrays:

var choosing, number: **array**[1..N] **of integer**;

Elements choosing[i] and number[i] are in the memory of processor i, and are initially zero. We must assume that the values in number[i] may become arbitrarily large. The mutual exclusion algorithm for processor i is shown in Figure 2.20. As with sequencers, this algorithm is based on the procedure commonly used in bakeries, in which a customer receives a number upon entering a store. The holder of the lowest number is the next one to be served.

The correctness of the algorithm rests on the truth of the following assertions [Lamport, 1974]:

1. If processors i and k are now in the bakery and i entered the bakery before k entered the doorway and took its number, then number[i] < number[k]. The phrase "entered the doorway" for process k refers to the time in the algorithm that choosing[k] = 1; "in the bakery" is the time span after choosing[k] returns to 0 through the time that process k exits its critical section. This assertion shows that processors enter their critical sections on a first-come, first-served basis.

2. If processor i is in its critical section and processor k (k ≠ i) is in the bakery, then (number[i], i) < (number[k], k). For ordered pairs of integers, (a, b) < (c, d) if a < c, or if a = c and b < d. This assertion implies that at most one

Figure 2.20 A Decentralized Mutual Exclusion Algorithm [From Lamport, 1974. Copyright © 1974 by Association for Computing Machinery. Reprinted by permission].

Mutual Exclusion Algorithm for Processor i

Shared Variables

var choosing, number: **array**[1..N] **of integer**;

loop

   . . .

   choosing[i] := 1;

   number[i] := 1 + max(number[1], . . ., number[N]);

   choosing[i] := 0;

   for j := 1 **to** N **do**

     L: **while** choosing[j] = 1 **do endwhile**;

     while number[j] $\neq$ 0 **and** (number[j],j) < (number[i],i) **do endwhile**

   endfor;

   Critical section;

   number[i] := 0;

   . . .

endloop

processor can be in its critical section at any time. It also shows, together with assertion 1, that processors enter their critical sections on a first-come, first-served basis.

3. Assume that only a bounded number of processor failures may occur. If no processor is in its critical section and there is a processor in the bakery that does not fail, then some processor must eventually enter its critical section. This assertion means that the system can only be deadlocked by a processor halting in its critical section, or by an unbounded sequence of processor failures and restarts. The latter can tie up the system as follows. If processor j continually fails and restarts while choosing[j] remains 1 "most of the time," then in the worst case processor i could loop forever at the statement labeled L.

Lamport's algorithm has the following properties:

1. Failure of a processor, including its memory unit, does not lead to a total system failure if the processor halts after its failure and any read from its memory after its halt gives a value of zero.

2. Since no interrupt inhibition is used, an external interrupt can be handled without delay.

2.9.3 Creation and Deletion of Semaphores and Sequencers

Semaphores, sequencers and other process synchronization variables are themselves *shared variables* that do not belong to any particular process. They must be kept under operating system control. They may be either predefined or created upon request. To allow dynamic creation and deletion of process coordination variables, primitives such as the following might be provided:

create-semaphore(name, initial value)
delete-semaphore(name)

Since the undisciplined use of these primitives might lead to chaos, many systems restrict their use. Another issue with dynamic creation and deletion of semaphores is main memory management. That is, the resident area of an operating system may have to be dynamically expanded to accommodate coordination variables and associated queues.

2.9.4   Misuse of Mechanisms

Every mechanism introduced in this chapter may be misused. For example, a **P** may appear without a needed matching **V**. These mistakes are extremely difficult to find, and testing of concurrent programs is an enormous task. These mechanisms should not be used in higher level languages or in application codes available to general users.

2.10   Summary

This chapter reviews some elementary ideas about processes and their synchronization. We see how a model of process systems supplies methods for establishing determinacy and for maximizing parallel execution. Fundamental ideas of process synchronization are reviewed, some classical problems are introduced, and several newer methods of synchronization are introduced and exemplified. A general picture of interprocess communication provides a framework for characterizing all the methods. Table 2.1 shows the wide variety of low-level process synchronization methods. Finally, implementation issues are discussed.

All the mechanisms of this chapter are suitable for programming operating system components at the lowest level. For higher level languages, we need more structured language elements. These are the subject of Chapter 3, which discusses concurrent programming.

Key Words

advance	**broadcast** operation	**cobegin-coend**
AND synchronization	busy waiting	communication link
await	change-priority	competition
Bernstein conditions	Cigarette Smoker's	consumer
blocked	Problem	cooperation

cooperation without mutual exclusion

create_mailbox operation

create-semaphore operation

critical section

deadlock

Dekker's algorithm

delete-semaphore operation

determinacy

Dining Philosopher Problem

direct communication

direct predecessor

disable interrupts

dispatching

enable interrupts

equivalent systems

event

event variable

eventcount

external fragmentation

firmware implementation

fork

indefinite delay

independent processes

indirect communication

internal fragmentation

interpretation

interprocess communication

join

lock instruction

logical link

mailbox

maximally parallel system

message

message communication

mutual exclusion problem

mutual noninterference

NOT synchronization

OR synchronization

P operation

Pboth

physical link

precedence relation

predecessor

private semaphore

process

process control block (PCB)

process creation

process termination

processor scheduling

producer

producer/consumer problem

psignal operation

pwait operation

read

reader/writer problem

ready

receive operation

redundant edge

replace operation

resume

running

semaphore

send operation

sequencer

short-term scheduling

signal

SP operations

starvation

successor

suspend

suspended-blocked

suspended-ready

SV operation

tagged messages

test-and-set instruction

ticket

transitive closure

V operation

virtual processor

wait operation

wait-or operation

weak reader preference solution

Questions

1. Define a sequencer and an eventcount. Discuss their advantages and disadvantages compared with semaphores.

2. Show a solution of the producer/consumer problem using sequencers and event-counts. Are there any methods to prevent unmatched use of **ticket, await,** and **advance** operations?

3. What problems does the solution shown in Figure 2.10 have? How can the problems be avoided?

4. Define a simultaneous P and a corresponding V. Can they be mixed with simple P and V operations?

5. Define a parameterized P operation and show its use for a general priority problem. What occasions require a parameterized P operation?

6. Show that an arbitrary condition can be stated if shared variables are allowed and a mutual exclusion mechanism is provided. What are the disadvantages of this approach?

7. State the advantages and limitations of the concurrent reading and writing method based on the Lamport's theorem.

8. Can you obtain mutual exclusion using only test-and-set instructions (namely, without using the interrupt disabling/enabling technique) in a uniprocessor system?

9. Which of the following statements are true:
   a. Two P operations working on different semaphores must be mutually excluded.
   b. It is not possible to intermingle simple P operations (with only one parameter) and simultaneous P operations in one system.
   c. The initial value of a semaphore cannot be zero.
   d. The value of a semaphore cannot be modified by an operation other than P and V.

10. Which of the following statements on the solution shown in Figure 2.4 are true:
    a. Only one producer can place a message into the buffer at a time.
    b. Only one consumer can take a message from the buffer.
    c. A producer and a consumer cannot simultaneously place and take a message into/from the buffer.
    d. It is not possible to modify the solution so that several producers can simultaneously place a message because there is only one buffer.

11. Which of the following statements on the solution shown in Figure 2.5 are true:
    a. The number of writers must be limited to one.
    b. Suppose that a reader is in the "read" stage and a writer has attempted a write operation. Another reader has then arrived. This reader will wait at P(wmutex).
    c. Suppose that a writer is in the "write" stage while one writer and three readers are waiting. When the writer has completed its write operation, one of the readers always get priority over the waiting writer.
    d. With simple P operations, it is not possible to write a solution that always prefers writers to readers.

12. In Figure 2.6, there is only one **advance**(In) in the producer specification. In Figure 2.4, the producer executes two **V** operations. Why is one **advance** sufficient?

13. Which of the following statements are true:

    a. Operations on a semaphore must be mutually excluded, whereas operations on a sequencer are not.

    b. A semaphore is useful for expressing mutual exclusion whereas a sequencer/eventcount scheme is not.

    c. A starvation problem will not arise in a system based on a sequencer.

    d. A sequencer/eventcount mechanism can assign processes more efficiently than a semaphore mechanism.

    e. It is not always easy to express an *AND* condition with **await** operations.

    f. It is not easy to express a *NOT* condition with **await** operations.

14. Does it make sense to provide both semaphores and sequencers in a single system? Justify your answer.

15. Show an example that cannot be stated with only simple **P** operations. Assume that no shared variables other than semaphores are allowed.

16. Show an example that cannot be stated with only simple and simultaneous **P** operations. Assume that no shared variables other than semaphores are allowed.

17. Compare and evaluate the **P/V, ticket/await/advance, and wait/post** mechanisms. Do this by exploring whether one is more *powerful* than another. Mechanisms have equal power if each can be implemented using the other; otherwise, one mechanism is more powerful than the other.

18. Exemplify case 3 of Lamport's theorem using the same example used in Section 2.6.1.

Problems

1. [Coffman, 1973, p. 80. Reprinted by permission of Prentice-Hall, Inc., Englewood Cliffs, N.J.] Suppose that, instead of a first-come, first-served semaphore queuing discipline, queuing is last-come, first-served. However, we still want to implement *safe* mutual exclusion for the critical sections of n cyclic processes. *Safe* means that no process can block indefinitely while other processes cycle arbitrarily often. For example, processes P_1 and P_2 can block P_3 forever if P_3 arrives second and P_1 and P_2 cycle alternatively through their critical sections.

   Consider a binary tree with n leaves, one for each process. Each internal node has an associated semaphore. The processes desiring to enter their critical sections perform **P** operations on successive semaphores from their leaves to the root of the tree, execute their critical section, and perform **V** operations in reverse order back down the tree.

    a. Show that this scheme implements safe mutual exclusion.

    b. Discuss how the shape of the binary tree can affect the relative speeds of the processes and enforce a priority scheme.

2. Is it necessary to extend the **await** operation to a simultaneous **await** and a parameterized **await** like the **P** operation in order to describe those problems that cannot be stated with simple **P** operations?

3. If the pairing of **P** and **V** is not proper, the system may be deadlocked or it may destroy data. Can you propose a way that a compiler can help avoid this error?

4. Is it possible to implement a semaphore for decentralized data (data on different processors' memories)? What about a sequencer and an eventcount?

5. A time-out facility is useful to detect a permanent wait in a **P** or any other wait operation. Write a specification for a **P** operation with time-out facility, assuming the existence of a timer interrupt and an associated process that you may specify.

6. Design a timer queue that accepts the following requests:

   a. Wake up after T seconds

   b. Wake up at time T

Be careful about the race condition between the expiration of the current interval and the setting of a new interval.

7. There are N blocks of storage, each of which holds one unit of information. Initially, these blocks are empty and linked on "freelist." Three processes communicate using shared memory in the following manner:

Shared Variables

var freelist, list1, list2: block;

Process 1

      var b: **ptr to** block;
      while true **do**
          begin
              b : = *unlink*(freelist);
              produce information in block b;
              link(b, list1)
          end

Process 2

      var x,y: **ptr to** block;
      while true **do**
          begin
              x : = *unlink*(list1); y : = *unlink*(freelist);
              use block x and produce information in block y;
              link(x, freelist); *link*(y, list2)
          end

Process 3

      var c: **ptr to** block;
      while true **do**

```
begin
        c := unlink(list2);
        consume information in block c;
        link(c, freelist)
end
```

Rewrite the code for the processes, using semaphores to implement the necessary mutual exclusion and synchronization. The solution must be deadlock-free and concurrency should not be unnecessarily restricted.

8. For a semaphore s, define:

$init[s]$ = initial value of s
$start\_P[s]$ = the number of times $P(s)$ has been started
$end\_P[s]$ = the number of times $P(s)$ has been completed
$end\_V[s]$ = the number of times $V(s)$ has been completed

A useful semaphore invariant is:

$$end\_P[s] = min(start\_P[s], init[s] + end\_V[s])$$

An abstract version of the bounded buffer problem is:

var empty, full, mutex: **semaphore** = (N, 0, 1);

Producer	Consumer
while true **do**	**while** true **do**
begin	**begin**
P(empty);	P(full);
get buffer from freelist;	get buffer from freelist;
...	...
put buffer on fullist;	put buffer on fullist;
V(full)	V(empty)
end	**end**

Prove that $0 \leq end\_P[empty] - end\_P[full] \leq N$.

9. The following table shows domains and ranges for a system of processes along with known precedence constraints:

Process	Domain	Range	Preceded By
P_1	v_5	v_4, v_7	
P_2	v_1, v_7	v_5	P_1
P_3	v_4	v_6	P_1
P_4	v_4, v_8	v_2	P_2
P_5	v_2	v_3, v_1	P_3
P_6	v_3	v_5	P_3
P_7	v_4	v_5, v_8	P_4, P_6

Add the minimum number of precedence constraints to make this system of processes determinate. Do not remove any constraints.

10. Work Problem 7 using sequencers and eventcounts.

11. Prove the lemma in Section 2.6.1. (*Hint:* Use induction on the number of digits m.) Use the lemma to prove Lamport's theorem.

12. Show how a semaphore can be implemented using eventcounts and sequencers. You may assume that a FIFO semaphore queue is sufficient.

References

Baer, J. L. (1973). "A survey of some theoretical aspects of multiprocessing." *ACM Computing Surveys* 5, 1, pp. 31–80.

Bernstein, A. J. (October 1966). "Analysis of programs for parallel processing." *IEEE Transactions on Computers* EC-15, 5, pp. 757–762.

Brinch-Hansen, P. (1973). *Operating System Principles*. Prentice-Hall, Englewood Cliffs, N.J.

Coffman, E. G., and P. J. Denning. (1973). *Operating System Theory*. Prentice-Hall, Englewood Cliffs, N.J.

Conway, M. (1963). "A multiprocessor system design." *Proceedings of the AFIPS Fall Joint Computer Conference,* pp. 139–146.

Denning, P. J., T. D. Dennis; and J. A. Brumfield. (October 1981). "Low contention semaphores and ready lists." *Communications of the ACM* 24, 10, pp. 687–699.

Dijkstra, E. W. (September 1965). "Solution of a problem in concurrent programming control." *Communications of the ACM* 8, 9, p. 569.

———. (1968). "Cooperation sequential processes." In *Programming Languages,* F. Geunys (Ed.), Academic Press, N.Y., pp. 43–112.

Eisenberg, M. A., and M. R. McGuire. (November 1972). "Further comments on Dijkstra's concurrent programming control problem." *Communications of the ACM* 15, 11, p. 999.

Gaines, R. S. (March 1972). "An operating system based on the concept of a supervisory computer." *Communications of the ACM* 15, 3, pp. 150–156.

Knuth, D. E. (May 1966). "Additional comments on a problem in concurrent programming control." *Communications of the ACM* 9, 5, pp. 321–322.

Kosaraju, S. R. (October 1973). "Limitations of Dijkstra's semaphore primitive and Petri nets." *Proceedings of the Fourth Symposium on Operating System Principles,* pp. 122–126.

Lamport, L. (August 1974). "A new solution of Dijkstra's concurrent programming problem." *Communications of the ACM* 17, 8, pp. 453–455.

———. (November 1977). "Concurrent reading and writing." *Communications of the ACM* 20, 11, pp. 806–811.

Lipton, R. J. (1974). "A comparative study of models of parallel computation." *15th Annual Symposium on Switching and Automata Theory,* pp. 145–155.

Maekawa, M. (1980). "A classification of process coordination schemes in descriptive power." *International Journal of Computer and Information Science* 9, 5, pp. 383–406.

Maekawa, M.; I. Yamazake; et al. (1982). "Experimental polyprocessor system (EPOS)—Operating system." *Proceedings of the 6th Annual IEEE Symposium on Computer Architecture.*

Patil, S. S. (February 1971). "Limitations and capabilities of Dijkstra's semaphore primitives for coordination among processes." *MIT Project MAC Computation Structure Group Memo 57,* MIT, Cambridge, Mass.

Peterson, G. L. (June 1981). "Myths about the mutual exclusion problem." *Information Processing Letters* 12, 3, pp. 115–116.

Presser, L. (1975). "Multiprogramming coordination." *ACM Computing Surveys* 7, 1, pp. 21–44.

Reed, D. P., and R. K. Kanodia. (February 1979). "Synchronization with eventcounts and sequencers." *Communications of the ACM* 22, 2, pp. 115–123.

Saltzer, J. H. (July 1966). "Traffic control in a multiplexed computer system." *MIT Project MAC Report MAC-TR-30,* MIT, Cambridge, Mass.

Vantigorgh, H., and A. Van Lamsweerde. (1972). "On an extension of Dijkstra's semaphore primitives." *Information Processing Letters,* 1, pp. 181–186.

Suggested Readings

Courtois, P. J.; R. Heymans; and D. L. Parnas. (1971). "Concurrent control with 'readers' and 'writers'." *Communications of the ACM* 14, 10, pp. 667–668.

Debruijn, N. G. (March 1967). "Additional comments on a problem in concurrent programming control." *Communications of the ACM* 10, 3, pp. 137–138.

Horning, J. J., and B. Randell. (1973). "Process structuring." *ACM Computing Surveys* 5, 1, pp. 5–30.

Kessels, J. L. W. (July 1977). "An alternative to event queues for synchronization in monitors." *Communications of the ACM* 20, 7, pp. 500–503.

Lamport, L. (March 1977). "Proving the correctness of multiprocess programs." *IEEE Transactions on Software Engineering* SE-3, 2, pp. 125–143.

————. (November 1985). "A Fast Mutual Exclusion Algorithm." Digital Equipment Corporation Systems Research Center Technical Report.

Maekawa, M. (1977). "Interprocess communications in a highly diversified distributed system." *Information Processing* 77, pp. 149–154.

Maekawa, M., and D. L. Boyd. (1974). "A model of concurrent tasks within jobs of a multiprogramming system." *Proceedings of the Eighth Annual Princeton Conference on Information Sciences and Systems,* Princeton University (March 28-29, 1974), pp. 97–101.

Maekawa, M., and Y. Morimoto. (July 1982). "A performance adjustment of an APL interpreter." *IEEE Transactions on Software Engineering* SE-8, 4, pp. 331–343.

Parnas, D. L. (March 1975). "On a solution to the cigarette smoker's problem (without conditional statements)." *Communications of the ACM* 18, 3, pp. 181–183.

Parnas, D. L., and H. Wurges. (October 1976). "Response to undesired events in software systems." *Proceedings of the 2nd International conference on Software Engineering.*

Peterson, J. L., and T. H. Bredt. (1974). "A comparison of models of parallel computation." *Information Processing 74,* North-Holland, pp. 466–470.

Schutz, H. A. (1979). "On the design of a language for programming real-time concurrent processes." *IEEE Transactions on Software Engineering* SE-5, 3, pp. 248–255.

Walden, D. C. (1972). "A system for interprocess communication in a resource sharing computer network." *Communications of the ACM* 15, 4, pp. 221–230.

Language Mechanisms   **3**
for Concurrency

3.1   Introduction

The process synchronization mechanisms described in Chapter 2 are at a level comparable to assembly language programming. While they are useful for implementing the primitives typically offered by operating system nuclei, they are too primitive to build large, reliable systems. For this we need higher level concepts integrated into modern programming languages so that correctness is supported and underlying hardware implementations are of no importance to the programmer. Any such language mechanism for parallel computation must be based on a computation model. Useful models include Petri nets [Peterson, 1981], the object model [Liskov and Zilles, 1975; Liskov, et al., 1977; Wulf, et al., 1976; Goldberg and Robson, 1983], the data flow model [Dennis, 1974; Dennis and Misunas, 1975; Arvind, et al., 1977; Arvind and Brock, 1982] and the actor model [Hewitt, 1973]. The Petri net model has been used as the basis for describing computations at a low level of detail; for large and complex systems, this model can lead to very large descriptions. The data flow model has been used to support ideas about parallel computation at the application level, but so far has not been influential in the design of operating systems facilities. Most of the mechanisms in this chapter are examples from the *object model* of computation (the actor model is similar in many ways). In the next section we briefly discuss this model and explain the major concurrent programming idea based on it. In subsequent sections we introduce a framework for analyzing mechanisms, examine a few mechanisms in use today, and finally discuss the concurrent processing features of the Ada* programming language.

3.2   The Object Model and Monitors

The object model of computation can be traced to the design of the Simula programming language [Dahl, et al., 1968]. Its purpose is to clearly define the com-

---

* Ada is a registered trademark of the U. S. Government, Ada Joint Program Office.

ponents of a system, which come in two varieties. First, there are "passive" *objects* with associated invariant properties that must hold at all times for the objects. If we consider the read/write mechanism of a moving-head disk to be an object, then some properties associated with the object are: The head may only move in one dimension, inward and outward; the head may stop only at predefined positions along its range of travel, over the cylinders of the disk; the head may be stopped over exactly one cylinder at a time; the time required to move from one position to another is positive, and the function describing the time required to move the head is a nondecreasing function of distance.

Operations are the second kind of object model components—the "active" portion. Operations perform actions on the passive objects and must preserve their invariant properties. Since only defined operations may inquire about the state of objects or alter the state, they completely define the behavior of the object. Using the moving-head disk example again, only the operation "move to cylinder N" to reposition the head may be necessary.

The object model is a general framework within which alternatives about object representation and interface must be chosen. It is often convenient to allow multiple *instances* of an object without requiring a completely repeated definition (multiple disks will each have an associated head mechanism). In addition, one may want to supply parameters to each instance (different disks may have a different number of cylinders). As with simpler objects in programming languages, it is convenient to allow the original declaration to be a *type,* of which instances are declared as other items in a language. In this context the object model is implemented as an *abstract data type*.

The two components of the object model find counterparts in the abstract data type. The passive objects are represented as a set of descriptions for internal data structures that retain the state of the object. These structures may in turn be defined by other abstract data types defined within the outer type. Initializing code that, when executed, provides the initial state for each instance of the type is also considered a passive object because it plays no role after instantiation. The most important feature is that objects of the abstract data type are not visible outside the type definition; they are *encapsulated*.

The active components of an abstract data type are the operations that may be performed on an instance. By far the most common mechanism for operation definition is the procedure declaration, but this is not strictly necessary. The operations are known globally. In some implementations a language must provide for the names of internally defined types to be known externally as well so that operations that are procedures may have parameters of proper types.

The *monitor* proposed by Hoare [Hoare, 1974] is an abstract data type implementation of the object model with additional capabilities for process synchronization with respect to resource objects of the type. The monitor has been widely used to manage resources in centralized computer systems, although later in this chapter we will see extensions for its use in distributed systems. Because of its importance, we describe its structure in some detail, exemplify its use (the examples are adapted from Hoare [1974]), and discuss some issues of usage and design.

3.2.1   Mechanisms

A monitor is a type used to manage an operating system resource, either hardware or software. A schematic structure is shown in Figure 3.1, and Figure 3.2 has the outline of a programming language representation. The *resource* managed by a monitor will be manifest in the local data of the monitor if it is a software resource, or it will be implicit if the monitor manages some hardware component. The *local data* that describes the state of the resource is used by a *scheduler* (usually an implicit

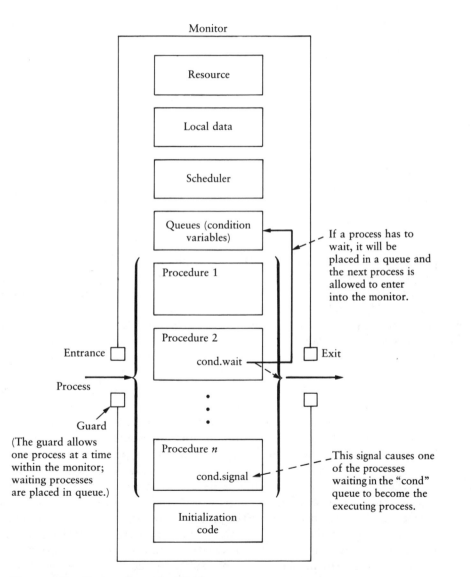

Figure 3.1   Components of a Monitor.

Figure 3.2   Language Structure of a Monitor.

Monitor_name: **monitor**
    Declarations of data local to the monitor
    . . .
    CV1, CV2, . . . : **condition**;
    . . .
    Declarations of procedures to implement operations
    . . .
    procedure Name(... formal parameters ...);
      begin
        . . .
        Procedure body may include
        "CVi.**wait**" and
        "CVi.**signal**" statements
        . . .
      end;
    . . .
    begin
      Initialization statements
      for local data
end

part provided by the programming language implementation) to control the order of resource allocation. *Condition variables* are distinguished local data items that are explicitly referenced by processes executing procedures; the associated *queues* hold processes that are blocked by each condition variable. Actual queue structures depend on the supplied scheduling disciplines. *Procedures* of a monitor implement the operations of the abstract data type. They are invoked by processes to acquire the resource, release it, or interrogate the state of the resource. *The monitor allows only one process to be active (executing a procedure) within the monitor at a time.* The *guard* (another implicit part of a monitor) performs this regulation. *Initialization code* is executed when an instance of the monitor is defined to initialize local data.

One monitor type is usually defined for each resource type, such as magnetic disk, magnetic tape, card reader, and line printer. If resource units are not interchangeable, they are either defined by separate monitor types or by parameterized types.

Since the monitor definition includes provision for mutually exclusive execution of any procedure, the procedures themselves need not be written to solve any associated problems (this has been one of the primary attractive features of monitors). However, it is common, during the execution of a procedure to perform a monitor operation, for an executing process to be delayed until a specified condition is satisfied. Simply exiting the procedure will not suffice because that does not provide the needed service to the executing process. On the other hand, the rule that only one process may execute in a monitor at a time precludes a busy waiting for the resource to become free. This is the purpose of condition variables: One is declared for each different condition that may cause an executing process to wait. Associated with each condition variable CV are three operations. A process that must be blocked executes CV.**wait** to join the queue of processes waiting in association with CV. This clears the way for another process to enter (or perhaps to resume execution in) a monitor procedure. Another process that alleviates a waiting condition associated with CV will execute CV.**signal** to cause one (if any) process waiting in association with CV to begin immediate execution. A third operation, CV.**queue,** returns *true* if any process is waiting in the queue associated with CV. Otherwise its value is *false*. Several points should be noted here.

First, the waiting queues associated with a condition variable may be implemented just as those associated with semaphores, as discussed in Chapter 2.

Second, the **signal** operation is defined to take no action if no process is waiting with the condition variable. This is different from the situation where the integer value of a semaphore is incremented when **V** occurs.

Third, unlike the unblocking action of the semaphore **V** operation, we describe the unblocking of **signal** to result in the immediate resumption of execution of an unblocked process. This is necessary because if the unblocked process becomes merely *ready* to execute, some other resource-consuming process may successfully execute a request. Later, the unblocked process will proceed under the assumption that the resource is still available. To prevent this, one can envision that the newly unblocked process *replaces* the signaling process in the monitor. The signaling process joins an "urgent" queue. A process on this queue is resumed if another process performs a CV.**wait** or exits its monitor procedure.

Next we will consider some simple examples of the use of monitors in process synchronization problems.

3.2.2 The Reader/Writer Problem

Although the reader/writer problem has several variations depending on the priority relation among readers and writers, a monitor can implement all variations because arbitrary local data in a monitor can maintain necessary information. As an example, a strong reader preference solution is shown in Figure 3.3. Variations of the reader/ writer problem include:

- Weak reader priority—An arriving writer waits until there are no more active readers.

- Strong reader priority—Conditions of the weak reader priority solution apply, but also a waiting reader has priority over a waiting writer.

- Writer priority—An arriving reader waits until there are no more active or waiting writers.

The local datum "busy" is initialized to *false* to indicate that whatever is being shared by readers and writers is not in use, and "readercount" keeps track of the number of concurrent reading processes. Two condition variables are declared since two kinds of waiting conditions are necessary.

Figure 3.3   A Strong Reader Preference Solution Based on Monitors [Hoare, 1978. Copyright © 1978 by Association for Computing Machinery. Reprinted by permission].

```
readers_and_writers: monitor
  var readercount: integer;
    busy: boolean;
    OKtoread, OKtowrite: condition;

  procedure startread;
    begin
      if busy then OKtoread.wait endif;
      readercount := readercount + 1;
      if OKtoread.queue then OKtoread.signal endif
    end startread;

  procedure endread;
    begin
      readercount := readercount − 1;
      if readercount = 0 then OKtowrite.signal endif
    end endread;

  procedure startwrite;
    begin
      if readercount ≠ 0 or busy then OKtowrite.wait endif;
      busy := true
    end startwrite;

  procedure endwrite;
    begin
      busy := false;
      if OKtoread.queue then OKtoread.signal
      else OKtowrite.signal endif
    end endwrite;

begin
    readercount := 0; busy := false
end readers_and_writers;
```

A reader process invokes the procedure "startread" before it performs a read operation. If the resource is being accessed by a writer, the reader blocks on the "OKtoread" condition; otherwise, it starts the read operation. The process tests whether there are any readers waiting in the queue of "OKtoread"; it does this via the primitive OKtoread.queue, which returns *true* if the queue is not empty—otherwise, it returns *false*. If any readers are waiting, one of them is activated by the OKtoread.signal operation and the new reader exits the monitor. If more processes are waiting, the newly activated process still in the monitor will activate yet another. In this way, all waiting reader processes will gain read access to the resource. Note that all waiting readers are consecutively resumed without interruption, during which the mutual exclusion of the monitor is passed on from one reader to another.

Figure 3.4   A Disk-Head Scheduler Based on Monitors [Hoare, 1978. Copyright © 1978 by Association for Computing Machinery. Reprinted by permission].

```
diskhead: monitor
   var headpos, maxcylinderindex: cylinderindex;
      direction: (up, down);
      busy: boolean;
      upsweep, downsweep: condition;

   procedure request(dest: cylinderindex);
      begin
         if busy then
            if headpos < dest or (headpos = dest and direction = up) then
               upsweep.wait(dest)
            else downsweep.wait(maxcylinderindex - dest)
            endif
         endif;
         busy := true; headpos := dest;
         Move disk head to cylinder dest
      end request;

   procedure release;
      begin
         busy := false;
         if direction = up then
            if upsweep.queue then upsweep.signal
            else
               direction := down; downsweep.signal
            endif
         else
            if downsweep.queue then
               downsweep.signal
            else
            direction := up; upsweep.signal
            endif
         endif
      end release;

begin
   headpos := 0; direction := up; busy := false
end diskhead;
```

A reader invokes the procedure "endread" after it completes its read operation. If no other reader is active, a waiting writer is activated (or if no writer is waiting, no action results).

A writer executes a similar sequence in "startwrite." It may proceed only when no readers and no other writer are active. Upon completing a write operation, the writer may awaken a reader or a writer in "endwrite." All readers have a higher priority than any writer, regardless of the order of their arrival.

This example also demonstrates a weakness of monitors as described. Since mutually exclusive execution is the rule, we cannot encapsulate the data shared by readers and writers within the monitor itself; simultaneous access by readers would be impossible. But by excluding the shared data from the monitor, we must once again rely on correct behavior by reader and writer processes. In this case, the monitor has not added to the reliability of the solution.

3.2.3   A Disk-Head Scheduler

Resource schedulers often use information about requests to dynamically determine the order in which requests will be satisfied. A disk-head scheduler is an excellent example of this. Figure 3.4 shows a solution based on the monitor mechanism. To reduce seek time, the algorithm gives preference to requests nearest the current cylinder. A simple "shortest seek time first" scheme would give preference to centrally located cylinders and, under heavy load, would keep requests for cylinders near edges waiting indefinitely. To prevent this, the algorithm sweeps in one direction until no outstanding requests "lie ahead" and then reverses to sweep cylinders in the other direction until requests in that direction are exhausted. This is the so-called LOOK algorithm, a variant of the SCAN class of disk-head scheduling methods.

Three local variables are necessary. The variable "headpos" retains the current head position, "direction" indicates whether the head is currently on upsweep or downsweep, and "busy" indicates whether the disk is currently servicing a request.

When it wishes to perform a disk operation, a process first invokes the procedure "request," with the cylinder number as a parameter. If the disk is not busy, headpos is set to the requested position, the disk head is moved as specified, and the process is allowed to perform its I/O operation. If the disk is busy, the request is placed in either the upsweep queue or the downsweep queue depending on the relative position of the head to the requested position. In this example, we show an enhanced **wait** primitive that accepts a parameter specifying the relative priority of the waiting process (smaller values are higher priorities). In this case requests in a queue are ordered according to their cylinder positions. A corresponding **signal** (executed by a process in "release" to relinquish control of the disk head) selects the request nearest the current head position in the current direction, or reverses direction if no processes are waiting in the current direction.

In this example the resource being managed is also outside the monitor, but it is a hardware object. If the head-positioning command is not executable outside of these operations, then this monitor has made a start on completely controlling the head mechanism. However, we still trust that a process will request the disk before performing an I/O operation, and will not neglect to execute the release operation.

3.2.4   Design and Usage Issues

Some inherent assumptions are made about the monitor construct described here to simplify its structure and implementation. While adequate in most cases, two issues should be discussed concerning alternative approaches.

Priorities

We have specified that when a process is awakened by a condvariable.**signal** operation, it must begin execution immediately. This assumption, however, may limit flexibility in CPU scheduling. The following are alternative methods:

1. Select the highest priority process among the processes that have been waiting and can now proceed, and let it run. As the selected process leaves the monitor, the process that signaled and awakened it runs (thus process switching is necessary) or may start to run, provided that a processor is available. In this way no other process can intervene between the **signal** operation and the start of the awakened process.

2. Select the highest priority process among those that have been waiting and can now proceed, and make it a "ready" process. The process that has issued the **signal** operation continues to run. The selected process will have had its program counter reset to the monitor entry point; eventually it reenters the monitor procedure and retests conditions since arbitrary process executions may have occurred in the monitor since it was unblocked. (It is assumed that the selected process has not changed any monitor state variables.)

3. The same as method 1 except that both the selected process and the process that has executed the **signal** operation become "ready." Which one runs next depends on the priority relation between the two.

4. Select all the processes that can proceed and make all of them "ready." These processes will reenter their monitor procedures in some order to check whether their conditions are met. The process that has executed the **signal** operation continues to run.

5. The same as method 4 except that the process that has executed the **signal** operation is also made "ready."

All of these alternatives are equally easy to implement. But two other criteria should be considered. The first is modularity and ease of use. The separation between scheduling and synchronization would be much easier in method 5 because the selection of a process is made only after the synchronization is completed. The process coordination mechanism should not be involved in process selection since any process coordination mechanism that must assume a certain scheduling discipline is less flexible in application.

The second criterion is overhead, often a penalty we pay for modularity and ease of use. The space cost is the same in each method. The execution time cost, however, is greater in methods 4 and 5 because processes reenter monitor procedures, perhaps repeatedly, until conditions are met.

Although it is not possible to determine the best method without defining the context in which it will be used, method 3 is flexible. The Mesa system [Lampson and Redell, 1980] has adopted mechanisms 2 and 4. In method 2, one process context switch is avoided and the selected process may run at some convenient future time. Mesa performs this type of process wakeup via a **notify** operation. Mesa also provides a **broadcast,** implementing method 4. The serializer, which will be described below, adopts method 4 as its only signaling mechanism.

Nested Monitor Calls

Software designers understand that a hierarchical structure is an appropriate form for a large program; operating system designers have also adopted this form. But in the presence of monitors, difficulties may arise. Suppose a monitor of a resource calls a procedure of another monitor, which in turn calls a procedure of still another monitor. In such *nested monitor calls,* deadlocks and loss of efficiency are probable. For example, a deadlock can occur via the following sequence. Process A calls a procedure of monitor M, which in turn calls a procedure of monitor N, in which process A is caused to wait. Process B is capable of executing in N to unblock process A. However, process B first calls a procedure of monitor M. Deadlock results because process B cannot enter monitor M since process A is still holding it. Loss of efficiency may occur because monitor M is held while process A is waiting in monitor N even if no deadlock occurs.

Solutions for this problem vary. Some operating systems are structured so that such deadlocks will never occur. They may be designed so that inner monitors keep processes waiting for only a short time, eliminating the deadlock possibility and keeping efficiency loss to a tolerable level.

One approach that has been proposed is to temporarily release ownership of all monitors entered when a process blocks in an inner monitor. This requires additional bookkeeping and overhead but increases flexibility. Programmers must assume that any monitor procedure invocation might cause a wait.

3.3   Analysis Framework for Mechanisms

The previous section introduced the monitor as a useful mechanism for resource management. To get a better understanding of such mechanisms, we now establish a framework in which to evaluate mechanisms that provide advanced capabilities. We develop some requirements and criteria for concurrent programming mechanisms, and briefly survey some extant or proposed systems. We will discuss a few of these in the remainder of the chapter.

3.3.1   Requirements

Much of the material in this section follows Bloom [1979]. Important requirements and constraints on concurrent programming mechanisms include the following:

1. Applicability to both centralized and distributed systems
2. Expressive power
3. Modularity
4. Ease of use
5. Program structure
6. Process failures and time-outs
7. Unanticipated faults and their recoveries

8. Real-time systems

We examine each of these in turn.

Applicability to Centralized and Distributed Systems

Centralized systems and distributed systems often need to interact. Ideally, a single-process synchronization mechanism for both local (in the same site) and remote (in a different site) processes would mask the geographical details about process residence. Most monitor implementations are applicable only to centralized systems.

Expressive Power

Two facets of *expressive power* are of interest. First, mechanisms must provide *exclusion constraints* on simultaneous execution so that correct solutions to problems can be formulated. Second, mechanisms should provide *priority constraints* for expressing priority relations among processes, so that efficient solutions can be devised. In either case, the constraints involve *conditions* that must be satisfied before we conclude that a process should execute, or that one process has priority over another. The constraints can be categorized on the basis of the kinds of information that may be included in the conditions, such as:

- The type of request (e.g., readers may have priority over writers)
- The time that a request was made (e.g., to implement fair scheduling)
- Parameters of the request (e.g., distance from the current disk-head position)
- Process information (e.g., for load-control purposes)
- Priority relations (e.g., taking into account assigned priorities)
- Local state of resources (e.g., the state of a set of buffers must affect execution decisions)
- History information (e.g., preventing indefinite delays)

One way to compare the expressive power of different mechanisms is to assemble a set of problems that we believe represents the kinds of situations we will encounter, and try to express correct and efficient solutions using each mechanism. We should be able to draw a few conclusions about how the mechanisms compare with each other.

A second approach is to examine each mechanism with respect to the kinds of information that may be used to influence exclusion and priority decisions. This is a more general approach, and should prove useful for many current and proposed mechanisms for concurrent programming.

Modularity

There are two differing views regarding operating system structuring. The first, motivated by systems with shared memory (*centralized systems*), is that an operating system consists of shared resources, whose accessibility must be regulated. The second, arising from *distributed systems* without shared memory, is that an operating system is a collection of coordinated processes whose interactions must be regulated. The first view is the traditional one; most process coordination mechanisms fall into this category. The low-level language constructs of Chapter 2 rely on common variables and provide little structuring capability. High-level language constructs provide more structuring capabilities, but until recently most also centered around shared resources.

In either centralized or distributed systems, two orthogonal criteria of *modularity* should be considered:

1. Resources, as abstract data types, must be separated from each other and should contain a synchronization and scheduling scheme as well as usual objects and operations of a sequential abstract data type.

2. The synchronization and scheduling aspects of a mechanism must be clearly separated from the operational and state retention aspects. Further, each part may have to be governed to some degree by global control, as in the case of deadlock prevention and scheduling. In such cases, these parts may have to be coordinated among resource modules. Thus, a multidimensional modularization is inevitable and important.

Ease of Use

Bloom has defined *ease of use* to be the simplicity of constructing a solution. If a complex problem can be broken down into simple, independent conditions, its solution can be expressed "additively." If the implementation of any one condition is dependent on other conditions, then, as the number of conditions increases, solutions become more and more difficult to construct. In addition, the solutions are very difficult to modify. A single change in one condition can cause the entire solution to become invalid.

One way to test whether a mechanism allows an independent implementation of conditions is to examine solutions to two similar synchronization problems. If the problems share some conditions, but not others, then the common conditions should be similarly implemented in both solutions. Reader/writer problems may be useful for this analysis since reader preference and writer preference examples have the same exclusion conditions, but dissimilar priority conditions.

The independence of condition implementations can be checked by seeing that the implementation of a constraint remains valid when other conditions are changed to use different information. Another reader/writer problem could be used for this purpose. For instance, a first-come, first-served condition does not change the exclusion condition, but uses additional information about the times at which requests were made.

Program Structure

When we use high-level process synchronization mechanisms, the relation between overall program structure and the mechanism is important. Path expression mechanisms (see Section 3.4.2) are appealing for this and other reasons. First, they are designed to be used as part of the definition of an abstract type, automatically associating the mechanism with the resource—and satisfying our modularity requirement. Second, since they are nonprocedural, they remove most of the implementation burden from the user. Third, path expression mechanisms can be incorporated into almost any programming system.

Monitors can be the basic unit of global program structuring. However, since many parts of an operating system do not require mutually exclusive access, other, more flexible forms of program structuring are required. The degree of similarity between the desired synchronization and the monitor's capabilities determines the latter's fitness. Another problem is a call from a monitor to a procedure not included in that or any monitor. If this invoked procedure causes a wait, serious problems such as deadlocks may occur. A solution to this problem is to release possession of the monitor as the procedure is called. The lock is reacquired when it returns to the monitor. The serializer mechanism is an extension of the monitor mechanism that supports this scheme. Serializers are introduced in Section 3.4.1.

Process Failures and Time-Outs

When a process fails for some reason, it may affect the progress of other processes as well. Therefore, the synchronization mechanism should ensure that such a *process failure* will not affect other processes. Two issues involved in process failures are detection of failure and recovery from it. Detection itself is very difficult. The following kinds of exceptions are common:

- A *time-out exception* to detect a process that has never responded
- Computational or operational exceptions that occur in the course of progress of a process

Among the many low-level process synchronization mechanisms introduced so far, few provide a time-out facility. Unstructured process coordination primitives such as the semaphore operations would need additional parameters in order to specify exception-handling procedures and return exception status. For structured mechanisms such as monitors and serializers, exception-handling procedures should be defined as part of the structure. When a process leaves a mechanism due to a time-out exception, it must release the resource just as if it had returned normally. This additional capability, however, causes extra overhead in both time and space. A simple mutual exclusion scheme may become several times slower and larger because it can handle time-out exceptions. In this case, the use of tiny critical sections or the like should be avoided as much as possible. Whenever process synchronization without mutual exclusion is possible, it should be employed. When mutual exclusion is unavoidable, one should seek efficient implementations in hardware or firmware.

Unanticipated Faults and Recovery

Even well-designed and tested systems contain residual faults. And having exception-handling procedures for all possible hardware and software errors is not feasible. The traditional approach is to provide exception-handling procedures for major errors and to neglect the minor errors, hoping they do not cause major damage or manifest abnormal states in one way or another. We call the first class of errors—exceptions for which exception-handling procedures are provided—*anticipated faults* and the second class—those for which exception-handling procedures are not provided—*unanticipated faults*. The first class is discussed, for example, in Goodenough [1975] and Parnas and Wurges [1976]. For the second class of faults, a program structure called a *recovery block* has been developed. A recovery block provides redundancy in the form of standby exception handlers, which can be added to programs to improve reliability [Horning, et al., 1974; Randell, 1975]. It allows a computation to be backtracked to an earlier state when an error occurs, and to proceed again using a possibly different algorithm. A recovery block is provided with a means to detect error (an acceptance test) and zero or more standby spares (alternatives). A recovery block can be considered an extension of the more traditional *check point and restart* facilities common in database management systems.

The effectiveness and applicability of recovery blocks remain to be seen. Particularly, it may be difficult to provide meaningful acceptance test conditions and suitable alternatives for nontrivial cases. Economy is another criterion. It is not certain whether these additional facilities are economically justified.

Real-Time Systems

The incorporation of concurrent programming techniques into *real-time* languages has not advanced as much as it has in operating system development languages [Roessler and Schenk, 1976]. ILIAD is a high-level language for programming real-time applications, with concurrent programming facilities [Schutz, 1979]. It provides primitives such as **activate, priority, await,** and **locking.** One form of the **await** operation expresses a time-out condition as

> **await** boolean-expression **for** time-expression

An additional feature is the **time** data type, which represents the time of day or a time duration, along with the built-in function **clock** and two forms of the **delay** statement.

Handling run-time errors is also important in real-time programming. One does not normally have the option of restarting an entire computation. Even unrecoverable errors must allow some orderly shutdown procedure to take place. In ILIAD, the programmer may specify an *error task* at link time. When an unrecoverable error is detected by the operating system, all shared resources in the system are unlocked, all tasks are terminated, and the error task is activated.

3.3.2   Languages and Systems

In this section we describe several basic concepts of concurrent programming, including:

- Monitors
- Messages
- Input/output statements

- Procedures
- Guarded commands

These concepts are basic building blocks of concurrent programming mechanisms. Monitors were introduced in Section 3.2.1. Messages are information transferred between processes. I/O statements can be used in a form of message passing. Procedures are subprograms invoked by programs. Guarded commands [Dijkstra, 1975] are commands guarded by conditions (these will reappear in our discussions of CSP and Ada). The guarded commands are executed only when the conditions are satisfied.

Mechanisms for concurrent programming can be classified according to how these basic building blocks are incorporated and which of them are emphasized. The following categories are important:

1. Extensions or variations of the monitor mechanism: serializers [Hewitt and Atkinson, 1979], Concurrent Pascal [Brinch Hansen, 1975], Modula [Wirth, 1977], Mesa [Lampson and Redell, 1980], and path expressions [Campbell and Habermann, 1974].

2. Message-passing mechanisms: Smalltalk [Goldberg and Robson, 1983], Gypsy [Good, et al., 1979], Plits [Feldman, 1979].

3. I/O statement-based mechanisms: communicating sequential processes (CSP) [Hoare, 1978].

4. Procedure-based mechanisms: distributed processes (DP) [Brinch Hansen, 1978], the communication port model [Mao and Yeh, 1980].

5. Integration of CSP and DP: Ada [Ichbiah, 1979].

6. Further integration: synchronizing resources (SR) [Andrews, 1981], the input tool process model (ITP) [van den Bos, et al., 1981].

In the next section we describe some of the mechanisms listed in categories 1 through 4. Section 3.5 describes Ada's tasking facility in detail.

3.4 Some Concurrent Programming Mechanisms

In this section we examine some examples of concurrent programming mechanisms that are organized in new ways. The schemes designed for shared memory systems, serializers, and path expressions are extensions to the monitor. Communicating sequential processes and distributed processes are meant for use in systems that communicate only via message passing.

3.4.1 Serializers

The *serializer* mechanism proposed by Hewitt and Atkinson [1979] is a more structured form of the monitor mechanism based on the actor model [Hewitt, 1973]. A serializer is analogous to the front desk of a hospital in that only one person can check in or out at a time. The hospital front desk schedules the entrance and exit of people into and out of the hospital. Various waiting rooms or "holes" are available

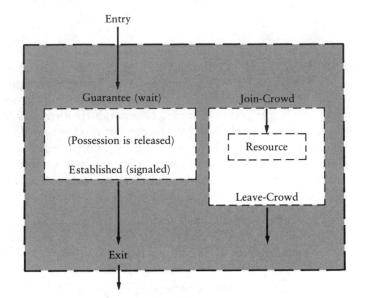

Figure 3.5   Schematic Diagram of a Serializer [Hewitt and
Atkinson, 1979, p. 11. Copyright © 1979 by
IEEE].

for people who are waiting so they do not monopolize the front desk. Figure 3.5
shows a schematic example of a serializer scheduling access to a protected resource.
Our description of a serializer follows Hewitt and Atkinson [1979].

Each arrow in the diagram shown in Figure 3.5 is labeled with the kind of
computational event it represents. All the events represented in the diagram are
serialized. An event corresponds to a process gaining or releasing possession of the
serializer; at most one process at a time may own the serializer. In the figure a
process is in possession of the serializer when it is executing in the shaded region of
the diagram.

Hewitt and Atkinson described the work of the serializer as follows [1979,
p. 11]:

> A typical simple sequence of events occurring in the use of a protected resource P begins
> with a SERIALIZER-REQUEST event in which the serializer receives a message M which is
> intended for the protected resource P. The request must eventually result in an ENTRY
> event which gains possession of the serializer, or a GUARANTEE event will cause a process
> to wait until some condition is true before proceeding. Such a request releases possession
> of the serializer. If execution of a process continues after a GUARANTEE event then the
> next event will be called an ESTABLISHED event because the condition is guaranteed to
> be true at the time. Thus each ESTABLISHED event regains possession of the serializer at
> a point in time when the condition is guaranteed to be true. When the proper condition
> for using a protected resource has been established, the possession of the serializer can
> be released by a JOIN-CROWD event which records that there is another process in the
> crowd (a crowd is an internal data structure of the serializer that keeps track of which
> processes are using the resource.) Next the message M is delivered to the protected
> resource P in a RESOURCE-REQUEST event. Eventually the protected resource P may pro-
> duce a reply to the request, called a RESOURCE-REPLY event. The RESOURCE-REPLY will

eventually result in a LEAVE-CROWD event which regains possession of the serializer and records that the process is no longer in the crowd using P. After this the process releases possession with an EXIT event, which causes a SERIALIZER-REQUEST event to occur.

Serializers are so-called because all events that gain and release possession of them are totally ordered in time. We assume that every serializer is written so that an event gaining possession is always followed by one releasing possession. In Figure 3.5 the interior of the serializer has two "holes" in which a process temporarily releases possession of the serializer. The purpose of a hole entered by a GUARANTEE event is to release possession while a process is waiting for some condition to be established so that it can proceed. This kind of hole is called a "waiting room." If a process in the waiting room has waited for a condition for a time longer than specified, it regains possession of the serializer via the TIME-OUT event. The purpose of a hole entered by a JOIN-CROWD event is to allow parallelism in the use of protected resources by releasing possession of the serializer so that other processes can gain possession. This kind of hole is called a "resource room." There may be any number of holes of either variety. This feature may support modular programming better than monitors because serializers can be sensibly nested inside one another.

Another difference between serializers and monitors is the automatic signaling mechanism of serializers: A waiting process is signaled when another process leaves a serializer. A signaled process must reexamine its waiting condition because a signal means only that the state of the resource may have changed. While this automatic signaling enhances verifiability and ease of use, it comes at the expense of efficiency. Still another difference is that the serializer mechanism provides a time-out facility. This makes I/O synchronization and fault tolerance problems easier to solve. As an example of the use of the serializer mechanism, we show a writer preference solution of the reader/writer problem (Figure 3.6). The notation is Lisp-like but should not be difficult to read because ample comments have been added.

3.4.2 Path Expressions

Path expressions as proposed by Campbell and Habermann [1974] are declarative synchronization specifications that control the execution by processes of the operations of an abstract data type. The code of calling processes contains no reference to synchronization primitives: Abstract operations may proceed only if allowed to do so by the controlling path expression. Likewise, the procedures that implement the operations of the abstract data type contain no synchronization: If one or more processes are executing the operation, it is because the path expression of the type has specified that it may occur. Path expressions have attracted interest because of their elegance and for a number of other reasons. They have been extended by Andler [1979], and are of interest for controlling parallelism in parallel applicative languages because they are nonimperative; see, for example, Oldehoeft and Jennings [1984], and Headington and Oldehoeft [1985]. Finally, research continues in developing automated reasoning tools that can analyze path expressions to find certain properties (such as deadlock) [Campbell, 1982]. We will describe both open path expressions as implemented in Path Pascal [Kolstad, 1980], and predicate path expressions as described by Andler [1979].

Figure 3.6   A Writer Preference Solution Based on
Serializers [Hewitt and Atkinson, 1979, p. 16.
Copyright © 1979 by IEEE].

((writers_priority = the_resource) ≡ ;to create a writers priority serializer
                                        for a resource
 (*create_serializer* ;create a serializer
  (*queues* : reader_q waiting_q) ;with two queues called reader_q and
                              waiting_q
  (*crowds* : writer readers) ;and two crowds called writer and readers
  (*entry* : ;on entry to the serializer
  (*message_cases* ;there are two cases for the message

    ((*read*(*using* := directions)) →
           ;receive a request to read the resource using directions
    (*guarantee*(or *empty* : readers)(*empty* : waiting_q))
    ;guarantee that there are no readers in the resoruce or that the
    waiting_q is empty
    (*wait_in* : reader_q)
    (*then* :
     (*guarantee*(*empty* : writer) ;guarantee that the writer crowd is empty
     (*wait_in* : waiting_q) ;wait in the waiting queue
    (*relay_to* : the_resource(*read*(*using* : directions)))
     ;then relay the message to the resource
     (*thru* : readers))))) ;passing through the readers crowd

    ((*write*(*using* := directions)) →
          ;receive a request to write in the resource using directions
    (*guarantee*(*empty* : readers writer))
    ;guarantee that there are neither readers nor a writer in the resource
    (*wait_in* : waiting_q) ;wait in the waiting_q
    (*relay_to* : the_resource(*write*(*using* : directions)))
    thru : writer)))))))

Open Path Expressions and Path Pascal

Path Pascal is an extended language that provides for declaration and simultaneous execution of processes (the symbol **process** appears instead of **procedure** in a process declaration) that share instances of abstract data types called **objects**. Object declarations may appear where a **record** declaration can, and have a similar bracketed structure. An object contains, in addition to a path expression (discussed below), the encapsulated data of the type, "entry" procedures and functions that define the operations, other internal procedures and functions, and an initialization block that is executed whenever an instance of the type appears. Neither the processes that reference operations nor the code in the operations themselves has any way of expressing synchronization constraints—this is the sole function of the path expression.

    Each object begins with a path expression bracketed with the symbols **path** and **end** that specifies how parallel execution of all operations must be constrained, if at all. Names in the path expression are entry procedure and function names; the remainder is composed of punctuation (resulting, unfortunately, in a very terse notation). Five syntactic structures are used to specify synchronization among processes using the operations:

1. A comma (,) separates path expression components and specifies no constraint.

2. A semicolon (;) separates subexpressions and specifies a *sequencer*. The number of initiations of what appears to the right may not exceed the number of completions of what appears to the left. For example,

    A; B

    specifies that the number of processes that exit procedure A must not be less than the number of processes that enter procedure B. A ";" has a higher precedence than a ",".

3. The construction "constant:(path-expression)" is a *resource restrictor*. The number of processes simultaneously active in the parenthesized item may not exceed the value of the constant. For example,

    10:(PUT)

    restricts to 10 the number of processes simultaneously executing PUT.

4. The construction "[path-expression]" is a *resource derestrictor*. As long as any process is executing in the bracketed item, another may freely join it. The first process to enter and the last process to leave affect the synchronization state in just the same way as the first and last readers in a reader/ writer problem.

5. Parentheses may be used for grouping and to alter default precedences.

The syntax of open path expressions can be summarized by the following rules in Backus-Naur form:

```
<list>      ::=    <seq> | <seq> ',' <list>
<seq>       ::=    <item> | <item> ';' <seq>
<item>      ::=    <unsigned-integer> ':' '(' <list> ')'
                 | '[' <list> ']'
                 | '(' <list> ')'
                 | <identifier>
```

Figure 3.7 displays the declaration for a Path Pascal object that implements a *bounded buffer*, the instantiation of two such buffers, and the form for referencing the operations. The path expression

path 10:(Place; Remove), 1:(Place, Remove) **end**

prevents the number of Place operations from falling behind the number of Remove operations (the ";" prevents underflow), proscribes the number of Place operations from running more than 10 ahead of the number of Remove operations [via "10:(Place; Remove)"], and restricts each Place and Remove to operate in respective mutual exclusion ["1:(Place, Remove)"] just as in a monitor implementation.

Figure 3.8 contains a weak reader preference solution to the reader/writer problem. The path expression

path 1:([read], write) **end**

allows just one of a single write operation or one or more concurrent read operations.

Figure 3.7   A Bounded Buffer Implementation Using Path
Expressions.

```
type boundedbuffer = object

    path 10: (Place; Remove), 1: (Place, Remove) end;

    type bufferrange = 0..9;
         message = char;
         bufferarray = array [0 .. 9] of message;

    var lastpointer, firstpointer: bufferrange;
        buffer: bufferarray;

    entry procedure Place(x: message);
      begin
         buffer[lastpointer] : = x;
         lastpointer : = (lastpointer + 1) mod 10
      end;

    entry procedure Remove(var x: message);
      begin
         x : = buffer[firstpointer];
         firstpointer : = (firstpointer + 1) mod 10
      end;

    init;
      begin lastpointer : = 0; firstpointer : = 0 end
    end;
    . . .
var BUF1, BUF2: boundedbuffer;
. . .
BUF1.Place(m); BUF2.Remove(n);
```

Implementation

In this section we investigate an efficient implementation of the Path Pascal version of this mechanism to further clarify its use and to expose and solve a problem in the original implementation. In Campbell [1979] a simple "compiler" is presented that accepts a path expression and produces a "prologue" and an "epilogue" to be inserted around each operation procedure body. These are largely constructed of semaphore operations to implement the semantics of path expressions. Table 3.1 is used in the following way. Beginning with the entire expression, find a row that matches in the first column with the form of the expression. The expression has a left context L and a right context R (already generated strings that appear around the expression). The result of a match is the production of one or two new, smaller expressions with contexts obtained from the original; these new expressions are given in the second column of the table. For some, new semaphores with initial values must be created—the third column of the table gives this information.

Figure 3.8 A Weak Reader Preference Solution Using Path
                Expressions.

type readwrite = **object**
  path 1: ([read], write) **end**;
  . . .
  Declarations for the encapsulated data
  . . .
  entry procedure read(**var** x: datatype);
    begin
      . . .
      Read the shared data
      . . .
    end;

  entry procedure write(x: datatype);
    begin
      . . .
      Write the shared data
      . . .
    end
end;

To exemplify, we translate the path expression for the bounded buffer problem in Figure 3.7.

1. The entire expression matches line 1 of the table—the expression is a comma-separated list. The resulting new expressions are "10:(Place; Remove)" and "1:(Place, Remove)", which we may process further in any order.

2. "10:(Place; Remove)" matches table row 3. A new expression "$P(S_1)$ Place; Remove $V(S_1)$" results and the new semaphore S_1 is initialized to 10.

3. The rest of the original expression matches line 3 as well. The resulting expression is "$P(S_2)$ Place, Remove $V(S_2)$", and a new semaphore S_2 has initial value 1.

4. The expression from step 2 is further processed by matching line 2 for separating semicolon-coordinated items. Two expressions "$P(S_1)$ Place $V(S_3)$" and "$P(S_3)$ Remove $V(S_1)$" result; the new semaphore S_3 has value 0. See that the original left context precedes the first new expression, and the original right context follows the second new expression.

5. The expression from step 3 matches line 1. Two new expressions "$P(S_2)$ Place $V(S_2)$" and "$P(S_2)$ Remove $V(S_2)$" are formed. In this case the left and right contexts are repeated around both new expressions.

All four of the expressions generated so far have been reduced to left and right contexts surrounding simple operation names. If each name had appeared just once

Table 3.1 A Compiler for Open Path Expressions

Current Expression	New Expressions	Semaphore Initialization
1. L <seq>,<list> R	L <seq> R	
	L<list> R	
2. L <item>;<seq> R	L <item> V(S_i)	$S_i = 0$
	P(S_i) <seq> R	
3. L n:(<list>) R	P(S_i) L <list> R V(S_i)	$S_i = n$
4. L [<list>] R	PP(C_i,S_i,L) <list> VV(C_i,S_i,R)	$S_i = 1, C_i = 0$
5. L (<list>) R	L <list> R	

with PP(C,S,L) = "P(S); C := C + 1; **if** C = 1 **then** L; V(S)"
and VV(C,S,R) = "P(S); C := C − 1; **if** C = 0 **then** R; V(S)"

in the original expression, these contexts would give the prologues and epilogues for synchronizing the operations. When, as in this case, names are repeated, the result is more than one pair of controlling strings. One solution to this problem is to nest them so that each name appears once. A possible nesting for this case is:

P(S_1); P(S_2); Place; V(S_2); V(S_3)
P(S_3); P(S_2); Remove; V(S_2); V(S_1)

This is what a programmer with only semaphores at his disposal might write: S_1 counts empty buffers, S_3 counts full buffers, and S_2 provides mutually exclusive execution of Place and Remove operations. It seems that the implementation problem is solved.

However, this is only one possible nesting for the preceding example. See that the other possibility leads to deadlock, and that there is no mechanical procedure to choose the correct nesting. In this example, one can reformulate the path expression so that each name appears only once, and the deadlock is then impossible; such a rearrangement is not always possible, however. Fortunately, a mechanism from Chapter 2, the *simultaneous* P operation, makes this problem disappear. If we replace all strings of consecutive P operations with an **SP** operation, and all consecutive V operations with a single **SV**, no deadlock can result. Either nesting results in

SP(S_1, S_2); Place; SV(S_2, S_3)
SP(S_3, S_2); Remove; SV(S_2, S_1)

The bounded buffer open path expression used here is not optimum because monitor-like mutual exclusion is not actually needed. Either

path 10:(Place; Remove), 1:(Place), 1:(Remove) **end**

or

path 10: (1:(Place); 1:(Remove)) **end**

allows the overlap of single Place and Remove operations. We encourage the reader to compile these expressions to verify this.

Predicate Path Expressions

Predicate path expressions (PPEs) are an extension of regular path expressions [Campbell and Habermann, 1974] and have been implemented as an experimental extension to Algol 68 [Andler, 1979]. Their salient feature is the introduction of predicates while retaining the sequential semantics (with operators to express parallelism) of regular path expressions. Philosophically, PPEs are distinctly different from OPEs since the latter are based on parallel semantics.

In PPEs, regular operators " + " (nondeterministic selection), ";" (sequencing), and "*" (repetition) are augmented by nonregular operators "{ }" (simultaneous execution identical to [ ] in OPEs) and "," (collateral execution). A predicate may be attached to a path element, restricting the use of the element until the predicate becomes true. This allows finer control over the operations of an abstract data type. In particular, an operation O is divided into phases with four distinct recognizable events ordered in time: req_O (request), act_O (activation), e_O (execution), and $term_O$ (termination). For each operation, the implementation environment maintains three nonnegative, monotonically increasing counters corresponding to three of the events: req(O), act(O), and term(O). Req(O) is incremented when a request for an O arrives at the instance of the abstract data type; act(O) is incremented when an O begins execution; and term(O) is incremented when the execution of an O terminates.

Informally, a predicate is a boolean function of linear relational expressions involving constants and counters for operands. As an example of the power of PPEs, the writers' priority variant of the reader/writer problem can be simply expressed as:

def ww = req(WRITE) − act(WRITE)
path ({READ[ww = 0]} + WRITE)*

Here, ww denotes the number of waiting writers.

The unrestricted use of "," and "*" operators leads to difficulties in implementation, so we will discuss restricted PPEs without these two operators. The syntax in Backus-Naur form is:

<restricted_PPE>	::=	**path** '(' <list> ')''*'
<list>	::=	<sequence> | <sequence> ' + ' <list>
<sequence>	::=	<item> | <item> ';' <sequence>
<item>	::=	'{' <list> '}' | <item> [<predicate>]
		| '(' <list> ')' | op_id
<predicate>	::=	<pred_term> | <predicate> **or** <pred_term>
<pred_term>	::=	<factor> | <pred_term> **and** <factor>
<factor>	::=	<rel_exp> | '(' <predicate> ')' | **not** <factor>
<rel_exp>	::=	<arith_exp> <rel_op> <arith_expr>
<arith_exp>	::=	<term_symb> | <term_symb> <sum_op>
		<arith_exp>
<term_symb>	::=	<event_ctr> | <nonneg_integer>
		| <nonneg_integer> <mult_op> <event_ctr>
<event_ctr>	::=	req(<op_id>) | act(<op_id>) | term (<op_id>)
<sum_op>	::=	+ | −

<mult_op>	::=	*
<rel_op>	::=	> | ≥ | = | ≠ | < | ≤

Table 3.2 outlines a compiler that transforms a PPE into a nondeterministic program C(PPE) using "guarded commands" [Dijkstra, 1975] and the parallel **cobegin-coend** construct. Updating of the counters is implicit in the generated code.

Two examples are given here to provide the flavor of specifying synchronization requirements using PPEs. For the OPE in the bounded buffer implementation of Figure 3.7, an equivalent PPE is

def num_full = term(Place) − act(Remove)
path (Place [num_full < 10] + Remove [num_full > 0])*

For the weak reader preference example in Figure 3.8, an equivalent PPE is

path ({READ} + WRITE)*

Table 3.2 A Compiler for Predicate Path Expressions

Expression	Program = C(Expression)
1. $E_1 + E_2$	**if** true → C(E_1)
	|true → C(E_2)
	endif
2. $E_1;E_2$	C(E_1);C(E_2)
3. E*	**if** true → null
	| true → C(E); C(E*)
	endif
4. E[predicate]	**if** predicate → C(E)
	|**not** predicate → halt
	endif
5. {E}	**if** true → C(E)
	|true → **cobegin** C(E)||C({E}) **coend**
	endif
6. operator O	code for O

Path expressions in either form seem to be excellent mechanisms that can be incorporated into any monitor-like structure. For ease of expression, examples can be constructed to demonstrate the advantages of each. Since mutually exclusive execution is not a requirement, many problems related to nested monitors do not arise and more efficient overlapped execution by processes is possible. However, as pointed out by Andrews [1983], priority conditions cannot be expressed directly in OPEs because ordinary variables are inaccessible. In PPEs, this condition is slightly eased since predicates allow access to implicit counters. On the other hand, path expressions provide a very high-level notation that allows separation of synchronization from the general procedure code and eases the problem of establishing correctness in a parallel environment.

3.4.3 Communicating Sequential Processes

Hoare's communicating sequential processes (CSP) [Hoare, 1978] recognized that synchronous input/output can be basic primitives of concurrent programming. In CSP, processes interact by means of input-output commands. Communication is synchronized by delaying an input (output) command in one process until a matching output (input) command is executed by another process. Under these conditions, the sending and receiving processes are said to correspond.

Since input-output commands transfer messages, CSP is based on message-passing (not shared memory) synchronization. But since messages are not buffered, their transfers are synchronously performed. In CSP, the correspondence between a sender (process executing an output command) and a receiver (process executing an input command) is made one-to-one by requiring that the sender or receiver be explicitly named. Process names are static and an upper limit on the number of processes must be stated in advance. These restrictions pose some problems, but the CSP notation presents clean and elegant mathematical-style solutions to a number of problems.

To exemplify the features of CSP, a solution of the bounded buffer problem with capacity 10, operated on by a single producer and a single consumer*

```
BUF:: buffer : (0..9) PORTION;
   in, out : INTEGER; in := 0; out := 0;
   *[in < out + 10; producer ? buffer(in mod 10) → in := in + 1
   □ out < in; consumer ? more ( ) → consumer ! buffer (out mod 10);
   out := out + 1
   ]
```

This defines the process "BUF". The producer process will include an output statement with the form

```
BUF ! p
```

to provide a value p as input to BUF, and the consumer will execute pairs of commands

```
BUF ! more(); BUF ? p
```

---

to write a message to BUF that a value is desired, and to read the value p written by BUF. The concurrency among processes is expressed by the notation

[code for P_1 | ... | code for P_n]

The notation

$[GC_1 \ \square \ GC_2 \ \square \ ... \ \square \ GC_n]$

gives an *alternative command,* where GC_i is a *guarded command* [Dijkstra, 1975]. Each guarded command has the form

<guard> → <command list>

The alternative command executes by evaluating each guard for *success* or *failure*. If the guard is a boolean expression, then success and failure correspond with *true* and *false*. If a guard contains an input command, it succeeds only when the preceding elements of the guard indicate success and the corresponding output statement is executed. If no guard succeeds, an error results. If one guard succeeds, its associated command list is executed. If more than one guard succeeds, one of the command lists associated with a successful guard is chosen *nondeterministically,* that is, by some "random" choice. The input command in a selected guard is executed before the command list to the right.

An alternative command can be executed repeatedly via the *repetitive command*

$*[GC_1 \ \square \ GC_2 \ \square \ ... \ \square \ GC_n]$

In a repetitive command the failure of all guards terminates the repetition instead of resulting in error. In the preceding BUF example, the repetitive command contains two guarded commands. Whenever out = in, the buffer is entirely empty and only the first guard can succeed, resulting in the (eventual) placement of a value in a buffer slot. When in = out + 10, only the second command can be enabled. After a consumer has written a request, the second command will read it; then a buffer element will be written to the consumer. Finally, when out < in < out + 10, either command may be enabled, depending on whether the producer writes a value first or the consumer writes a request first.

We now present several additional examples to illustrate the power of CSP. The following example shows how a subroutine can be simulated in CSP [Hoare, 1978]:

```
[ X:: *[ . . .
     Y!entry( input parameters );
     Y?return( output parameters );
     . . .
   ]
|
  Y:: *[ X?entry( parameters );
     . . .
     X!return( results expressions )
   ]
]
```

The names of entry points in the caller and sender must match in order for the two to correspond.

This next example shows how a static array of processes may be used to model recursion in computing the value of a factorial [Hoare, 1978]:

```
[ fact(i:1.. maxproc)::
  *[ n: INTEGER;
     fact(i − 1)?n →
        [ n = 0 → fact(i − 1)!1
        □ n > 0 → fact(i + 1)!n − 1;
          temp: INTEGER;
          fact(i + 1)?temp;
          fact(i − 1)!n*temp
        ]
   ]
| fact(0)::USER ]
```

Note that each process communicates with its neighbors in exactly the same way that an invocation, in conventional recursion, communicates with its successor and predecessor invocations.

The final example shows how an array of processes USER can access a semaphore encapsulated by a process SEM [Hoare, 1978]:

```
SEM:: sem:INTEGER; sem := 0;
  *[(i:1..maxproc) USER(i)? V() → sem := sem + 1
  □ (i:1..maxproc) sem > 0; USER(i)? P() → sem := sem − 1
  ]
```

Since CSP processes are sequential, SEM can rendezvous with only one USER process at a time, thereby providing a critical section for the updating and testing of sem.

Notice how concisely solutions to the various synchronization problems can be described in CSP. CSP, however, has a number of serious limitations such as the requirement that processes explicitly name each other, the lack of a recursive call construct, and lack of a message-buffering mechanism to provide for asynchronous communication. Also, the fact that an individual sequential process is used to encapsulate a resource makes the expression of concurrent access to the resource difficult (without compromising the encapsulation). See, for example, Problem 18.

3.4.4 Distributed Processes

Another mechanism based on synchronous message passing is distributed processes (DP) [Brinch Hansen, 1978]. In DP, processes communicate by means of *common procedures*. A process P calls a procedure OP defined within another process Q via:

call Q.OP(expressions, variables)

Before the procedure OP is executed, the *expressions* are evaluated and are assigned to OP's *input* parameters. When OP exits, the values of its *output* parameters are assigned to the *variables* of the call. Parameter passing between processes may be implemented either by copying in shared memory or by message passing between processes without shared memory. As in CSP, DP uses guarded commands to implement nondeterminism. In addition, a *guarded region* enables a process to wait until a choice among several statements can be made. If none of the alternatives are possible in the current state, the process postpones the execution of the guarded region. Since many aspects of DP are generalized and incorporated into Ada, we discuss the concurrent programming features of Ada rather than DP in detail in the remainder of this chapter.

3.5   Ada Concurrent Programming Mechanisms

Ada is the result of a lengthy development effort by the U. S. Department of Defense [U.S. Dept. of Defense, 1983] to define a standard programming language for *embedded applications* in which computer systems are part of larger physical systems such as aircraft or communications systems. The result is a large, Pascal-like language that has capitalized on much of the programming language design research of the 1970s. In the context of this chapter we will see that the design of Ada allows concurrent processes to execute by either shared memory or message passing (making it a promising candidate for widespread use), but the synchronization mechanisms present some challenges in terms of efficient implementation.

Before we can discuss Ada's concurrency mechanisms, we must briefly review the overall structure of Ada programs. (See, for example, Barnes [1981] and Habermann and Perry [1983] for references useful to experienced programmers.) Ada is designed to be useful to teams of programmers for constructing large programs, so hierarchical modularity is an important need. The *package* is the fundamental program building block. Versions of packages are used to implement blocks of type and data declarations to be shared among subprograms (or processes), abstract data types (with parameters to customize different instantiations—*generic packages*), or subprogram libraries. To promote the idea of data encapsulation, a package declaration has two parts: the *package specification* and the *package body*. The former contains those definitions needed by an Ada compiler when compiling a module that references the package: names of procedures that may be referenced from outside the package, type definitions to allow proper declarations of procedure parameters, perhaps even constants and variables to be visible outside the package. The latter contains hidden data objects, internal procedures, and the bodies of publicly known procedures named in the specification. In the syntax descriptions of this section { ... } denotes zero or more occurrences of the enclosed entity, and [...] denotes zero or one occurrence.

Procedures, package specifications, package bodies, and task specifications and task bodies (both discussed below) are separate units of compilation. Each may refer to previously defined package or task specifications, and contain new ones. An Ada program is a collection of these elements, with a single procedure designated as the main program. The package concept is the feature that has attracted the attention of potential Ada users from beyond the original embedded systems application area.

Package Specification

package Name **is**
    Declaration of visible
    procedures (headers only),
    necessary types, constants,
    and variables.
end;

Package Body

package body Name **is**
    Declaration of local procedures,
    types, constants, and variables,
    and complete bodies of visible
    procedures.
begin
    Initialization statements to
    execute for each instantiation.
[**exception**
    Exception handlers for
    this package.]
end;

3.5.1 Task Declaration and Initiation

Tasks are processes in Ada. Like packages, their specification and implementation are separate. Instead of making procedures, types, and so on visible, the purpose of a task specification is to "export" *task entries* that are similar in structure to procedures because they allow parameters and are referenced as if they were ordinary procedures. Tasks can be declared in procedures, packages, program blocks, or other tasks. Unlike CSP procedures, tasks can access variables in their global environments. Ada tasks unify the concepts of monitor and process, a direct influence from DP, mentioned above.

Task Specification

task [**type**] Name **is**
    entry specifications
end;

Task Body

task body Name **is**
    Declarations as found in
    any procedure
begin
    Statements of the task
exception
    Exception handlers for
    this task
end;

Ada's method of task initiation is different from that of earlier languages with multiprocess facilities. Instead of providing an explicit task initiation statement like PL/1 or Path Pascal, an Ada task begins execution as soon as it is instantiated. That is, when execution enters the scope of definition of a task, execution begins. In many instances one wants tasks to be runnable for the entire program execution, so it is common for the declaration of Ada tasks to reside in the main procedure.

3.5.2   Entries and the Accept Statement

An **entry** specification has the same syntactic structure as the header of a procedure: A name is followed by a parenthesized list of formal parameters. Corresponding to an entry are one or more **accept** statements in the executable part of the task body. An **accept** statement has the form

```
accept Entryname(formal parameters) do
    Statements forming the
    body of this entry
end Entryname;
```

Corresponding with a task **entry** E (and associated executable **accept** statements) of a task T are *entry calls* in other tasks with the form "T.E(actual parameters)." The qualification is necessary only to disambiguate the reference when two or more entries with the same name are established by different tasks. An **accept** statement executes when normal processing reaches it *and* another task executes a corresponding entry call statement. This synchronization between two tasks is the Ada *rendezvous*. Execution of the statements of the **accept** then occur in T, while execution in the calling task *waits* until those statements in T are complete. Thus from the point of view of the calling task, both the syntax and the semantics are that of a usual procedure reference. This is an example of a more widely used process synchronization mechanism called the *remote procedure call*; see Welsh and Lister [1981] for a comparison of the Ada rendezvous with similar mechanisms. The entry concept has roots in the common procedure of DP, and the rendezvous is found in the matchup of input and output commands in CSP and the mechanisms of DP.

With these structures we can specify a simple single-element buffer managed by an Ada task; see Figure 3.9. The two operations, Place and Remove, are identified

Figure 3.9 An Ada Task for Simple Message Passing.

```
task SimpleBuffer is
    entry Place( x: in message);
    entry Remove( x: out message);
end;

task body SimpleBuffer is
    buffer: message;
begin
    loop
        accept Place( x: in message) do
            buffer := x;
        end Place;
        accept Remove( x: out message) do
            x := buffer;
        end Remove;
    end loop;
end SimpleBuffer;
```

in the task specification. The task body eternally repeats the **accept** statement pair for Place and Remove. Note that the parameter to Place is of *directionality* **in** and that of Remove is **out.**

3.5.3 The Select Statement

The Ada task synchronization techniques discussed so far are not sufficient to solve problems of greater complexity than that of the preceding example. Tasks need to respond to events in an unpredictable order. To allow for this capability, one of three forms of a **select** statement may be used. Syntactically, we have [U.S. Dept. of Defense, 1983]:

select_statement:: = selective_wait|conditional_entry_call | timed_entry_call.

The *selective_wait* statement provides a called task with a sophisticated means for selecting from a set of alternatives, each of which may depend on an associated Dijkstra-like guard.

```
selective_wait :: =
select
   select_alternative
{ or
   select_alternative}
[ else
   {statement}]
end select;

select_alternative :: =
   [ when condition = > ] selective_wait_alternative

selective_wait_alternative :: =
   accept_alternative | delay_alternative | terminate_alternative

accept_alternative :: = accept_statement {statement}
delay_alternative :: = delay_statement {statement}
terminate_alternative :: = terminate;
```

At least one accept alternative must be present in a selective wait.

An alternative in a selective_wait statement is said to be *open* if it does not have a prefixed guard (**when** condition) or if the condition in the prefixed guard is true. The following rules define the execution of a selective_wait:

1. All guards are first evaluated to determine the set of open alternatives. If an open alternative starts with a **delay** statement, then the corresponding delay expression is immediately evaluated (see Rule 3).

2. An open alternative whose statement body begins with an **accept** statement may be selected for execution if a rendevous is possible.

3. The remaining statements, following the **delay** statement in an open alternative starting with a **delay**, will be selected for execution if no other alternative is selected before the specified duration has elapsed.

4. An open **terminate** alternative will be selected only if termination of this task is required (see Section 3.5.5).

5. If no open alternative can be immediately selected or all alternatives are closed, then the **else** alternative, if present, is selected. If an **else** is not present and open alternatives exist, execution is delayed until an open alternative can be selected. If an **else** is not present and all alternatives are closed, an error exception is raised (see Section 3.5.5).

With this mechanism, we can implement an Ada task that encapsulates a bounded buffer and provides operations Place and Remove. Figure 3.10 shows the task. Note that buffer underflow and overflow are not possible. When the buffer is neither completely empty nor completely full, either alternative of the **select** statement may be chosen. Each alternative includes code that follows the **accept** block. In some situations, it is important to factor as much code out of the **accept** block as possible to achieve a higher degree of asynchronous execution among the called and the calling tasks. Unlike the final Path Pascal version, it is not possible for this task to be servicing both a Place and Remove request simultaneously.

Figure 3.11 illustrates use of the **else** alternative and the **delay** statement.

A conditional_entry_call statement allows a caller to cancel a call if a rendezvous is not immediately possible. The syntax is

```
select
    entry_call_statement {statement}
else
    {statement}
end select;
```

An example of this is the program segment

```
select
    stack.push(params)
else
    {statements to do something else}
end select;
```

The timed_entry call is a simple variation of the previous form. Its syntax is

```
select
    entry_call_statement {statement}
or
    delay_alternative
end select;
```

Figure 3.10   A Bounded Buffer Using an Ada Task.

```
task BoundedBuffer is
  entry Place(x: in message);
  entry Remove(x: out message);
end;

task body BoundedBuffer is
  N: constant : = 10;
  buffer: array(0..N − 1) of message;
  i, j: integer range 0..N − 1 : = 0;
  count: integer range 0..N : = 0;
begin
  loop
    select
      when count < N =>
      accept Place(x: in message) do
        buffer(i) : = x;
      end Place;
      i : = (i + 1) mod N; count : = count + 1;
    or
      when count > 0 =>
      accept Remove(x: out message) do
        x : = buffer(j);
      end Remove;
      j : = (j + 1) mod N; count : = count − 1;
    end select;
  end loop;
end BoundedBuffer;
```

In the following example, the call on push is canceled if a rendezvous is not started in 10 seconds:

```
select
  stack.push(params)
or
  delay 10.0
end
```

The three forms of the select give both the calling and called tasks significant control over rendezvous possibilities.

Figure 3.12 presents a complete Ada program, which is found in Habermann and Perry [1983]. In this example, the tasks are defined in the body part of the package TABLE and, consequently, their existence is not known to a user. Upon instantiation of a variable X of type TABLE, an internal task *TManager* is instantiated.

Figure 3.11 A Line Server in an Ada Task.

```
task line_server is
    entry signal(params);
    entry enable;
    entry disable;
end line_server;

task body line_server is
    type inhibit is (on, off);
    service: inhibit : = off;
begin
    loop
        select
            when service = on = > accept signal(params) do ... end;
        or
            accept enable do service : = on; end
        or
            accept disable do service : = off; end
        or
            delay 2; print("no signal");
        end select;
    end loop;
end line_server;
```

When the user calls X.LOOKUP, an eventual rendevous takes place with entry LOOKUP in *TManager*. During the rendezvous, two parallel tasks ODD and EVEN of type *SearchTask* are instantiated. One of the two tasks will be aborted while the other will terminate normally.

3.5.4 Real-Time Processing

Real-time processing is readily supported by the select statement. The **else** alternative and the **delay** statement in the selective_wait both provide ready escapes in the event that no open alternatives exist or that open alternatives are unduly delayed in their selection. Using the conditional or timed entry calls, the calling task can ensure that it will not be blocked due to the inability of the called task to complete a rendezvous.

Another feature that is useful both in real-time processing and in broader scheduling contexts is the *COUNT* attribute. Used in an expression, the value of the term "entry_name *'COUNT*" is the number of tasks waiting for a rendezvous at the corresponding **accept** entry_name statement. Finally, the scheduling discipline at any **accept** statement is based on the *static* priority (if specified) of the tasks.

Figure 3.12 An Ada Program with Multiple Tasks
[Habermann and Perry, 1983].

```
generic tsize: NATURAL : = 354; — tsize is an even number
package TABLE is

   subtype key is STRING(1..4);
   subtype tindex is INTEGER range 0 .. (tsize-1);

   function ENTER ( k: in key) return tindex;
   function LOOKUP( k: in key) return tindex;

   toverflow: exception;

end TABLE;

package body TABLE is

   blank: constant key : = (others = > ' ');
   table: array(0 .. (tsize-1)) of key : = (others = > blank);

   task TManager is
      entry LOOKUP( k: in key; t: out tindex);
      entry RESULT(q: in tindex);
   end TManager;

   task type SearchTask is
      entry SEARCH ( k: in key; start: in tindex);
   end Search Task;

   function HASH( k: in key) return tindex is
   begin
      return (character'POS(k(1)) * character'POS(k(2)) *
              character'POS(k(3)) * character'POS(k(4))) mod tsize;
   end HASH;

   function ENTER( k: in key) return tindex is ... end ENTER;

   function LOOKUP( k: in key) return tindex is
      t: tindex;
   begin
      TManager.LOOKUP( k, t); return t;
   end LOOKUP;

   task body TManager is
      start, cur: tindex;
   begin
      loop
         accept LOOKUP( k: in key; t: out tindex) do
            declare
               ODD, EVEN: Search Task;
```

(continued next page)

Figure 3.12 *(continued)*

```
        begin
          start : = HASH( k);
          ODD.SEARCH( k, (start + 1) mod tsize);
          EVEN.SEARCH( k, start);
          accept RESULT(q: in tindex) do
            cur : = q;
          end RESULT;
            if (cur − start) mod 2 = 0 then abort ODD;
            else abort EVEN; end if; — correct iff size is even
            t : = cur;
        end;
      end LOOKUP;
    end loop;
  end TManager;

  task body SearchTask is
    clay: key;
    locindex: tindex;
  begin
    accept SEARCH( k: in key; start: in tindex) do
      clay : = k; locindex : = start;
    end SEARCH;
    while table(locindex) /= clay loop
      locindex : = (locindex + 2) mod tsize;
    end loop;
    TManager.RESULT(locindex);
  end SearchTask;

end TABLE;
```

3.5.5   Termination and Exceptions

Normal termination of a task occurs when it reaches the end of its code sequence and all *dependent* tasks (those that were declared in this task and initiated because this task started) have terminated. Executing a **select** alternative that consists of **terminate** is equivalent to reaching the end of a task's code. Finally, a task (and all its dependent tasks) will terminate when any other task executes an **abort** statement that names this task. If an aborted task is waiting at a rendezvous, processing depends on its role. If it is the calling task, the called is unaffected. If it is the called task, the exception "TASKING-ERROR" is raised in the caller.

The task structure may contain a final section beginning with the symbol **exception**. This section contains the *exception handlers* for this task. Each handler has the form

       when Exception_name => statement

where an Exception-name is a predefined condition such as TASKING-ERROR or NUMERIC-ERROR, or an identifier declared to have type **exception.** Statements in the "normal" part of the task code may include statements of the form

       raise Exception-name;

to signal that normal execution is to be abandoned and that the associated handler is to be executed instead. It is possible for an exception to be raised without the presence of an associated handler. In a task, this results in termination of the task, and the exception signal is *not* reported elsewhere. Exceptions raised and not handled in other kinds of program units (procedures, packages) may be *propagated* to the units that referenced them. In either case Ada follows a *termination* model rather than a *resumption* model: That is, normal execution does not resume at the point that the exception was raised.

    Figure 3.13 shows a task encapsulating a shared vector of integers with entries Obtain and Replace. The task has a defined exception "vecrange" that will be raised if a call supplies an illegal subscript. The result, in addition to the output that the exception handler produces, is that the Shared_Vector task terminates and a calling task has the predefined exception TASKING-ERROR raised. Note also that, since the square of the value supplied in Replace is stored, a NUMERIC-ERROR exception is also possible.

3.5.6 Ada and Concurrent Programming Requirements

We briefly review the capabilities of Ada with respect to the requirements on concurrent programming mechanisms discussed in Section 3.3. Ada is an excellent tool on several counts. Since it has the capability for tasks to share memory, and since entry calls may be performed by message passing, multiprocess Ada programs can be developed on both centralized and distributed systems. The hierarchical modularity imposed by the package concept is deemed to be one of Ada's strong features. And since the language was originally designed to solve problems that involve real-time processing and anticipated faults, we should not be surprised to find features for this purpose.

    In terms of expressive power, local task state influences the **select** statement and history information is programmable in terms of time-outs, but no priority queuing is possible. In many instances Ada is more complex to use than other concurrent programming languages. The problem lies in the necessity for an active task to be present among tasks communicating information or competing for resources. This extra task must rendezvous with tasks doing useful work, thereby making them less efficient than they might otherwise be. The program structure, which allows only the monitor-style of mutually exclusive access, loses some possibilities for concurrent execution. Finally, like most systems, handling unanticipated faults is beyond Ada's capabilities.

Figure 3.13 An Exception Handler in an Ada Task.

```
task Shared_Vector is
  entry Obtain( index: in INTEGER; rslt: out INTEGER );
  entry Replace( index, val: in INTEGER );
end Shared_Vector;

task body Shared_Vector is
  vec: array(1..N) of INTEGER;
  vecrange: exception;
begin
  loop
    select
      accept Obtain( index: in INTEGER; rslt: out INTEGER ) do
        if index < 1 or index > N then raise vecrange;
        else rslt : = vec(index);
        end if;
      end Obtain;
    or
      accept Replace( index, val: in INTEGER ) do
        if index < 1 or index > N then raise vecrange;
        else vec(index) : = val * val;
        end if;
      end Replace;
    end select;
  end loop;
exception
  when vecrange =>
      begin PUT("Shared_Vector index out of range"); PUT(index); end;
end Shared_Vector;
```

3.6 Summary

In this chapter we have examined two approaches for high-level synchronization and communication among processes. The first is the monitor and its extensions and variants. These explicitly or implicitly rely on the existence of a shared memory for information exchange; low-level methods of the preceding chapter are useful in implementing them. The other depends on message passing (or input/output) and may be implemented in centralized systems or those without shared memory. Ada has been influenced by representatives of this group, and so has applicability to both kinds of systems. The reader will find Andrews [1983] an excellent survey of the material presented here. Chapters 6 and 7 cover important issues in the design and control of distributed processing systems.

Key Words

abstract data type	expressive power	process failures
Ada tasking	guarded commands	process time-outs
alternative command	I/O statements	real-time systems
anticipated faults	message passing	recovery block
bounded buffer	modularity	rendezvous
centralized systems	monitor	repetitive command
check point and restart	nested monitor calls	reusable resources
	nondeterminism	scheduling
distributed systems	object model	serializer
ease of use	package	unanticipated faults
encapsulated	path expressions	
error task	priority constraints	
exclusion constraints		

Questions

1. How many queues are associated with the monitor shown in Figure 3.3?

2. Suppose that the **if** statement of the procedure "startread" of the monitor shown in Figure 3.3 is replaced with

   while busy **do** OKtoread.**wait endwhile**;

   Does the monitor still perform the intended task? Justify your answer.

3. Suppose that every conditional statement containing a condvariable.**wait** is replaced with

   while not condition **do** condvariable.**wait endwhile**;

   Is it then true that an awakened process need not be immediately executed? Justify your answer.

4. State the advantages and disadvantages of two process activation mechanisms: (a) the explicit and immediate activation of a process employed in the monitor mechanism, and (b) the implicit activation used in the serializer.

5. Show an example of nested monitor calls that illustrates a deadlock possibility. Show another example that illustrates only inefficiency.

6. Which of the following statements are true?

   a. Several processes can concurrently attempt to invoke procedures of the same monitor.

   b. Several processes can concurrently execute different procedures of the same monitor.

   c. Monitors are processes.

   d. A condvariable.**signal** can activate several processes.

   e. The queue discipline used for the queues associated with condition variables must be first-come, first-served (FCFS).

   f. A process waiting for an entry to the monitor is activated by a condvariable.**signal**.

   g. The queue discipline used for the entry queue to the monitor must be FCFS.

   h. A monitor must run in an interrupt-inhibited mode.

7. How are the requirements on concurrent programming mechanisms listed in 3.3.1 related to each other?

8. Which of the following statements are true?

   a. Monitors are passive objects.

   b. Tasks in Ada can be either passive or active objects.

   c. A call to an entry of a task in Ada may block the calling process.

   d. If a call to an object is a blocking primitive, parameters can be passed by value, message, or reference.

9. Explain why it is difficult to write an explicit priority problem using path expressions. What other types of problems are difficult to write using path expressions?

10. Which of the following statements are true?

   a. A task in Ada maintains only a single queue.

   b. An interrupt is not allowed in an Ada task.

   c. If several tasks (processes) call the same entry of a task, they all are reactivated when the corresponding **accept** statement has been executed.

   d. In Ada tasking, parameters passed by an entry call can be updated simultaneously by the calling and called tasks.

11. Does the Ada tasking facility solve the problems with monitors discussed in Section 3.2.4?

12. Compile the following open path expressions into code involving P and V operations. In each case explain the overall effect of the synchronization specified.

   a. **path** 1:(A;B), 1:(B;A) **end**

   b. **path** 1:(1:(A),B) **end**

   c. **path** 1:([open_read; read; close_read], (open_write; write; close_write)) **end**

Problems

1. Show a writer preference solution of the reader/writer problem based on a monitor.

2. Write a solution of the dining philosophers problem based on the monitor mechanism.

3. Write a solution of the dining philosophers problem that avoids starvation. Use a monitor.

4. Show a process coordination example that requires each of the following items:
   a. Type of request
   b. Times at which requests were made
   c. Request parameters
   d. Process information
   e. Priority relation
   f. Local state of resource
   g. History information

5. Indicate how each of the items listed in the preceding question could be incorporated in the monitor mechanism.

6. Indicate how each of the items listed in Problem 4 can be incorporated or used with the **P** and **V** (including simultaneous **P** and parameterized **P**) scheme.

7. Extend the monitor mechanism to incorporate a time-out facility.

8. Write a reader preference solution in Ada of the reader/writer problem. To avoid the indefinite postponement of writers, a writer must be allowed to enter after it has waited for three readers. Also, if more than two writers are waiting, they all should be allowed immediately after the current reader completes.

9. Write a solution of the dining philosophers problem in Ada. No philosopher may skip a chance to eat more than three times.

10. Write a solution of the producer/consumer problem using path expressions.

11. Convert the following open path expressions into predicate path expressions:
    a. **path** A **end**
    b. **path** A,B **end**
    c. **path** n:(A) **end**
    d. **path** A; [B] **end**

12. Convert the following predicate path expressions to open path expressions.
    a. **path** (A + B)*
    b. **path** (A, B)*
    c. **path** (A; B)*

13. Solve Problem 1 of Chapter 2 using an Ada task rather than semaphores.

14. Use Ada tasks to implement a LOOK disk scheduler. Assume the code exists to implement the disk operation DISKIO and focus on the synchronization aspects.

15. Use Ada tasks to encapsulate a data object accessed by readers and writers so that a writer preference solution is implemented that obeys the predicate path expression

    path ({read[ww = 0]} + write)*

    Assume the code for read and write exist.

16. Use Ada tasks to implement the open path expression

path (E,F); 1:(C,D;G) **end**

Assume the code for procedures E,F,C,D,and G exists.

17. Construct a Hoare monitor that implements the synchronization equivalent to the predicate path expression

    path ({P} + {Q})∗

18. Assume a collection of CSP user processes X(1..100) exists, each of which both reads and writes a database. Construct a CSP solution that allows for simultaneous reads. (*Hint:* For N users, use N copies of the database, each of which is encapsulated by a single process. Be careful how you handle a write.) Assume the code for actual reading and writing already exists and concentrate on the synchronization aspects of the problem. Does your solution give priority to readers or writers?

19. Show how the basic monitor mechanism can be implemented via semaphores. Be sure to define all necessary semaphores and other variables needed to manage the entry and exit conditions, the condition variables, and the urgent queue.

20. Repeat problem 19 using sequencers and eventcounts.

21. We have seen how semaphores can be used to implement open path expressions. Is there a reasonable implementation using sequencers and eventcounts?

22. Can we always avoid nested monitor calls? If yes, are there any constraints that should be imposed on system structures?

23. Can we write an I/O supervisor using the Ada tasking capability? If yes, write one. If no, indicate necessary extensions.

24. Show how the Ada tasking mechanism can be implemented based on the semaphore mechanism.

25. Do Problem 24 based on the sequencer/eventcount mechanism.

26. Write a solution to the multiple producer/consumer problem using Ada tasks that send and receive messages directly among themselves. Make sure that each message is received by one and only one consumer and that every producer and consumer is treated fairly. No centralized task is allowed.

27. Write a resource allocator in Ada that allocates resources $R_1, R_2, \ldots, R_n$. A process may make several requests simultaneously. Each resource R_i consists of t_i units. A request is given by a vector $(r_1, r_2, \ldots, r_n)$, where r_i is the number of units of resource R_i requested. Employ an aging technique to avoid indefinite postponement.

28. Assume the following monitor implementation of a P and V operation:

```
semaphore: monitor
  begin
    num_p_start, num_p_end, num_v: integer;
    cond: condition;
    procedure P;
```

```
        begin
          num_p_start : = num_p_start + 1;
          if num_p_start > num_v then cond.wait endif;
          num_p_end : = num_p_end + 1
        end;
      procedure V;
        begin
          num_v : = num_v + 1;
          if num_p_end < num_p_start then cond.signal endif
        end;
  begin
    num_p_start : = num_p_end : = num_v : = 0
  end semaphore;
```

Using "preconditions" and "postconditions" on sequence of statements, prove that the semaphore invariant num_p_end = min(num_v, num_p_start) is true for the above implementation of the P and V operations.

References

Andler, S. (1979). "Predicate path expressions." *Sixth Annual ACM Symposium on Principles of Programming Languages,* San Antonio, TX., pp. 226–236.

Andrews, Gregory R. (October 1981). "Synchronizing resources." ACM *Transactions on Programming Languages and Systems* 3, 4, pp. 405–430.

———. (March 1983). "Concepts and notations for concurrent programming." *ACM Computing Surveys* 15, 1, pp. 3–43.

Arvind; K. P. Gostelow; and W. Plouffe. (November 1977). "Indeterminacy, monitors and dataflow." *Proceedings of the Sixth ACM Symposium on Operating Systems Principles, Operating Systems Review* 11, 5, pp. 159–169.

Arvind, and J. D. Brock. (1982). "Streams and managers." *Lecture Notes in Computer Science* 143 (Eds. M. Maekawa and L. A. Belady), Springer-Verlag, pp. 452–465.

Barnes, J. G. P. (1981). *Programming in Ada.* Addison-Wesley, Reading, Mass.

Bloom, T. (1979). "Evaluating synchronization mechanisms." *Proceedings of the Eighth ACM Symposium on Operating System Principles,* pp. 24–31.

Brinch Hansen, P. (June 1975). "The programming language Concurrent Pascal." *IEEE Transactions on Software Engineering* SE-1, 2, pp. 199–207.

———. (1978). "Distributed processes: a concurrent programming concept." *Communications of the ACM* 21, 11, pp. 934–941.

Campbell, R. H. (July 1979). "Path expressions in Pascal." University of Illinois Technical Report.

———. (September 1982). "A definition of open path expressions." University of Illinois Technical Report UIUCDCS-R82-1102.

Campbell, R. H., and A. N. Habermann. (1974). "The specification of process synchronization by path expressions." *Lecture Notes in Computer Science,* 16, Springer-Verlag Publishing, pp. 89–102.

Dahl, O. J.; B. Myhrhaug; and K. Nygaard. (May 1968). *Simula-67—Common Base Language*. Norsk Regnesentral, Norway.

Dennis, J. B. (1974). "First version of a data flow procedure language." *Lecture Notes in Computer Science* 19 (Eds. G. Good and J. Hartmanis), Springer-Verlag, pp. 362–376.

Dennis, J. B., and D. P. Misunas. (January 1975). "A preliminary architecture for a basic data-flow processor." *Proceedings of the Second Annual Symposium on Computer Architecture,* pp. 126–132.

Dijkstra, E. W. (August 1975). "Guarded commands, nondeterminancy and formal derivation of programs." *Communications of the ACM* 18, 8, pp. 453–457.

Feldman, J. A. (June 1979). "High-level programming for distributed computing." *Communications of the ACM,* 22, 6, pp. 353–369.

Goldberg, A., and D. Robson. (1983). *Smalltalk-80: The Language and Its Implementation*. Addison-Wesley, Reading, Mass.

Good, D. I.; R. M. Cohen; and A. Keeton-Williams. (1979). "Principles of proving concurrent programs in Gypsy." *Proceedings of the Sixth Annual ACM Symposium on Principles of Programming Languages,* San Antonio, TX., pp. 42–52.

Goodenough, J. B. (December 1975). "Exception handling: issues and proposed notation." *Communications of the ACM* 18, 12, pp. 683–696.

Habermann, A. N., and D. E. Perry. (1983). *Ada for Experienced Programmers*. Addison-Wesley, Reading, Mass.

Headington, M. R., and A. E. Oldehoeft. (1985). "Open predicate path expressions and their implementation in highly parallel computing environments." *Proceedings of the International Conference on Parallel Processing,* pp. 239–246.

Hewitt, C. (1973). "A universal modular actor formalism for artificial intelligence." *Proceedings of the International Joint Conference on Artificial Intelligence.*

Hewitt, C. E., and R. R. Atkinson. (1979). "Specification and proof techniques for serializers." *IEEE Transactions on Software Engineering,* SE-5, No. 1, pp. 10–23.

Hoare, C. A. R. (1974). "Monitors: an operating system structuring concept." *Communications of the ACM* 17, 10, pp. 549–557.

———. (1978). "Communicating sequential processes." *Communications of the ACM* 21, 8, pp. 666–677.

Horning, J. J.; H. C. Lauer; et al. (1974). "A program structure for error detection and recovery." *Lecture Notes in Computer Science* 16, Springer-Verlag Publishing, pp. 177–193.

Ichbiah, J. D. (June 1979). "Rationale for the design of the ADA programming language." *ACM SIGPLAN Notices* 14, 6, part B.

Kolstad, R. B., and R. H. Campbell. (1980). "Path Pascal user manual." University of Illinois Computer Science Department Technical Report TR-UIUCDCS-F-80-893.

Lampson, B. W., and D. D. Redell. (1980). "Experience with processes and monitors in Mesa." *Communications of the ACM* 23, 2, pp. 105–117.

Liskov, B. H., and S. Zilles. (1975). "Specification techniques for data abstraction." *IEEE Transactions on Software Engineering* SE-1, 1, pp. 7–19.

Liskov, B. H., et al. (August 1977). "Abstraction mechanisms in CLU." *Communications of the ACM* 20, 8, pp. 564–576.

Mao, T. W., and R. T. Yeh. (March 1980). "Communication port: a language concept for concurrent programming." *IEEE Transactions on Software Engineering* SE-6, 2, pp. 194–204.

Oldehoeft, A. E., and S. F. Jennings. (May 1984). "Dataflow resource managers and their synthesis from open path expressions." *IEEE Transactions on Software Engineering* SE-10, 3, pp. 244–257.

Parnas, D. L., and H. Wurges. (October 1976). "Response to undesired events in software systems." *Proceedings of the Second International Conference on Software Engineering.*

Peterson, J. L. (1981). *Petri Nets Theory and the Modeling of Systems.* Prentice-Hall, Englewood Cliffs, N.J.

Randell, B. (June 1975). "System structure for software fault tolerance." *IEEE Transactions on Software Engineering* SE-1, 6. pp. 220–232.

Roessler, R. and K. Schenk, eds. (October 1976). *A Languages Comparison.* (Developed by the Long Term Procedural Languages Committee—Europe, International Purdue Workshop on Industrial Computer Systems), Purdue University. W. Lafayette, IN.

Schutz, H. A. (1979). "On the design of a language for programming real-time concurrent processes." *IEEE Transactions on Software Engineering* SE-5, 3, pp. 248–255.

U.S. Department of Defense. (January 1983). *Military Standard Ada Programming Language.* ANSI/MIL-STD-1815A, Washington D.C.

van den Bos, Jan; Rinus Plasmeijer; and Jan Stroet. (July 1981). "Process communication based on input specifications." *ACM Transactions on Programming Languages and Systems* 3, 3, pp. 224–250.

Welsh, J. and A. Lister. (March 1981). "A comparative study of task communication in Ada." *Software Practice and Experience* 11, 3, pp. 257–290.

Wirth, N. (January 1977). "Modula: a programming language for modular multiprogramming." *Software-Practice and Experience* 7, 1, pp. 3–84.

Wulf, W. A., et al. (December 1976). "An introduction to the construction and verification of Alphard programs." *IEEE Transactions on Software Engineering* SE-2, 4, pp. 253–265.

Suggested Readings

Baer, J. L. (1973). "A survey of some theoretical aspects of multiprocessing." *Computing Surveys* 5, 1, pp. 31–80.

Boebert, W. E.; W. R. Franta; et al. (1978). "Kernel primitives of the HXDP executive." *Proceedings of the IEEE COMPSAC Conference.*

Brinch Hansen, P. (1973). *Operating System Principles.* Prentice-Hall, Englewood Cliffs, N.J.

Brinch Hansen, P., and J. Staunstrup. (May 1978). "Specification and implementation of mutual exclusion." *IEEE Transactions on Software Engineering* SE-4, 5, pp. 365–370.

Bryant, R. E., and J. B. Dennis. (1982). "Concurrent programming." *Lecture Notes in Computer Science* 143 (Eds. M. Maekawa and L. A. Belady), Springer-Verlag, pp. 426–451.

Campbell, R. H., and R. B. Kolstad. (October 1–3, 1980). "A practical implementation of path expressions." *Proceedings of the Tenth International Symposium on Fault-Tolerant Computing,* Tokyo, Japan.

———. (September 1980). "An overview of Path Pascal's design." *ACM SIGPLAN Notices* 15, 9, pp. 13–24.

Conway, M. (1963) "A multiprocessor system design." *Proceedings of the AFIPS Fall Joint Computer Conference,* pp. 139–146.

Dijkstra, E. W. (1968). "Cooperating sequential processes." In *Programming Languages* (Ed. F. Genuys), Academic Press, New York, pp. 43–112.

Habermann, A. N. (March 1972). "Synchronization of communicating processes." *Communications of the ACM* 15, 3, pp. 171–176.

Hirose, K.; K. Segawa; N. Saito, et al. (1981). "Specification technique for parallel processing: process-data representation." *Proceedings of the AFIPS National Computer Conference,* pp. 407–413.

Horning, J. J., and B. Randell. (1973). "Process structuring." *ACM Computing Surveys* 5, 1, pp. 5–30.

Kessels, J. L. W. (July 1977). "An alternative to event queues for synchronization in monitors." *Communications of the ACM* 20, 7, pp. 500–503.

Lamport, L. (April 1983). "Specifying concurrent program modules." *ACM Transaction on Programming Languages and Systems* 5, 2, pp. 190–222.

Lauer, H. E., and R. M. Needham. (October 1978). "On the duality of operating system structures." *Proceedings of the Second International Symposium on Operating Systems,* Le Chesnay, France. [Reprinted in *ACM Operating Systems Review* 13, 2, pp. 3–19.]

Lipton, R. J. (1974). "A comparative study of models of parallel computation." *Proceedings of the 15th Annual Symposium on Switching and Automata Theory,* pp. 145–155.

Liskov, B. (December 10–12, 1979). "Primitives for distributed computing." *Proceedings of the Seventh Symposium on Operating Systems Principles,* Pacific Grove, California, pp. 33–42.

Maekawa, M. (1977). "Interprocess communications in a highly diversified distributed system." *Information Processing 77,* pp. 149–154.

———. (1980). "A classification of process coordination schemes in descriptive power." *International Journal of Computer and Information Science* 9, 5, pp. 383—406.

Peterson, J. L., and T. H. Bredt. (1974). "A comparison of models of parallel computation." *Information Processing 74,* pp. 466–470.

Saltzer, Jerome H. (1978). "Research problems of decentralized systems with largely autonomous nodes." *ACM Operating Systems Review* 12, 1, pp. 43–52.

Shaw, A. C. (1978). "Software descriptions with flow expressions." *IEEE Transactions on Software Engineering* SE-4, 3, pp. 242–254.

Shrivastava, S. K., and J-P. Banatre. (1978). "Reliable resource allocation between unreliable processes." *IEEE Transactions on Software Engineering* SE-4, 3, pp. 230–241.

Silberschatz, A. (1979). "Communication and synchronization in distributed systems." *IEEE Transactions on Software Engineering* SE-5, 6, pp. 542–546.

Vantiborgh, H., and A. van Lamsweerde. (1979). "On an extension of Dijkstra's semaphore primitives." *Information Processing Letters* 1, pp. 181–186.

Walden, D. C. (April 1972). "A system for interprocess communication in a resource sharing computer network." *Communications of the ACM* 15, 4, pp. 221–230.

Wirth, N. (1977). "Toward a discipline of real-time programming." *Communications of the ACM* 20, 8, pp. 577–583.

Wulf, W. A., et al. (December 1976). "An introduction to the construction and verification of Alphard programs." *IEEE Transactions on Software Engineering* SE-2, 4, pp. 253–265.

Deadlock 4

4.1 Introduction

Deadlock is the *permanent* blocking of a set of processes that either compete for system resources or communicate with each other. Unlike other aspects of process management, deadlock is a problem that defies efficient solution in the general case. If deadlock is ignored in the design stage, it must later be detected by some means, and then processes must be terminated and restarted to recover from it. Alternatively, process behavior can be constrained (or systems can be restricted) at the design stage so deadlock does not occur. Resource utilization must suffer under these regimens.

In this chapter we follow the development found in Holt's thesis [Holt, 1971] and a later tutorial [Holt, 1972]. First, we introduce the deadlock problem. Second, we introduce some definitions and results from graph theory that allow a model of deadlock to be constructed in Section 4.4. This model is useful because the only elements are processes and resources. Processes compete for resources or communicate by producing and consuming resources. The abstract nature of the model means that results are widely applicable and do not depend on the characteristics of particular operating systems. This first, completely general, model captures the nature of deadlock but, unfortunately, fails to help us develop algorithms for coping with the problem. Section 4.5 considers some restrictions on the general model. These models depict frequently occurring special situations wherein efficient and useful approaches to the deadlock problem are available. Recovery from deadlock is considered in Section 4.6. Deadlock can be prevented by system design; this is the subject of Section 4.7. Section 4.8 considers how the methods considered in this chapter are combined in the design of complete operating systems.

4.2 The Deadlock Problem

In this section we define terms used in the rest of the chapter, give examples of deadlock, explain the characteristics of resource types, and introduce policies for dealing with deadlock.

4.2.1 Definition of Deadlock

A computer system may be abstractly represented by a pair of sets (Σ, Π), where

Σ = {All possible allocation states of all system resources}
Π = {Processes}

Each element in Σ represents one possible state in the distribution of the resources. Each process in Π is a function that, for each system state in Σ, maps to another set of states (possibly empty).

For example, let $\Sigma = \{S, T, U, V\}$ and $\Pi = \{P_1, P_2\}$. There are only four possible system states; actions by the two processes cause the system to change from state to state. Suppose the possible actions by the two processes are:

$$P_1(S) = \{T, U\} \quad P_2(S) = \{U\}$$
$$P_1(T) = \varnothing \quad P_2(T) = \{S, V\}$$
$$P_1(U) = \{V\} \quad P_2(U) = \varnothing$$
$$P_1(V) = \{U\} \quad P_2(V) = \varnothing$$

where, for example, $P_1(S) = \{T, U\}$ means that when P_1 is in state S, it may operate to change the system to state T or state U. When the range is $\varnothing$, the process may not operate when the system is in the given state. One may show the states graphically by using nodes for the possible states and arcs for the possible state changes. The arcs are labeled with the process that can effect that state change. The example above is also defined by:

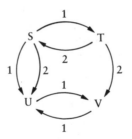

An *operation* by process i changes the system state from, say, S to T. We abbreviate this by writing $S{\rightarrow}i{\rightarrow}T$. In the figure, $S{\rightarrow}1{\rightarrow}U$, $T{\rightarrow}2{\rightarrow}V$, and so forth. If a sequence of operations by processes i, j, . . . , k is possible ($S{\rightarrow}i{\rightarrow}T$, $T{\rightarrow}j{\rightarrow}U$, . . . , $V{\rightarrow}k{\rightarrow}W$), we abbreviate sequences by $S{\rightarrow}^*{\rightarrow}W$.

With this minimal setting, we can define some terms relating to deadlock in an unambiguous way.

- A process P_i is *blocked in state S* if there exists no T so that $S{\rightarrow}i{\rightarrow}T$. In the figure, P_1 is blocked in state T because there is no arc labeled 1 starting at node T.

- Process P_i is *deadlocked in state S* if P_i is blocked in S and, for all states T with $S{\rightarrow}^*{\rightarrow}T$, P_i is blocked in T. No matter how other processes change the system state, there will never be an opportunity for P_i to perform an operation. In the figure, P_2 is deadlocked in states U and V. P_1 is not deadlocked in T because, for example, $T{\rightarrow}2{\rightarrow}S$ unblocks P_1.

- If there is a process P_i deadlocked in S, then S is a *deadlock state*.

- If all processes P_i are deadlocked in S, then S is a *total deadlock state*. In the figure, there are no total deadlock states, but U and V are deadlock states.

• State S is *secure* if S is not a deadlock state and, for any state T reachable from S (S→*→T), T is not a deadlock state.

Here is an example that will help make these abstract ideas more concrete: Two processes compete for exclusive access to a disk file D and the only tape drive T in a system. Both cyclic programs perform these operations:

P_1:		P_2:
0: ...	0:	...
while (true) **do**		**while** (true) **do**
1: Request(D);	1:	Request(T);
2: ...	2:	...
3: Request(T);	3:	Request(D);
4: ...	4:	...
Release(T);		Release(D);
5: ...	5:	...
Release(D);		Release(T);
endwhile		**endwhile**

As each process executes its cycle, it may be in one of six states relative to the ownership of system resources, as seen here:

	P_1:		P_2:
0:	Holds no resources	0:	Holds no resources
1:	Holds none, requests D	1:	Holds none, requests T
2:	Holds D	2:	Holds T
3:	Holds D, requests T	3:	Holds T, requests D
4:	Holds D and T	4:	Holds T and D
5:	Holds D, T released	5:	Holds T, D released

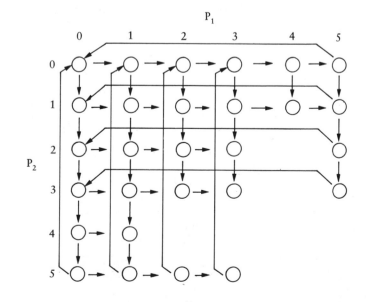

A state of this system S_{ij} reflects that P_1 is in state i while P_2 is in state j. The possible system states are found in the preceding graph. Horizontal arrows (left or right) are state changes due to actions by P_1, and vertical arrows (up or down) are state changes due to the action of P_2.

Both P_1 and P_2 are deadlocked in S_{33}: It is a total deadlock state. States S_{23} and S_{32} are deadlock states because P_2 and P_1 are deadlocked in the states, respectively. P_1 is blocked in states S_{14}, S_{32}, and S_{35}. P_2 is blocked in states S_{23}, S_{41}, and S_{53}. There are no secure states.

4.2.2 Examples of Deadlock

Deadlock may involve any number of processes and resources in simple or complicated ways.

As a first example, consider the two processes competing for disk file D and tape drive T in the example of the preceding section. Deadlock occurs if each process holds one resource and requests the other. Although this example can be regarded as a system design error, its occurrence in practice is real and often embedded in complicated program logic to the extent that a priori detection is difficult, if not impossible. Strategies to cope with this type of problem include imposing constraints on system design so that certain resources are requested in a particular order.

For a second example, suppose the main memory space required for activation records of processes is dynamically allocated. Suppose the total space consists of 20K bytes and two processes require memory in the following way:

P_1:	P_2:
Request 8K bytes	Request 7K bytes
Request 6K bytes	Request 8K bytes

As in the previous example, deadlock occurs if both processes progress to their second request. Note that the processes are not incorrectly designed since neither requests more than the total space in the system. Strategies to cope with this type of problem include the preemption of main memory through paging or requiring processes to specify in advance the maximum amount of memory space needed.

As a third example, suppose two communicating processes have the structure:

P_1:	P_2:
. . .	. . .
Receive (P_2,M)	Receive (P_1,M)
. . .	. . .
Send (P_2,M')	Send (P_1,M')

Design errors such as these may occur at isolated places in very large programs and may be difficult to detect. The actual occurrence of deadlock may be infrequent and may occur only after the system has been in service for many years.

In each of these examples, deadlock occurs because processes request resources held by other processes and, at the same time, hold resources requested by these same processes. This is a fundamental characteristic of deadlock.

Deadlock is similar to *starvation,* since each of these involves one or more processes that are permanently blocked and waiting for the availability of resources. The two, however, are distinctly different phenomena. A deadlocked process waits for resources (held by another process) that will never be released. Starvation occurs when some process waits for resources that periodically become available but are never allocated to that process due to some scheduling policy. An example of starvation is a process waiting for the simultaneous availability of two tape drives. An endless sequence of processes request, are allocated, and release tape drives such that either two drives are never simultaneously available or, if they are available, they are allocated to a higher priority process.

4.2.3 Resource Types

Resources can be divided into two classes: *reusable* and *consumable*. Each class has distinct properties that are reflected in the various strategies designed to deal with the deadlock problem.

A reusable (serially reusable) resource is characterized by the following properties:

- There is a fixed total inventory. Additional units are neither created nor destroyed.
- Units are requested and acquired by processes from a pool of available units and, after use, are returned to the pool for use by other processes.

Examples of serially reusable resources are processors, I/O channels, main and secondary memory, devices, channels, busses, and information such as files, databases and mutual exclusion semaphores. The first two examples of the last section illustrate deadlock involving serially reusable resources.

A consumable resource type is characterized by the following properties:

- There is no fixed total number of units. Units may be created (produced or released) or acquired (consumed) by processes.
- An unblocked producer of the resource may release any number of units. These units then become immediately available to consumers of the resource.
- An acquired unit ceases to exist.

Examples of consumable resources are interrupts and signals, messages, and information in I/O buffers. The third example in the previous section illustrates deadlock involving messages.

In general, deadlock may involve any combination of classes of resources, both reusable and consumable. The classes of resources present in any system or subsystem affects the manner in which the deadlock problem can be handled. This will become clear in subsequent sections.

4.2.4 Deadlock Policies

Methods for coping with deadlock fall into three categories. In this chapter we will see examples from each class. The first policy is *detection and recovery*. Here no action is taken to keep deadlock from occurring. Rather, system events may trigger the execution of a detection algorithm. When the group of deadlocked processes is identified, some of them must be terminated (or rolled back to an earlier state if checkpoint information is available) in order to break the deadlock. This approach is satisfactory in some computer systems if the frequency of deadlock is low and the cost of recovery is reasonable because the utilization of system resources is not degraded during normal operation. Efficient detection algorithms will be discussed in Sections 4.5.1 and 4.5.3.

A second class of deadlock policies is *prevention*. Here the system design prevents entry into a state from which future deadlock is inevitable. This is accomplished by denying at least one of the four following conditions, all of which are necessary for deadlock to occur:

1. *Mutual Exclusion:* Processes hold resources exclusively, making them unavailable to other processes.
2. *Nonpreemption:* Resources are not taken away from a process holding them; only processes can release resources they hold.
3. *Resource Waiting:* Processes that request unavailable units of resources block until they become available.
4. *Partial Allocation:* Processes may hold some resources when they request additional units of the same or other resources.

Deadlock is prevented by designing the resource management sections of an operating system so that one of the conditions cannot occur. Denying any condition inevitably degrades utilization of system resources, but is appropriate in systems for which deadlock carries a heavy penalty (real-time systems controlling chemical or nuclear processes, or systems that monitor or control hospital intensive care units, for example). We will see examples of prevention policies in Sections 4.4 and 4.7.

Avoidance is the third type of deadlock policy. This refers to methods that rely on some knowledge of future process behavior to constrain the pattern of resource allocation. Once again a degradation in resource utilization is inevitable. Often, a subset of resources for which deadlock is especially expensive is managed with an avoidance policy, while detection and recovery suffices for other resources in the same system. Future information may be reasonably easy for a system to deduce or for a user to supply in some instances, but may be impossible to deduce or obtain from a user in other cases. A generalization of a method you may already know (the Banker's Algorithm) is found in Section 4.5.3.

4.3   Concepts from Graph Theory

Before we can introduce the model, we must discuss a few terms and results from graph theory.

- A *directed graph* (digraph) is a pair (N,E), where N is a nonempty set of nodes and E is a set of edges. Each edge is an ordered pair of nodes.

- A *bipartite graph* is one in which all the nodes in N divide into two disjoint subsets π and ρ so that all edges consist of a node from each subset. An interesting result of bipartite graphs will help us determine the efficiency of a detection algorithm later; that is, if the subsets contain m and n nodes, respectively, then the maximum number of nonidentical edges is 2mn.

- Node z is a *sink* if there are no edges (z,b).

- Node z is an *isolated node* if there are no edges (z,b) or (b,z).

- A *path* is a sequence (a,b,c, . . . , y, z) of at least two nodes for which (a,b), (b,c), . . . , (y,z) are edges.

- A *cycle* is a path with the same first and last node.

- The *reachable set* of a node z is the set of all nodes to which there is a path beginning with z. The reachable set of z may contain z itself if there is a cycle.

- A *knot* K is a nonempty set of nodes with the property that, for each node z in K, the reachable set of z is exactly the knot K.

In Figure 4.1 we see a bipartite graph with nodes N = {a,b,c,d} and edges E = {(a,b), (a,b), (a,c), (c,d), (d,c)}. All edges connect between nodes in the two sets {a,d} and {b,c}. Node b is a sink, (c,d,c) is a cycle, and {c,d} is a knot. Note that from now on we will allow multiple edges from one node to another.

Some results of knots will be the basis for future deadlock detection algorithms:

- If a digraph has a knot, then it has a cycle.

- No node in a knot is a sink.

- There is no path from a node in a knot to a sink.

- A digraph is free of knots if and only if, for each node z, z is a sink or there is a path from z to a sink.

In the next section we introduce the graph model of completely general systems of processes and resources.

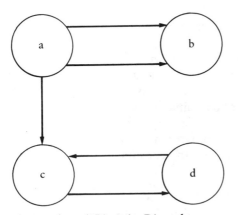

Figure 4.1   A Bipartite Digraph.

4.4   The General Model

A general resource system model consists of a nonempty set $\pi = \{ P_1, \ldots, P_n \}$ of processes and a nonempty set $\rho = \{ R_1, \ldots, R_m \}$ of resources. The set ρ is partitioned into two disjoint subsets, ρ_r and ρ_c, representing reusable and consumable resources, respectively. Associated with each resource R_j is the current number of available units $r_j \geqslant 0$. Associated with each reusable resource R_j is the total number of units $t_j > 0$. For each consumable resource R_j there is a nonempty set of processes that produce units of R_j.

4.4.1   General Resource Graph

A particular state in the general resource system model is completely described by the number of units of each resource that each process requests, the number of units of each reusable resource held by each process, and the current available inventory of each resource. For each state there is a corresponding bipartite digraph:

- Nodes N = {Processes} ∪ {Resources}. To distinguish between them in figures, we draw processes as square boxes, □, and resources as round circles, ○. For reusable resources R_j, we represent the total inventory t_j by placing small tokens in the circle for R_j. For consumable resources, the tokens represent the number of currently available units r_j.
- Edges E are of three types:

  Request edges (P_i, R_j) connect process to resources. They represent units of R_j that have been requested but not yet obtained.

  Assignment edges (R_j, P_i) connect resources to processes. These arcs signify units of reusable resources R_j currently held by P_i.

  Producer edges (R_j, P_i) connect consumable resources to processes that produce them. These are permanent identifiers of the producers P_i of R_j.

Notice that the graph is bipartite. Since request and assignment edges may appear and disappear with state changes (as we will soon see), and producer edges are permanent, we draw request and assignment edges using solid arrows, and producer edges with dashed arrows.

In Figure 4.2 we see a *general resource graph,* with two processes, P_1 and P_2, and two resources, R_1 and R_2. Process P_1 holds two units of reusable resource R_1. R_1 has a total inventory of four units. Process P_2 also holds one unit of R_1, requests one unit of R_2, and is the only producer of consumable resource R_2. R_2 has a current inventory of one unit. Observe the structural similarity between Figures 4.1 and 4.2.

Graphs representing states in the general resource system model obey some reasonable restrictions with respect to reusable and consumable resources. For reusable resources:

- The number of assignment edges directed from R_j cannot exceed t_j.
- At all times the available units $r_j = t_j - $ (number of edges directed from R_j).

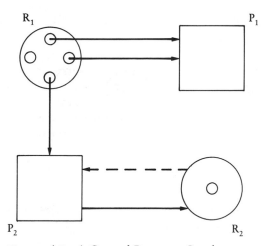

Figure 4.2 A General Resource Graph.

- For each process P_i, [number of request edges (P_i,R_j)] + [number of assignment edges (R_j,P_i)] $\leq t_j$.

For consumable resources:

- Edge (R_j,P_i) exists if and only if P_i produces R_j.
- The inventory r_j at any time is constrained only to be nonnegative. This means that systems containing consumable resources may have an infinite number of states.

4.4.2 Operations on Resources

Processes perform operations that change the state of the general resource system. Each state has a corresponding graph. Here we describe the operations that processes execute—*requests, acquisitions,* and *releases*—and the corresponding graph alterations necessary to reflect these new states. All the operations are constrained by the resource restrictions above.

REQUESTS If process P_i has *no* outstanding requests (that is, if it is executable), then it may request units of any number of resources R_j, R_k, ... To reflect this in the graph, add edges (P_i,R_j), (P_i,R_k), . . . in multiplicities corresponding to the number of units of each resource requested.

ACQUISITIONS If process P_i has outstanding requests, and for each requested resource R_j, the number of requested units does not exceed the current inventory r_j (that is, if *all* requests are grantable), then P_i may acquire *all* requested resources. The graph is altered as follows. For each request edge (P_i,R_j) to a reusable resource, reverse the edge direction to make it an assignment edge (R_j,P_i). Each request edge to a consumable resource disappears, simulating the consumption of units by P_i. In either case each inventory r_j is reduced by the number of units of R_j acquired or consumed by P_i.

RELEASES   If process P_i has no outstanding requests (that is, if it is executable), and there are assignment or producer edges (R_j,P_i), then P_i may release any subset of the reusable resources it holds or produce any number of units of consumable resources for which it is a producer. Assignment edges from reusable resources disappear from the graph, but producer edges are permanent. Inventories r_j are incremented by the number of units of each resource R_j released or produced.

Consider again the system state in Figure 4.2. The successive states shown in Figures 4.3(a), 4.3(b), and 4.3(c) reflect the following three operations, respectively:

(a) P_1 requests one unit of R_1 and two units of R_2. Edge (P_1,R_1) and two edges (P_1,R_2) appear in the graph. Since P_1's requests are not all satisfiable, P_1 is blocked in this state.

(b) P_2's request for one unit of R_2 is granted. Since R_2 is consumable, the request edge (P_2,R_2) disappears. A token disappears from R_2.

(c) P_2 produces three units of R_2. Three tokens appear in R_2. P_1 is no longer blocked in this state.

The next subsection discusses the characterization of deadlock in terms of general resource system graphs.

4.4.3   Necessary and Sufficient Conditions for Deadlock

In this section we introduce the concept of graph reduction and derive conditions that relate reducibility of a resource graph to deadlock. A *graph reduction* reflects an optimistic view about the behavior of a process. In particular, a reduction by a process P_i simulates the acquisition of any outstanding requests, the return of any

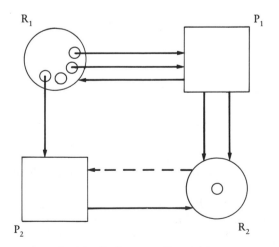

Figure 4.3(a) P_1 Request Operation.

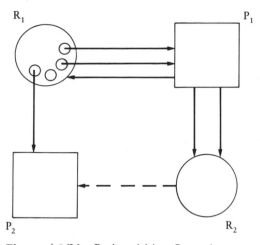

Figure 4.3(b) P_2 Acquisition Operation.

allocated units of a reusable resource, and, if P_i is a producer of a consumable resource, the production of a "sufficient" number of units to satisfy all subsequent requests by consumers. In the case of a consumable resource R_j, the new inventory is represented by ∞ to indicate that all future requests for R_j are grantable.

Formally, a graph may be *reduced* by a nonisolated node, representing an unblocked process P_i, in the following manner:

- For each resource R_j, delete all edges (P_i, R_j) and if R_j is consumable, decrement r_j by the number of deleted request edges.
- For each resource R_j, delete all edges (R_j, P_i). If R_j is reusable, then increment r_j by the number of deleted edges. If R_j is consumable, set $r_j = \infty$.

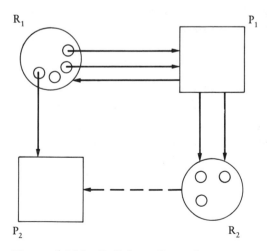

Figure 4.3(c) P_2 Release Operation.

A reduction of a graph by a process node P_i may lead to the unblocking of another process node P_j, thereby making P_j a candidate for the next reduction. A graph is said to be *completely reducible* if there exists a sequence of graph reductions that reduces the graph to a set of isolated nodes. Figure 4.4 illustrates a reduction sequence applied to a completely reducible graph.

The manner in which graph reductions are related to the deadlock problem is stated in the following result:

THEOREM 4.1

A process P_i is not deadlocked in state S if and only if there exists a sequence of reductions in the corresponding graph that leaves P_i unblocked.

This result follows from two observations:

1. Such a sequence of reductions explicitly demonstrates the manner in which a blocked process P_i may become a runnable process.

2. If a blocked process is to become runnable, then some sequence of process executions must exist to unblock it.

An immediate consequence of this result is:

COROLLARY

If a graph is completely reducible, then the state it represents is not deadlocked.

While Theorem 4.1 and its corollary are important for characterizing properties of deadlocked states, they do not, by themselves, provide the basis for practical algorithms for deadlock detection. The reasons for this impracticality are illustrated in two examples.

First, reducibility may be dependent on the order of the reductions. This is illustrated in Figure 4.5, where the only possible sequence of reductions leading to a completely reduced graph is $P_1 P_2$. This suggests that an algorithm for detecting deadlock may have to, in the most general case, inspect n! possible reduction sequences, yielding a worst-case time complexity of $O(mn!)$, where m is the number of resource types and n is the number of processes. Second, the converse to the corollary is not true, as illustrated by the example in Figure 4.6. This graph may be reduced by either process node P_1 or process node P_2, after which no reductions are possible. Clearly neither process is deadlocked, although deadlock is imminent. Thus, the corollary provides a conclusion of no deadlock if the graph is completely reducible, but fails to provide a conclusion if the graph is not reducible (see, however, Problem 3).

In order to derive practical algorithms for dealing with deadlock, certain constraints must be imposed on the behavior of the system of processes. The first such constraint deals with the occurrence of grantable requests.

A system state is *expedient* if all processes requesting resources are blocked. In such systems, a new allocation of resources can take place only at the time of a request or at the time of a release. Expediency is not considered a major restriction since most practical systems naturally follow such an allocation policy.

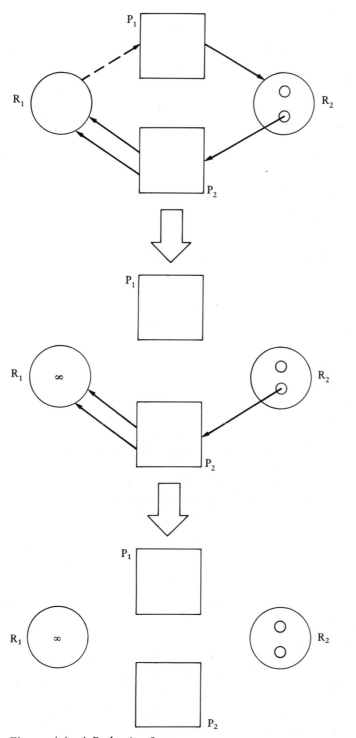

Figure 4.4 A Reduction Sequence.

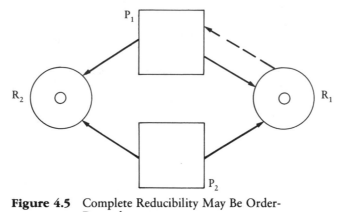

Figure 4.5   Complete Reducibility May Be Order-
Dependent.

Combined with an important necessary condition, we have the following result for a general resource system:

THEOREM 4.2

A cycle is a necessary condition for deadlock. If the graph is expedient, a knot is sufficient condition for deadlock.

The necessity of a cycle follows from the observation that absence of a cycle implies the existence of a linear ordering of process nodes following arcs from processes to resources to processes. The reverse listing of processes alone gives a reduction sequence for completely reducing the graph. The sufficiency of a knot follows from the observation that each process node in a knot is directly or indirectly waiting for other process nodes in the knot to release resources. Since all are waiting on each other, no process node in a knot can be reduced.

If a general resource graph is not expedient, then a knot is not a sufficient condition for deadlock. This is demonstrated by the example in Figure 4.7. Expe-

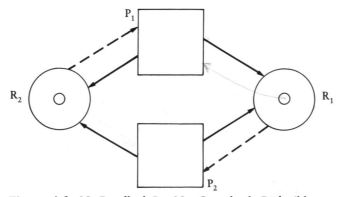

Figure 4.6   No Deadlock But Not Completely Reducible.

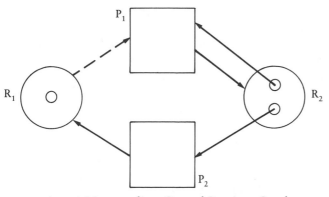

Figure 4.7 A Nonexpedient General Resource Graph.

diency will be assumed throughout the remainder of this chapter. Figure 4.7 also demonstrates that the presence of a cycle in a general resource graph is not a sufficient condition for deadlock. This is true even for expedient systems.

4.5 Special Cases with Useful Results

By further restricting general resource systems, we can obtain useful approaches to managing deadlock in situations common to current computer systems.

4.5.1 Single-Unit Requests

In these systems a process may have at most one outstanding request for a single unit of some resource. These *single-unit request* systems are also expedient. Some message-passing systems are examples of systems with these characteristics. Deadlock may be efficiently detected in this case.

In the most general case of Section 4.4, the existence of a knot in an expedient graph implied a deadlock state. The following three facts lead to two efficient detection algorithms.

First, if a graph is a deadlock state, then a knot exists. If we were to assume that there is no knot, then each process P_i is either a sink (it is not blocked), or there is a path $(P_i, R_j, P_k, \ldots, P_x, R_y, P_z)$ so that node P_z is a sink. The sink must be a process because of expedience. Then P_z is not blocked and we can reduce the graph by P_z. Node R_y is a resource, and reduction by P_z must have increased R_y's inventory. Since P_x is requesting just one unit of R_y, it is no longer blocked and we reduce by P_x. We continue up the path in this way until P_i is no longer blocked. Thus, there is no deadlock. Combined with the second part of Theorem 4.2, we see that the existence of a knot is equivalent to deadlock in single-unit request systems, and graph-knot detection algorithms can be used to determine the existence of deadlock.

Second, any two reduction sequences lead to the same irreducible state. The truth of this statement relies on two propositions. (1) If two sequences of reductions are applied to a state S, and the two sequences contain the same processes in different order, then the resulting state is the same in either case. This is true because each reduction removes the same edges in either sequence, so the same end result is achieved. (2) In a state S, if we could reduce the graph by P_i, but instead we reduce the graph by other processes to state T, then T is still reducible by P_i. This is true because reusable inventories clearly do not decrease in the alternate reduction to T, and expedience prevents inventories of consumable resources from declining. These propositions allow one to verify that any two reduction sequences that yield irreducible states must be permutations of each other; then these two states must be identical. This fact is important because it eliminates the need to consider reduction sequences that are permutations of each other, and the exponential cost of searching for an irreducible state is reduced to a polynomial cost.

Third, process P is not deadlocked in state S if and only if P is a sink or on a path to a sink. This fact leads to an effective method for checking if a particular process is deadlocked.

On the basis of these facts, two useful algorithms are now available. The first detects the presence of a knot to determine the presence or absence of deadlock. The expression "L ∥ F" appends the node F to the node list L (if it does not already exist in L).

ALGORITHM 4.1

Is state S a deadlock state?

```
L : = [List of sinks in state S]
for the next N in L do
    for F so that (F,N) is an edge do
        L : = L∥F
    endfor
endfor
Deadlock : = {Nodes} ≠ L
```

List L begins as a list of initial sinks. The outer loop processes through L to find nodes F that are on a path of length 1 from sink nodes (or paths to sinks) already found. These nodes are appended to L. When the outer loop reaches these added nodes, new nodes that are two steps from the original sinks are appended. When the entire list L has been processed, it will contain all nodes that are not participating in a knot. If this is not all nodes, then {Nodes} − L is the group of processes and resources defining the deadlock condition.

The second algorithm attempts to find a path from a process P to a sink in order to establish that P is not deadlocked.

ALGORITHM 4.2

Is process P deadlocked?

```
Deadlock : = true; L : = [P]
for the next N in L while Deadlock do
    for each F so that (N,F) is an edge do
```

> **if** F is a sink **then** Deadlock : = *false*
> **else** L : = L ‖F
> **endif**
> **endfor**
> **endfor**

The list L initially contains P, the process in question. We travel on all the paths from nodes in L to neighbor nodes F. If a neighbor is a sink, the algorithm terminates, reporting no deadlock. Otherwise the neighbor is appended to L for possible later processing. If the entire list is processed and no sink is found, then P is part of a knot and is deadlocked.

Each of these algorithms executes in time proportional to the number of edges in the graph. Since our graphs are bipartite with n processes and m resources, we know that the algorithms execute in $O(mn)$ time. Further, the second algorithm is likely to terminate quickly under most circumstances.

Thus, continual deadlock detection can be done at a reasonable cost. When process P requests an unavailable unit, the second algorithm should be executed. As a potentially cheaper but less immediate alternative, the first algorithm should "occasionally" be executed.

4.5.2 Consumable Resources Only

In some system models, reusable resources may not be present. For example, models of operating systems that rely solely on message passing may depict only consumable resources. We assume that each process is a producer or consumer of at least one resource. Although we cannot obtain an efficient detection algorithm for reasons explained in Section 4.4, we can *prevent* deadlock by a conservative system design method.

We define the *claim-limited graph* of the *consumable resource system* to be the graph corresponding to the special state in which all inventories are exhausted and each consumer of each resource requests one unit. Figure 4.8 shows a simple example. Clearly, this may be a desperate situation. If there are no producer processes that consume no resources, all processes must remain blocked and hence deadlocked. The result that leads to a scheme for preventing deadlock is:

> A consumable resource system is secure from deadlock if and only if its claim-limited graph is completely reducible.

This result can be used to analyze a computer system during its design. When all resources, and consumer and producer processes are known, the claim-limited graph is constructible. Its complete reducibility means that the system cannot enter a deadlock state. However, this is a very strong deadlock prevention criterion and thus results in poor resource utilization. It is useful in consumable resource systems for which deadlock prevention is an absolute requirement.

The following example demonstrates why the result is often too strong to be of practical value. It is assumed that a "send" operation does not cause a process to

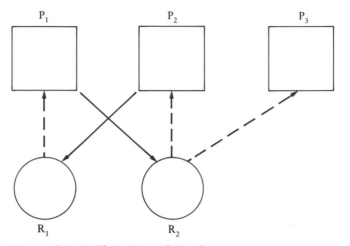

Figure 4.8 A Claim-Limited Graph.

become blocked. Here the claim-limited graph of the message-passing system is not reducible even though the system is deadlock-free:

P_1: **while** *true* **do**
    begin
        produce M
        send (P_2,M)
        receive (P_2,L')
    end

P_2: **while** *true* **do**
    begin
        produce L
        send (P_1,L)
        receive (P_1, M')
    end

This system results in the claim-limited graph shown in Figure 4.9.

4.5.3   Reusable Resources Only

A *reusable resource system* is a special case of a general resource system in which there are only reusable resource types. Assuming expediency, efficient algorithms can be defined for all three policies: detection, prevention, and avoidance. Each of these policies will be examined in subsequent sections.

Detection in Reusable Resource Systems

The following major result provides necessary and sufficient conditions for the existence of deadlock, establishing the basis for efficient deadlock detection:

THEOREM 4.3
Let S be any state of a reusable resource system. Any sequence of reductions of the corresponding graph leads to a unique graph that cannot be reduced. S is not deadlocked if and only if S is completely reducible.

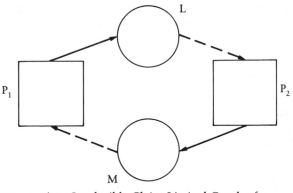

Figure 4.9 Irreducible Claim-Limited Graph of a Deadlock-Free System.

The first statement follows from the observation that a reduction never decreases the number of available units of a resource. As a consequence, reducibility is not order-dependent and any two reduction sequences that leave the graph in an irreducible state must necessarily involve the same set of process nodes. For the second statement, it was shown in Section 4.4.3 that complete reducibility implies absence of deadlock. To establish the necessity of the condition, note that if S is not deadlocked, then no process is deadlocked. From the first statement, it follows that any reduction sequence leads to a completely reduced graph.

Theorem 4.3 provides the basis for efficient deadlock-detection algorithms. The first of these algorithms is appealing because of its simplicity:

ALGORITHM 4.3
Detection in reusable systems (simple version):

> L : = [List of process nodes];
> finished : = *false*;
> **while** ((L $\neq \emptyset$) **and not** finished) **do**
> > P : = First process in L by which graph can be reduced;
> > **if** P $\neq$ nil **then** Reduce graph by P; Remove P from L
> > **else** finished : = *true*
> > **endif**
> **endwhile**

Upon completion of Algorithm 4.3, L $\equiv$ [List of deadlocked processes]. The algorithm has an $O(mn^2)$ worst-case time complexity since a reduction can involve m resource nodes, the selection of P on the *ith* pass of the loop may require inspection of $(n - i + 1)$ nodes, and n total passes may be required.

At the expense of extra storage, a more efficient algorithm is available. The following data structures are assumed to be maintained by this system:

- *wait_count:* Associated with each process, this denotes the number of resources for which the process is currently waiting.

• *ordered_requests:* Associated with each resource, this is a list of processes that request units. This list is maintained in increasing order of units requested.

ALGORITHM 4.4

Detection in reusable systems (ordered requests):

```
L : = [List of nonisolated process nodes];
list_to_be_reduced : = [List of nonisolated process nodes
whose wait_count is 0];
while (list_to_be_reduced ≠ ∅) do
   Select P from list_to_be_reduced;
   for R ∈ {Resources assigned to P} do
      Increase available units of R by number of units assigned to P;
      for each process Q in ordered_requests for this R
      whose request can be satisfied do
         Decrease wait_count of Q by 1;
         if wait_count of Q = 0 then
            Add Q to list_to_be_reduced
         endif
      endfor
   endfor;
   Remove P from L
endwhile
```

Upon completion of Algorithm 4.4, L ≡ [Deadlocked processes]. Since the selection of Q does not require a search of *ordered_requests*, the time complexity of this algorithm is O(mn).

The next example illustrates the use of Algorithm 4.4. Consider a system of three processes, P_1, P_2, and P_3, and three reusable resources, R_1, R_2, and R_3, with total units of 2, 3, and 2, respectively.

1. Initial State
   wait_count: 0 for all processes
   ordered_requests: empty for all resources

2. P_1 requests and acquires two units of R_3.
   wait_count: 0 for all processes
   ordered_requests remains unchanged
   The deadlock detection algorithm is not applied since all *wait_counts* are zero.

3. P_3 requests and acquires two units of R_2.
   The *wait_counts* and *ordered_requests* remain unchanged

4. P_3 requests two units of R_3.
   wait_count[P_3] = 1, all other *wait_counts* are 0
   ordered_request[R_3] = {P_3}, all other *ordered_requests* are empty
   The deadlock detection algorithm is applied with L = {P_1,P_3} and

list_to_be_reduced = {P$_1$}. The algorithm terminates in one pass with the conclusion that deadlock does not exist.

5. P$_2$ requests and acquires two units of R$_1$.
    The *wait_counts* and *ordered_requests* remain unchanged

6. P$_2$ requests two units of R$_2$.
    wait_count[P$_1$] = 0, *wait_count*[P$_2$] = *wait_count*[P$_3$] = 1
    ordered_requests[R$_1$] = $\varnothing$, *ordered_requests*[R$_2$] = {P$_2$},
    ordered_requests[R$_3$] = {P$_3$}
    The deadlock detection algorithm is applied with L = {P$_1$,P$_2$,P$_3$} and list_to_be_reduced = {P$_1$}. The algorithm reduces P$_1$, P$_3$, and finally P$_2$.

7. P$_1$ requests a unit of R$_1$.
    wait_count: 1 for all processes
    ordered_requests[R$_1$] = {P$_1$}, *ordered_requests*[R$_2$] = {P$_2$}
    ordered_requests[R$_3$] = {P$_3$}
    The deadlock algorithm is applied with L = {P$_1$,P$_2$,P$_3$} and list_to_be_reduced = $\varnothing$. No processes are reducible and the algorithm terminates with the conclusion that all three processes are deadlocked.

A requirement of Algorithm 4.4 is that the system maintain the *wait_count* and *ordered_requests* data structures. However, this information allows efficient allocation to waiting processes when units of a resource are released.

Since only unsatisfiable requests for resources can cause a deadlock in reusable resource systems, detection needs to be performed only at request time and, consequently, deadlock is detected as soon as it occurs. Assuming that the system does not already contain a deadlock at the time of such a request, Algorithms 4.3 and 4.4 can be made more efficient by terminating them as soon as it has been determined that a reduction sequence involves the requesting process.

Avoidance in Reusable Resource Systems

The method presented in this section requires that each process be able to anticipate its maximum total resource requirements, called its *claim*, at any point during execution. Clearly no process can be allocated more than its claimed resources. The original algorithm for this process was first proposed for a single resource by Dijkstra [1968], and was called the "Banker's Algorithm." It was extended to multiple resources by Habermann [1969].

Formally, let c$_{ij}$ denote the claim of process P$_i$ for resource R$_j$, where $0 \leq c_{ij} \leq t_j$, and let C[1:n,1:m] denote the claim matrix for n processes and m resources. For a given state, the *maximum-claim graph* reflects the projected worst-case future state and is constructed from the graph of the current state by adding additional request edges (P$_i$,R$_j$), called *claim edges,* until the number of request edges plus the number of assignment edges (R$_j$,P$_i$) is equal to c$_{ij}$. These claim edges are denoted by dotted edges. A state is defined as *safe* if its corresponding maximum-claim graph is deadlock-free. A *maximum-claim reusable resource system* is one in which all states are safe.

Whenever a process makes a request, the following algorithm is executed.

ALGORITHM 4.5

Avoidance

1. Project the future state by changing the request edge to an assignment edge.
2. Construct the maximum-claim graph for this state and analyze it for deadlock. If deadlock exists, then defer granting the request; otherwise, grant the request.

Figures 4.10(a), 4.10(b), and 4.10(c) show an execution of the deadlock-avoidance algorithm for a system of two processes, P_1 and P_2, and two reusable resource types, R_1 and R_2, consisting of 3 and 2 units, respectively. Figure 4.10(a) depicts the initial safe state along with the claim matrix. Figure 4.10(b) depicts a request by P_1 for a unit of R_2, along with the corresponding maximum-claim graph for the projected state. Since the maximum-claim graph contains a deadlock, the request by

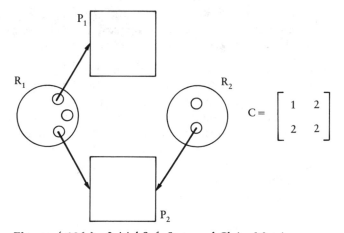

$$C = \begin{bmatrix} 1 & 2 \\ 2 & 2 \end{bmatrix}$$

Figure 4.10(a)   Initial Safe State and Claim Matrix.

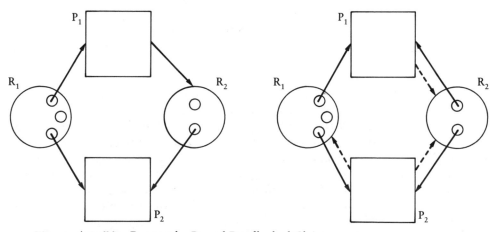

Figure 4.10(b)   Request by P_1 and Deadlocked Claim-Limited Graph.

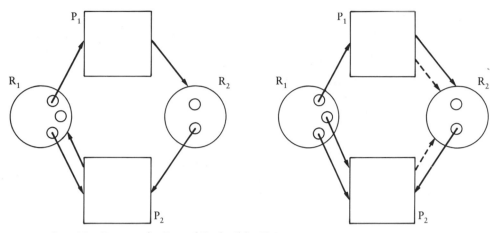

Figure 4.10(c)   Request by P_2 and Reducible Claim-Limited Graph.

P_1 cannot be safely granted now. Figure 4.10(c) shows that a subsequent request by P_2 for a unit of R_1 can be safely granted.

Given an initial safe state, the deadlock-avoidance algorithm will ensure that every successive state will also be safe. However, although the algorithm is useful in specific circumstances involving particular resource types, there may be major costs associated with its use. First, the algorithm must be executed for every request prior to granting it. Second, the restriction on resource allocation may severely degrade system resource utilization. Unless the claims are simultaneously realized by the processes, it is impossible to actually reach the pessimistic state represented by a maximum-claim graph. Thus, if the claims are not precise, many requests may be deferred when they might in fact be safely granted. In many cases it is impossible for a user to estimate resource requirements accurately.

4.6   Recovery from Deadlock

Recovery from deadlock requires the *rollback* of one or more deadlocked processes. An extreme case of rollback is to abort a process and restart it at its beginning. If the system has a checkpoint/restart facility, then only partial rollback may be required, although the rollback may involve more than the deadlocked processes. In many database processing systems, discriminate rollback of an application is possible; this typically requires a restart only of the current transaction. Whenever rollback occurs, the system must guard against repeated deadlock involving the same processes. The countermeasures may involve raising the priority according to the number of rollbacks or the use of timestamps.

Regardless of the degree of rollback, the ideal selection is one that minimizes the cost of reexecuting the rolled-back processes. Numerous factors may be involved in determining the cost of restarting an individual process: priority, type and amount of current resource allocation, number of processes affected, amount of service received, and amount of service required to finish.

For general resource systems, the cost of executing an optimal recovery algorithm may be prohibitive. Let c_i denote the cost of recovery for process i and let P_1, ..., P_k denote the set of deadlocked processes. Select a subset of deadlocked processes P_{i_1}, ..., P_{i_q} for removal so that (1) deadlock is resolved, and (2) $c_{i_1} + \cdots + c_{i_q}$ is a minimum. Such a cost-recovery algorithm for n processes, given in Holt [1971], has an $O(n(n + (n - 1) + \cdots + n!))$ worst-case execution time and $O(n * n!)$ worst-case storage requirements. For the special case of a reusable resource system with n processes and m resource types, a more efficient algorithm can be found that has $O((m + n)^2)$ time and space requirements [Purdom, 1968].

Simple and fast algorithms have been devised for suboptimal recovery from deadlock. The following algorithm [from Holt, 1971], is applicable to reusable resource systems and has O(mn) execution time.

ALGORITHM 4.6

Recovery:

    L = [Processes ordered by increasing termination cost];
    while (L ≠ ∅) **do**
        Select next P from L;
        Terminate P and remove P from L;
        Use deadlock-detection Algorithm 4.4 to reduce as many processes as
        possible, removing all liberated processes from L
    end

If continuous deadlock detection is feasible, then a simple, fast suboptimal recovery algorithm is to abort the requesting process.

4.7   Prevention by System Design

As mentioned in Section 4.2.4, deadlock prevention is accomplished by designing the system so that one of four necessary deadlock conditions is denied. A prevention policy is attractive from the point of view that run-time overhead, required for deadlock testing in each of the other two policies, is avoided. In general, it is not practical to execute a deadlock-detection algorithm each time a process requests, acquires, or releases a shared variable. There are three important prevention methods: collective requests, ordered requests, and preemption [Havender, 1968].

In the *collective-requests method,* a process requests and is allocated all resources that it will need during any moment of its execution. New requests are allowed only if the process first releases everything that it has been allocated. This method denies the partial allocation condition necessary for deadlock to exist. The method is simple and effective, but may seriously degrade utilization of system resources since a process may hold resources for extended periods of time during which they are not needed. Starvation is another potential difficulty since a process with large resource requirements may be indefinitely blocked. For example, processes with large memory requirements may fit into this category. The usual countermeasures to starvation are *aging* or running such a job at a designated period of time when demand is usually low. If a large job is run during a peak period, an accounting question is raised since it is not clear who should be charged for other idled resources. Although the method of collective requests has clear disadvantages, it is a particularly useful approach in dealing with shared variables when it is known that the duration of use will be short.

In the *ordered requests method,* a fixed ordering $C_1, \ldots, C_k$ is imposed on resource classes, each containing one or more resources. If a process holds a resource in class C_i, it can only request resources of classes C_j for $j > i$. This method denies the existence of a cycle in the resource graph that Theorem 4.2 established as a necessary condition for deadlock. Although the ordered-request method is more efficient than the collective-request method, it still may seriously degrade system performance. Since the order of resource usage differs from one process to another, processes may be forced to request and be allocated resources unnecessarily early. If resources are reordered, programs optimized for an old ordering may need to be redesigned. Since requests for an already allocated resource are not allowed without release of all resources in this and subsequent classes, a typical approach may be for a process to request the maximum quantity at each stage. In spite of the potentially serious impact on resource utilization, the ordered-resource approach is a common technique used to prevent deadlocks.

Preemption is a third method used to prevent deadlock. For some resource types or processes, however, the penalty is too high to make this method effective. This is particularly true for real-time applications, where it may be impossible to recover a previous system state. Even if recovery is possible, the cost of restarting a long-running process may be too high. Resources commonly considered preemptible include the processor in time-shared systems, main memory in swapping systems or virtual memory systems, and access to data in transaction-based systems.

4.8   Total System Design

Deadlock control in operating systems typically involves a mixture of several policies, and several methods within each policy. Most operating systems are hierarchically organized in layers, each of which modifies and extends the capabilities of the underlying layer. A primitive operation in one layer is implemented in terms of operations in lower layers. This leads to a natural ordering of groups of resources— resources used in higher levels are requested before resources in lower levels. Within each group, other techniques described in this chapter for dealing with deadlock may be employed. The following is a list of resource types and commonly used policies [Howard, 1973]:

- *Swap space in secondary memory:* Preallocate the maximum amount of space needed by each process.

- *Job or job-step resources:* Resources, such as files and special I/O devices, are typically needed for the duration of job or job step. A common approach in batch-processing systems is to use an avoidance strategy since considerable information about future resource usage can be deduced from job-control statements. Another approach might be to use a collective-request prevention strategy, with new allocations occurring at the beginning of each job step and all allocations released at the end of each job step. Some systems use only deadlock detection for files.

- *Main memory for user jobs:* Preemption is the most effective approach in a paging, segmentation, or swapping system. If this is not possible, main memory should be included in the class of job resources.

- *Internal system resources:* Resources such as control blocks, buffers, and semaphores are included in this class. Since access is frequent, a prevention strategy such as resource ordering is a typical choice. The hierarchical nature of the system may provide a natural choice for the ordering. If ordering is difficult, a collective-request method may be used. For example, see the simultaneous P operation in Chapter 2.

4.9   Summary

Deadlock is a difficult problem with no single solution to fit all circumstances. The three general policies are detection, avoidance, and prevention. In a general resource system, a cycle in the resource graph is a necessary but not sufficient condition for deadlock existence. On the other hand, complete reducibility of the resource graph is a sufficient but not necessary condition for absence of deadlock. As a consequence, there are no known efficient algorithms for the completely general case. Imposing certain constraints, however, allows for the derivation of efficient algorithms for detection and avoidance.

Assuming expedience and single unit requests, a knot in the resource graph and complete reducibility are both necessary and sufficient conditions for deadlock. Necessary and sufficient conditions for a consumable resource system to be secure from deadlock is the total reducibility of the claim-limited graph. These latter two results are important in the design of message-based systems.

In reusable resource systems, complete reducibility of the resource graph is both necessary and sufficient for existence of deadlock. Efficient algorithms can be devised for both deadlock detection and deadlock avoidance.

Three important prevention methods employed in many operating systems are collective resource requests, ordered resource requests, and preemption. Most operating systems are designed using combinations of policies and methods.

Key Words

acquisition operation	avoidance	claim
aging	bipartite graph	claim-limited graph
assignment edges	blocked	

collective-requests method	isolated node	release operation
completely reducible	knot	request edges
consumable resource	maximum-claim graph	request operation
consumable resource system	maximum-claim reusable resource system	resource waiting
cycle	mutual exclusion	reusable resource
deadlock state	nonpreemption	reusable resource system
deadlocked	ordered-requests method	rollback
detection and recovery	partial allocation	secure
directed graph	path	single-unit requests
expedience	preemption	sink
general resource graph	prevention	starvation
graph reduction	producer edges	total deadlock state
	reachable set	

Questions

1. Consider a system consisting of two processes, P_1 and P_2, and two reusable resources, R_1 and R_2, each of which has an inventory of one unit. In this system, shared read operations are allowed, but write operations require exclusive access. Each process requests access to both resources, in unpredictable order, prior to releasing them both. The type of access (read or write) is also unpredictable. Describe the state transition graph, similar to that found in Section 4.2.1, and identify all deadlock states. Define whatever notation you need to simplify the description of states.

2. Consider a system consisting of one reusable resource with a total inventory of two units and two processes, each of which may request both units (one or both at a time).

   a. Assuming deadlock detection, describe the state transition diagram, similar to that found in Section 4.2.1. Define whatever notation you need to simplify the description of states.

   b. Suppose deadlock prevention is used for this system. Describe the modified state transition graph. Consider collective requests and ordered requests.

3. Should the following items be considered resources? If yes, should they be reusable resources or consumable resources?

   a. terminal
   b. cassette tape drive
   c. floppy diskette
   d. CPU
   e. general CPU registers
   f. relocation register
   g. cache memory
   h. program status register
   i. I/O channel
   j. paged or segmented main memory

k. page or segment table register   l. main memory with relocation register
m. I/O buffer   n. channel command program
o. program code   p. disk file
q. semaphore   r. interrupt signal
s. message buffer   t. OS process running in main memory
u. disk space   v. user process running in main memory

4. Why is it important to allow an AND condition in P operations from the viewpoint of deadlock?

5. For each of the following, construct the general resource graph and determine if the graph is completely reducible:

a. R_1, R_2, R_3 are reusable resources with total respective inventories of 2, 2, and 3 units. Process P_1 is allocated one unit each of R_2 and R_3 and is requesting 2 units of R_1; process P_2 is allocated 1 unit of R_1 and is requesting 2 units of R_3; and process P_3 is allocated 1 unit each of R_1 and R_2 and is requesting 3 units of R_3.

b. Same as part (a) except R_1 has a total inventory of 3 units.

c. R_1 and R_2 are consumable resources, each with a current inventory of 0 units. Process P_2 is a producer of R_1, and processes P_2 and P_3 are producers of R_2. P_1 is requesting 1 unit of R_1, and P_2 is requesting 1 unit of R_2.

d. R_1 and R_3 are reusable resources with total respective inventories of 2 and 5 units. R_2 is a consumable resource with a current inventory of 0 units. P_1 is allocated 3 units of R_3 and is requesting 2 units of R_1; P_2 is allocated 1 unit of R_1 and is requesting 3 units of R_2; and P_3 is a producer of R_2 and is requesting 4 units of R_3.

e. R_1 and R_3 are consumable resources, each with a current inventory of 1 unit. R_2 is a reusable resource with a total inventory of 2 units. P_1 is a producer of R_1 and is requesting 1 unit of R_1, 2 units of R_2, and 1 unit of R_3; P_2 is a producer of R_3 and is requesting 1 unit each of R_1 and R_2; and P_3 is requesting 1 unit each of R_1 and R_3.

6. Assume a maximum-claim reusable resource system with four processes and three resource types. The claim matrix is given by

$$C = \begin{bmatrix} 4 & 1 & 4 \\ 3 & 1 & 4 \\ 5 & 7 & 13 \\ 1 & 1 & 6 \end{bmatrix}$$

where C_{ij} denotes maximum claim of process i for resource j. The total units of each resource type are given by the vector (5 8 16). The allocation of resources is given by the matrix

$$A = \begin{bmatrix} 0 & 1 & 4 \\ 2 & 0 & 1 \\ 1 & 2 & 1 \\ 1 & 0 & 3 \end{bmatrix}$$

where A_{ij} denotes the number of units of resource j that are currently allocated to process i.

a. Determine if the current state of the system is safe.

b. Determine if the granting of a request by process 1 for 1 unit of resource 1 can be safely granted.

c. Determine if the granting of a request by process 3 for 6 units of resource 3 can be safely granted.

Problems

1. On the basis of Theorem 4.1, construct an algorithm to detect if a general resource graph is completely reducible. Determine the order of complexity of your algorithm.

2. Prove that the following two allocation policies prevent deadlock:

   a. ordered requests   b. collective requests

3. Prove or give a counterexample: If a general resource graph is not totally reducible, then deadlock is imminent.

4. Provide a detailed formal proof of Theorem 4.2.

5. Prove that the existence of a cycle is a necessary and sufficient condition for deadlock to exist in a system in which all resources have an inventory of 1 unit.

6. Discuss how the prevention and avoidance of deadlocks would affect operating system structure and performance. Also discuss how it would affect user friendliness. (*Hint:* Deadlock prevention is usually designed in two stages: (1) reduce the number of resources and competition that must be considered; and (2) apply deadlock-prevention methods. Use avoidance methods on the remaining resources.)

7. Discuss criteria for selecting a deadlock policy among the following strategies:

   a. No provision for deadlock detection, avoidance, and prevention except for operator observance of system behavior

   b. Detection only (when a deadlock is detected, all deadlocked jobs are aborted by the operator)

   c. Detection and resolution

   d. Prevention only

   e. Avoidance and detection and resolution

   f. Prevention and detection and resolution

   g. Prevention and avoidance and detection and resolution

Can these strategies coexist in one system or must a system uniformly adopt one strategy for all resources? If they can coexist, what are the criteria for doing so?

8. Extend the deadlock-avoidance algorithm (Algorithm 4.5) in Section 4.5.3 to a general resource system.

9. Extend the collective-requests and ordered-requests allocation policies to a system of shared logical resources. Prove that your policies prevent deadlock.

References

Dijkstra, E. W., (1968). "Co-operating sequential processes." In *Programming Languages* (Ed. F. Genuys), Academic Press, New York. pp. 43–112.

Habermann, A. N., (July 1969). "Prevention of system deadlocks." *Communications of the ACM* 12, 7, pp. 373–377, 385.

Havender, J. W., (1968). "Avoiding deadlock in multitasking systems." *IBM System Journal* 7, 2, pp. 74–84.

Holt, R. C., "On deadlock in computer systems." (January 1971). Ph.D. thesis, Cornell University. [Reissued as Technical Report CSRG-6, University of Toronto, Computer System Research Group (1972).]

———. (September 1972). "Some deadlock properties of computer systems." *Computing Surveys* 4, 3, pp. 179–196.

Howard, J. H., Jr. (July 1973). "Mixed solutions for the deadlock problem." *Communications of the ACM* 16, 7, pp. 427–430.

Purdom, P. W., (July 1968). "A transitive closure algorithm." Technical Report 33, Department of Computer Science, University of Wisconsin, Madison.

Suggested Readings

Ahuja, V. (1979). "Algorithm to check network states for deadlock." *IBM Journal of Research and Development* 23, 1, pp. 82–86.

Bittman, P., and K. Unterauer. (October 1978). "Models and algorithms for deadlock detection." *Proceedings of the Second International Symposium on Operating Systems,* Rocquencourt, France.

Coffman, E. G., Jr.; M. J. Elphick; and A. Shoshani. (1971). "System deadlocks." *ACM Computing Surveys* 3, 2, pp. 67–78.

Dijkstra, E. W. (1972). "A class of allocation strategies inducing bounded delays only." *Proceedings of the AFIPS Spring Joint Computer Conference* 40, pp. 933–936.

Fontano, R. O., (June 1972). "A concurrent algorithm for avoiding deadlocks in multiprocess multiple resource systems." *ACM Operating System Review* 6, 1 and 2, pp. 72–79.

Frailey, D. J., (May 1973). "A practical approach to managing resources and avoiding deadlocks." *Communications of the ACM* 16, 5, pp. 323–329.

Gligor, V., and S. Shattuch. (September 1980). "On deadlock detection in distributed systems." *IEEE Transactions on Software Engineering* SE-6, pp. 435–440.

Gold, E. M., (1978). "Deadlock prediction: easy and difficult cases." *SIAM Journal of Computing* 7, 3, pp. 320–336.

Habermann, A. N. (1974). "A new approach to avoidance of system deadlocks." *Lecture Notes in Computer Science* 16 (Ed. E. Gelenbe and C. Kaiser), Springer-Verlag , N.Y., pp. 163–170.

———. 1978. "System deadlocks." In *Current Trends in Programming Methodology*, Vol. III (Ed. K. Mani Chandy and Raymond T. Yeh), Prentice-Hall, Englewood Cliffs, N.J., pp. 256–297.

Holt, R. C. (January 1971). "Comments on prevention of system deadlocks." *Communications of the ACM* 14, 1, pp. 36–38.

Hutchison, D. A.; J. S. Riordan; and S. A. Mahmoud. (October 1977). "A recursive algorithm for deadlock preemption in computer networks." *Information Processing* 77, Toronto, pp. 241–246.

King, P. F., and A. J. Collmeyer. (1973). "Database sharing—an efficient mechanism for supporting concurrent processes." *Proceedings of the AFIPS National Computer Conference* 42, pp. 271–275.

Lomet, D. B. (1980). "Subsystems of processes with deadlock avoidance." *IEEE Transactions on Software Engineering* SE-6, pp. 297–304.

Murphy, J. E. (1968). "Resource allocation with interlock detection in a multi-task system." *Proceedings of the AFIPS Computer Conference* 33, pp 1169–1176.

Parnas, D. L. and A. N. Habermann. (1972). "Comment on a deadlock prevention method." *Communications of the ACM* 15, 9, p. 840 (with reply by R. C. Holt, pp. 840–841).

Pirkola, G. C. (June 1975). "A file system for a general-purpose time-sharing environment." *Proceedings of IEEE* 63, 6, pp. 918–924.

Rypka, D. J., and A. P. Luciado. (1979). "Deadlock detection and avoidance for shared logical resources." *IEEE Transactions on Software Engineering* SE-5, pp. 465–471.

Sherman, S. W.; J. C. Browne; and J. H. Howard. (1974). "A comparison of deadlock prevention schemes using a trace driven model." *Proceedings of the ACM National Conference.*

———. (1975). "Trace driven studies of deadlock control and job scheduling." *Lecture Notes in Computer Science* 26 (Ed. Goos and Hartmanis), pp. 386–395.

Shoshani, A., and A. J. Bernstein. (November 1969). "Synchronization in a parallel-accessed data base." *Communications of the ACM* 12, 11, pp. 604–607.

Virtual
Memory

ᶜʰᵏ

5

5.1   Introduction

Historically, the conservation of main storage has been an important consideration in program design. With only a few thousand bytes available, saving a few hundred could mean the difference between successfully executing a program and failing because too little memory was available. Programmer-designed overlay structures reused portions of storage for different purposes at different points during execution. Hardware advances have made large amounts of inexpensive memory possible, but memory management considerations have not disappeared. And, inevitably, the magnitude of problems for which computer solutions are sought has grown. In place of specific overlay structures for each program, a general-purpose virtual memory system is often provided to users. *Virtual memory* is an illusion supported by system hardware and software that a user has a vast linear expanse of useful storage. In fact, however, a much smaller *real memory* is used to hold portions of a user's program during execution. The efficient preservation of this illusion is the subject of this chapter.

We first review some fundamental concepts. Then we cover a class of virtual memory management methods called *stack algorithms,* which provide solutions to two important problems. This class is also relevant to the remainder of the chapter. An approach to managing storage by linking process management with memory management, called *working sets* is then presented. An introduction to models of virtual memory follows. Next, we discuss *clock algorithms*; noteworthy results have recently been published concerning them. Finally, we introduce the idea of restructuring programs to improve their performance in virtual memory systems.

5.2   Background and Review

In addition to the mythical virtual memory and the actual real memory just mentioned, a third component, the *auxiliary memory,* plays an important role. The operating system and hardware divide virtual memory into *pages* of identical size and divide real memory into *page frames*. Pages reside in auxiliary memory and may, in addition, occupy a page frame in real memory. When an executing program refers to a particular item in virtual memory, the reference proceeds normally if the item is also *resident* in a page frame. Otherwise, a *page-fault interrupt* occurs to enable the operating system to adjust the contents of real memory to make a retry of the reference successful. A *page table* holds information about the whereabouts of each page; either it supplies the page frame address or it gives the auxiliary memory address. Conceptually, the page table is a vector indexed by the left bits of a virtual address. The right bits provide an offset into the identified page. Both system hardware and system software cooperate to make virtual memory work.

5.2.1   Hardware Support

The most important hardware component in a virtual memory system is an *address translation device* that accepts an effective address generated by instruction execution for a byte in virtual memory and produces a real memory address to that byte in some page frame. If the page table were an ordinary vector stored in real memory itself, the address translation device would be intolerably slow. Instead, special associative registers and caches hold parts of page tables so that the translation is overlapped with other CPU activity to make the translation time acceptable. If the required page is not resident in some frame, the translation device causes the page-fault interrupt to initiate software activity.

Two additional hardware components that are not strictly required are bit vectors with an entry for each page frame in real memory. The first, called the *use bits,* are set whenever pages in the associated frames are referenced. The second, the *dirty bits,* are set whenever pages in the associated frames are targets of memory-modification instructions. Operating system software can use these bits to improve its management activities. If the use bit of a particular frame has remained off for an interval, the content of that frame is a page to which the program has made no recent reference. If the dirty bit is off, then the copy of the page in auxiliary memory is still up-to-date, and the contents of the frame need not be written back. While these bit vectors are not necessary, some discussions in this chapter will assume their existence.

5.2.2   Page-Fault Rate and Principle of Locality

During the course of executing a program, the processor generates a sequence of virtual page references

$$\omega = r_1 \, r_2 \ldots r_t \ldots r_T$$

called the *reference string.* To remove the effects of other processes, we view this string as being generated in *virtual time* or *process time,* the time seen by the individual process. We define a *virtual time unit (vtu)* to be the average amount of time required to make a reference to main memory. Let F denote the average amount of time (*vtu*s) to service a page fault. If p is the probability of a page fault, then the *effective access time* of the process is defined by

$$EAT = 1 + p * F$$

and the *duty factor* of a process is defined to be

$$DF = \frac{|\omega|}{|\omega| * 1 + p * |\omega| * F} = \frac{1}{1 + p * F}$$

EAT measures the effective speed at which a process executes and DF measures the ability of a process to use the processor. For small values of p, DF and EAT are approximate reciprocals of each other. As an example, suppose that a *vtu* is 1 μs and disk access time is 10 ms. Then $F = 10^4$ and EAT $\simeq 1 + 10^4 * p$. If p is in the range $(10^{-4}, 10^{-3})$, then EAT is in the range $(2, 11)$ and DF is in the range $(\frac{1}{11}, \frac{1}{2})$.

Reference strings typically range from tens of thousands to millions of references in length and may involve many distinct pages. Based on current technology, a very low page-fault rate p is required for acceptable performance. Even in a multiprogrammed environment, the degree of multiprogramming is typically not large enough to compensate for large values of p. Suppose we require a process to execute in a main memory (or a memory partition) smaller than the program size in virtual memory. Even then small values of p occur in practice because of a property exhibited by most programs called *locality of reference*. This property says that, at any instant, there is a favored subset of all pages that have a high probability of being referenced in the near future. The following example illustrates the *principle of locality*.

Suppose the program statement

for i **in** 1..n **do** A[i] : = B[i] + C[i] **endfor**

is executed in a memory with page size of 1000 words. Let n = 1000. Using a register machine (with registers denoted by Ri), the machine language version of this program, loaded in main memory starting at address 4000, might appear as:

4000	(R1) ← ONE	Establish index register for i
4001	(R2) ← n	Establish n in R2
4002	compare R1,R2	Test i > n
4003	branch greater 4009	
4004	(R3) ← B(R1)	Access B[i] using index register R1
4005	(R3) ← (R3) + C(R1)	Add C[i] using index register R1
4006	A(R1) ← (R3)	Store sum in A[i] using index register R1
4007	(R1) ← (R1) + ONE	Increment i
4008	branch 4002	
	...	
6000-6999	storage for A	
7000-7999	storage for B	
8000-8999	storage for C	
9000	storage for ONE	
9001	storage for n	

The reference string generated by this loop is

$$494944(47484649444)^{1000}$$

consisting of over 11,000 references (but involving only five distinct pages).

5.2.3   Software Components

Both operating system software and user processes behave in ways that make virtual memory efficient. The former implements explicit policies, and the latter have implicit characteristics that follow expected patterns.

Operating System Policies

Several alternatives exist for the operating system designer for handling page-fault interrupts and other aspects of virtual memory management. Each choice enforces a component of the set of policies for memory management. We briefly review them here.

FETCH POLICY   The determination about *when* a page migrates from auxiliary memory to a page frame constitutes the fetch policy. There are two alternatives. The simpler is called *demand fetching* because a page comes into real memory only when a page-fault interrupt results from its absence. The characteristics of auxiliary memory (such as disks with seek and rotational delays preceding information transfer) encourage forms of *prepaging* in which pages other than the one demanded by a page fault are brought into page frames. The utility of this scheme has not been established. However, when a process is initiated (or reactivated) it may be advantageous to immediately preload some pages to prevent frequent page faults.

PLACEMENT POLICY   Determining *where* in real memory a page is to reside is irrelevant in a *paged-memory system* because the address translation hardware will use any element of the page table with equal efficiency. *Placement policies* are important, however, in *pure-segmentation systems,* where the parts of a program are variable in size and the minimization of external fragmentation in main memory is an issue. Recent systems that support segmentation also provide paging at a lower level so that segments need not reside in contiguous memory locations, once again rendering a placement policy unimportant. Because modern segmented memory is supported by paging, we do not discuss pure segmentation.

REPLACEMENT POLICY   Replacement policy has been much studied over the last two decades. The decision about which page to *replace* when all frames have resident pages can have a great effect on the frequency of subsequent page faults. General-purpose approaches rely on the locality of reference to make decisions. Since the correlation between recent referencing history and near-future referencing patterns is high, realizable replacement policies try to predict future references from past behavior. The set of pages to which accesses are being made changes relatively slowly; if the operating system can accurately determine what this subset is and keep it in real memory, page faulting can be greatly reduced. Both program and data structures contribute to this tendency. The desirable subset that ought to be in real memory is sometimes called a *resident set* or a *locality*.

Several common replacement policies will be useful in this chapter. All are *demand replacement* policies: No prepaging is done, and replacement occurs only when real memory is full. For any pair of fetch and replacement policies, the processing of virtual memory references results in a sequence of memory states. Specifically, corresponding to a reference string ω is a sequence of real memory states

$$M_0, M_1, \ldots, M_t \ldots, M_T$$

where M_0 is the initial state, usually empty. Real memory has m page frames. A reference to r_t causes a transition from M_{t-1} to M_t:

$$M_t \leftarrow M_{t-1} + X_t - Y_t$$

where X_t is the set of pages fetched because of the reference to r_t, and Y_t is the set of pages removed from real memory. A demand algorithm defines the transition of memory states by

$$M_t \leftarrow \begin{cases} M_{t-1} \text{ if } r_t \text{ in } M_{t-1} \\ M_{t-1} + r_t \text{ if } r_t \text{ not in } M_{t-1} \text{ and } |M_{t-1}| < m \\ M_{t-1} + r_t - y \text{ for some } y \text{ in } M_{t-1} \text{ if } r_t \text{ not in } M_{t-1} \text{ and } |M_{t-1}| = m \end{cases}$$

Replacement policies vary in how the page y is selected for removal from real memory:

- *Least recently used:* LRU replaces the page in real memory whose last reference was the longest in the past. A faithful implementation of LRU requires hardware support to maintain a stack of pages referenced, an expensive prospect. However, a policy based on examining use bits and dirty bits approximates LRU well. By dividing all frames into four classes according to the value of the pair (use bit, dirty bit), the page to replace is chosen from the first nonempty class in [(0,0), (0,1), (1,0), (1,1)]. All use bits must be periodically reset [Shaw, 1974].

- *Optimal replacement:* OPT selects for replacement the page that will be referenced next the longest time in the future. If a page is not referenced again, its future reference time is ∞. Several pages may have value ∞; any can be selected and optimality is preserved. Although this is not a realizable policy, it is valuable in simulations to determine the best possible paging behavior for a reference string.

- *First-in, first-out:* A FIFO policy is extremely easy to implement with a pointer rotating circularly among the page frames. Unfortunately, the performance of FIFO is inferior to that of LRU.

- *Last-in, first-out:* LIFO ensures that a page will be removed as soon as another page is referenced. This may have utility in specific cases of sequential references.

- *Least frequently used:* LFU replaces the page whose total usage count is the smallest. Implementing LFU accurately requires expensive hardware, and other methods generally outperform it.

- *Most recently used:* MRU replaces the most recently accessed page.

A distinction can be made between replacement policies that consider *all* pages in real memory for replacement and those that choose only among the pages of the process that generated the fault. The former are *global* policies and the latter are *local. Page stealing* is possible with a global policy; a page of one process may be replaced in a frame with the page for another process. The dichotomy between local and global policies is well summarized by Carr [1984]:

> Local algorithms have gained considerable popularity among the research community because they are easier to analyze and use in multiprogram system models. Global algorithms are more popular with operating system designers because of their simplicity of implementation and minimal overhead.

MAIN STORAGE ALLOCATION POLICY   Allocation policies can be divided into two categories based on how main memory is allocated. A *fixed-allocation policy* gives a process a fixed number of pages in which to execute, while a *variable-allocation policy* allows the page frames held by a process to vary over the lifetime of the process. The former implies a local page replacement policy while the latter allows either a local or global policy. If a process has a fixed number of page frames, difficulties arise if the allocation is too small. Difficulties may also arise if the program makes a *phase transition* from one locality to another. Two properties characterize a reasonable page-replacement algorithm:

1. If a program is executing in a locality whose size exceeds the size of the fixed partition, then the algorithm should do a good job of making the best of a bad situation; that is, on the average it should do a respectable job in attempting to minimize the number of page faults.
2. The algorithm should quickly adapt to a phase transition.

If the amount of main memory exceeds the size of the largest locality, then property 1 is not a factor and one may argue the merits of various page-replacement algorithms. For example, consider the MRU and LFU policies previously mentioned. Both are poor choices for satisfying property 2. The following reference string (for a fictitious program) shows the execution of two program loops:

$$\omega = (123)^r (456)^s$$

If the program executes in a partition of three page frames, then both MRU and LFU have difficulties. MRU incurs $3(1 + s)$ faults and LFU incurs $3(1 + \min(r,s))$ faults. LIFO also fails to adapt to a phase transition. On the other hand, the LRU and FIFO policies each incur the minimum number of page faults (six), readily adapting to the phase transition. Most page replacement algorithms used in practice are variants or enhancements of the LRU or FIFO algorithms.

CLEANING POLICY   A cleaning policy is the opposite of a fetch policy. It determines *when* a page that has been modified will be written to auxiliary memory. In *demand cleaning* a dirty page will be written only when selected for removal by the replacement policy. A *precleaning* policy writes dirty pages before their page frames are needed, converting them to clean, resident pages. If a form of precleaning is implemented, the writing of a dirty page need not make it unavailable for use during the transfer. The operating system resets the dirty bit as output is initiated; if a process modifies it during the transfer, the dirty bit is set and the page must be cleaned again subsequently. A careful balance is necessary between cleaning dirty pages and fetching needed pages. A static priority given to one or the other can result in management problems [Carr, 1984].

LOAD-CONTROL POLICY Without a mechanism to control the number of active processes, it is very easy to *overcommit* a virtual memory system. Each process is actively referencing some subset of its virtual pages. If the sum of the sizes of these subsets exceeds the number of page frames, then frequent faulting will occur. The virtual memory management overhead becomes so great that a precipitous decrease in system performance is visible as soon as the memory overcommitment occurs. A system in this state is said to be *thrashing*. Figure 5.1 shows a typical curve. As the multiprogramming level increases, one would expect that throughput would increase up to the level of system capacity and then decline slowly due to increasing overhead. Instead, throughput falls dramatically because active processes require more real memory than is available. Question 6 illustrates concretely the concept of thrashing.

Global-replacement policies are more susceptible to thrashing because they lack mechanisms to gauge the memory required by individual processes and hence the total demand. A local policy can measure the page-faulting rate of individual processes and determine if more page frames (or fewer) are required. The *working set* virtual memory management method, discussed in Section 5.4, is especially attractive in this regard. Section 5.6 includes a discussion of a global policy that shows promise in handling the load control problem well.

Process Behavior

No action by processes in execution is required to implement virtual memory. Attempts have been made to describe how code should be written or data structures arranged

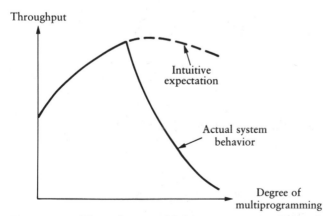

Figure 5.1 Throughput vs. Multiprogramming Level with Thrashing.

to improve virtual memory performance [Brawn, 1968; McKellar, 1969]. However, one of the advantages of automatic memory management is the freedom from explicit action by processes (or programmers). Success relies on programs exhibiting locality in memory references. An automatic procedure for improving locality is discussed in Section 5.7.

5.3   Stack Algorithms

In this section we investigate a class of replacement algorithms called *stack algorithms* [Mattson, et al., 1970; Coffman and Denning, 1973] that have the *inclusion property*. This property allows the computation of the cost of processing a particular reference string for all memory sizes of interest in only one pass over the string, and to predict the cost of executing a particular string in an expanded memory. First, we define what we mean by cost.

5.3.1   Cost Function

If the replacement policy is fixed, the *cost* of processing virtual memory references depends both on the amount of real memory (m page frames) and the particular reference string ω. This in turn determines the contents of X_t and Y_t, the successive fetch and replacement sets. Since many pages in Y_t may be clean, and page writes can be overlapped with other processing, we ignore the latter.

Let $f(k)$ be the cost of a page-fetch operation that obtains k pages from auxiliary memory. The function is normalized by

$$Z = \text{Time}_{delay} + \text{Time}_{transfer}$$

the time required to fetch a single page, so $f(1) = 1$. In keeping with practical algorithms, we assume that

$$f(0) = 0, f(k) \geq f(1) \text{ for } k \geq 1, f(k + 1) \geq f(k) \text{ for all } k$$

Then the cost $C(m,\omega)$ is given by

$$C(m, \omega) = \sum_{t = 1}^{T} f(|X_t|)$$

If a demand replacement is in effect, $0 \leq |X_t| \leq 1$, and

$$C(m, \omega) = \sum_{t = 1}^{T} |X_t|$$

Notice that for auxiliary memory with moving parts,

$$f(k) = \frac{\text{Time}_{delay} + k \times \text{Time}_{transfer}}{Z}$$

and so f(k) < k × f(1) = k. If electronic auxiliary memory is used,

$$f(k) = k \times \frac{\text{Time}'_{delay} + \text{Time}'_{transfer}}{Z}$$

with f(k) = k × f(1) = k. This leads to the following result.

THEOREM 5.1

[From Mattson, et al., 1970] *Suppose f(k) ⩾ k. Then for any page-replacement algorithm, there exists a demand algorithm with a cost function that does at least as well for* all *memory sizes and reference strings.*

Because effective prepaging algorithms are generally difficult to find and analyze, most virtual memory implementations using disks and drums use demand-paging algorithms. Further, in anticipation that electronic auxiliary memory will be common in the future, nearly all research has focused on demand algorithms.

5.3.2   Definition of a Stack Algorithm

To expand the notation for memory states, $M(m,\omega)$ is the state of real memory after processing reference string ω in m frames, with initial memory state $\emptyset$. A replacement algorithm is a *stack* algorithm if it satisfies the *inclusion property:*

$$M(m,\omega) \subseteq M(m + 1,\omega) \text{ for all m and } \omega$$

Equivalently, we can express the inclusion property as follows. Given ω, there is a permutation of the virtual pages labeled 1, 2, . . . , n called the *stack*

$$S(\omega) = [s_1(\omega), \ldots, s_n(\omega)]$$

so that for all m,

$$M(m,\omega) = \{s_1(\omega), \ldots, s_m(\omega)\}$$

That is, the contents of real memory consisting of m frames is always identified by the first m elements of $S(\omega)$.

For a stack algorithm processing $\omega = r_1, \ldots, r_t, \ldots$, a sequence of stacks $S_1, \ldots$, $S_t, \ldots$ can be constructed so that the memory state sequence for each value of m is just the first m pages in the stacks. The LRU replacement policy results in a stack algorithm. It is easy to see that, for LRU,

$$M(m,\omega) = \{m \text{ most recently referenced pages}\} \subseteq M(m + 1, \omega)$$

On the other hand, FIFO is *not* a stack algorithm, as can be seen from the processing of a reference string in two memory sizes. Figure 5.2(a) shows processing in three page frames; the same string is processed in four frames in Figure 5.2(b). The final memory contents in the two cases show that $M(3,\omega) = \{5,1,2\} \not\subseteq \{5,2,3,4\} = M(4,\omega)$.

Nonstack algorithms such as FIFO also exhibit an unusual property called *Belady's anomaly* [Belady, et al., 1969]. It is not always true that $C(m,\omega)$ is a nonin-

ω	1	2	3	4	1	2	5
M	1	1	1	4	4	4	5
	-	2	2	2	1	1	1
	-	-	3	3	3	2	2

(a) FIFO Processing in Three Frames.

ω	1	2	3	4	1	2	5
M	1	1	1	1	1	1	5
	-	2	2	2	2	2	2
	-	-	3	3	3	3	3
	-	-	-	4	4	4	4

(b) FIFO Processing in Four Frames.

Figure 5.2 FIFO Processing.

creasing function of m; consider Figures 5.3(a) and 5.3(b) in which a reference string is processed in three and then four page frames. The references that result in page fetches are marked with $*$. In the former, $C(3,\omega) = 9$, but in the latter, $C(4,\omega) = 10$.

5.3.3 Stack-Updating Procedure

We need a method of describing how to obtain the stack S_{t+1} from S_t. First we make some observations about how the movements of pages in a stack are restricted. Define the *stack distance* of a page p as its position in $S(\omega)$. Let $d_p(\omega) = k$ if $s_k(\omega) = p$. If p has not yet been referenced, it does not appear in $S(\omega)$ and $d_p(\omega) = \infty$. Note that a fault occurs in an m-frame memory on the last element p of ωp if $d_p(\omega) > m$.

ω	1*	2*	3*	4*	1*	2*	5*	1	2	3*	4*	5
M	1	1	1	4	4	4	5	5	5	5	5	5
	-	2	2	2	1	1	1	1	1	3	3	3
	-	-	3	3	3	2	2	2	2	2	4	4

Figure 5.3(a) Belady's Anomaly: Three Frames.

ω	1*	2*	3*	4*	1	2	5*	1*	2*	3*	4*	5*
M	1	1	1	1	1	1	5	5	5	5	4	4
	-	2	2	2	2	2	2	1	1	1	1	5
	-	-	3	3	3	3	3	3	2	2	2	2
	-	-	-	4	4	4	4	4	4	3	3	3

Figure 5.3(b) Belady's Anomaly: Four Frames.

Observation 1: Since the most recently referenced page p must be in memory of any size (and, in particular, for m = 1), we must have $d_p(\omega p) = 1$.

Observation 2: Stack algorithms are demand algorithms, so a page that is not referenced may not be brought into memory of any size, so $d_q(\omega) \leq d_q(\omega p)$ if $p \neq q$.

Observation 3: If some page q resides in the stack at position k below the referenced page p, observation 2 tells us that it cannot move up the stack. If it could move down the stack, a reference to p in a k-frame memory would result in the removal of q even though no fault had occurred. Hence, such a page does not move in the stack at all: $s_k(\omega p) = s_k(\omega)$ if $d_p(\omega) < k$.

As a result of these observations, we have a general picture in Figure 5.4 of how stack elements move. The referenced page p moves to the top of the stack, the elements from position 1 through $d_p(\omega) - 1$ arrange themselves into positions 2 through $d_p(\omega)$, and the pages below $d_p(\omega)$ are unchanged.

To more clearly define how the dynamic section of stack is actually sorted out, we define *priority algorithms*. A paging algorithm is a priority algorithm if, associated with each reference r_t in ω, there is a priority list L_t with two properties:

1. The priority list L_t is an ordering (by decreasing priority) of the distinct pages referenced so far. This list is independent of the memory size in which a process executes.

2. For all real memory sizes m, the page q removed from real memory as a result of referring to r_{t+1} is the lowest priority page (according to L_t) that is also resident. Refer to this page as $q = \min[M]$. Note that $\max[M]$ also has a reasonable meaning. We will extend the notation to select the lower or higher priority of two individual pages as well.

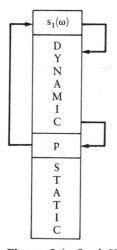

Figure 5.4 Stack Updating Procedure: General Motion.

Priority algorithms are stack algorithms. If memory of size m + 1 contains pages M ∪ {y} (for any page y), then the page to be removed upon a fault is min[M ∪ {y}] = min[min[M], y], the lower priority page between that which would be removed from M and the page y. This is just an alternative definition of a stack algorithm.

Stack algorithms are also priority algorithms. The stack algorithms mentioned in this chapter all have a method of ordering pages independently of real memory size:

LRU   Orders by increasing time to last reference

OPT   Orders by increasing time to next reference

LFU   Orders by decreasing frequence of reference
        (any deterministic tie-breaker will do)

LIFO   Orders by increasing time of real memory entry

One may be tempted to include FIFO in this list, since it also orders pages by time of entry to real memory. However, consider processing ω = 123412 in three and four page frames.After processing ω, the two alleged priority lists would be (3, 4, 1, 2) and (1, 2, 3, 4). Page 2 precedes page 4 in the former, but follows it in the latter. No single priority list suffices independently of real memory size (and FIFO orders only pages in real memory, not all pages referenced), so FIFO is not a priority algorithm and there is no contradiction.

Only in LRU do the stack S and the priority list L coincide. In all other stack algorithms, both must be explicitly maintained in order to perform stack updating. Specifically, we define the stack-updating procedure in terms of the priority of pages. If $S(\omega)$ is a stack in which $d_p(\omega) = k$, we define each stack element $s_i(\omega p)$ by

$$s_i(\omega p) = \begin{cases} p & \text{if } i = 1 \\ \max\,[s_i(\omega), \min\,[M(i - 1, \omega)]] & \text{if } 1 < i < k \\ \min\,[M(k - 1, \omega)] & \text{if } i = k \\ s_i(\omega) & \text{if } i > k \end{cases}$$

To summarize, the referenced page (at position k) moves to the top element of the new stack, and the page displaced from the top position and the page originally in the second position are compared. The "max" page becomes the page in the second position of the new stack, and the "min" page is compared with the page in the original third position. This comparison continues until the "min" page not placed into the new stack at position k − 1 falls into the empty position at position k. Pages below position k do not move. Figure 5.5 gives a diagram of stack movement, with a circle, ◯, used to represent the comparison of two page priorities.

An example of processing a reference string using optimal replacement is shown in Figure 5.6. At each reference r_t, the stack S_t is formed using S_{t-1} and L_{t-1}; then the new priority list L_t is obtained.

5.3.4 Calculating Cost Function

One attractive property of stack algorithms is that the cost of fetching pages for any reference string can be computed for all memory sizes in one pass over the string

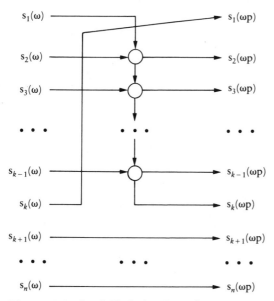

Figure 5.5 Stack Updating Procedure: Priority Operator.

by using the procedure described here. Define a vector with elements $c_k =$ the number of times that a page p moved from position $d_p = k$ to position 1 in the stack because it was referenced. Then the cost of processing the string is

$$C(m,\omega) = \sum_{k=m+1}^{n} c_k + c_\infty$$

where c_∞ is the number of times a new page was referenced and n is the number of distinct pages in ω.

A tableau like the one exemplified in Figure 5.7 can be used to manually process small examples, and gives the method for programming a simulator that processes large reference strings.

ω	1	2	3	4	1	2	3	2	3	1
S_t	1	2	3	4	1	2	3	2	3	1
	-	1	1	1	4	1	2	3	2	2
	-	-	2	2	2	4	1	1	1	3
	-	-	-	3	3	3	4	4	4	4
L_t	1	1	1	1	2	3	2	3	1	1
	-	2	2	2	3	2	3	1	2	2
	-	-	3	3	1	1	1	2	3	3
	-	-	-	4	4	4	4	4	4	4

Figure 5.6 Stack and Priority List Updating: OPT Replacement.

ω	1	2	3	4	1	2	3	2	3	1	
S_t	1	2	3	4	1	2	3	2	3	1	
	-	1	1	1	4	1	2	3	2	2	
	-	-	2	2	2	4	1	1	1	3	
	-	-	-	3	3	3	4	4	4	4	
L_t	1	1	1	1	2	3	2	3	1	1	
	-	2	2	2	3	2	3	1	2	2	
	-	-	3	3	1	1	1	2	3	3	
	-	-	-	4	4	4	4	4	4	4	
d_p	∞	∞	∞	∞	2	3	4	2	2	3	$C(m,\omega)$
c_1	0	0	0	0	0	0	0	0	0	0	10
c_2	0	0	0	0	1	1	1	2	3	3	7
c_3	0	0	0	0	0	1	1	1	1	2	5
c_4	0	0	0	0	0	0	1	1	1	1	4
c_∞	1	2	3	4	4	4	4	4	4	4	-

Figure 5.7   Calculating Cost Function.

5.3.5   The Extension Problem

When a demand-paging algorithm processes a reference string ω in real memory with m frames, and only information available at the time of faults may be recorded, can we predict performance in a real memory with m + k frames? The answer to this *extension problem* is yes only if the paging algorithm is a stack algorithm. Such an algorithm allows one to predict the performance of a memory management system before actually installing additional storage by recording information only at fault times, not at each reference.

At each fault, record a pair of virtual page numbers (p_i, q_i), where p_i is the page referenced that caused the fault and will be brought into real memory, and q_i is the page that will be removed. Also record the priority lists at each fault that were used to determine which page was to be replaced. Then, with this information we can maintain the stack segment $[s_{m+1}, \ldots, s_{m+k}]$.

Given $[(p_i, q_i)]$, construct a new sequence by considering two cases as follows:

1. The stack distance for p_i exceeds m + k. Hence a fault will also occur in m + k frames. Using the priority list recorded at fault i, update the stack segment to find the page q_i' that will be removed from the larger memory. Emit (p_i, q_i') into the new sequence. See Figure 5.8(a).

2. The stack distance for p_i lies in the range [m + 1, m + k]. Then no fault will occur in the larger memory. Simply update the stack segment and emit no entry into the new sequence. See Figure 5.8(b).

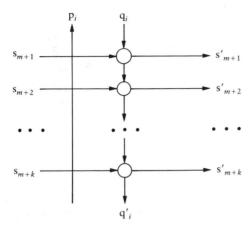

Figure 5.8(a) Extension Problem: Fault Occurs in Larger
Memory.

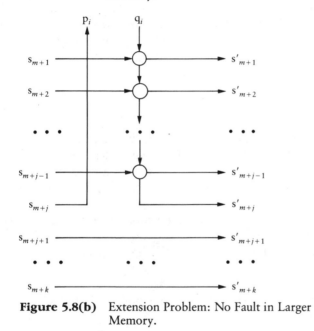

Figure 5.8(b) Extension Problem: No Fault in Larger
Memory.

As an example, if we recorded the sequence from the example in Figure 5.7
along with priority lists (using three page frames), we would have obtained:

(p_i, q_i)	$(1, -)$	$(2, -)$	$(3, -)$	$(4, 3)$	$(3, 4)$
L_{i-1}	−	1	1	1	3
	−	−	2	2	2
	−	−	−	3	1
	−	−	−	−	4

To predict paging behavior in four frames, we need to maintain only the stack element in position 4, $s_4(\omega)$. Each initial fault is unchanged in the new sequence, but at the pair $(3, 4)$ we recognize that $s_4(\omega) = 4$ and no fault results from this string in four frames. We correctly predict that four faults will occur in the larger memory.

Clearly, the stack segment is necessary for the operation of this procedure. If the paging algorithm does not have the stack property, the problem cannot be solved with only this amount of information.

5.4   Working Sets

In a multiprogramming system we have conflicting policies for process and memory management. To maximize throughput we should have as many active processes as possible to keep processor and device utilization high. To minimize page-fault overhead, each process should have as much real memory as possible. If we limit the number of active processes too much, throughput can suffer; if we do not control them enough, thrashing can result. Working sets can help determine the optimum point between policies for process and memory management.

5.4.1   Definition of Working Set

The *working set* with parameter Δ for a process at time t, $W(t, \Delta)$, is the set of pages that have been referenced in the last Δ time units [Denning, 1968; Denning, 1970]. Δ is the *window size*, and it is a tuning parameter. Since Δ is a time measure, and we are considering multiprogramming systems, Δ must measure process time rather than real time. If Δ is large enough so that the working set contains pages being frequently accessed, and small enough to contain no more, the working set is a reliable way to obtain a description of the needs of a process. Observe that $| W(t, \Delta) |$ can vary over time. If a process executes for Δ time units and uses only a single page, then $| W(t, \Delta) | = 1$. Working sets can also grow as large as the number of pages n of a process if many different pages are rapidly addressed.

The importance of working sets is that they link memory and process management via the *Working Set Principle:*

> A process may execute only if its working set is resident in main memory. A page may not be removed from main memory if it is in the working set of an executing process.

This means that, if the working set of a process contains those pages currently needed, frequent page faulting is eliminated. The working set of a process may not be affected by the execution of other processes. By limiting the number of active processes to a group whose working sets will fit in real memory, memory overcommitment is avoided and thrashing is eliminated. The working set strategy is a local policy that allows the number of page frames used by executing processes to vary.

If a process has run long enough to have established a working set, and is then blocked or otherwise suspended from execution, its working set can be expected to disappear from real memory. When reactivated, the Working Set Principle dictates that all of its former working set should be prepaged back before execution resumes. If care is taken, the transfer of a working set into real memory can be much less costly than moving it using the normal faulting mechanism page by page.

5.4.2 Properties of Working Sets

Working sets exhibit some interesting properties that make them attractive for memory management. First, as mentioned, the size of a working set can vary. Specifically, $1 \leq |W(t, \Delta)| \leq \min(\Delta, n)$. This means we can avoid allocating a fixed partition of real memory for a process.

In addition, working sets are inclusive: $W(t, \Delta) \subseteq W(t, \Delta + 1)$. This is similar to the inclusive nature of stack algorithms; working set management will not exhibit Belady's anomaly.

Finally, a graph of working set size versus time will show that, for many programs, periods of relatively constant sizes alternate with periods of much larger sizes. This reflects periods of fairly constant locality followed by rapid changes to a new locality. Since Δ is constant for the process, the working set size temporarily increases as new pages rapidly join the working set. Later, as pages no longer in use leave the working set (also at a rapid pace), the working set size falls to another stable level. Figure 5.9 shows a typical graph of working set size. This phenomenon can also be seen in a plot of page number referenced versus time; see Figure 5.10 [Hatfield and Gerald, 1971] for an example. The rectangular areas show that for long periods of time (horizontal dimension) a well-defined subset (vertical dimension) of pages is being referenced. See also that the shifts to new localities occur

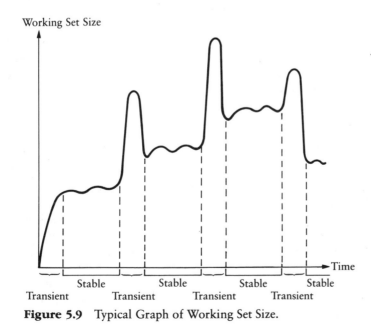

Figure 5.9 Typical Graph of Working Set Size.

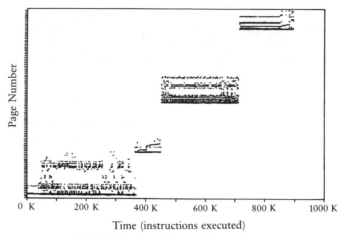

Figure 5.10   Working Sets: Page Referenced vs. Time.
[Copyright © 1971 by International Business
Machines. Reprinted by permission.]

quickly. In addition, the relationship between the mean working set size and the
page-fault rate is established in Problem 10.

A study of page faults under the working set discipline disclosed some interesting phenomena [Kahn, 1976]. Stable phases covered nearly all the process time
(98%). Nearly half of the faults occurred during the other 2% of process time while
phase transitions were in progress. Fault rates during transitions were 100 to 1000
times higher than during stable phases. Finally, the observed phases were relatively
insensitive to the choice of working set window size Δ.

Several variations on simple working sets have been proposed. Denning proposed using different Δ values for code pages and data pages since they are likely to
exhibit totally different localities. The page-fault-frequency algorithm [Chu and
Opderbeck, 1972] achieves a reverse feedback by altering Δ to match a target fault
rate. Dealing with abrupt changes in locality is the goal of the damped working set
algorithm [Smith, 1976].

5.4.3   Implementation

The realization of a working set policy for process and memory management requires
either additional hardware or some compromises in the original definition. We
discuss representatives in each category.

In Morris [1972] we find a design for an implementation of the working set
concept in the Maniac II computer system that is similar to a proposal in Denning
[1968]. In addition to page table base and limit registers and an associative memory
to implement paging efficiently, the Maniac II design has a *working set register,* a
page-frame register associated with each frame, and a *T-register.* The working set
register is a bit map that identifies which page frames hold pages of the running
process. Each page-frame register contains a counter that is periodically incremented

if the associated working set register bit is set; the counter associated with a non-running process's page is not incremented. When a counter in a page-frame register overflows, an *alarm bit* in the page-frame register is set to indicate that the page in this frame is no longer in the working set of the process. Each time a page in a frame is referenced, the counter in that page-frame register is reset to zero (the alarm bit is also reset). The T-register controls the frequency of updating counters. At a page fault, the frames with alarm bits set indicate pages eligible for removal from real memory. Process switching requires replacing the contents of the working set register but not alteration of any page-frame registers.

An approximation to the working set policy as described here was implemented in an extant time-sharing system [Rodriguez-Rosell and Dupuy, 1973]. The IBM 360/67 computer system provided use bits with each page frame. The quantum of processor time is divided into subintervals of T time units corresponding to a working set window size. At the beginning of an entire quantum all use bits are reset. After each subinterval pages in frames not referenced are marked as candidates for replacement by setting the *absent bit* in the appropriate page-table entries, and then all use bits are again reset. If the process subsequently references such a page before its actual removal, a page fault results but the only effect is the return of the page to the working set of the process. Accurate accounting for the sizes of working sets is complicated by the special handling of information in shared pages outside of this mechanism. However, the installation of this scheme successfully eliminated the thrashing phenomenon.

5.5 Models of Virtual Memory

Models that represent the behavior of programs in virtual memory have been of interest to researchers since the development of virtual memory itself. They have value in testing proposed modifications to systems, for capturing essential characteristics of workloads, and for understanding the effects of virtual memory management policies. A good model is easier to work with than long traces of actual executions. In Spirn [1977] we see a dichotomy between classes of models. One class, called *extrinsic models,* uses information about observed behavior to construct a description that is representative of more particular instances. The other class, *intrinsic models,* uses what is known about the internal nature of program behavior to build a mathematical structure that displays results similar to observed behavior. If one approach is used, the other can be used to validate the first model. We will discuss one virtual memory model of each class.

5.5.1 An Extrinsic Model—Lifetime Curves

This simple description of a program's behavior is generated by processing a reference string for a range of memory sizes m to obtain *mean lifetimes* L(m). A lifetime is a period of execution that is uninterrupted by a page fault, measured in process time or in number of main memory references. If the residence set has a variable size, as in the working set method, other parameters (such as the working set window size Δ) are manipulated to vary mean residence set size (see Problem 9). The curve L(m) versus m is the *lifetime curve* and the *fault rate* is 1/L(m).

Ideally, a lifetime curve is S-shaped, as shown in Figure 5.11. For small memory sizes, faulting is frequent and lifetimes are short. As available real memory increases, lifetimes increase as expected. However, above a certain threshold the increase in mean lifetime grows less rapidly. The "primary knee" of the concave-down portion of the curve is the point where L(m)/m is maximal. The knee phenomenon has been attributed to two sources [Spirn, 1977]:

1. A reasonable explanation is the concept of locality. After a sufficient number of frames is allocated, a further increase in real memory has a small effect on fault rates and hence on lifetimes. It has been proposed [Denning and Kahn, 1975] that the primary knee corresponds to the average size of localities that span stable phases in residence set composition, and that this real memory allocation is optimal.

2. When a page is first referenced, it always causes a fault. For a reference string of length k that touches n distinct pages, the lifetime curve L(n) is approximated by k/n. When real memory allocation approaches n page frames, the mean lifetime is strongly influenced by the length of the reference string. This may lead one to conclude that, beyond the primary knee, a lifetime curve is an unreliable model of program behavior. Although we may not be very interested in this area of the curve, studies have shown that initial page loads can be a major contributor to the existence of the primary knee [Carr, 1984].

Nevertheless, a lifetime curve is easy to generate from an actual program trace and therefore it has the advantage of being derived from real data.

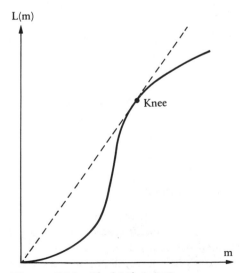

Figure 5.11   Ideal Lifetime Curve.

5.2.2 An Intrinsic Model—LRU Stack

The LRU *stack model* of program behavior arose because the LRU replacement policy was seen to give good performance. It is a relatively simple intrinsic model, and the stack-updating procedure is easy to understand (see Section 5.3.3). Its origins are found in Shemer and Shippey [1966], and in Shemer and Gupta [1969].

In this model we assume that successive stack positions $p_{t-1}(r_t)$ at which the references r_t occur are independent random variables drawn from the probability distribution

$$\text{Prob}[p_{t-1}(r_t) = i] = a_i$$

with cumulative distribution

$$A_i = \text{Prob}[p_{t-1}(r_t) \leq i] = \sum_{j=1}^{i} a_j$$

Given an initial stack s_0 (often assumed to be $[1, 2, \ldots, n]$), we obtain a sequence of stack distances from the distribution above and, from that, generate a reference string. Strings generated this way are called LRU *reference strings*.

LRU reference strings can be constructed that exhibit statistical behavior similar to that of actual programs. If $a_k = 1$, $a_i = 0$ for $i \neq k$, a looping reference string results:

$$\omega = k, k - 1, k - 2, \ldots, 2, 1, k, k - 1, \ldots$$

If $a_1 \geq a_2 \geq \cdots a_n$, then stack positions near the top are favored. In this case, we are not surprised that the LRU replacement policy is optimal [Coffman and Denning, 1973]. One could empirically obtain estimates of these probabilities by processing reference strings of interest and observing stack positions.

The LRU stack model, along with some other models, was validated in Spirn [1977] by comparing its behavior with that observed when actual reference strings were processed with a working set method. The needed probabilities for stack positions were obtained empirically by observing those that actually occurred. The reference strings were all short enough so that they do not include phase transitions. Within a single locality, the LRU stack model was seen to be the most acceptable model of the program's virtual memory behavior.

5.6 Clock Algorithms

Versiors of replacement algorithms have long existed that resemble the simple versions of the methods in this section. Recent work has shown that they can be enhanced to provide good alternatives to purely local policies [Carr and Hennessey, 1981; Carr, 1984]. This section is based on that research. Clock algorithms implement forms of global-replacement policies. Envision the page frames of real memory arranged circularly, as on a clock face. A pointer travels clockwise among the frames. Whenever a page must be selected for replacement, the pointer is advanced to the next frame containing a page that satisfies some particular criterion. If no criterion at all is used, the next page in turn is selected for replacement, implementing the global FIFO method. By using the following scheme, global LRU is approximated. When a page frame is examined, its use bit is checked and then cleared. If the page has been referenced, the pointer is advanced to the next frame. If not, the page is replaceable, and the pointer is left at the following frame. If frames remain unused with equal probability for a given length of time over all frames, the clock algorithm will find the highest density immediately ahead of the pointer, so the pointer should not have far to travel.

When a page has been deemed replaceable by the criterion in effect, it is processed differently if its dirty bit is set. In that case the page is queued for cleaning and the clock scan proceeds to the next page. Usually the page has been cleaned by the time it is considered again, and is then replaced. This generates a relatively even stream of requests to clean pages and avoids long waits for page writes followed by reads. See Figure 5.12 [Carr and Hennessey, 1981]; we refer to this as the Clock algorithm.

5.6.1   A Working Set Approximation—WSClock

The clock algorithm framework can be supplied with different criteria in order to approximate the replacement methods described in this chapter; we describe one here, the *WSClock algorithm*. This algorithm approximates a working set method for pages of processes in combination with global replacement by updating information about pages as the pointer passes over them. As a frame is considered, its use bit is tested and reset as usual. If the bit was already set, its time of last reference is assumed to be the current process time PT and is stored in association with that frame in LR[f]. If the bit was not set, the page is replaceable if $PT - LR[f] > T$, the working set window parameter.

This method has two inaccuracies. First, the estimate of the last reference is more accurate when the pointer is rapidly moving among the frames. Second, the algorithm operates on resident pages (frames, actually) instead of all pages. It is, however, a low-overhead approximation to the standard working set method.

Standard working set schemes do not distinguish among replaceable pages. By approximating it in the clock algorithm framework, the replaceable pages are ordered in a manner that approximates LRU. Also, no data structure is needed to keep track of pages not in working sets; they are found as needed.

5.6.2   Load-Control Methods

Since the clock algorithm in all its forms is still a global replacement scheme, load control is important to avoid memory overcommitment. The method in the next section applies to both WSClock and Clock mechanisms. In the sections after this, specific techniques for each are described.

LT/RT Load Control

Carr describes a method called *loading-task/running-task* load control (LT/RT). This method distinguishes between *loading tasks*, which have few resident pages that will

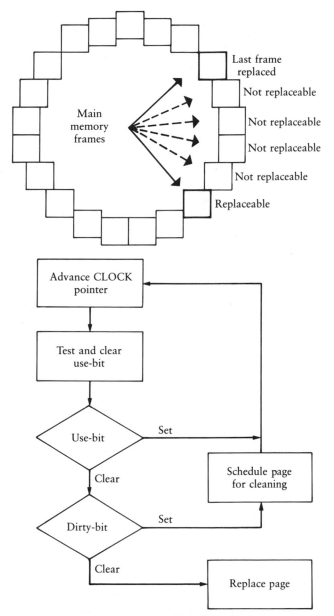

Last frame replaced

Not replaceable

Not replaceable

Not replaceable

Not replaceable

Replaceable

Main memory frames

Advance CLOCK pointer

Test and clear use-bit

Use-bit

Set

Clear

Dirty-bit

Set

Clear

Schedule page for cleaning

Replace page

Figure 5.12   Clock Algorithm [From Carr and Hennessy, 1981. Copyright © 1981 by Association for Computing Machinery. Reprinted by permission.]

fault frequently as needed pages are referenced, and *running tasks,* which have needed pages resident and fault infrequently. It is used instead of prepaging the resident sets of newly activated tasks. LT/RT uses a parameter τ to distinguish between the classes. A newly activated task is a loading task initially. As long as its lifetimes (intervals between successive faults) do not exceed τ, it remains a loading task. Whenever a lifetime longer than τ occurs, the task becomes a running task until it terminates or is deactivated. The LT/RT regime limits the number of loading tasks to some number L, a second parameter of the method.

WSClock Load Control

Since the WSClock mechanism considers only resident pages, the resident set of a process is defined to be its working set (for running, not loading, processes). WSClock detects *memory overcommitment* when an entire lap of the frames completes without encountering a replaceable page. When this occurs, the page-cleaning queue is examined. If there is an outstanding request for a page to be cleaned, it is processed to yield a replaceable page. Failing that, memory is overcommitted and a process must be deactivated.

Clock Load Control

In the absence of direct information about the memory demands of processes, as in the working set or WSClock methods, some adaptive feedback control mechanism is necessary, or a global replacement algorithm such as Clock will overcommit memory and cause thrashing. Denning, et al. [1976] suggested two possibilities for global policies. The first, the *L = S criterion,* adjusts the multiprogramming level so that the mean time between faults is the same as the mean time required to process a page fault. The second, the *50% criterion,* attempts to keep the utilization of the auxiliary memory device used for paging at 50%.

The Clock load-control mechanism attempts to keep the rate of pointer travel C near an optimal rate C_0. We will describe below a method to estimate C by $\hat{C}$. If $\hat{C} < C_0$, the pointer rate is slower than desired, meaning either that few faults are occurring or that the pointer finds replaceable pages without moving very far. In either case, the multiprogramming level may be increased. $\hat{C} > C_0$ indicates either a high fault rate or the fact that the pointer must travel long distances to find a replaceable page. This means a memory overcommitment; a process must be deactivated.

In addition to C_0, three other parameters control the computation of $\hat{C}$ and its comparison with C_0. The first, δ, controls the frequency with which the load-control mechanism is invoked at times t_i. The more frequently load control is executed, the more responsive the system is to changes that are needed, but then the load-control algorithm itself causes more overhead. A small δ also introduces more variability in successive estimates. Each time, an estimate of clock pointer rate, called c_i, is computed. The second parameter, α, is the exponential smoothing weight used to combine c_i with $c_{i-1}, c_{i-2}, \ldots$ into a current average $\hat{C}_i$. A large α puts more weight on the latest c_i, allowing faster response to changes, but it also contributes to variation in the estimate. The third parameter, ϕ, governs how the comparison between C_0 and $\hat{C}_i$ is done. $\hat{C}_i$ is acceptable if it lies in $[C_0 - \phi, C_0 + \phi]$; no changes in multiprogramming level are necessary. A small ϕ results in quicker system response but incurs the cost of frequent process activation and deactivation.

An exponential smoothing method is used to compute $\hat{C}_i$ because it incorporates all previous interim measures c_i and requires no explicit storage of previous measures. At each execution of the Clock load-control mechanism, compute

$$Y_i = c_i + \alpha\, Y_{i-1}$$

and

$$Z_i = 1 + \alpha\, Z_{i-1}$$

with $Y_0 = Z_0 = 0$. Then

$$\hat{C}_i = Y_i \,/\, Z_i.$$

Choosing a Process to Deactivate

In either the WSClock or Clock methods, *process deactivation* must occur when memory overcommitment is detected. Carr lists six possibilities (in addition to a random choice):

1. The *lowest priority process* [Denning, 1980]: This implements a policy decision and is unrelated to performance issues.
2. The *faulting process* [Fogel, 1974]: This is an intuitive idea, since the faulting process may not have its working set resident, and deactivating it eliminates the need to satisfy this page request.
3. The *last process activated*: This is the process least likely to have its working set resident.
4. The *smallest process*: This will require the least future effort to reload.
5. The *largest process*: This obtains the most free frames in an overcommitted memory, making additional deactivations unlikely soon.
6. The *largest remaining quantum process*: This approximates a *shortest processing time first* scheduling discipline.

5.6.3 Simulation Results

In Carr [1984], we find an extensive description of a simulation model for virtual memory designed to compare the many alternative management policies. The reference strings from executing eight heavily used programs were captured and processed for simulator input. We report results germane to the discussion in this section.

Process Deactivation Policies

No differences were observed among selecting the process with the smallest resident set, the one most recently activated, or the one with the largest remaining quantum. The other alternatives exhibited inferior performance.

LT/RT Control

The parameter τ should not be too small, or a process will be deemed running before its resident set has been acquired; if τ is too large, efficient processing continues, so the LT/RT control mechanism is robust in that regard.

The number L of loading processes allowed was optimal when L was set to the number of auxiliary memory paging devices in use. This was limited to L = 1 or 2 in the simulations.

Clock Load Control

The mechanism proved very insensitive to the value of the parameters δ, α, and ϕ after tuning the simulation model to an appropriate value for C_0. This does not mean it was ineffective, because it often caused changes in multiprogramming level. Instead, the LT/RT mechanism had a larger effect.

Relative Performance

The WSClock and Clock mechanisms were compared with each other and with an exact implementation of a working set policy. All were independently tuned for their best performance. Carr's simulation showed that all three performed almost exactly as well in maintaining a high utilization (with similar mean multiprogramming levels), as shown in Table 5.1. Several comments will be helpful here. First, the Clock method performed much worse before tuning than the untuned WSExact and WSClock methods. This may indicate that careful tuning is more important for Clock, because its feedback mechanism is less direct than those based on working sets. Second, the Clock algorithm is simpler to implement and should use less system capacity to execute than the others, making it attractive to operating system designers. Third, WSClock performs as well as an exact working set algorithm, and is simpler to implement.

5.7   Program Restructuring

Users of systems that provide virtual memory facilities are encouraged to view virtual memory as a seamless, linear extent of memory without internal structure. However, it is easy to see that the arrangement of program modules in virtual memory determines the page coresidence of the modules, which explains the potential for page

Table 5.1   Comparison of Working Set, WSClock, and Clock Algorithms

Algorithm	Utilization	Mean MPL
WSExact	.6211	5.25
WSClock	.6164	5.01
Clock	.6177	5.27

faults when modules reference each other. A method for improving the locality of programs and therefore their virtual memory performance—*program restructuring*—is given in this section, which is based on some of the work in Johnson [1975].

Other work in this area can be found in Hatfield and Gerald [1971], Kobayashi [1977], Comeau [1967], Ferrari [1974], and Ferrari and Kobayashi [1977]. Ferrari and others showed that program restructuring can reduce page faults by 50%. Hatfield restructured the nonresident component of an operating system and improved overall system throughput significantly. *The structure of a program in virtual memory can have a larger impact on performance than the choice of page-replacement algorithm.*

A program whose memory reference behavior varies significantly depending on particular input data is not a good candidate for restructuring based on the trace of a particular execution. Fortunately, however, many programs exhibit memory reference patterns that are relatively insensitive to the information being processed; their restructuring expense should be recovered quickly if the program is heavily used [Hatfield and Gerald, 1971].

It has been suggested that with the advent of electronic auxiliary memory, page sizes will decrease and working sets or their analogues will more nearly represent the exact needs of an executing process, thus making program reorganization unnecessary [Denning, 1980]. Unfortunately, these technologies have not yet had widespread impact.

5.7.1 Theoretical Bounds on Paging Performance

In this section we describe upper and lower limits on the kinds of behavior possible by programs executing in virtual memory. In the next section we will see that these bounds can be approached by actual programs. The bounds we discuss here are widely applicable in that they apply to any program restructuring, with other parameters fixed but arbitrary. Johnson [1975] derives some additional bounds that apply to all restructurings but constrain the values of other parameters. They are often tighter than those presented here.

Paging Performance Model

First, we introduce some definitions that will allow the expression of theoretical limits on paging performance. Let

m_P = size of primary memory M_P

N = page size in bytes

A = $a^1, \ldots, a^T$; the virtual address trace of a program's execution

P = $p^1, \ldots, p^T$; the virtual page trace of execution; $P = A \div N$

F = $f^1, \ldots, f^T$; a sequence of sets of pages. f^i is the set of pages fetched in response to reference a^i. F also represents the page-fetch policy in effect.

R = $r^1, \ldots, r^T$; a sequence of sets of pages removed as a result of references in A. R also stands for the page-replacement policy in effect.

$$FF_P = \sum_{t=1}^{T} |f^t|;$$ the total number of page fetches associated with processing reference string A.

It is FF_P that we intend to minimize. Note that $FF_P = FF_P(\ m_P, N, A, F, R\ )$. The size of primary memory, the page size, the fetch policy, and the replacement policy all affect the number of pages fetched. However, we concentrate on the effect of A, the virtual address trace.

A program consists of a set of m relocatable *sectors* $Q = \{\ S_1, \ldots, S_m\ \}$. The program's structure is determined by the order of its sectors in virtual memory, a *sector ordering*, $SO = S_1, \ldots, S_m$, where Q is an unordered set and SO is an ordered sequence. There are m! sector orderings for each Q. The sector ordering SO of Q determines its virtual address trace A and hence its page trace P. So, we can model program behavior by a sector ordering and a *sector trace*, $ST = S^1, \ldots, S^T$. Let n = the number of pages of size N used to hold Q. We define an n-way restructuring of Q as a partition $II = \{\ II_1, \ldots, II_n\ \}$, where $\bigcup_{i=1}^{n} II_i = Q$, $II_i \cap II_j = \emptyset$ if $i \neq j$, and $\sum_{sk \in \pi_i} |\ S_k\ | \leq N$. Then the number of page fetches actually depends on a particular partition of the sectors and the sector trace:

$$FF_P = FF_P(\ m_P, N, II, ST, F, R\ ).$$

Sectoring Performance Model

Assume the existence of a sector memory composed of sector frames, each of which can hold any single program sector exactly. Here the unit of information transfer is the sector, not the page. We want to set up a *sectoring performance model* to characterize sector movement in such a memory system independently of any particular sector ordering. As before, we introduce some definitions:

m_S = size of sector memory M_S

ST = $S^1, \ldots, S^T$; a program sector trace

F_d = $f_d^1, \ldots, f_d^T$; a sequence of sectors fetched in response to references in ST. F_d is always demand fetching for sector memory.

R = $r^1, \ldots, r^T$; a sequence of sectors removed as a result of references in ST; also the sector replacement policy in effect.

FF_S = $\sum_{t=1}^{T} |f_d^t|$; the total number of sector fetches associated with processing sector reference string ST.

Here $FF_S = FF_S(\ m_S, ST, F_d, R\ )$.

A Lower Bound

For this bound, fix an integer k that is the maximum number of sectors that any page may contain.

THEOREM 5.2

For any partition Π_{any}, *the minimum number of page fetches is bounded below by*

$FF_P(\ m_P,\ N,\ \Pi_{any},\ ST_{any},\ F_{any},\ R_{any}\ ) \geq$
$(1/k)\ \times\ FF_S(\ m_S = k \times m_P\ ,\ ST = ST_{any},\ F_d,\ R_{opt}\ )$

Notice here that sector memory is k times larger than paged memory, and that the sector virtual memory system uses optimal replacement, a stack algorithm. This means that one can compute FF_S for any $k \times m_P$ in just one pass over ST.

Theorem 5.2 is applicable in any virtual memory system; unfortunately, as k increases, this bound becomes progressively weaker.

An Upper Bound

THEOREM 5.3

For demand fetching, LRU replacement, and any partition Π_{any}, *the number of page fetches is bounded above by*

$FF_P(\ m_P,\ N,\ \Pi_{any},\ ST_{any},\ F_d,\ R_{LRU}\ ) \leq FF_S(\ m_S = m_P,\ ST = ST_{any},\ F_d,\ R_{LRU}\ )$

Note here that sector memory is the same size as page memory, and both are governed by demand fetching and LRU replacement.

This simple example of lower and upper bounds computation shows that even when $\frac{2}{3}$ of a program fits into primary memory, a wide variation in performance is possible. Let $m_P = 2$, $k = 3$ sectors per page, $F = F_d$, $R = R_{LRU}$. Consider a program Q = { abcdefghi } composed of nine sectors, each of size N/3. Suppose we have derived the sector trace

ST = aehae hbdgb dgaeh bficf ibeha dgadg.

To obtain a lower bound on the number of page fetches, apply Theorem 5.2 after computing $FF_S(\ m_S = 6,\ ST,\ F_d,\ R_{opt}\ )$, as shown in Table 5.2(a). A lower bound on the number of page fetches is $\frac{12}{3} = 4$.

We get an upper bound by computing $FF_S(m_S = 2,\ ST,\ F_d,\ R_{LRU}\ )$, as demonstrated in Table 5.2(b), and applying Theorem 5.3. Here an upper bound is 30 page fetches. An exercise will demonstrate that these bounds can be achieved by different partitions.

5.7.2   An Experiment

To explore heuristics for automatic program restructuring, Johnson [1975] used the following procedure:

1. Record a virtual instruction trace from program execution and, using the ordering of sectors in virtual memory, along with their sizes, map this to a sector trace.

Table 5.2(a) Example: Lower Bound Computation

ST	=	aehae	hbdgb	dgaeh	bficf	ibeha	dgadg
F_d	=	aeh	bdg		fic	a	dg
R_{opt}	=				gda	c	fi
M_S	=	aehae	hbdgb	dgaeh	bficf	ibeha	dgadg
		aahh	eebbg	gddae	ebffc	fibeh	aaggd
		eea	aaadd	bbbbb	hebii	cfibe	hddaa
			heaa	aagda	ahebb	bcfib	ehhhh
			hee	eeegd	dahee	eecfi	beeee
			hh	hhhhg	gdahh	hhhcf	ibbbb

Table 5.2(b) Example: Upper Bound Computation

ST	=	aehae	hbdgb	dgaeh	bficf	ibeha	dgadg
F_d	=	aehae	hbdgb	dgaeh	bficf	ibeha	dgadg
R_{LRU}	=	aeh	aehbd	gbdga	ebefi	cfibe	hadga
M_S	=	aehae	hbdgb	dgaeh	bficf	ibeha	dgadg
		aeha	ehbdg	bdgae	hefic	fibeh	adgad

2. Construct an *intersector reference matrix* C. This is an m × m matrix in which C[i, j] and C[j, i] reflect the strength of the connection between sectors i and j of the program. We will examine below a useful heuristic for this construction.

3. Use C to partition sectors into blocks with a *clustering procedure*. A clustering heuristic is also included here.

4. Insert the ordered blocks into the virtual address space.

5. Simulate the paging behavior of the restructured program (using LRU replacement).

6. Compare the performance of the restructured program with theoretical lower bounds, and compare the performance of intentionally bad partitions with upper bounds.

Building the Intersector Reference Matrix

Johnson [1975] explored six heuristic procedures for building an intersector reference matrix that captured the relative strength of bonds between pairs of sectors. One that proved useful over a wide range of memory sizes is called the *Outside the working set model*, and it uses the idea of a sector working set

$$W_S(t, \Delta) = \{ \textit{Sectors referenced in the interval } t - \Delta \text{ to } t \}$$

The algorithm is

```
C ← [0];
for t ← 1 to T do
   if S^t = S_j and S_j ∉ W_S(t − 1,Δ) then
      forall S_i ∈ W_S(t − 1,Δ) do C[i,j] ← C[i,j] + 1 endfor;
      C[j,j] ← C[j,j] + 1
   endif
endfor
```

For each sector in the sector trace, if it is not a member of the current working set when encountered, increment its strength with the members of the working set. An appropriate value for Δ, the sector working set window size, is a value near the parachor or "knee" of the curve $FF_S(\ m_S,\ \text{ST},\ F_d,\ R_{opt}\ )$ versus m_S. Since OPT is a stack algorithm, a suitable value for Δ in the matrix construction algorithm can be had with a single preliminary pass over the sector trace. Results are relatively insensitive to the choice of Δ. Note that $C[j, j]$ is the number of sector fetches for S_j, and $C[i, j] + C[j, i]$ is the number of page fetches that will *not* occur if sectors S_i and S_j co-reside in a page.

Clustering Procedure

Eleven heuristics for ordering sectors in virtual memory were explored; we present one here that was widely successful in Johnson's experiments. The idea is to begin with individual sectors and build ever larger clusters of sectors until only one, the desired sector ordering, remains:

1. Initially define m clusters $G_1, \ldots, G_m$, one sector per cluster.
2. Find clusters G_x and G_y that maximize $\sum\limits_{i \in G_x} \sum\limits_{j \in G_y} C[i,j]$
3. Concatenate G_x and G_y, preserving their respective internal orders.
4. Repeat until only one cluster remains.

Note that most of the double summation values can be reused as the clustering algorithm iterates. The sectors are arranged as dictated by the final cluster in virtual memory without regard to page boundaries.

Experimental Results

Each of the intersector reference matrix construction heuristics was used on some actual sector traces, and the results were combined with several clustering procedures to compare relative improvements. The pair described here together give a useful algorithm for restructuring programs. In a specific example, a virtual memory trace of just over two million references involving nearly 100 sectors was recorded and converted to a sector trace. The program was restructured using the two heuristics described here; in addition, the program was restructured by sorting the sectors according to their sizes. Several curves appear in Figure 5.13. The graph presents the total number of page fetches FF_P versus the number of page frames M_P. Curves A and B are, respectively, theoretical lower and upper bounds on the number of page fetches for all sector orderings. Curve C is the performance of the original, unrestructured program. Curve D represents the improved program, and Curve E is the performance of the program whose sectors are ordered by size.

From Figure 5.13 we see that, over a broad range of memory sizes, the reorganization reduced the number of page fetches by about 50% when compared with the original version. A bad ordering can approach the theoretical worst case in paging behavior, and a heuristic reordering of program sectors can approximate the theoretically minimum number of page fetches. Any random ordering is likely to fall between these two, but there is real danger that a thoughtless ordering will be very expensive to execute.

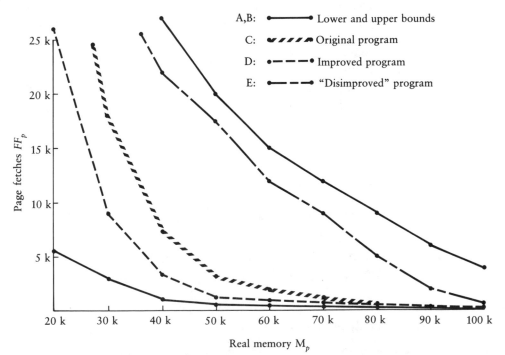

Figure 5.13   Program Restructuring: Bounds and Performance Curves.

5.8 Summary

In this chapter we first reviewed the fundamental ideas about virtual memory management. Then we used the concept of stack algorithms to show how to evaluate the paging cost of a program in all memory sizes simultaneously and to predict paging behavior in larger memories. The working set principle ties together memory management and process management to prevent overcommitment of storage. Models of virtual memory are useful for testing system changes and for enhanced understanding. Recent research in clock algorithms has demonstrated that simple versions of this global method can compete with more complex local approaches. Finally, program restructuring can significantly improve the performance of programs executing in virtual memory. Together these results mean that the automatic management of main storage can be very effective.

The trend toward virtual memory implementations on smaller systems continues, and one can expect that it will soon be common on personal computers.

Key Words

address translation device

auxiliary memory

Belady's anomaly

cleaning policy

clock algorithm

clustering procedure

cost function

demand cleaning

demand fetching

demand replacement

dirty bits

duty factor

effective access time

extension problem

extrinsic model

fault rate

fetch policy

first-in, first-out (FIFO) replacement

fixed-allocation policy

global-replacement policy

inclusion property

intersector reference matrix

intrinsic model

L = S criterion

last-in, first-out (LIFO) replacement

least frequently used (LFU) replacement

least recently used (LRU) replacement

lifetime

lifetime curve

load-control policy

loading-task/running-task load control

local replacement policy

locality of reference

LRU reference string

LRU stack model

memory overcommitment

most recently used (MRU) replacement

optimal replacement (OPT)

Outside the working set model

page

page-fault interrupt

page frame

page stealing

page table

paged-memory system

phase transition

placement policy

precleaning

prepaging

principle of locality

priority algorithm

process deactivation

process time	sector	variable-allocation policy
program restructuring	sector ordering	
pure-segmentation system	sector trace	virtual memory
	sectoring performance model	virtual time
real memory		window size
reference string	stack algorithm	working set
replacement policy	stack distance	Working Set Principle
resident page	thrashing	WSClock algorithm
resident set	use bits	50% criterion

Questions

1. Which of the following statements are true?
   a. The placement policy has no consequence in paging systems.
   b. Demand paging is optimal in terms of the number of page faults.
   c. Prepaging reduces the number of page faults.
   d. Initially loaded demand fetch reduces the page-transfer time because a number of pages are initially brought into memory by one or a few I/O operations.

2. Why is LRU difficult to implement?

3. Show a page-reference string that exhibits each of the following phenomena:
   a. FIFO performs better than LRU.
   b. RANDOM performs better than LRU.
   c. LRU performs better than LIFO.

4. What measures should be taken in each of the following cases?
   a. High CPU utilization and little paging traffic between memory and disks
   b. High CPU utilization and moderate paging traffic
   c. High CPU utilization and heavy paging traffic
   d. Low CPU utilization and little paging traffic
   e. Low CPU utilization and heavy paging traffic

5. If a large number of programs is kept in main memory, there is almost always another ready program when a page fault occurs. Thus, CPU utilization can be kept high. If, however, we allocate a large memory space to each of a few programs, then each program produces a smaller number of page faults. Thus, CPU utilization can be kept high. Are these two arguments correct? Which policy should be preferred?

6. This problem illustrates thrashing. Main storage consists of 90 page frames. Nine identical programs reside in main storage and make references according to the string

   $$\omega = (0123456789)^{\infty}$$

Note that the fault rate of each program is zero and the CPU utilization is 100%. Assume that a tenth program, identical to the others, is loaded, so each program now has nine frames. Compute the page-fault rate, effective access time, and duty factor for each program, assuming an LRU replacement policy and a page fault time of 10^4 virtual time units.

7. Compare the advantages and disadvantages of a pure demand paging policy and an initially loaded demand fetch policy from various viewpoints.

8. What kinds of programming practices can reduce page faults?

9. Can a compiler produce code that makes it easy to detect a transition between phases?

10. Suppose that a computer executes each instruction in 1 μs, where each instruction makes two memory accesses. Assume the following:

    (1) Ninety percent of the accesses are made through the associative registers. In this case no paging overhead is incurred

    (2) When an access is made through a page table, overhead of a half microsecond is incurred.

    (3) Each page faults incurs a 20-msec overhead.

    Compute the page-fault rate that keeps the effective instruction execution time below 1.2 μs.

11. Consider the following program:

    ```
    var A, B: array[1..1000] of integer;
    for I in 1..1000 do
       A[I] := A[I] + B[I]
    endfor;
    ```

    Assuming that an integer occupies a word, compute the number of page faults generated by the program in each of the following cases:

    a. Two page frames of size 100 words can be allocated to arrays *A* and *B* at any time.

    b. Three page frames of size 100 words can be allocated to arrays *A* and *B* at any time.

    c. Ten page frames of size 100 words can be allocated to arrays *A* and *B* at any time.

    d. Two page frames of size 500 words can be allocated to arrays *A* and *B* at any time.

    Compute results for two policies FIFO and LRU. Assume that the code and variable I are placed in another page frame and no instruction fetch or access to variable I produces a page fault. Also assume that main memory is initially empty.

12. Compute the number of page faults generated by the following program under the same assumptions as those of Question 11:

```
var A, B: array[1..1000] of integer;
for I in 1..1000 do
   A[1001 − I] := A[I] + B[I]
endfor;
```

13. Show that the theoretical bounds computed in Section 5.7.1 [using Tables 5.2(a) and 5.2(b)] can be achieved by carefully designed partitions.

Problems

1. Suppose the paging hardware of a computer system is designed so that each entry in the page table has an invalid bit, but no use bit. We want to implement a memory management policy that requires an analysis of use bits. Describe how a "low-cost" mechanism to record the use of pages can be implemented in software.

2. This problem is meant to show that page size has a complex effect on performance. Assume that the total amount of real memory is fixed.

   a. Give an example showing that *doubling* the page size can reduce page faults.

   b. Give an example showing that *halving* the page size can reduce page faults.

3. Apply the intersector reference matrix construction algorithm and clustering procedure discussed in Section 5.7.2 to the sector trace of Table 5.2. First it will be necessary to find an appropriate window size for the matrix construction algorithm by examining the curve $FF_S(\,m_S, ST, F_d, R_{opt}\,)$ versus m_S. Produce the resulting page trace, and compare its performance with the theoretical lower bound computed in Section 5.7.1.

4. Devise an antithetical clustering procedure using the data of Problem 3 to obtain a page organization that gives the *worst* possible performance.

5. Suppose that the sector trace in Table 5.2 is actually a page trace. Compute the cost of processing this reference string for all memory sizes of interest using LRU replacement. Repeat for optimal replacement.

6. In the never-ending search for good theoretical lower bounds on paging behavior, Miss Ann Alyze has conjectured that

$$FF_P(\,m_P, N, II_{any}, ST_{any}, F_d, R_{LRU}\,) \geqslant$$
$$FF_S(\,m_S = k \times m_P, ST_{any}, F_d, R_{LRU}\,)\,/\,k$$

This conjecture is based on the following reasoning:

> If each page holds k sectors, sector memory could hold the same number of sectors as paged memory. So k sector fetches are needed to do what one page fetch does. If all pages contain sectors that are used together, then dividing FF_S by k should do the trick.

Consider the program Q = {a, b, c, d, e, f, g, h, i, j, k, l} wherein each sector has size N/3 running in three page frames. Let k = 3. Consider the looping sector trace ST = (feab hdlk gjci)". Find a partition II that disproves the conjecture. What is the trend as n increases?

7. For the program Q = {a, b, c, d, e, f, g, h} made up of eight sectors of size N/2, and a sector trace ST = (acdb efbg hacd aefb), apply Theorems 5.2 and 5.3 to obtain theoretical lower and upper bounds on paging behavior for m_P = 1, 2, and 3. Are there partitions that achieve these bounds?

8. Suppose A denotes a nondemand page-replacement algorithm. Show how to construct a demand paging algorithm A' that satisfies Theorem 5.1. (*Hint:* A' must simulate, in its internal state, the behavior of A.)

9. Consider the high-level program segment:

for i **in** 1 .. n **do** A[i] : = i; B[i] : = n − i + 1 **endfor**;
for i **in** 1 .. n **do**
    temp : = 0;
    for j **in** i .. n **do** temp : = temp + A[n + i − j] * B [j] **endfor**;
    C[i] : = temp
endfor

Using a register machine (with registers denoted by Ri), the machine language version of this program is loaded in virtual address space (with page size of 1000 words) as follows:

2983	(R1) ← ONE	Index i
2984	(R2) ← n	Loop Bound
2985	compare R1,R2	Test i > n
2986	branch_greater * + 8	
2987	A(R1) ← (R1)	Compute A[i]
2988	(R0) ← n	Compute B[i]
2989	(R0) ← (R0) − (R1)	
2990	(R0) ← (R0) + ONE	
2991	B(R1) ← (R0)	
2992	(R1) ← (R1) + ONE	Increment i
2993	branch * − 8	
2994	(R1) ← ONE	Index i
2995	(R2) ← n	Loop Bound
2996	compare R1,R2	Test i > n
2997	branch_greater * + 20	
2998	(R0) ← ZERO	temp ← 0
2999	temp ← (R0)	
3000	(R3) ← (R1)	Index j
3001	(R4) ← n	Loop Bound
3002	compare R3,R4	Test j > n
3003	branch_greater * + 11	
3004	(R0) ← n	Compute A[n + i − j]
3005	(R0) ← (R0) + (R1)	
3006	(R0) ← (R0) − (R3)	

3007	$(R5) \leftarrow A(R0)$	
3008	$(R6) \leftarrow B(R3)$	Compute B[j]
3009	$(R5) \leftarrow (R5) * (R6)$	
3010	$(R5) \leftarrow (R5) + temp$	
3011	$temp \leftarrow (R5)$	
3012	$(R3) \leftarrow (R3) + ONE$	Increment j
3013	branch $*$ $-$ 11	
3014	$C(R1) \leftarrow (R5)$	Compute C[i]
3015	$(R1) \leftarrow (R1) + ONE$	Increment i
3016	branch $*$ $-$ 20	
	...	
6000	Storage for C	
7000	Storage for ONE	
7001	Storage for n	
7002	Storage for temp	
7003	Storage for ZERO	
8000	Storage for A	
9000	Storage for B	

Upon execution of this program segment, the following reference string is generated:

$$\omega = 272722(28272272927222)^n$$
$$272722(272733733(373338393373737333)^{n-i+1}3637322)^n$$

a. Assume $n = 10$. Write a program to analyze the run-time behavior if a working set memory management policy is used. In particular, your program should print a table:

$$\Delta = \text{window size}$$
$$P(\Delta) = \text{total number of page faults}$$
$$W(\Delta) = \text{average working set size}$$
$$F(\Delta) = \frac{P(\Delta)}{|\omega|} = \text{average page fault rate}$$

b. Plot the following curves: Δ vs. $P(\Delta)$, Δ vs. $W(\Delta)$, and Δ vs. $1/F(\Delta)$ for Δ ranging from 1 to 200.

c. From the plot of Δ vs. $1/F(\Delta)$, explain the precise cause of all knees in terms of program (or reference string) structure.

10. Let $\omega = r_1 \cdots r_t \cdots r_T$ be a reference string, and assume a working set memory management policy. Define Δ, $P(\Delta)$, $W(\Delta)$, and $F(\Delta)$, as in Problem 9. Further, let $w(t, \Delta)$ denote the working set size at time t and $w(\Delta)$ denote the average working set size over the entire reference string. Show that, for large T, $F(\Delta)$ is approximately $w(\Delta + 1) - w(\Delta)$, that is, F is the derivative of the mean working set size.

References

Belady, L. A.; R. A. Nelson; and G. S. Shedler. (June 1969). "An anomaly in space-time characteristics of certain programs running in a paging environment." *Communications of the ACM* 12, 6, pp. 349–353.

Brawn, B., and F. G. Gustavson. (1968). "Program behavior in a paging environment." *Proceedings of the AFIPS Fall Joint Computer Conference* 33, pp. 1019–1032.

Carr, R. W. 1984. *Virtual Memory Management.* UMI Research Press, Ann Arbor, Mich.

Carr, R. W., and J. L. Hennessy. (December 1981). "WSClock—a simple and efficient algorithm for virtual memory management." *Proceedings of the Eighth Symposium on Operating System Principles,* pp. 87–95.

Chu, W. W., and H. Opderbeck. (1972). "The page fault frequency replacement algorithm." *Proceedings of the AFIPS Fall Joint Computer Conference,* pp. 597–609.

Coffman, E. G., and P. J. Denning. 1973. *Operating System Theory.* Prentice-Hall, Englewood Cliffs, N.J.

Comeau, L. (October 1967). "A study of the effect of user program optimization in a paging system." *Proceedings of the First ACM Symposium on Operating System Principles.*

Denning, P. J. (May 1968). "The working set model for program behavior." *Communications of the ACM* 11, 5, pp. 323–333.

———. "Virtual memory." (September 1970). *ACM Computing Surveys* 2, 3, pp. 153–189.

———. (January 1980). "Working sets past and present." *IEEE Transactions on Software Engineering* SE-6, 1, pp. 64–84.

Denning, P. J., and K. C. Kahn. (November 1975). "A study of program locality and lifetime functions." *Proceedings of the Fifth ACM Symposium on Operating System Principles,* pp. 207–216.

Denning. P. J., et al. (1976). "Optimal Multiprogramming." *Acta Informatica* 7, pp. 197–216.

Ferrari, D. (November 1974). "Improving locality by critical working sets." *Communications of the ACM* 17, 11, pp. 614–620.

Ferrari, D., and M. Kobayashi. (April 1977). "Program restructuring algorithms for global LRU environments." *Proceedings of the International Computing Symposium 1977,* pp. 277–283.

Fogel, M. (January 1974). "The VMOS paging algorithm." *Operating Systems Review* 8, 1, pp. 8–17.

Hatfield, D. J., and J. Gerald. (1971). "Program restructuring for virtual memory." *IBM Systems Journal* 10, 3, pp. 168–192.

Johnson, J. W. (March 1975). "Program restructuring for virtual memory systems." Project MAC TR-148, MIT, Cambridge, Mass.

Kahn, K. C. (August 1976). "Program behavior and load dependent system performance." Ph.D. dissertation, Computer Science Department, Purdue University, W. Lafayette, Ind.

Kobayshi, M. (1977). "A set of strategy independent restructuring algorithms." *Software—Practice and Experience* 7, 5, pp. 585–594.

Mattson, R. L.; J. Gecsei; D. R. Slutz; and I. L. Traiger. (1970). "Evaluation techniques for storage hierarchies." *IBM Systems Journal 9*, 2, pp. 78–117.

McKellor, A., and E. G. Coffman (March 1969). "The organization of matrices and matrix operations in a paged multiprogramming environment." *Communications of the ACM 12*, 3, pp. 153–165.

Morris, J. B. (October 1972). "Demand paging through utilization of working sets on the Maniac II." *Communications of the ACM 15*, 10, pp. 867–872.

Rodriguez-Rosell, J., and J. Dupuy. (April 1973). "The design, implementation, and evaluation of a working set dispatcher." *Communications of the ACM 16*, 4, pp. 247–253.

Shaw, A. *The Logical Design of Operating Systems.* 1974. Prentice-Hall, Englewood Cliffs, N.J.

Shemer, J. E., and S. C. Gupta. (July 1969). "On the design of Bayesian storage allocation algorithms for paging and segmentation." *IEEE Transactions on Computers* C-18, 7, pp. 644–651.

Shemer, J. E., and B. Shippey. (December 1966). "Statistical analysis of paged and segmented computer systems." *IEEE Transactions on Computers* EC-15, 6, pp. 855–863.

Smith, A. J. (September 1976). "A modified working set paging algorithm." *IEEE Transactions on Computers* C-25, 9, pp. 907–914.

Spirn, J. R. *Program Behavior: Models and Measurements.* 1977. Elsevier North-Holland Publishing, N.Y.

Suggested Readings

Aho, A. V.; P. J. Denning; and J. D. Ullman. (January 1971). "Principles of optimal page replacement." *Journal of the ACM 18*, 1, pp. 80–93.

Alderson, A.; W. C. Lynch; and B. Randell. (1972). "Thrashing in a multiprogrammed paging system." In *Operating Systems Techniques* (Eds. C. A. R. Hoare and R. H. Perrott), Academic Press, London, pp. 152–167.

Arden, B., and D. Boettner. (October 1969). "Measurement and performance of a multiprogramming system." *Proceedings of the Second ACM Symposium on Operating Systems Principles,* pp. 130–146.

Baer, J., and G. R. Sager. (March 1976). "Dynamic improvement of locality in virtual memory system." *IEEE Transactions on Software Engineering* SE-1, pp. 54–62.

Batson, A. P. (November 1976). "Program behavior at the symbolic level." *Computer 9*, 11, pp. 21–28.

Batson, A. P., and R. G. Bundage. (January 1977). "Segment sizes and lifetimes in ALGOL 60 programs." *Communications of the ACM 20*, 1, pp. 36–44.

Batson, A. P.; S. Ju; and D. Wood. (March 1970). "Measurements of segment size." *Communications of the ACM 13*, 3, pp. 155–159.

Belady, L. A. (1966). "A study of replacement algorithms for virtual storage computers." *IBM Systems Journal 5*, 2, pp. 78–101.

Belady, L. A., and C. J. Kuehner. (1969). "Dynamic space-sharing in computer systems." *Communications of the ACM 12*, 5, pp. 282–288.

Bryant, P. (May 1975). "Predicting working set sizes." *IBM Journal of Research and Development* 19, 3, pp. 221–229.

Chamberlin, D. D.; S. H. Fuller; and L. Liu. (1973). "An analysis of page allocation strategies for virtual memory systems." *IBM Journal of Research and Development* 17, pp. 404–412.

Coffman, E. G., Jr., and L. C. Varian. (July 1968). "Further experimental data on the behavior of programs in a paging environment." *Communications of the ACM* 11, 7, pp. 471–474.

DeMeis, W. M., and N. Weizer. (1969). "Measurements and analysis of a demand paging time sharing system." *Proceedings of the ACM National Conference,* pp. 201–216.

Denning, P. J. (1968). "Thrashing: its causes and prevention." *Proceedings of the AFIPS Fall Joint Computer Conference* 33, pp. 915–922.

———. (1972). "On modeling program behavior." *Proceedings of the AFIPS Spring Joint Computer Conference* 40, pp. 937–944.

Denning, P. J., and G. S. Graham. (June 1975). "Multiprogrammed memory management." *Proceedings of the IEEE* 63, 6, pp. 924–939.

Denning, P. J., and K. C. Kahn. (1976). "An $L = S$ criterion for optimal multiprogramming." *Proceedings of the ACM SIGMETRICS International Symposium on Computer Performance Modeling, Measurement and Evaluation,* pp. 219–229.

Denning, P. J., and S. C. Schwartz. (March 1972). "Properties of the working-set model." *Communications of the ACM* 15, 3, pp. 191–198.

Doran, R. W. "Virtual memory." (October 1976). *Computer* 9, 10, pp. 27–37.

Easton, M. C. (March 1978). "Model for database reference strings based on behavior of reference clusters." *IBM Journal of Research and Development* 22, pp. 197–202.

Easton, M. C., and B. T. Bennett. (February 1977). "Transient-free working set statistics." *Communications of the ACM* 20, 2, pp. 93–99.

Ferrari, D. (1974). "Improving program locality by strategy-oriented restructuring." *Information Processing 74: Proceedings of IFIP Congress 74,* pp. 266–270.

———. (May 1975). "Tailoring programs to models of program behavior." *IBM Journal of Research and Development* 19, pp. 244–251.

———. (November 1976). "The improvement of program behavior." *Computer* 9, 11, pp. 39–47.

Fine, G. H.; C. W. Jackson; and P. V. McIsaac. (1966) "Dynamic program behavior under paging." *Proceedings of the ACM National Conference,* pp. 223–228.

Franklin, M. A.; G. S. Graham; and R. K. Gupta. (March 1978). "Anomalies with variable partition paging algorithms." *Communications of the ACM* 21, 3, pp. 232–236.

Freibergs, I. F. (1968). "The dynamic behavior of programs." *Proceedings of the AFIPS Fall Joint Computer Conference,* pp. 1163–1167.

Gupta, R. K., and M. A. Franklin. (August 1978). "Working set and page fault frequency paging algorithms: a performance comparison." *IEEE Transactions on Computers* C-27, 8, pp. 706–712.

Hatfield, D. J. (January 1972). "Experiments on page size, program access patterns, and virtual memory performance." *IBM Journal of Research and Development* 16, 1, pp. 58–62.

Hoare, C. A. R. (August 1973). "A structured paging system." *The Computer Journal* 16, 3, pp. 209–215.

Hoare, C. A. R., and R. M. McKeag. (1972). "A survey of store management techniques." In *Operating Systems Techniques* (Eds. C. A. R. Hoare and R. H. Perrot), Academic Press, London, pp. 117–151.

Joseph, M. (February 1970). "An analysis of paging and program behavior." *The Computer Journal* 13, 1, pp. 48–54.

Krzesinski, A., and P. Teunissen. (1978). "A multiclass network model of a demand paging computer system." *Acta Informatica* 9, pp. 331–343.

Kuck, D. J., and D. H. Lawrie. (1970). "The use and performance of memory hierarchies: a survey." *Software Engineering* 1, Academic Press, New York, pp. 45–78.

Lau, E. J. *Performance Improvement of Virtual Memory Systems.* 1982. UMI Research Press, Ann Arbor, MI.

Lau, E. J., and D. Ferrari. (January 1983). "Program restructuring in a multilevel virtual memory." *IEEE Transactions on Software Engineering* SE-9, 1, pp. 69–79.

Liptay, J. S. (1968). "Structural aspects of the System/360 model 85: II—the cache." *IBM Systems Journal* 7, 1, pp. 15–21.

Madison, A. W., and A. P. Batson. (May 1976). "Characteristics of program localities." *Communications of the ACM* 19, 5, pp. 285–294.

Masuda, T. (1978). "Analysis of memory management strategies for multiprogrammed virtual storage systems." *Journal of Information Processing* 1, 1, pp. 14–24.

McKellar, A., and E. G. Coffman. (March 1969). "The organization of matrices and matrix operations in a paged multiprogramming environment." *Communications of the ACM* 12, 3, pp. 153–165.

Nishigaki, T. (January 1983). "Experiments on the knee criterion in a multiprogrammed computer system." *IEEE Transactions on Software Engineering* SE-9, 1, pp. 79–86.

Oliver, N. A. (1974). "Experimental data on page replacement algorithms." *Proceedings of the AFIPS National Computer Conference* 43, pp. 179–184.

Organick. E. I. 1972. *The MULTICS System: An Examination of Its Structure.* MIT Press, Cambridge, Mass.

Parent, M., and D. Potier. (1977). "A note on the influence of program loading on the page fault rate." *Acta Informatica* 8, pp. 359–370.

Potier, D. (November 1977). "Analysis of demand paging policies with swapped working sets." *Proceedings of the 6th ACM Symposium on Operating Systems Principles,* pp. 125–131.

Prieve, B. G., and R. S. Fabry. (May 1976). "VMIN—an optimal variable space page replacement algorithm." *Communications of the ACM* 19, 5, pp. 295–297.

Randell, B. (July 1969). "A note on storage fragmentation and program segmentation." *Communications of the ACM* 12, 7, pp. 365–372.

Randell, B., and C. J. Kuehner. (May 1968). "Dynamic storage allocation systems." *Communications of the ACM* 11, 5, pp. 197–304.

Rodriguez-Rosell, J., and J. P. Dupuy. (November 1976). "Empirical data reference behavior in data base systems." *Computer* 9, pp. 9–13.

Sadeh, E. (November 1975). "An analysis of the performance of the page fault frequence

(PFF) replacement algorithm." *Proceedings of the 5th ACM Symposium on Operating Systems Principles,* pp. 6–13.

Sayre, D. (December 1969). "Is automatic 'folding' of programs efficient enough to replace manual?" *Communications of the ACM* 12, 12, pp. 656–600.

Slutz, D. R., and I. L. Traiger. (October 1974). "A note on the calculation of average working set size." *Communications of the ACM* 17, 10, pp. 563–565.

Smith, A. J. (January 1977). "Two simple methods for the efficient analysis of memory address trace data." *IEEE Transactions on Software Engineering* SE-3, pp. 94–101.

————. (March 1978). "A comparative study of set associative memory mapping and their use for cache and main memory." *IEEE Transactions on Software Engineering* SE-4, pp. 121–130.

————. (September 1978). "Sequentiality and prefetching in data base systems." *ACM Transactions on Database Systems,* pp. 223–247.

————. (December 1978). "Sequential program prefetching in memory hierarchies." *Computer* 11, 12, pp. 7–21.

Spirn, J. R., and P. J. Denning. (1972). "Experiments with program locality." *Proceedings of the AFIPS Fall Joint Computer Conference* 41, pp. 611–621.

Tannenbaum, A. S. (March 1978). "Implications of structured programming for machine architecture." *Communications of the ACM* 21, 3, pp. 237–246.

Trivedi, K. S. (September 1976). "Prepaging and applications in array algorithms." *IEEE Transactions on Computers* C-25, pp. 915–921.

Tuel, W. G., Jr. (September 1976). "An analysis of buffer paging in virtual storage systems." *IBM Journal of Research and Development* 20, pp. 518–520.

Turner, R., and B. Strecker. (November 1977). "Use of the LRU stack depth distribution for simulation of paging behavior." *Communications of the ACM* 20, 11, pp. 795–798.

Vareha, A. L.; R. M. Rutledge; and M. M. Gold. (October 1969). "Strategies for structuring two-level memories in a paging environment." *Proceedings of the Second ACM Symposium on Operating System Principles,* pp. 54–59.

Weizer, N., and G. Oppenheimer. (1969). "Virtual memory management in a paging environment." *Proceedings of the AFIPS Spring Joint Computer Conference* 34, p. 234.

Wilkes. M. V. (February 1973). "The dynamics of paging." *The Computer Journal* 16, pp. 4–9.

Winograd, J.; S. J. Morganstein; and R. Herman. (October 1971). "Simulation studies of a virtual memory, time-shared, demand paging operating system." *Proceedings of the Third ACM Symposium on Operating Systems Principles,* pp. 149–155.

Wolman, E. (January 1965). "A fixed optimum cell-size for records of various lengths." *Journal of the ACM* 12, 1, pp. 53–70.

Wulf, W. A. (October 1969). "Performance monitors for multiprogramming systems." *Proceedings of the Second ACM Symposium on Operating Systems Principles,* pp. 175–181.

Distributed 6
Systems

6.1 Introduction

This chapter deals with fundamental concepts in the design of software for distributed systems. By a *distributed system,* we mean a collection of independent computers and some communication facility for exchanging messages. By a distributed computation, we mean a collection of processes on two or more of these computers, which need to communicate to achieve some objective. We assume that the computers do not have a common shared memory, so the process synchronization mechanisms described in Chapters 2 and 3 are, for the most part, not applicable. In these types of systems, or *networks* as we shall call them, message passing must serve as the basis for distributed synchronization. The purpose of this chapter is twofold. First, we describe a structured approach to the design of reliable software for network systems. Second, we describe some methods for process synchronization as would be required at the traditional operating system or application software levels.

Networks can be classified as *local area networks (LANs)* or wide area (long-haul) networks. LANs are characterized by their confinement to a smaller geographic area, such as a room, building, or plant site. Typical physical communication media for an LAN include twisted pairs, coaxial cables, and optical fibers. Long-haul networks are characterized by their larger geographic span, and typically involve communication media such as telephone lines and microwave and satellite links.

When computers or processes communicate by exchanging messages, there must be a set of *protocols* (established rules) to govern the manner in which communication is allowed to take place. Various levels of protocols are required. For example, synchronization between a sender and receiver may be necessary to ensure that buffer capacities are not exceeded and messages are not lost. Protocols may be needed to effect such functions as efficient routing from one node to another, avoiding congestion in the network, and recovering from transmission errors or lost messages.

The model introduced in this chapter is based on the ISO Reference Model of Open Systems Interconnection. Sections 6.2 through 6.5 discuss the lower five layers of this model, which establish reliable message transmission among processes and guarantee that messages are received in the same order in which they were sent. There is a major overlap of this material with that found in conventional textbooks on computer networks. As such, these sections serve only to summarize the vast amount of material that is available. The reader who is familiar with layered systems for computer networks may elect to skip these sections.

Sections 6.6 through 6.11 constitute the major thrust of this chapter and deal with the use of message passing for the coordination of high-level processes. While the focus of attention is the mutual exclusion problem, the concepts are at the very heart of most distributed process synchronization techniques. As a result, the discussion establishes a fundamental basis for forming network programs at the traditional operating system level. Several important algorithms are presented and classified according to their degree of distribution and efficiency.

6.2 Layered Structures

The model network architecture used in this chapter is a *layered structure*, a collection of layers that interface with hardware functions at the lowest level and incorporate application programs at the highest level. Figure 6.1 shows a three-layer model consisting of a communication device, an operating system layer, and an application layer. This figure illustrates the relative position of the functions of an operating system in the computer network. Network architectures proposed by the international standardization bodies and various vendors are more elaborate in that numerous sublayers and corresponding functions are specified.

6.2.1 The Reference Model of Open Systems Interconnection

Although there is no generally accepted universal model for the various types of distributed systems, the *International Organization for Standardization's Reference Model of Open Systems Interconnection (ISO OSI Reference Model)* and the National Bureau of Standards model serve as the primary bases for our description of the functions of a network [ISO, 1981; ISO, 1982a, b, c; NBS, 1983a, b, c, d, e, f]. In addition to ISO and NBS reports, other sources of information include Myers [1982], Tanenbaum [1981], and Zimmermann [1980]. The ISO OSI Reference Model was primarily designed with wide area networks in mind and, as illustrated in Figure 6.2, it defines seven layers. Each layer logically communicates with the corresponding layer on another host. This communication is termed *peer-to-peer communication*.

Communication between two hosts requires the participation of all nodes on some path between these hosts. Each intermediate node must perform the functions required by the three lowest layers of the ISO OSI Reference Model. For this reason, special-purpose processors, called *communications processors* or *front-end processors*, often serve as intermediate nodes. The collection of such processors, along with their interconnection, constitutes a communication subnet, as depicted in Figure 6.3.

The protocol for peer-to-peer communication at layer *k* is called the *layer k protocol*. In an actual implementation, messages are passed vertically down the layers at the source site, transmitted horizontally in the physical layer, and finally passed vertically up the layers at the receiving site. This is shown in Figure 6.2 by the solid

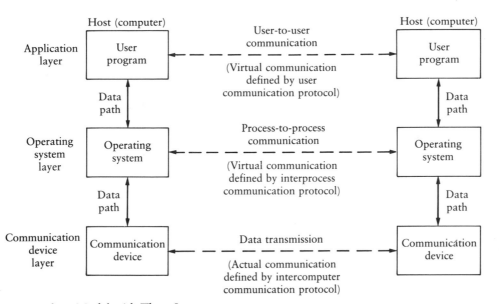

Figure 6.1 Model with Three Layers.

line. Each layer at the sending site performs some function on the information, attaches a *header,* and sends the packaged result to the next lower layer. At the receiving site, each layer removes the header associated with its level and performs the necessary work based on this information. Figure 6.4 shows this system of *enveloping.*

The lowest three layers in Figure 6.2 provide the basic communication service; these correspond to the communication device layer shown in Figure 6.1. This service is, for the most part, provided by a communication subnet depicted in Figure 6.3. The middle two layers and the top two layers in Figure 6.2 correspond to the operating system layer and the application layer, respectively, in Figure 6.1.

The functions of the seven layers of the ISO OSI Reference Model can be summarized as follows:

1. The physical layer is concerned only with the transmission of a raw bit stream between two nodes or sites. Electrical details such as the representation of 0s and 1s, the number of pins there will be in the network connector, *full-duplex* or *half-duplex* transmission, and the time duration of a bit signal must be defined in this level.

2. The data-link layer introduces reliability by providing functions for recovering from transmission errors. Regulation of the rate at which transmission flows between two directly connected nodes is also done at this level.

3. The network layer breaks a message into packets and controls both routing through the network and congestion in order to provide for high performance.

4. The transport layer provides reliable host-to-host communication and network independence by hiding the details of the communication network.

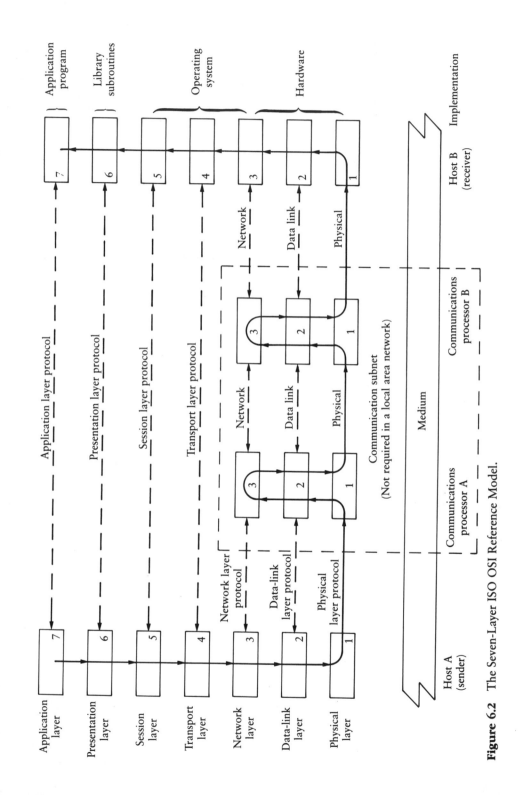

Figure 6.2 The Seven-Layer ISO OSI Reference Model.

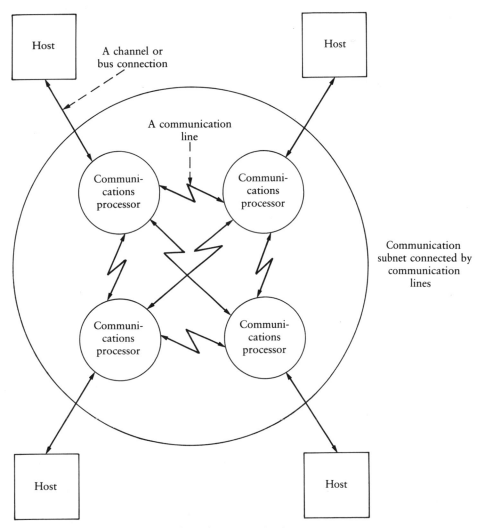

Figure 6.3   Computer Network and Communication
Subnet.

5. The session layer manages process-to-process communication. In particular,
   it establishes, manages, and closes connections between processes and also
   handles certain aspects of synchronization (such as buffering) and recovery.

6. The presentation layer provides the facilities for commonly performed data
   transformations such as text compression, encryption, and virtual terminal
   capabilities. These functions are often provided as a collection of library
   routines.

7. The application layer consists of the collection of user programs. Activity is
   initiated at this level by some process attempting to communicate with another
   process.

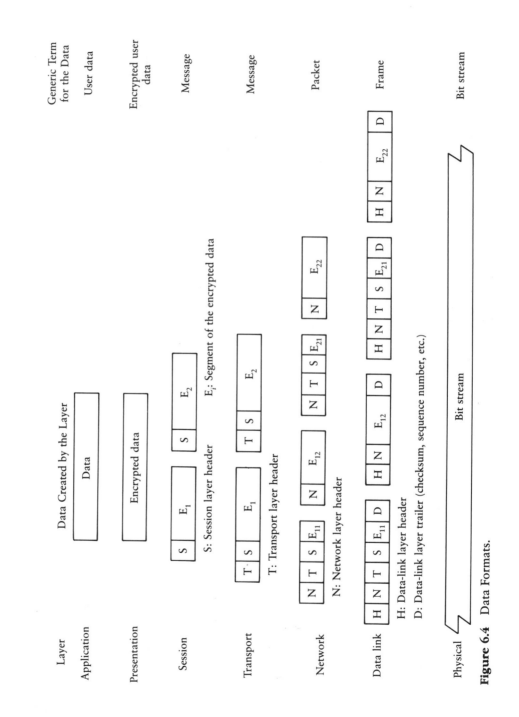

Figure 6.4 Data Formats.

This principle of structuring a network as a hierarchy of layers is widely accepted and is the basis for the design of almost all distributed systems. In the ISO OSI Reference Model, each layer is designed to be relatively independent. Modification or replacement of an implementation of one layer can be done without major impact on the enclosing layers as long as the newly implemented layer delivers the same functional service to the layer above and calls out the functional service of the layer below.

In an actual implementation, many of the functions found in the bottom three layers of the ISO Model are likely to be placed in hardware while the remaining layers are typically software functions. In this chapter, we will focus attention on the top layers.

6.2.2 The Local Area Network Reference Model

The IEEE Standards Project 802 Local Network Standards Committee has proposed a model that serves the same purpose for local area networks as the ISO OSI Reference Model does for long-haul networks [IEEE, 1982]. This *LAN reference model,* as depicted in Figure 6.5, was developed within the framework of the ISO OSI Reference Model and can be considered as a particular implementation of physical and data-link layers. A further elaboration of this model [Myers, 1982] is shown in Figure 6.6 and is called the *implementation reference model.*

The purpose of the logical link control sublayer is to initiate the interchange of control signals, organize data flow, interpret commands, generate responses, and carry out the functions of error detection and recovery. Two protocols are enforced. Type 1 protocol allows for the exchange of data units without having to go through the formalities of establishing a link connection. Type 2 protocol provides for a link connection along with the functions of acknowledgment, flow control, and error recovery. The purpose of the media access control is to support media-dependent functions, such as those described in Section 6.3.1. The functions of data encapsulation/decapsulation and data transmit/receive management are provided by the physical signaling sublayer. The encodement and decodement of signals sent to and received from the medium are performed by the physical medium attachment.

Standards for a local area network within the ISO model have also been proposed by other organizations such as American National Standards Institute [Burr, 1983].

6.2.3 Implementation Strategies

While actual implementations usually provide most of the functions of the seven layers in the ISO model, the number of layers and the division of duties among the layers will vary from one implementation to another. Figure 6.7 shows one possible implementation. A user process may communicate with either local or remote processes. "Interface 1" directs a call to either the interprocess communication facility or the session layer, depending on whether the target process is local or remote. "Interface 2" provides I/O services. The network layer of the host computer could be moved to a communications processor.

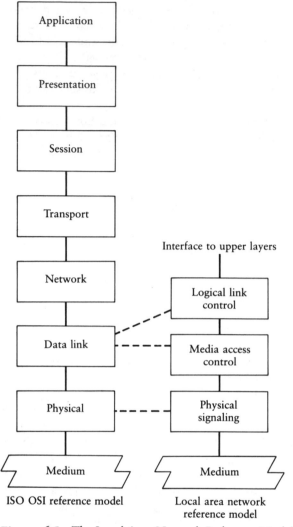

Figure 6.5   The Local Area Network Reference Model
[Myers, 1982. Copyright © 1982 by IEEE].

6.3   The First Three Layers

6.3.1   The Physical Layer

The major function of the *physical layer* is to provide a facility for transmitting a raw bit stream through the network. In this layer, there is no concern with how the bits are grouped or with recovery from transmission errors.

There are two basic approaches to using the transmission capacity (*bandwidth*) of the physical communication medium: *circuit switching* and *packet switching*.

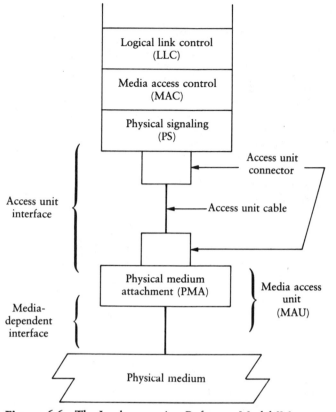

Figure 6.6   The Implementation Reference Model [Myers, 1982. Copyright © 1982 by IEEE].

With circuit switching, a fixed amount of transmission capacity is reserved when the source (sender) initiates a conversation. When the conversation is terminated, this bandwidth resource is deallocated. Circuit switching is best suited to those circumstances where the bandwidth requirements do not vary much over the duration of the conversation. With packet switching, the capacity of the communication medium is allocated on a demand basis. The unit of demand is a *packet* of information—typically 10–1000 bytes long. Because of the limitation in the size of a packet (fixed in many implementations), data must be sent as a sequence of packets. Packet switching is well-suited for bursty, short communication. The next few sections briefly describe several common communication media that are used for the physical layer.

Telephone Systems

Used mostly by long-haul networks, a telephone network is divided into two components: *local loops* and *trunks*. A local loop connects a telephone to a switch, typically using a pair of copper wires with a low bandwidth capacity. A trunk, with

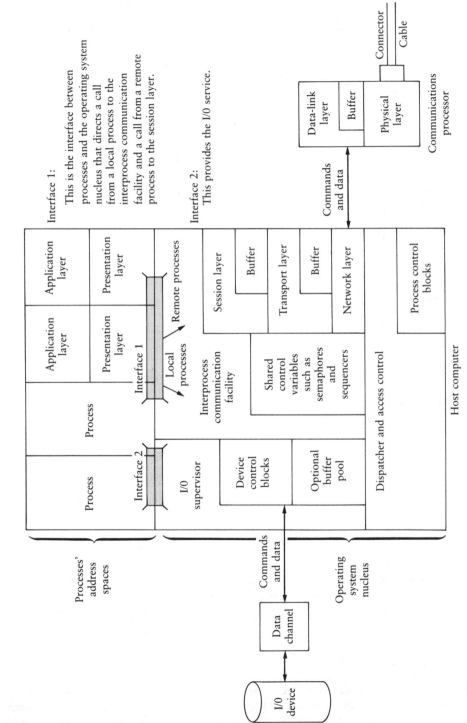

Figure 6.7 A Possible Implementation Structure of the Seven Layers in a Host Computer.

high-bandwidth capacity, connects switches and typically uses such media as microwave relays, fiber optics, or even copper wires. High bandwidth is achieved through multiplexing to allow for the simultaneous transmission of thousands of unrelated calls.

A local loop is not well-suited for sending digital signals because of the low bandwidth. Instead, a *modem* (short for "modulator/demodulator") is used to convert digital signals (from a computer) to analog signals. This conversion is performed by modulating a sine wave. There are three common techniques for modulation: amplitude modulation (AM), frequency modulation (FM), and phase modulation (PM). Their normal uses and corresponding baud rates are shown in Table 6.1. A modem is also used for demodulation from analog to digital signals. The RS-232-C interface is among the best known physical layer standards that utilizes analog signaling. The RS-449 standard is a more recent and more elaborate standard that is upward compatible with RS-232-C.

Communication Satellites

A communication satellite, placed in orbit above the equator at an altitude of approximately 23,000 miles, relays radio or television signals between ground stations in its purview. This type of communication has several important advantages: economy over long distances, high bandwidth with high reliability, and broadcast capability.

Local Area Networks

Three commonly used protocols for controlling access to LAN media are: *CSMA/CD* (carrier-sense multiple-access with collision detect), token bus, and token ring. The *Ethernet* concept [Metcalfe and Boggs, 1976] provided early impetus for the development of CSMA/CD local area networks. With the CSMA/CD access protocol, all stations continuously monitor the medium (have *carrier sense*). A station defers transmission if it detects that some other station is currently transmitting data. If simultaneous transmission does occur, it is detected by the transmitting stations and

Table 6.1 Standard Use of Modulation Methods

Data Transmission Rate (Bit/second)	Modulation Method
≤ 300	FM
≤ 1200	FM
2400	PM (4 phases)
4800	PM (8 phases)
9600	AM·PM

FM: Frequency modulation
PM: Phase modulation
AM: Amplitude modulation

retransmission is attempted after some delay. Repeated delays are avoided by assigning a different (usually random) delay time to each station. The probability of a "collision" increases with the load. Perhaps the most important advantages of CSMA/CD are its simplicity and the fact that it is easily implemented using inexpensive chips.

With the token bus protocol, a broadcast topology is assumed. A centralized controller allocates the token to a requesting site, or the token can be passed from the finished site to the next site. A site may transmit only if it has the token.

The token ring protocol assumes a logical sequential (ring) topology, in which a token is passed from one site to the next. There are three common methods for allocating the bandwidth:

1. The ring is divided into *time slots* with each slot having empty/used bits indicators. If a slot is empty, it may be used by some site for transmission.

2. A *control token* is circulated on the ring. Any site that captures the token is allowed to transmit and, upon completion, this site places the control token back on the ring.

3. *Register insertion* refers to a technique by which a transmitting site may insert a message, if necessary, between any two existing messages in transit on the ring. Local buffer storage must be available to support this method. The waiting time to initiate transmission is small, but the total transmission time varies.

Some standards for digital interfaces have been developed by CCITT (Consultative Committee on International Telegraphy and Telephony). One such standard for connecting a host to a network is X.21 [Bertine, 1980].

6.3.2 The Data-Link Layer

The *data-link layer* provides for reliable data transmission (error control) and *data flow control*. A message is partitioned into *frames* and each frame is passed to the physical layer for transmission. For long-haul networks, three common techniques are used to effect this partition: *character count, character stuffing,* and *bit stuffing.* In the first method, the header of each frame contains a count field that specifies the length of the frame. By simply counting the characters, the receiving or intermediate sites can determine where one frame stops and the next begins. In the second method, a distinguished character is used to delimit the end of a message. If this special character should happen to occur as a normal character in the text of the message, an escape character is stuffed in front of it to differentiate this point from the actual end-of-frame. If an escape character should happen to occur in the text, an additional escape character is stuffed in front of it. The third method, bit stuffing, is probably the most common technique in use today. In this method, each frame is delimited by a special end-of-frame character, denoted by the bit pattern 01111110. To prevent the occurrence of this special bit pattern in the normal text of the message, a zero bit is stuffed into the stream whenever five consecutive 1s appear in the data stream.

While any of these three methods can also be used in local area networks, a popular technique for LANs is to simply use a signal on the transmission medium to synchronize the sender and receiver prior to sending a frame.

Error detection is typically performed by including a *checksum* in a trailer field attached to each frame. Most checksum algorithms are based on modulo-2 polynomial arithmetic. Typically, the checksum is used to detect errors but not to correct them since correction requires, on the average, the transmission of more bits than would be required for error detection and retransmission of the frame.

The second major function of the data link layer, flow control, is required to synchronize the message-passing activity over a physical link. Unlike the partitioning of a message into frames and error detection, both of which can be done in the hardware, flow control is more likely to be implemented in the software.

One algorithm for flow control is the *stop-and-wait protocol,* a method that requires the sender to wait for explicit permission from the receiver before sending the next frame. Transmission errors are handled through the use of a *negative acknowledgment* to request the retransmission of an incorrect frame and the concept of a *time-out* if an acknowledgment is not returned within a reasonable time. A simple stop-and-wait protocol is inefficient if the transmission time is large, such as with satellite channels, since there can be only one outstanding unacknowledged frame at any instant. Multiple outstanding unacknowledged frames are provided for by a *sliding window protocol*. This requires the use of a sequence number to validate that the frames are received in proper order.

HDLC (high-level data link control), developed by ISO, is a protocol that incorporates the ideas of frames, error control, and flow control. The format of an HDLC frame is shown in Figure 6.8. Only the address of the receiver station appears in the frame. The "sequence" field contains the number of the current frame. Error recovery, by means of retransmission, may be initiated either by the receiver (negative acknowledgment) or by the sender (acknowledgment time-out). Flow control is performed by using a fixed-size window and by requiring the sender to wait when the receiver does not appear to have enough free buffers. Layer 2 of X.25, recommended by CCITT, is a permissible version of HDLC [Rybczynski, 1980].

In HDLC, one correspondent on a physical link is designated to be the *primary station,* which is responsible for flow control and error control. The other correspondent is designated to be the *secondary station;* this station operates in either *normal response mode* (it never transmits data unless it is instructed to do so by the primary station) or *synchronous response mode* (it may begin transmission without being instructed to do so by the primary station). The primary station uses the poll bit (P/F) to instruct the secondary station to transmit packets.

By use of the *balanced mode,* each station assumes both primary and secondary roles, thereby achieving even higher throughput. Called a *combined* station, each can initiate transmission at any time. Figure 6.9 illustrates this concept for two host nodes, A and B. Initially, both begin sending frames. Every information frame, denoted by I, is identified by a sequence number S. The receipt of information frames is acknowledged by returning the sequence number of the next expected information frame in the "next" field. This is denoted by R in the figure. Whenever possible, an acknowledgment is *piggybacked* onto an information frame. Otherwise, a receive

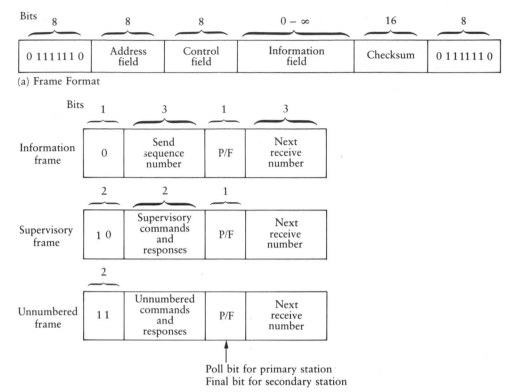

(a) Frame Format

(b) Control Byte

Figure 6.8 HDLC Frame Format.

ready (RR) supervisory frame can be used to send an acknowledgment. If an error occurs in transmission of a frame (for example, as in the frame with $S = 2$ from host B in Figure 6.9), the receiving host repeatedly asks for the same frame. This can be seen in the information frames with $S = 5$ to 1 from host A. If a sending host times-out prior to receiving an acknowledgment, all the frames after and including the frame that was incorrectly received are retransmitted.

6.3.3 The Network Layer

The *network layer* is concerned with *routing* and *congestion control*. These functions are typically not of concern in LANs. There are two basic approaches for implementing these functions. The first approach is the use of a *virtual circuit,* whereby a fixed route is established through the network to connect two hosts. To establish this connection, a setup packet is first transmitted in order to choose a route between the sending and receiving hosts and to initialize the communications processors along the route. Subsequent packets of information, for this extended conversation, are simply sent along this fixed route (circuit). The *datagram* approach requires no

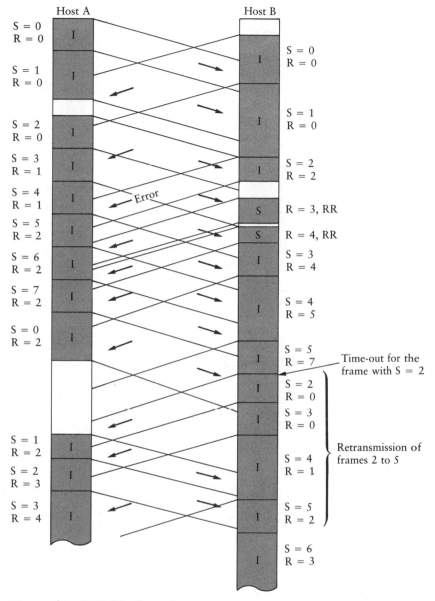

Figure 6.9   HDLC in Operation.

predetermined connection. Instead, a separate routing decision is made for each individual packet (datagram). The datagram approach is well suited for short and bursty communication. The virtual circuit approach is better suited for longer communication with predictable bandwidth requirements. For example, the transfer of a large file that must be broken into a sequence of packets might be best handled by a virtual circuit approach. The protocol X.25, which was defined by CCITT, is perhaps

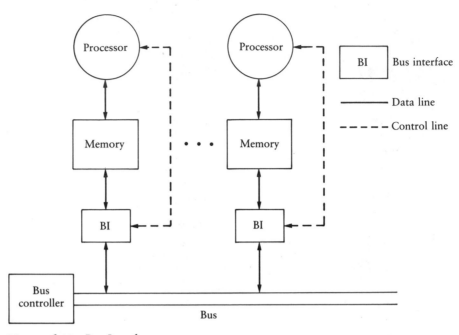

Figure 6.10   Bus Interface.

the best known protocol standard for the network layer [Rybczinski, 1980].[1] It utilizes the concept of a virtual circuit.

6.3.4   Multicomputer Organizations

A multicomputer organization with a common bus interconnection allows for a major simplification of the lowest three layers. These functions are typically performed by a general bus controller and a bus interface (BI) for each computer. A generalized structure of a such a system is shown in Figure 6.10. Responding to commands from an associated processor, a BI communicates with this processor in initiating and terminating data transmission. To effect data transmission, BIs communicate with each other according to a protocol imposed by the bus controller (see Sections 6.2.2 and 6.3.1). The bus may be multiplexed either byte/word-wise or packet-wise. In the former case, multiple bytes are carried simultaneously (streamed) over the bus, an approach that is highly suited for high data-rate transmission between computer memories. Packet-wise multiplexing is better suited for data transmission involving a slower I/O device. In a multicomputer organization, a simple transmission service typically provides primitives such as

---

[1]Actually, X.25 is the collective name for all three basic layers, with X.21 as the physical layer.

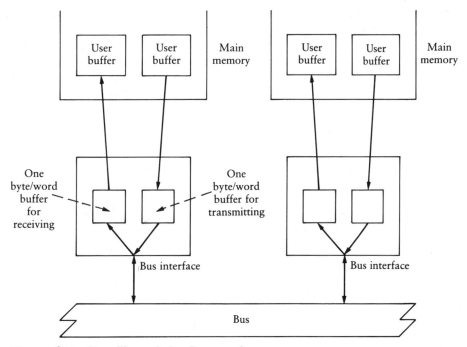

Figure 6.11 Data Transmission Between Computers.

request (destination, write command address)

request (source, read command address)

send-interrupt (destination, interrupt word)

where a command has the form: *read/write, data address, data size*. A request with
a *write* command causes the BI to initiate the transmission of *data size* units of data
from the memory area starting at *data address* to the *destination* computer. The BI
uses a byte or word buffer, as illustrated in Figure 6.11. It is assumed that the receiver
(destination computer) has already issued a request with a *read* command so that
its BI is ready to receive data. The *data address* and *data size* fields for a *read* have
a similar interpretation. The amount of information transmitted is limited by the
minimum of the two sizes specified by the hosts. The completion of a read or write
request results in a conventional interrupt being sent to the issuing processor.

Synchronization of read and write requests between the source and destination
computers is accomplished through use of the *send-interrupt* primitive. This is illustrated in Figure 6.12. The sender executes a *send-interrupt,* causing an interrupt to
occur in the destination processor. The associated *interrupt word* carries information
needed by the receiver to allocate an input buffer. The receiver then executes a *read*
request command and a *send-interrupt* to inform the sender that the receiver is ready.
Upon receiving this latter interrupt, the sender transmits the data using a *write*
request command. Flow control between the sender and receiver is performed using
a stop-and-wait protocol or some other usually simple protocol tailored to the spe-
cifics of the hardware.

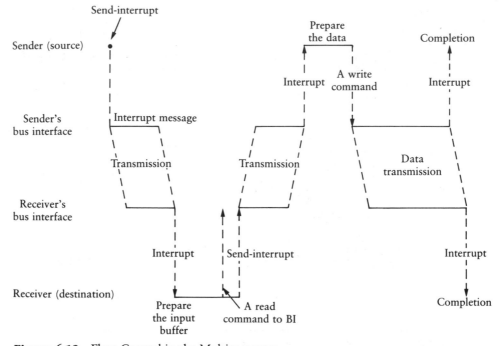

Figure 6.12   Flow Control in the Multicomputer Organization.

6.4   The Middle Two Layers

6.4.1   The Transport Layer

The purpose of the *transport layer* is to provide reliable *host-to-host* communication and to hide all details of the communication subnet from the session layer. The software that implements this layer is called the *transport station* or *transport entity*. The entities that request the transport services, usually representing hosts, are called *transport users*. A transport station establishes and tears down connections between transport users, and performs such services as blocking, segmenting, multiplexing, buffering, flow control, sequence control, and error control. Connections are full-duplex, and messages in each direction are sequentially numbered for the purposes of sequencing and error.

The standards for the transport protocol, drafted by ISO, specify the following services: connection establishment, graceful termination, abrupt termination, status reporting, data transfer, expedited data transfer, and connectionless data transfer. For each of these services, there are five primitives that define the functionality and interface to/from the transport layer from/to the higher layers:

1. Request (user to transport station)
2. Indication (transport station to user)

3. Response (user to transport station)
4. Confirm (transport station to user)
5. Cancel (user to transport station)

Table 6.2 illustrates the protocol followed by two hosts in successfully establishing a transport connection.

The *destination* and *source transport addresses* identify the end transport users. The user can specify requirements for the *quality of service* in terms of throughput, transit delay, reliability, and relative priority of the connection. The transport stations negotiate to select the corresponding *class of service,* protocol options, and size of a sliding-window sequence space. The *buffer management* parameter is used to indicate the amount of buffer space to be allocated. The *security parameters* indicate the level of security associated with the connection establishment attempt and the subsequent transfer of user data.

Peer-to-peer communication between transport stations is accomplished by sending and receiving transport-protocol-data-units (TPDUs). Ten TPDU types are defined to support the following functions: connection request (CR), connection confirm (CC), disconnect request (DR), disconnect confirm (DC), graceful close request (GR), TPDU error (ERR), transfer data (DT), transfer expedited data (XPD), acknowledge (AK), and expedited acknowledgment (XAK). A TPDU has the following structure with the maximum size negotiated during connection establishment:

Header
    Length Indicator Field   Indicates length of header
    Fixed Part   Control information including type of TPDU
    Variable Part   Optional parameters
Data   Used only for DT and XPD

Table 6.2 Transport Protocol Followed by Two Hosts

Host	Command	Parameters	Direction
A	CONNECT.request	Destination and source transport addresses Quality of service, buffer management, security parameters, data	User to Station
B	CONNECT.indication	Destination and source transport addresses, quality of service, security parameters, data	Station to User
B	CONNECT.response	Quality of service, buffer management, security parameters, data	User to Station
A	CONNECT.confirm	Quality of service, security parameters, data	Station to User

Through the use of unique identifiers assigned to a connection by each transport station multiple connections between transport stations are possible.

If the network layer is reliable, a simple two-way request-acknowledge protocol can be be used to establish a connection. If the network layer is unreliable, a three-way handshake procedure is commonly used to establish a connection. The need for such a protocol arises since a transmission failure might lead to the establishment of an incorrect connection. The following example illustrates how this might happen:

INCORRECT CONNECTION

- Station A sends a CR TPDU with the starting sequence number 600. This TPDU gets lost in the network.
- Station B receives an old delayed CR TPDU with the sequence number 200 from A.
- Station B sends a CC TPDU with the starting sequence number 1000. This TPDU gets lost.
- Station A receives an old delayed CC TPDU with the sequence number 700 from B.

A connection is established with A sending message 600 but B expecting message 200. Similarly, B sends message 1000: but A expects message 700. Both stations will continuously respond with ERR TPDUs. The *three-way* handshake procedure prevents establishment of wrong connections [Tomlinson, 1975]. In this case

CORRECT CONNECTION

- Station A sends a CR TPDU with the starting sequence number 600.
- Station B returns a CC TPDU with its own starting sequence number 1000 and acknowledges 600.
- Station A sends an AK TPDU with sequence number 601 and acknowledgment 1000.

The connection is established only when A and B have both received the proper TPDUs. The starting sequence number is, in general, required to prevent the occurrence of duplicate messages in the network.

In order to gracefully terminate a connection between transport users, the CLOSE.request and CLOSE.indication primitives are used. The initiating user issues a CLOSE.request, resulting in the transport station sending a GR TPDU (after sending all pending data TPDUs). The GR TPDU contains the sequence number of the last data TPDU so the peer transport station can be sure that all data has been received. The peer transport station responds with an AK TPDU and informs its transport user by means of a CLOSE.indication. Termination of the other direction of the connection is accomplished by the same sequence. The connection is terminated when both directions have been closed. This termination procedure works if the network level is reliable. If it is not reliable, the peer station cannot be sure that the AK has arrived and the termination has been successfully completed. Unfortunately, extending the protocol with more AK TPDUs does not change the circumstances, since there is no guarantee that the last AK will be received.

The transfer of data between two transport users is accomplished by use of DATA.request (by the the sending user) and DATA.indication (by the receiving user). The transport station may divide the data and send a sequence of data TPDUs. Upon receipt of one or more data TPDUs, the peer station sends an AK TPDU.

Although flow control is performed in the data-link and network layers, the problem is more acute in the transport layer since a large number of transport connections may be open. It is important to achieve high throughput without over-committing the available buffer space. A stop-and-wait protocol would severely limit the throughput, and dynamic assignment of buffers to connections on a demand basis invites deadlock or unfair allocation. Therefore, more complicated protocols and buffer management are required.

Two basic flow control techniques are the *sliding window,* and *M and N pacing.* The sliding window method can be used for a connection that has a dedicated set of buffers. Figure 6.13 illustrates a sliding window with a sequence number space equal to 8 and a window size of 3. The window size, directly related to the size of the buffer space, determines the maximum number of data units that can be accom-modated. Both the sending and receiving stations maintain individual windows of the same size. The sending station is allowed to transmit a data unit that falls within its window. If the receiving station receives a data unit with a sequence number that does not fall within the range of the receiver's window, the data unit is discarded. An acknowledgment of sequence number $S + 1$ by the receiver indicates receipt of data units up to and including the data unit with sequence number S. At this time, the receiver's window is rotated so that its left edge is at $S + 1$. Upon receiving an

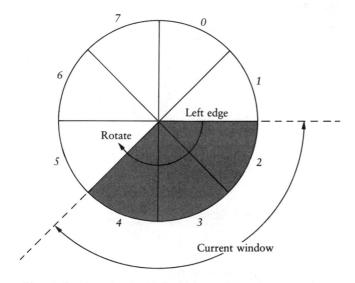

The window is maintained in both the sending and receiving hosts. The sending host's window is rotated to the left when an acknowledg-ment is received, while the receiving host's window is rotated when it has returned an acknowledgment.

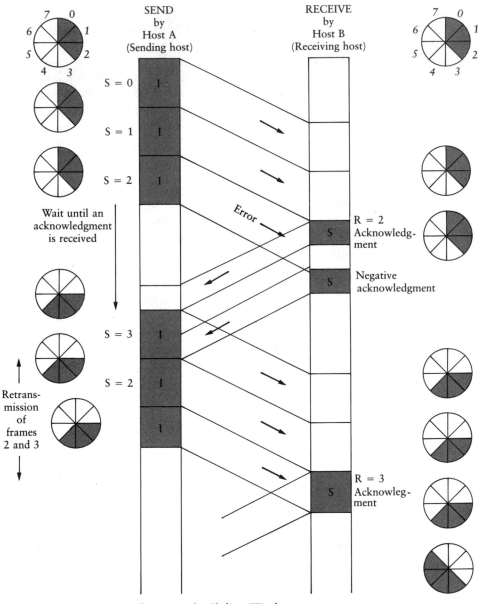

Figure 6.14 Data Transfer Using the Sliding Window
Method.

acknowledgment, the sender rotates its window to the same point. Figure 6.14
illustrates the use of sliding windows in flow control.

Figure 6.15 illustrates the M and N pacing method. The sending station sends
a request for N buffers. When the receiving station returns an acknowledgment, the
sender is free to transmit N data units. In order to utilize this otherwise lost bandwidth between the request and the acknowledgment, the receiver may send a *per-*

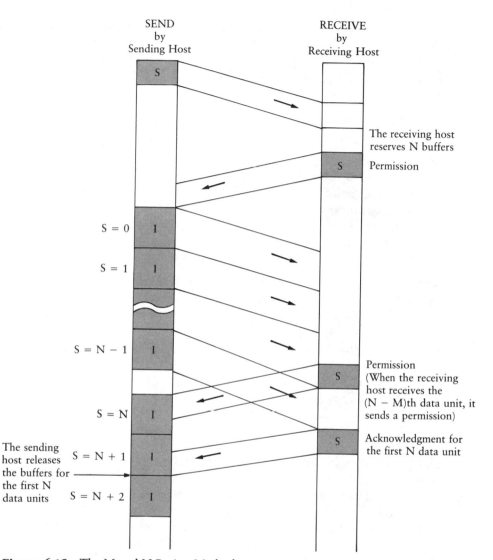

Figure 6.15 The M and N Pacing Method.

mission when it has received $(N - M)$ data units, where M is generally an increasing function of the delay between the sending and receiving hosts. The value of M may vary from 2 or 3 for a terrestrial network (if there are no intermediate hosts that must handle the data) to 30 or more for satellite links.

Other services provided by the transport layer include:

Connectionless service: A user may send a single-unit data without the overhead of establishing and tearing down a connection.

Expedited data service: A user may send a limited amount of information, bypassing the normal flow control.

Abrupt termination: A user can inform the correspondent that the connection has been terminated. The normal protocol for closing the connection is bypassed and pending data will be lost.

Status service: A user can inquire about the status of a correspondent.

6.4.2   The Session Layer

While the transport layer maintains connections between hosts, the *session layer* maintains connections (called *sessions*) between specific pairs of processes. Many networks do not distinguish between these layers, and even the ISO OSI Reference Model is vague on this point. The session layer service may provide a set of primitives similar to that of the transport layer. In fact, multiple sessions could be multiplexed on the same transport layer connection. Generally at most one session can be open between two processes at any point in time.

Other services provided by the session layer include:

Quarantine service: A group of messages on the receiving side is buffered until the session layer on the sending side sends an explicit release. This facility allows for the construction of a collection of messages as an atomic unit, as might be needed in a database system.

Dialog control: This facility supports asynchronous message communication between processes. If the sender does not block, it may have multiple requests outstanding for the same session. The dialog control ensures that the replies are matched with the corresponding requests.

6.5   Proprietary Network Architectures

Many computer and/or network vendors have developed their own network architectures. Several are contrasted with the ISO model in this section. Although they are distinctly different, they also have many common features and the current trend is toward the international standards described in previous sections. Early architectures include IBM'S *System Network Architecture (SNA)* and Digital Equipment Corporation's *Digital Network Architecture (DNA),* also known as *DECnet.* Well-known local area networks include Ethernet by Xerox.

The layers of SNA are shown in Figure 6.16. Since the first layer is identical to layer 1 of the ISO OSI Reference Model, it is not explicitly shown. The *link control* layer corresponds directly to layer 2 of the ISO model. SDLC (synchronous data link control), a permissible subset of HDLC, is used. The *path control* layer is basically equivalent to layer 3, although it differs in detail. The functions of layers 4, 6, and 7 of the ISO model are distributed somewhat differently in the *transmission control, data flow control,* and *network addressable units (NAU) services* layers. Users access the network by means of NAUs that are actually access ports.

Figure 6.17 shows the layers of DNA. The digital data communications management protocol (DDCMP) layer corresponds to layer 2 of the ISO model. The trans-

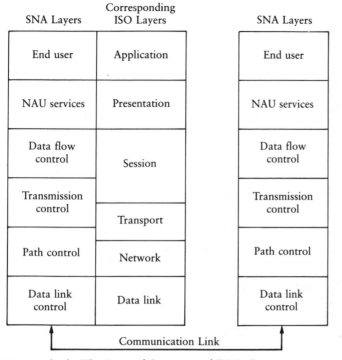

SNA Layers	Corresponding ISO Layers	SNA Layers
End user	Application	End user
NAU services	Presentation	NAU services
Data flow control	Session	Data flow control
Transmission control		Transmission control
	Transport	
Path control	Network	Path control
Data link control	Data link	Data link control

Communication Link

Figure 6.16 The Layered Structure of IBM's System Network Architecture (SNA).

port layer and network services protocol (NSP) layer perform, in general, the functions of layers 3 and 4 of the ISO model. DNA has no layer that corresponds to layer 5 of the ISO model. The application (A) layer includes program service functions such as remote file access, file transfer, terminal control, and database transaction requests.

Xerox's Ethernet is an LAN that implements CSMA/CD. Named after the hypothetical substance *ether,* which was once thought to be a medium for propagating radiation, the transmission media could include coaxial cable, twisted pairs, optical fibers, or radio. Figure 6.18 shows a typical Ethernet configuration. As shown in Figure 6.19, the packet format is extremely simple. This is generally true for local area networks because of their usual high reliability and topological simplicity.

The reader is referred to Meijer and Peters [1982] for a description of these and numerous recently developed network architectures.

6.6 Distributed Process Management

Processes interact with each other, either in a cooperative effort to achieve a common objective, or in competition for resources. Chapters 2 and 3 illustrated how such interaction may be accomplished in shared memory systems. The concern in this

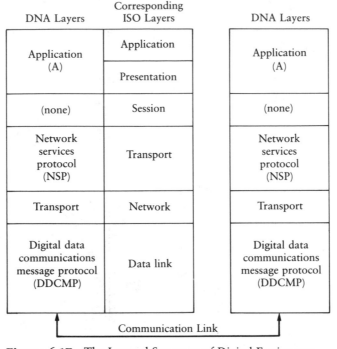

DNA Layers	Corresponding ISO Layers		DNA Layers
Application (A)	Application		Application (A)
	Presentation		
(none)	Session		(none)
Network services protocol (NSP)	Transport		Network services protocol (NSP)
Transport	Network		Transport
Digital data communications message protocol (DDCMP)	Data link		Digital data communications message protocol (DDCMP)

Communication Link

Figure 6.17 The Layered Structure of Digital Equipment Corporation's Digitial Network Architecture (DNA or DECnet).

section is with process interaction in a distributed system. The focus of attention is on mutual exclusion since this is the basis for process coordination. At this level of the network, we assume that a reliable underlying message-passing system is in place, such as that provided by layers 1–5 of the ISO OSI Reference Model.

6.6.1 Issues in Distributed Algorithms

The Characterization of Distributed Algorithms

Algorithms for mutual exclusion may vary from fully centralized to fully distributed. In a fully centralized control, one node is designated as the control node; this controls access to a shared object. Whenever a node wishes to gain access to the shared object, it sends a REQUEST message to the control node, which returns a REPLY (permission) message when the shared object becomes available (allocated) to the node. A centralized algorithm is characterized by the following properties:

1. Only the central (control) node makes a decision.
2. All necessary information is concentrated in the central control node.

Some variations of this idea exist, such as the idea that the central control can migrate from node to node. The weaknesses of this type of system are its vulnerability

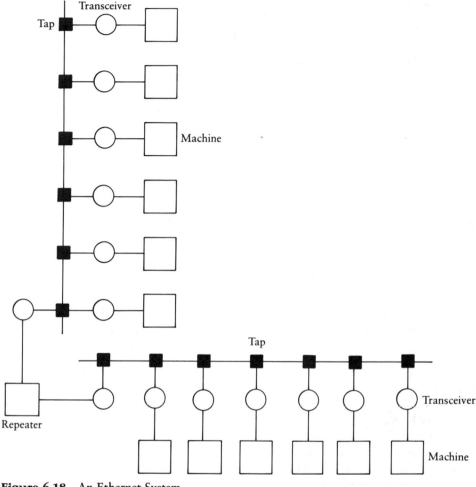

Figure 6.18 An Ethernet System.

to failure of the central control and the possibility that the central control may become a bottleneck. If these problems can be tolerated, then the central control method is suitable.

A "fully distributed" algorithm is characterized by these properties:

1. All nodes have an equal amount of information.
2. All nodes make a decision based solely on local information.
3. All nodes bear equal responsibility for the final decision.
4. All nodes expend equal effort in effecting a final decision.
5. Failure of a node, in general, does not result in a total system collapse.

In practice, there are very few fully distributed algorithms. Some algorithms, for example, may dictate that every node bears an equal amount of responsibility, while

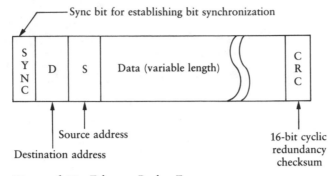

Figure 6.19 Ethernet Packet Format.

the amount of effort to obtain mutual exclusion is not equal. For other algorithms, the reverse might be true. Still others may lead to a total collapse of the system if even a single node fails.

Regardless of the manner and degree of distribution, there are two fundamental assumptions common to all *distributed algorithms:*

Assumption 1: Each node has only a partial picture of the total system and must make decisions based on this information.

Assumption 2: There exists no system-wide common clock.

This latter assumption is a major constraint since the temporal ordering of events is a fundamental concept in our view of computer systems. To say that an event *a* occurred before event *b* in a distributed system is not precise for two reasons. First, there may be a delay (message transmission time) between the actual occurrence of an event and the time that it is actually observed. Second, if each node contains a physical clock, inaccuracies would lead to a variance in their readings. In order to establish a firm basis for the design of distributed algorithms, we must find a way to circumvent this impression.

Ordering of Events in a Distributed System

In this section, we discuss a method attributed to Lamport [Lamport, 1978] for ordering events in a distributed system without using physical clocks. We assume that processes are sequential, so that events within a single process are totally ordered in time. Furthermore, we assume that the event of "sending" a message occurs before the event of "receiving" the same message. These assumptions naturally provide a partial ordering of events in the system, which is termed the *happened-before relation*. Denoted by "→", the happened-before relation is precisely defined as follows:

1. $a \rightarrow b$

   (i) if *a* and *b* are events in the same process such that *a* occurs before *b*, or

   (ii) if *a* is the sending of a message by one process and *b* is the receipt of the same message by another process.

2. The relation is transitive: If $a \to b$ and $b \to c$, then $a \to c$.

3. If no ordering exists between two distinct events, that is, if $a \nrightarrow b$ and $b \nrightarrow a$, then a and b are said to be *concurrent*.

We want to introduce a system of logical clocks whose values reflect this relation.

For each process P_i, we assume a logical clock C_i exists that assigns a number $C_i(a)$ to an event a in that process.[2] This logical clock C_i can be implemented by a counter. We denote by C the system of clocks C_i. For a system of logical clocks C to be correct, the following condition must hold:

Clock Condition
For any events a and b, if $a \to b$, then $C(a)$ must be less than $C(b)$.

The clock condition is satisfied if the following two conditions hold:

Condition 1
For two events a and b in process P_i, such that a comes before b, $C_i(a) < C_i(b)$.

Condition 2
If a is the event of sending a message m by process P_i and b is the receipt of m by process P_j, then $C_i(a) < C_j(b)$.

Conditions 1 and 2 can be satisfied by implementing the clocks so that the following conditions hold:

• P_i increments C_i between any two successive events.

• If a denotes the event of sending a message m by process P_i, then the message m bears the *timestamp* $T_m = C_i(a)$.

• When the message m is received, process P_j sets C_j to a value that is greater than or equal to its present value and greater than T_m.

It is now possible to induce a total ordering on the collection of events in our distributed system. Event a in process P_i precedes (denoted by $=>$) event b in process P_j if and only if

1. $C_i(a) < C_j(b)$, or

2. $C_i(a) = C_j(b)$, and $P_i << P_j$, where the relation $<<$ is an arbitrary total ordering of the processes.

A simple way to implement the relation $<<$ is to assign a unique process number to each process and to define $P_i << P_j$ if $i < j$.

6.6.2 Requirements for Distributed Mutual Exclusion Algorithms

Numerous algorithms have been proposed to implement mutual exclusion in a distributed system [Lamport, 1978; Thomas, 1979; Gifford, 1979; Ricart and Agra-

---

[2]Actually, the clock could be associated with the node on which the process is running.

wala, 1981; Maekawa, 1985]. Although they differ in requirements and objectives, these *distributed mutual exclusion algorithms* share several common assumptions and characteristics:

1. A distributed system consists of N nodes, uniquely numbered from 1 to N. Each node contains a process that makes a request for mutually exclusive access to the resource. This request is communicated to other processes.
2. The *pipelining* property holds—that is, messages sent from one process to another are received in the same order in which they are sent.
3. Every message is correctly delivered to its destination in a finite amount of time.
4. The network is fully connected; for example, each process can send messages directly to every other process.

Assumptions 2 and 3 are assumed to be realized by the methods described in Sections 6.2–6.5.

In our model of a distributed system, each process not only issues a request to access the resource, but also serves as an arbitrator to resolve requests that overlap in time. In order to arbitrate requests, any pair of two requests must be made known to at least one of the arbitrators. Suppose, for example, that process i must obtain a permission from each member of a subset S_i of the processes in the network in order to access the resource. Then, in order to ensure mutual exclusion for processes i and j, there must exist at least one arbitrating process common to S_i and S_j. This is formally stated as

(a) *Pairwise Nonnull Intersection Property:* $S_i \cap S_j \neq \phi$ for any combination of i and j, $1 \leq i,j \leq N$.

Assuming this property, mutual exclusion is guaranteed if every process i that requests access to the resource obtains permission from every member of S_i. This property is a necessary condition for enforcing mutual exclusion. In addition, the following properties are desirable:

(b) *Equal Effort Rule:* $|S_1| = \cdots = |S_N| = K$ where $|S_i|$ denotes the size of S_i.
(c) *Equal Responsibility Rule:* Every process j, $1 \leq j \leq N$, is contained in exactly the same number D of S_i's, $1 \leq i \leq N$.
(d) S_i, $1 \leq i \leq N$, always contains process i.

Properties (b) and (c) are necessary for a fully distributed algorithm. Property (d) is included simply to reduce by one the numbers of messages to be sent and received.

It should be noted that a centralized algorithm would designate a single process as a controller (arbitrator). This controller is contained in every S_i and thus it satisfies property (b) with $K = 1$. However, it violates property (c) because the controller node is the only node contained in every S_i.

6.7 Lamport's Algorithm

In addition to the requirements for distributed mutual exclusion, Lamport's problem [Lamport, 1978] requires that requests for a resource be granted in the order in which they are made. This is a nontrivial problem even if central control is used. For example, suppose process P_1 sends a request to a central scheduler process P_0 and a message to P_2 announcing the request. Upon receiving the message, P_2 also sends a request to P_0. It is possible that P_2's request will reach P_0 before P_1's request and that P_0 will grant access to P_2. This violates the requirement of the problem.

The following distributed algorithm, known as *Lamport's algorithm,* satisfies all requirements of the problem. The underlying assumptions are:

1. A request message REQUEST from process P_i is timestamped with (T_i, i), where $T_i = C_i$ is the clock value for process i associated with sending the message.

2. Each process maintains a *request queue,* initially empty, that contains REQUEST messages ordered by the relation $=>$.

The algorithm is defined by the following five rules. It is assumed that each rule forms a locally indivisible operation.

1. When process P_i requests a resource, it puts that message on its own request queue and sends a REQUEST(T_i, i) to every other process.

2. When process P_j receives the REQUEST(T_i, i) message, it returns a timestamped REPLY message and places the message on its request queue.

3. Process P_i is allowed to access the resource when the following two conditions are satisfied:

   (i) P_i's own REQUEST message is at the front of its queue.

   (ii) P_i has received a message from every other process with a time stamp later than (T_i, i).

4. To release the resource, process P_i removes the REQUEST message from its own queue and sends a timestamped RELEASE message to every other process.

5. When process P_j receives P_i's RELEASE message, it removes P_i's REQUEST message from its queue.

Verification that the algorithm is correct follows from these observations:

1. Rule 3(ii), together with the assumption that messages are received in order, guarantees that P_i has learned about all requests that preceded its current request.

2. Since the relation $=>$ totally orders requests, Rule 3(i) permits one and only one process to access the resource at any constant.

This algorithm satisfies conditions (b) and (c) for a distributed algorithm as stated in Section 6.6.2. In fact, every process maintains all information and actually simulates a central scheduling process. The total number of messages required to obtain and release access to a resource is $3(N - 1)$: $(N - 1)$ REQUEST messages, $(N - 1)$ REPLY messages, and $(N - 1)$ RELEASE messages.

6.8   Ricart and Agrawala's Algorithm

Ricart and Agrawala's algorithm [Ricart and Agrawala, 1981] solves the same mutual exclusion problem but it is more efficient than Lamport's solution in that at most $2(N - 1)$ messages are required. As before, the request queues are totally ordered by the $=>$ relation. The following steps describe the refinement to Lamport's algorithm:

1. When process P_i requests a resource, it sends a REQUEST(T_i, i) message to every other process.

2. When process P_j receives the REQUEST message, it performs the following operations:

   (i) If P_j is not currently requesting the resource, it returns a (timestamped) REPLY message.

   (ii) When process P_j is requesting the resource and the time stamp of its request (T_j, j) precedes (T_i, i), process P_i's REQUEST is retained; otherwise, a REPLY message is returned.

3. When process P_i receives a REPLY message from every other node, it is granted the resource.

4. When process P_i releases the resource, it returns a REPLY for each pending REQUEST message.

The state transition diagram for each process is shown in Figure 6.20.

An Ada version of Ricart and Agrawala's algorithm is presented below. The distributed system consists of N processes, uniquely numbered from 1 to N. Each process is actually implemented by two Ada tasks: USER_TASK and MUTUAL_EXCLUSION. USER_TASK is a user task that requests use of the resource. MUTUAL_EXCLUSION is a task that performs the algorithm on behalf of the user task. This latter task defines five entries: INVOKE, which is called by the user task to request access to the resource, WAIT to wait for a permission, RELEASE to release the resource, and RECEIVE REQUEST and RECEIVE_REPLY, which are used to receive REQUEST and REPLY messages from other MUTUAL_EXCLUSION tasks.

```
task body USER_TASK is
begin
   .
   .
   .
   MUTUAL_EXCLUSION.INVOKE;
```

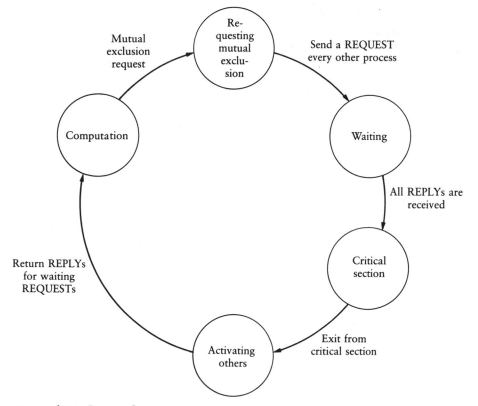

Figure 6.20 Process States.

```
MUTUAL_EXCLUSION.WAIT;
critical section;
MUTUAL_EXCLUSION. RELEASE;
    .
    .
    .
end USER_TASK;

task MUTUAL_EXCLUSION is
    entry INVOKE;
    entry WAIT;
    entry RELEASE;
    entry RECEIVE_REQUEST (k: in INTEGER; j: in INTEGER);
        k: the sequence number of the REQUEST
        j: the number of the node that sent the REQUEST
    entry RECEIVE_REPLY;
end;
```

```
task body MUTUAL_EXCLUSION is
  me : constant := ···; --the node's unique number
  N : constant := ···; --the number of nodes in the system
  OSN : INTEGER := 0; --the sequence number to be assigned to the next local
                        --request
  HSN : INTEGER := 0; --the highest sequence number seen in any REQUEST
                        --message sent or received
  ORC : INTEGER := 0; --the number of REPLY messages still expected
  RCS : BOOLEAN := FALSE; --TRUE when this node is requesting access to
                            --its critical section; otherwise FALSE
  RD : array (1..N) of BOOLEAN := (FALSE,FALSE, ··· ,FALSE);
            --RD(j) is TRUE when this node is deferring a REPLY to
            --node j's REQUEST message

  S : SEMAPHORE := 1; --interlock access to the above local shared data

begin
  loop
    select
      accept INVOKE do
        OSN := HSN + 1;
        RCS := TRUE;
        ORC := N - 1;
        for j in 1..N loop
          if j ≠ me then send a REQUEST message to node j;
          end if;
        end loop;
      end;
    or
      when ORC = 0 =>
      accept WAIT;
    or
      accept RELEASE do
        RCS := FALSE;
        for j in 1..N loop
          if RD(j) then
            send a REPLY(j) message;
            RD(j) := FALSE;
          end if;
        end loop;
      end;
    or
      accept RECEIVE_REQUEST (k: in INTEGER,
                  j: in INTEGER) do
        declare
          DEFER : BOOLEAN;
```

```
      begin
        HSN := max(HSN,k);
        DEFER := RCS and ((k>OSN) or
              (k=OSN and j>me));
        if DEFER then RD(j) := TRUE;
        else send a REPLY(j) message;
        end if;
      end;
    end;
  or
    accept RECEIVE_REPLY do
      ORC := ORC − 1;
    end;
  end select;
  end loop;
end MUTUAL_EXCLUSION;
```

Inspection of this algorithm reveals several important features:

1. All requests will be totally ordered since

   a. A new request is assigned a sequence number (OSN) that is greater than the sequence number of any previous REQUEST known to the node; and

   b. Ties, which occur among the REQUESTs sent by nodes that are not yet aware of each other's request, are resolved by the node numbers.

   This total ordering provides the desired mutual exclusion.

2. Control is fully distributed.

3. Deadlock cannot occur since no cycle of waiting nodes can occur.

4. Starvation cannot occur since ordering is first-come, first-served, and no node dominates any other node.

5. The algorithm is independent of the characteristics of the communication system.

6. The algorithm requires at most $2(N - 1)$ messages to service a request.

6.9 Maekawa's Square-Root Algorithm

6.9.1 Other Improvement Techniques

Several techniques can be used to reduce even further the number of messages required to implement distributed mutual exclusion. The Thomas majority consensus rule [Thomas, 1979] is based on the idea that permission to access the resource is needed only from a majority of the processes. Correctly implemented, no two processes can acquire a majority vote on their requests since the intersection of the two majorities is a nonnull set of arbitrators. Therefore, at least one arbitrator will vote favorably for one request and unfavorably for the other. The number of messages required to obtain permission to access a resource is, in the best case, $N/2$. Extensions of this method, proposed by Gifford [1979] and Skeen [1982], allow some processes to cast more than one vote (that is, to cast a weighted vote). In weighted voting schemes, it is sufficient to obtain a majority of the total votes, although not necessarily from a majority of the arbitrators, in order to access the resource. By proper distribution of the votes, the algorithm can be varied from centralized to distributed. For instance, if one process is given all the votes, while all others are given no votes, the algorithm reduces to a central control.

It is clear that Lamport's algorithm, Ricart and Agrawala's algorithm, and Thomas's algorithm satisfy properties (a), (b) and (c) of Section 6.6.2, with $K = D = N$. In general, the weighted voting algorithms do not satisfy property (c). If the total weight is not equally distributed among the processes, then the resulting algorithm is not fully distributed.

Maekawa's square-root algorithm further reduces the number of required messages by choosing a minimum K and a minimum D that satisfy conditions (b) and (c).

6.9.2 Theoretical and Conceptual Basis for Maekawa's Algorithm

In order to motivate Maekawa's algorithm, we restate here the conditions of Section 6.6.2 for a distributed algorithm:

(a) $S_i \cap S_j \neq \phi$ for any combination of i and j, $1 \leq i, j \leq N$.

(b) $|S_1| = \cdots = |S_N| = K$.

(c) Any j, $1 \leq j \leq N$, is contained in D S_i's, $1 \leq i \leq N$.

(d) S_i, $1 \leq i \leq N$, always contains i.

Maekawa's square-root algorithm satisfies all four properties and, in addition, is optimal in that it minimizes the values of K and D. From properties (c) and (d), each member of S_i can be contained in $(D - 1)$ other subsets. Therefore, the maximum number of subsets that satisfies property (a) is given by $(D - 1)K + 1$. In order for K to be minimized for a given N, we have

$$N = (D - 1)K + 1$$

Furthermore, $K = D$ must always hold since N must be KN/D, the total number of members divided by the number of duplications of each member. N is thus related to K by

$$N = K(K - 1) + 1$$

Under the constraints of conditions (a) through (d), it is clear from this discussion that K gives the optimal value for a given N. Within a fractional error, we see that $K = \sqrt{N}$.

The problem of finding a set of S_i's that satisfies these conditions is equivalent to finding a *finite projective plane* of N points. It is known that there exists a finite projective plane of order k if k is a power p^m of a prime p [Albert and Sandler, 1968]. This finite projective plane has $k(k + 1) + 1$ points. Hence, in our terms, a set of S_i's exists if $(K - 1)$ is a power of a prime. For other values of K, we can create a set of S_i's by relaxing, to a small extent, conditions (b) and (c). For values of N that cannot be expressed as $K(K - 1) + 1$, we can still apply the method by creating a set of S_i's for a larger N and then discarding some sets. The creation of S_i's is discussed later. Figure 6.21 shows examples for $K = 2$, 3, 4, and 5.

Each node in the system executes an identical algorithm. The algorithm is based on the idea that i is allowed to access the resource if it is able to lock all members of S_i. If successful, then property (a) guarantees that no other node j will be able to lock all of its members. If it is unsuccessful, then it waits for an already locked

Figure 6.21   Mutually Nondisjoint Subsets of Integers.

$S_1 = \{1, 2\}$
$S_3 = \{1, 3\}$
$S_2 = \{2, 3\}$

(a) $K = 2$

$S_1 = \{1, 2, 3\}$
$S_4 = \{1, 4, 5\}$
$S_6 = \{1, 6, 7\}$
$S_2 = \{2, 4, 6\}$
$S_5 = \{2, 5, 7\}$
$S_7 = \{3, 4, 7\}$
$S_3 = \{3, 5, 6\}$

(b) $K = 3$

$S_1 = \{1, 2, 3, 4\}$
$S_5 = \{1, 5, 6, 7\}$
$S_8 = \{1, 8, 9, 10\}$
$S_{11} = \{1, 11, 12, 13\}$
$S_2 = \{2, 5, 8, 11\}$
$S_6 = \{2, 6, 9, 12\}$
$S_7 = \{2, 7, 10, 13\}$
$S_{10} = \{3, 5, 10, 12\}$
$S_3 = \{3, 6, 8, 13\}$
$S_9 = \{3, 7, 9, 11\}$
$S_{13} = \{4, 5, 9, 13\}$
$S_4 = \{4, 6, 10, 11\}$
$S_{12} = \{4, 7, 8, 12\}$

(c) $K = 4$

$S_1 = \{1, 2, 3, 4, 5\}$
$S_6 = \{1, 6, 7, 8, 9\}$
$S_{10} = \{1, 10, 11, 12, 13\}$
$S_{14} = \{1, 14, 15, 16, 17\}$
$S_{18} = \{1, 18, 19, 20, 21\}$
$S_2 = \{2, 6, 10, 14, 18\}$
$S_7 = \{2, 7, 11, 15, 19\}$
$S_8 = \{2, 8, 12, 16, 20\}$
$S_9 = \{2, 9, 13, 17, 21\}$
$S_{11} = \{3, 6, 11, 17, 20\}$
$S_3 = \{3, 7, 10, 16, 21\}$
$S_{13} = \{3, 8, 13, 15, 18\}$
$S_{12} = \{3, 9, 12, 14, 19\}$
$S_{15} = \{4, 6, 12, 15, 21\}$
$S_4 = \{4, 7, 13, 14, 20\}$
$S_{17} = \{4, 8, 10, 17, 19\}$
$S_{16} = \{4, 9, 11, 16, 18\}$
$S_{19} = \{5, 6, 13, 16, 19\}$
$S_5 = \{5, 7, 12, 17, 18\}$
$S_{21} = \{5, 8, 11, 14, 21\}$
$S_{20} = \{5, 9, 10, 15, 20\}$

(d) $K = 5$

member to be freed, at which time the member is locked. Deadlock is prevented by requiring a node to yield if the timestamp (sequence number) of its request is larger than the timestamp of any other request. Like the previous algorithms, the total ordering relation $=>$ on the nodes is an underlying requirement. The following is a conceptual description of the algorithm:

1. Node i requests mutually exclusive access by sending a timestamped REQUEST message to every member of S_i. Node i itself pretends to have received a REQUEST.

2. On receiving a REQUEST message, each member of S_i checks to see if it is locked for some other request. If not, it sets a lock for the REQUEST and then returns a LOCKED message to i. This REQUEST is called the LOCKED_REQUEST. If a LOCKED_REQUEST already exists, the received REQUEST is placed on a local WAITING QUEUE that is ordered in increasing order by timestamp. A test is then made to determine whether the current LOCKED_REQUEST or any other waiting REQUEST at the node has a timestamp that precedes the time-stamp of the received REQUEST. If one does, a FAILED message is returned to node i. Otherwise, an INQUIRE message is sent to the node originating the current locking REQUEST to inquire whether this originating node has suc-ceeded in causing a lock to be set in all of its members. If an INQUIRE has already been sent for a previous REQUEST and its reply message (either RELIN-QUISH or RELEASE) has not yet been received, it is not necessary to send an INQUIRE.

3. When a node i receives an INQUIRE message, it returns a RELINQUISH message if it knows that it will not succeed in causing a lock to be set in all of its members; that is, it has received a FAILED message from at least one of its members. By doing this, the node frees its member node to service a request with an earlier timestamp. This also serves to prevent the creation of a permanent cycle, thereby preventing deadlock. If the node has succeeded in causing a lock to be set in all of its members, it is free to access the resource. Upon completion, it returns a RELEASE message. If an INQUIRE message has arrived before it is known whether the node will succeed or fail to lock all of its members, a reply is deferred until this becomes known. If an INQUIRE message has arrived after the node has sent a RELEASE message, it is simply ignored.

4. When a member node receives a RELINQUISH message, it releases the lock on the associated LOCKED_REQUEST and places it in the WAITING QUEUE after first removing from the queue the REQUEST with the earliest timestamp. This removed request becomes the new LOCKED_REQUEST and a LOCKED message is returned to the node that originated the request.

5. If all members of S_i have returned a LOCKED message, node i is allowed to access the resource.

6. Upon completion, node i sends a RELEASE message to each member of S_i.

7. When a node receives a RELEASE message, it deletes this LOCKED_REQUEST and forms a new LOCKED_REQUEST for the earliest REQUEST, if any, in the

WAITING QUEUE. A LOCKED message is returned to the node originating the new designated LOCKED_REQUEST. If the WAITING QUEUE is empty, no action is taken.

A formal proof that Maekawa's algorithm enforces mutual exclusion while preventing deadlock and starvation is left as an exercise (see Problem 14).

6.9.3   Implementation Details of Maekawa's Algorithm

Each node has one control task that manages access to the resource and one user task that invokes requests access. These tasks are specified below for node i.

Although it is easy to write communications between tasks in different nodes using Ada's entry call capability, we have chosen to use message transfers for the following reasons:

- Message transfers are explicitly visible, and our concern is with the number of messages required to effect mutual exclusion.

- The specification of Ada's entry call has the undesirable effect of suspending the calling task until the accept statement has completed execution.

A message transmission is performed by a primitive SEND with the assumed syntax:

SEND *(message (parameter), destination)*

```
package body Node_i is
  type Request_block is
    record
      Sequence_number: INTEGER;
      Node_number: INTEGER;
    end record;
  type Inquire_block is
    record
      Request : Request_block;
      Locking_request : Request_block;
      Target_node_number : INTEGER;
    end record;

task body User_task is --the user task that invokes mutual exclusion
begin
      .
      .
      .
  Mutual_exclusion_manager.Invoke; --request mutual exclusion
  Mutual_exclusion_manager.Test_if_locked; --wait for all members to be locked
  Critical Section;
  Mutual_exclusion_manager.Release; --release the REQUEST
      .
      .
      .
end User_task;
```

task Mutual_exclusion_manager **is** --this task acts as an agent who creates mutual
--exclusion
    entry   Invoke; --called when the node invokes mutual exclusion
    entry   Test_if_locked; --used to wait until all the members of S_i have been
--locked
    entry   Release; --called to send RELEASE messages
    entry   Receive_REQUEST (Request: **in** Request_block);
--the following entries are called by
--service tasks when respective messages are received
    entry   Receive_INQUIRE (Inquire: **in** Inquire_block);
    entry   Receive_FAILED;
    entry   Receive_LOCKED (Sequence_number_seen: **in** INTEGER);
    entry   Receive_RELINQUISH;
    entry   Receive_RELEASE (Sequence_number_seen: **in** INTEGER);
end;

task body Mutual_exclusion_manager **is**
    i: **constant** INTEGER; --this node's unique number
    K: **constant** INTEGER; --the number of members of S_i
    S: **array** $(1..K)$ **of** INTEGER; --the node numbers of the members of S_i
    Locked_flag : BOOLEAN : = FALSE; --TRUE if this node is locked
    Locking_request: Request_block; --REQUEST locking this node
    Highest_sequence_number: INTEGER : = 0; --the highest sequence number
--seen in any REQUEST message sent, received or observed
    Current_sequence_number: INTEGER; --contains the sequence number of the
--current REQUEST and is incremented by 1 when this node
--completes the current mutual exclusion request
    Locked_count: INTEGER; --the number of member nodes locked
    Failed_count: INTEGER; --the number of nodes that are already locked for
--other REQUESTs
    Waiting_queue: **queue of** Request_block : = $\emptyset$;
--REQUESTS outstanding at this node; they are queued in the
--decreasing order of precedence
--the following primitives are allowed:
--Insert (Waiting_queue, T) inserts a component T
--Remove (Waiting_queue) removes the most preceding component
--and returns it
--Head (Waiting_queue) returns the value of the most preceding
--component; if the queue is empty, it returns (∞, ∞) where ∞ is the largest
--number representable by this machine
--Count (Waiting_queue) returns the number of components in the
--queue
    Inquire_sent: BOOLEAN : = FALSE; --An INQUIRE message was sent and is
--waiting for a RELINQUISH or RELEASE

Outstanding_inquiry: **array** (1..K) **of** Inquire_block;
                              --contains outstanding INQUIRE messages
Outstanding_inquiry_count: INTEGER; --the number of messages contained
                    --in Outstanding_inquiry

procedure Lock_this_node (Request: **in** Request_block) **is**
        --this procedure is used to lock this node
begin
  Locked_flag : = TRUE;
  Locking_request : = Request;
  if Request.Node_number = i **then**
    Locked_count : = Locked_count + 1;
  else
    SEND (LOCKED(Highest_sequence_number), Request.Node_number);
  end if;
end Lock_this_node;

procedure Failed_to_lock (Request: **in** Request_block) **is**
        --this is called when failed to lock this node
begin
  if Request.Node_number = i **then**
    Failed_count : = Failed_count + 1;
  else
    SEND (FAILED, Request.Node_number);
  end if;
end Failed_to_lock;

procedure Relinquish_this_node **is** --called to relinquish this node for the most
                --preceding REQUEST

begin
  Inquire_sent : = FALSE; --the inquiry has now been accomplished
  Insert (Waiting_queue, Locking_request);
  Lock_this_node (Remove(Waiting_queue));
end Relinquish_this_node;

procedure Send_RELINQUISH (Relinquish: **in** Inquire_block) **is**
  --used to send a RELINQUISH message if necessary
begin
  if Current_sequence_number = Relinquish.Locking_request.Sequence_number **then**
    if Locked_count ≠ K **then**
      if Failed_count > 0 **then**
        Locked_count : = Locked_count − 1;
        if Relinquish.Target_node_number = i **then** Relinquish_this_node;
        else SEND (RELINQUISH, Relinquish.Target_node_number);
        end if;

```
        else --now register an INQUIRE for a possible later RELINQUISH upon
                        --receiving a FAILED
          Outstanding_inquiry_count := Outstanding_inquiry_count + 1;
          Outstanding_inquiry (Outstanding_inquiry_count) := Relinquish;
        end if;
      end if;
    end if;
end Send_RELINQUISH;

procedure Send_INQUIRE (Inquire: in Inquire_block) is
  --used to send an INQUIRE message
begin
if Inquire.Locking_request.Node_number = i then
    Send_RELINQUISH (Inquire); --pretend that an INQUIRE has been sent
                               --and received
    else
      SEND (INQUIRE (Inquire), Inquire.Locking_request.Node_number);
    end if;
end Send_INQUIRE;

procedure Wait_or_return (Request : in Request_block) is
        --used to register a lock request and to return a FAILED or send an
        --INQUIRE
begin
  if Locking_request < Request or Head(Waiting_queue)< Request then
    Failed_to_lock (Request);
  else if not Inquire_sent then
        Send_INQUIRE ((Request, Locking_request, i));
        Inquire_sent := TRUE;
     end if;
  end if;
  Insert (Waiting_queue, Request);
end Wait_or_return;

procedure Try_to_lock (Request: in Request_block) is
begin
  if Locked_flag then
    Wait_or_return (Request);
  else
    Lock_this_node (Request);
  end if;
end Try_to_lock;

procedure Release_this_node is --called to release this node
begin
  Inquire_sent := FALSE; --the inquiry is cleared
  Locked_flag := FALSE;
  if not Count (Waiting_queue) = 0 then
```

```
        Lock_this_node (Remove(waiting_queue));
      end if;
  end Release_this_node;

begin
  loop
    select
      accept Invoke do
        declare
          Request: Request_block : = (0, i); --REQUEST originating at this node
        begin
          Request.Sequence_number : = Highest_Sequence_number + 1;
          Highest_sequence_number : = Request.Sequence_number;
          Current_sequence_number : = Request.Sequence_number;
          Locked_count : = 0;
          Failed_count : = 0;
          Outstanding_inquiry_count : = 0;
          for j in 1..K loop
            if S(j) = i then Try_to_lock (Request);
            else send (REQUEST (Request), S(j));
            end if;
          end loop;
        end;
      end Invoke;
    or
      accept Receive_REQUEST (Request: in Request_block) do
        Highest_sequence_number : =
          max (Highest_sequence_number, Request.Sequence_number);
        Try_to_lock (Request);
      end Receive_REQUEST;
    or
      accept Receive_INQUIRE (Inquire: in Inquire_block) do
        Send_RELINQUISH (Inquire);
      end Receive_INQUIRE;
    or
      accept Receive_FAILED do
        Failed_count : = Failed_count + 1;
        for I in 1..Outstanding_inquiry_count loop
          Send_RELINQUISH (Outstanding_inquiry (I));
        end loop;
Outstanding_inquiry_count : = 0;
      end Receive_FAILED;
    or
      accept Receive_LOCKED (Sequence_number_seen: in INTEGER) do
        Highest_sequence_number : = max (Highest_sequence_number,
          Sequence_number_seen);
```

```
            Locked_count : = Locked_count + 1;
        end Receive_LOCKED;
    or
        accept Receive_RELINQUISH do
            Relinquish_this_node;
        end Receive_RELINQUISH;
    or
        when Locked_count = K =>
        accept Test_if_locked;
    or
        accept Release do
            Current_sequence_number : = Current_sequence_number + 1;
                --indicate that the current mutual exclusion request is over
            for j in 1..K loop
                if S(j) ≠ i then send (RELEASE (Highest_sequence_number), S(j));
                else Release_this_node;
                end if;
            end loop;
        end Release;
    or
        accept Receive_RELEASE (Sequence_number_seen: in INTEGER) do
            Release_this_node;
            Highest_sequence_number : = max (Highest_sequence_number,
                Sequence_number_seen); --update Highest_sequence_number
        end Receive_RELEASE;
    end select;
  end loop;
end Mutual_exclusion_manager;
end Node_i;
```

6.9.4 An Example Using Maekawa's Algorithm

Assume a 13-node network using the square-root algorithm. The logical clock at each site is initialized to zero. The member sets S_i are shown in Figure 6.22(a). Suppose that nodes 7, 8, and 11 all request access to the resource and the following scenario of events takes place:

1. Node 11 is the first to request access. Its REQUESTS arrive at nodes 12 and 13, where they become the LOCKED_REQUEST, but its REQUEST to node 1 is still in transit.

2. Node 7 then requests access. Its REQUESTS arrive at nodes 2 and 10, where they become the LOCKED_REQUEST, but its REQUEST to node 13 is still in transit.

3. Node 8 then requests access. It sends REQUESTS to nodes 1, 9, and 10, but fails at node 10 because node 10 already has a LOCKED_REQUEST.

4. The REQUEST message originating at node 11 arrives at node 1, while the REQUEST message from node 7 arrives at node 13. Node 1 then returns a FAILED and node 13 sends an INQUIRE message to node 11.

This set of events creates the system state depicted in Figure 6.22(a) where nodes 7, 8, and 11 have formed a momentary cycle. Node 8 receives a FAILED message and cannot enter its critical section. Likewise, node 11 cannot enter its critical section because it receives a FAILED message from node 1. Node 7 is waiting because it has not received a LOCKED message from all of its member nodes.

When an INQUIRE message is received at node 11, node 11 knows that it cannot enter its critical section and it returns a RELINQUISH message to node 13. This causes node 13 to be released in favor of the oldest REQUEST in its waiting queue, which is the REQUEST from node 7. This becomes the LOCKED_REQUEST and node 13 returns LOCKED to node 7. Node 7 can then access the resource. This is depicted in Figure 6.22(b).

Upon completion, node 7 sends a RELEASE message to its member nodes, causing the REQUESTs to be deleted. This will cause the REQUEST from node 8 to become the LOCKED_REQUEST at all of its member nodes, and node 8 accesses the resource. Finally node 11 is allowed to access the resource.

Suppose, instead of this scenario, that a REQUEST from node 3 had arrived at node 13 after the INQUIRE message was sent but before the RELINQUISH message from node 11 arrived at node 13. In this case, since this latter REQUEST precedes any REQUEST at node 13, and since it is known that an INQUIRE had been sent, the REQUEST waits for a RELINQUISH. When the RELINQUISH message is received at node 13, the REQUEST from node 3 becomes the LOCKED_REQUEST at node 13 instead of the REQUEST from node 7. This will be the case at all of node 3's member nodes when node 8 sends a RELINQUISH to node 3.

6.9.5 A Comparative Message Traffic Analysis

In this section, we present a numerical comparison of Maekawa's and Ricart and Agrawala's algorithms under the conditions of both light and heavy demands. Table 6.3 gives a numerical comparison of the number of messages required by each of the two algorithms.

Table 6.3 Numerical Comparison

N	$\sqrt{N}$ Algorithm	Ricart and Agrawala's Algorithm
3 ($K = 2$)	3	4
7 ($K = 3$)	6	12
13 ($K = 4$)	9	24
21 ($K = 5$)	12	40
133 ($K = 12$)	33	264
381 ($K = 20$)	57	760

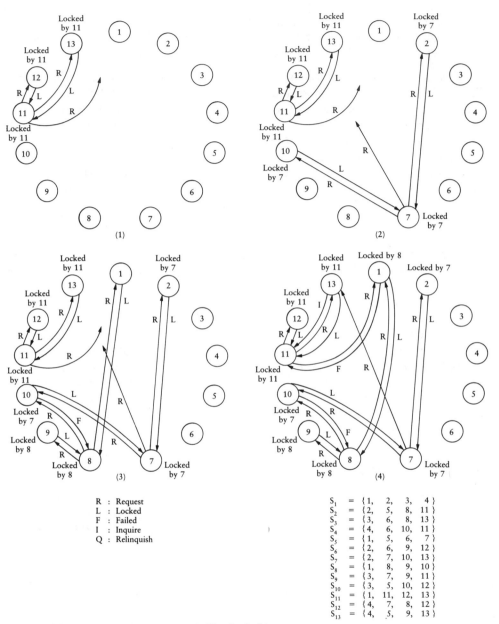

R : Request
L : Locked
F : Failed
I : Inquire
Q : Relinquish

$S_1 = \{ 1, \quad 2, \quad 3, \quad 4 \}$
$S_2 = \{ 2, \quad 5, \quad 8, \quad 11 \}$
$S_3 = \{ 3, \quad 6, \quad 8, \quad 13 \}$
$S_4 = \{ 4, \quad 6, \quad 10, \quad 11 \}$
$S_5 = \{ 1, \quad 5, \quad 6, \quad 7 \}$
$S_6 = \{ 2, \quad 6, \quad 9, \quad 12 \}$
$S_7 = \{ 2, \quad 7, \quad 10, \quad 13 \}$
$S_8 = \{ 1, \quad 8, \quad 9, \quad 10 \}$
$S_9 = \{ 3, \quad 7, \quad 9, \quad 11 \}$
$S_{10} = \{ 3, \quad 5, \quad 10, \quad 12 \}$
$S_{11} = \{ 1, \quad 11, \quad 12, \quad 13 \}$
$S_{12} = \{ 4, \quad 7, \quad 8, \quad 12 \}$
$S_{13} = \{ 4, \quad 5, \quad 9, \quad 13 \}$

(a) Circular locking

Figure 6.22   An Example.

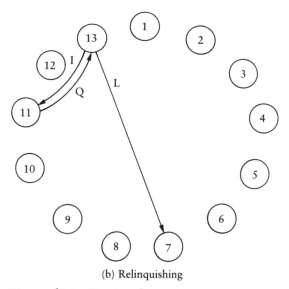

(b) Relinquishing

Figure 6.22   Continued

When the demand is light, *contention* rarely occurs and the square-root algorithm requires a total of $3(K - 1)$ messages for each request for access: $(K - 1)$ REQUEST messages, $(K - 1)$ LOCKED messages, and $(K - 1)$ RELEASE messages. The numbers appear in the second column. On the other hand, Ricart and Agrawala's algorithm requires $2(N - 1)$ messages. The numbers appear in the third column.

Under a heavy demand, a new REQUEST will most likely fail to become the LOCKED_REQUEST at its member nodes. Thus, we expect to have $(K - 1)$ REQUEST messages, $(K - 1)$ FAILED messages, $(K - 1)$ LOCKED messages to effect mutual exclusion, and $(K - 1)$ RELEASE messages to release the REQUEST. Altogether $4(K - 1)$ messages are required per request to access the resource. If a new REQUEST initiated from a node that has neither issued a REQUEST nor participated in the algorithm as a member node for a certain period of time, it will most likely precede other REQUESTs. It then causes an INQUIRE message to be sent, for which a RELINQUISH is returned. In this case, $(K - 1)$ REQUEST messages, $(K - 1)$ INQUIRE messages, $(K - 1)$ RELINQUISH messages, and $(K - 1)$ LOCKED messages are required to effect mutual exclusion, yielding a total of $5(K - 1)$ messages per request to access the resource. This is the worst case because a RELINQUISH message is not needed when the node is already accessing the resource. Furthermore, it is expected that under heavy demand almost all nodes will participate in the algorithm either as a requester or an arbitrator.

6.9.6   The Formation of Member Sets S_i

In any algorithm, the choice of a set of S_i's significantly impacts the number of messages required to effect mutual exclusion. It is particularly important for the square-root algorithm. Ideally, the set of S_i's should be symmetric, and the size of each subset should be minimized. As previously mentioned, these two conditions are both satisfied when there exists a finite projective plane of N points. Although it is known that a finite projective plane of order k exists if k is a power of a prime, very little is known about general finite projective planes for other values of k. The Bruck-Ryser Theorem states that there exists no finite projective plane of order k if either $k - 1$ or $k - 2$ is divisible by 4 and if k cannot be expressed as the sum of two integral squares ($k \neq a^2 + b^2$ for a and b nonnegative integers) [Albert and Sandler, 1968]. If a corresponding finite projective plane does not exist or if N cannot be expressed as $K(K - 1) + 1$, one or both of the above two conditions must be sacrificed. We will show two methods to create a near-optimal set of S_i's.

Method 1

Suppose that $(K - 1)$ is not a power of a prime number. Then there may not exist a corresponding finite projective plane. However, we can create a set of S_i's for this value of $L = K$ by the following method:

1. First, create a symmetric set of M S_i's where $(M - 1)$ is a power of a prime number and M is the smallest integer larger than L. Each component is contained in M subsets.

2. Next, replace each component greater than $N = L(L - 1) + 1$ in this set of S_i's by a number less than or equal to $N = L(L - 1) + 1$. (We assume that each replacement uses a different number.) Then each component will be contained in L subsets of the resulting set of S_i's. This set of S_i's is not symmetric in the sense that the size of the S_i is not always L.

Using this set of S_i's, the mutual exclusion algorithm produces slightly unbalanced performance because some node may have to send one or more extra messages. This is not considered to be serious since the largest difference between L and M is only 2 for $K \leq 20$ ($L = 15$ and $M = 17$) and only 4 for $K \leq 50$ ($L = 34$ and $M = 38$).

When N cannot be expressed as $K(K - 1) + 1$, a similar technique can be used to create a set of S_i's. As an example, let $N = 5$. We first create a set of S_i's for $M = 7$, using the method described in Section 6.9.2, and then replace nodes 7 and 6 with 5 and 4, respectively, discarding S_6 and S_7. This produces the following set of S_i's:

$$S_1 = \{1, 2, 3\}$$
$$S_2 = \{2, 4\}$$
$$S_3 = \{3, 5, 4\}$$
$$S_4 = \{1, 4, 5\}$$
$$S_5 = \{2, 5\}$$

Method 2

Consider an $L \times L$ grid and number the L^2 grid points from 1 to L^2. Define the subset S_i to be the set of grid points on the row or the column passing through point *i*. Then it is clear that $S_i \cap S_j \neq \phi$ for any *i* and *j*, $1 \leq i, j \leq L^2$. The set of S_i's is symmetric in the sense that $|S_i| = 2L - 1$ for all *i*, and any *i* is contained in $(2L - 1)$ subsets. In this construction, $|S_i| = 2\sqrt{N} - 1$ for any *i*. Therefore the number of messages needed to effect mutual exclusion is about twice as many as required by the previous method.

If *N* is not a square of an integer, we can create a larger grid. Any fractional row or column is completed by complementing its missing part from another row or column when the S_i's are determined.

6.10 Miscellaneous Considerations

The analysis in the previous sections assumes that the network is fully connected, that is, that a direct communication link exists between any two nodes. If this is not the case, the optimality of an algorithm for mutual exclusion must take into consideration the additional factor of the total number of *hops* (through intermediate nodes) that are required to send a message from the source host to the destination host. In addition, other special characteristics of the network might allow for further optimization.

6.10.1 Special Network Topologies

If the topology of the network is a ring, the algorithm should be modified to reduce the number of messages and minimize the number of hops. The following modification to the algorithm eliminates the need for REPLY messages:

1. The node requesting access to the resource sends a REQUEST to its neighbor on the ring. (Note that messages traverse in one direction on the ring.)
2. The neighbor interrogates the REQUEST message. If the REQUEST has priority, it is sent to the next neighbor. Otherwise, it is deferred.
3. When the REQUEST message is eventually returned to the initiating node, access to the resource is allowed.

N hops are required for a REQUEST message. The algorithm is optimal in terms of the number of hops and the number of messages.

If the topology of the network allows for broadcast messages, a node needs to send only one REQUEST message instead of $(N - 1)$.

6.10.2 Management of Message Sequence Numbers

If traffic is heavy and all nodes are participating in making requests to access the resource, the logical clocks will be closely synchronized. As a result, the tie-breaking rule will tend to slightly favor lower-numbered nodes. This can generally be avoided by using a random increment of the sequence number. In fact, a deliberate priority can be introduced by allowing high priority nodes to use small increments and low priority nodes to use large increments.

6.10.3   Dynamic Changes to the Network Topology

A node that joins the network must perform the following steps:

1. Interrogate some active node to obtain a list of participating nodes.
2. Assign to itself a unique node number.
3. Have its node number placed on every other node's list of participating nodes.
4. Acquire an appropriate value for its initial timestamp.

Some trial and error may be required in step 1 in order to locate an active node. If the concept of a "sponsor" node is used and the sponsor is active, then the trial and error can be avoided. Step 2 can be fairly complex if the dynamic assignment of node numbers is allowed. A simple and practical approach is to assign a fixed unique number to each node, regardless of whether or not it is active. In step 4, the timestamp of the new node must be set greater than the timestamp of any REQUEST message that would already have been received if the new node had been continuously active. This requires communicating with other nodes. Until this condition is met, the new node cannot request access to the resource and must defer sending a REPLY message for an incoming REQUEST message. A new node can determine its timestamp by several methods. But the method of asking all other nodes for their timestamp is perhaps the most practical.

A node that voluntarily leaves the network must notify all other nodes of its intention to leave. Upon acknowledgment from all other nodes, it is allowed to leave the network. While waiting for acknowledgments, the departing node may not participate in any communication that will affect mutual exclusion (for example, it cannot request further access to the resource and must return a REPLY to any REQUEST that it receives).

A time-out mechanism must be used to detect the failure of a node. Upon sending a REQUEST message, a requesting node starts a timer. If the timer expires, the timer is reset and a probe message is sent to the node that has not returned a REPLY. Upon time-out, prior to receiving a response to the probe message, the node that has not responded is considered to have failed. A procedure similar to a voluntary removal must be initiated.

6.10.4   Elimination Algorithms

The algorithms introduced so far are essentially based on deferral: A reply is deferred until a certain condition is satisfied. Another type of algorithm is based on the process of *elimination*. In this approach, messages from a node that cannot be a contender are simply discarded. The motivation comes from algorithms designed to designate by consensus a unique node (for instance, the highest numbered node) to replace a lost control token in a token ring bus. One algorithm, from Chang and Roberts [1979], is designed for a ring and requires an average of $O(N \log N)$ hops. In the worst case, it requires $O(N^2)$ hops. It is assumed that the ring allows message flow in only one direction. Hirschberg and Sinclair's algorithm requires $O(N \log N)$ hops in the worst case [Hirshberg and Sinclair, 1980]. The ring allows each node to send messages in both directions.

6.10.5 Other Approaches

All of the process synchronization techniques described in this chapter are based on the assumption that a reliable message-passing system, such as that provided by layers 1–4 of the ISO OSI Reference Model, is in place. An alternative is to use Lamport's approach, which was described in Chapter 2. This method provides a way to achieve mutual exclusion at the lowest possible level without relying on any atomic operations such as the sending and receiving messages [Lamport, 1986a]. A primitive communication mechanism can be defined, leading to a family of solutions to the n-process mutual exclusion problem, ranging from a requirement of one communication bit per process (with possible process starvation) to n! communication bits per process (which satisfies every reasonable requirement for fairness and fault-tolerance) [Lamport, 1986b].

6.11 A Comparative Order Analysis

Section 6.9.5 presented a numerical comparison of Maekawa's and Ricart and Agrawala's algorithms. In this section, we present a more complete comparison of the orders of the two methods, along with a fully centralized algorithm. Lamport's algorithm and Thomas's algorithm are not included since their performances are essentially the same as that for Ricart and Agrawala's algorithm, differing only by a constant factor. Table 6.4 summarizes the results.

In requesting access to a resource, a node sends only one REQUEST to the control node in the fully centralized algorithm, whereas $(\sqrt{N} - 1)$ and $(N - 1)$ messages are required, respectively, for the other two algorithms. This is the major penalty that must be paid in a distributed algorithm.

In order for a mutual exclusion algorithm to operate, each (control) node must have control information, both dynamic and static. The dynamic information consists of such things as the status of the related nodes; the static information consists of such things as the total number of nodes and the node numbers. If the dynamic information is duplicated in other nodes, the removal of a (control) node does not cause a loss of dynamic information. Hence a failed node can simply be removed. However, if static information is maintained in each (control) node, it must be modified when some node is removed. In Ricart and Agrawala's algorithm, a node removal causes no loss of dynamic information but requires a modification of the static information in each node. This requires $O(N)$ messages. In the fully centralized algorithm, on the other hand, all dynamic information is lost by the removal of the control node whereas no static information is lost. A backup controller is required to take over the failed controller and $O(N)$ messages are required to regain the dynamic information.

In the $\sqrt{N}$ algorithm, a node removal results in the loss of dynamic information about $(\sqrt{N} - 1)$ nodes, and another node must logically take over the role of a failed node. The lost dynamic information can be regained by $O(\sqrt{N})$, instead of $O(N)$, messages. The static information also needs to be modified in only $(\sqrt{N} - 1)$ nodes. The numbers of these $(\sqrt{N} - 1)$ nodes are known from the information

Table 6.4 Comparision of Distributed Mutual Exclusion Algorithms

	Fully Centralized Algorithm (one control node)	$\sqrt{N}$ Algorithm	Ricart and Agrawala's Algorithm
The number of nodes to which a REQUEST must be sent	1	$\sqrt{N} - 1$	$N - 1$
The number of nodes about which each (control) node keeps dynamic information	N	$\sqrt{N}$	N
The number of nodes, dynamic information about which is lost by a (control) node failure	N	$\sqrt{N}$	1
The number of nodes about which each (control) node keeps static information	0	$\sqrt{N}$	N
Removal of a (control) node	Need a backup control node	Dynamically possible	Dynamically possible
Overtaking by another node	Need a backup control node	Dynamically possible	Not necessary

about all S_i's kept in each node. This information itself needs to be modified in only those $\sqrt{N}$ nodes that are concerned with a modification. Therefore, it is generally expected that the $\sqrt{N}$ algorithm requires fewer messages than the other two algorithms to recover from node failure.

6.12 Summary

The major thrust of this chapter was the use of message passing for the coordination of high-level processes. The coordination of high-level processes assumes the services of a reliable and orderly message-passing system. The five lower layers of the ISO

Reference Model of Open Systems Interconnection were described to illustrate to the reader how this can be accomplished. Several important algorithms for distributed mutual exclusion were presented and classified according to their degree of distribution and efficiency. These algorithms require the ability to order events in a network system, and the discussion showed how this can be accomplished. It should be noted that, in a real system, a suitable algorithm must take into consideration numerous factors including network topology, network size, reliability, extensibility, and requirements for performance.

While the focus of attention was on the mutual exclusion problem, the discussion establishes the fundamental basis for forming network programs at the traditional operating system level. These ideas are further extended in Chapter 7.

Key Words

balanced mode
bandwidth
bit stuffing
carrier sense
character count
character stuffing
checksum
circuit switching
clock condition
collision detection and retransmission
communications processor
congestion control
contention
control token
CSMA/CD
data flow control
data-link layer
datagram
destination transport address
dialog control
Digital Network Architecture (DNA)
distributed

algorithm
distributed mutual exclusion algorithm
distributed (decentralized) systems
enveloping
equal effort rule
equal reponsibility rule
Ethernet
frames
front-end processor
happened-before relation
HDLC
implementation reference model
ISO OSI Reference Model
Lamport's algorithm
layer k protocol
layered structure
local area network (LAN)
M and N pacing

Maekawa's square-root algorithm
network
network layer
normal response mode
packet switching
peer-to-peer communication
physical layer
piggyback
primary station
protocol
quarantine service
register insertion
Ricart and Agrawala's algorithm
routing
secondary station
security parameters
sessions
session layer
sliding window protocol
stop-and-wait protocol

synchronous response mode	time slots	transport event
	three-way	transport layer
System Network Architecture (SNA)	connection	transport station
	timestamp	transport users
time-out	transport entity	virtual circuit

Questions

1. Place array processors, pipelined processors, uniprocessor centralized computer systems, multiprocessor systems, multicomputer systems, local area networks, and wide area networks in the spectrum of degree of decentralization of control, and then summarize important differences between them.

2. Suppose that a data transmission in circuit switching requires a sequence of:

   REQUEST (from sender to receiver)
   ACKNOWLEDGMENT (from receiver to sender)
   DATA (data transmission from sender to receiver)
   ACKNOWLEDGMENT (from receiver to sender)
   CLOSE (from sender to receiver)

   Define the time to perform each of these operations to be T except for DATA, which requires time $T + DL$, where D is a constant and L is the length of data in bytes. A packet transmission, however, requires T for a packet of 100 bytes. An acknowledgment is returned from the receiver to the sender every N packets. Compute the threshold value of L at which both circuit switching and packet switching perform at the same data transmission rate.

3. Why do the modern protocols use a bit stuffing technique to partition a bit stream into frames?

4. Draw a figure showing HDLC in operation when station A is designated a primary station, and station B works in normal response mode. (See Figure 6.8.)

5. Compute the maximum data transmission rate of HDLC working in balanced mode. Use the following variables:

   S : The CPU time to process a frame transmission request

   R : The CPU time to process a received frame

   T : The data transmission time to transmit a frame containing L information bytes

   F : The size of a frame in bytes

   E : Error rate

   If you have made any additional assumptions, state them.

6. Suppose that a system has adopted the following set of operations for the transport layer service:

   CONNECT
   CONNECT REJECT

SEND
RECEIVE
SEND INTERRUPT MESSAGE
DISCONNECT.

Describe how the following services are incorporated into these operations:

Transport-connection establishment service

Transport-connection graceful termination service

Transport-connection data transfer service

Transport-connection expedited data transfer service

Also state how the following primitives are incorporated:

Request primitive

Indication primitive

Response primitive

Confirm primitive

7. How many TPDUs are transferred between two hosts for the following services?
   a. Transport-connection establishment
   b. Transport-connection graceful termination
   c. A transfer of data that requires N TPDUs
   d. A transfer of expedited data

8. In connection establishment and tear-down, why is it easier to perform these services if one host is designated as the master while the other is designated as the slave?

9. Compute the maximum data transfer rate of sliding window with window size W. Use the following variables:

   S : The CPU time in the sender node to process a packet transmission request regardless of its type

   R : The CPU time in the receiver node to process a received packet regardless of its type

   T : The time to transmit a packet containing L information bytes over a communications line

   C : The time to transmit a control packet over a communications line

   Assume that the sending and receiving operations of a node can be performed in parallel and that no transmission errors will occur. If you have made any additional assumptions, state them.

10. Compute the maximum data transfer rate for M and N pacing. Use the variables defined in Question 9.

11. Suppose that a global network creates a million messages per minute and continues to run for 10 years. How many bits are necessary to distinguish every message? How would you implement this sequence number?

12. Compare the producer/consumer problem in centralized systems with flow control and pacing in distributed systems. (They essentially solve the same problem in different contexts.) Compare the methods used to solve them in terms of complexity. In centralized systems, mutual exclusion of larger items is built based on mutual exclusion of smaller items. Is there any similar hierarchy in the control of shared (in a broader sense) information in distributed systems?

13. Which of the following statements concerning the total ordering relation $=>$ are true? Justify your answer.

    a. An event a that happened before event b in physical time, will always satisfy $a => b$.

    b. If each process increments its logical clock by a different number, the total ordering relation $=>$ will not hold.

    c. If the delay of message transfer varies from time to time, the total ordering relation $=>$ will not hold.

    d. If the total ordering of processes, $<<$, changes during the operation of the system, the total ordering relation $=>$ will not hold.

14. In what senses can Lamport's algorithm and Ricart and Agrawala's algorithm be called "distributed" algorithms?

15. In what senses is the $\sqrt{N}$ algorithm a "distributed" algorithm?

16. Show an example sequence of operations involving a RELINQUISH message for the $\sqrt{N}$ algorithm working on a network of 13 nodes.

17. Show that the $\sqrt{N}$ algorithm is optimal if no centralized control or control token passing is used.

18. Devise a solution (algorithm) of the distributed producer/consumer problem, following these guidelines:

    a. A consumer polls producers when it becomes ready to accept a message.

    b. If it finds a producer that has a message ready, then it selects the producer and receives the message; otherwise, it goes to sleep.

    c. Similarly, a producer polls consumers when it creates a message.

    d. If it finds a consumer that is ready to accept a message, it sends the message to the consumer; otherwise, it goes to sleep.

Problems

1. Design the "Interface 1" and "Interface 2" shown in Figure 6.7 so that the underlying hardware structure (either distributed or centralized) is transparent to users.

2. Devise criteria to decide whether communications processors should be used to off-load the protocol work from host computers.

3. How can you make the underlying hardware structure transparent to users? Discuss this in terms of interprocess communications. Describe methods and evaluation criteria.

4. Write a high-level specification of an HDLC processing program.

5. Write a high-level language specification of an interprocess communications facility for a multicomputer organization.

6. Write a high-level language specification of the transport and session layers' services.

7. Write a high-level specification of a sliding window processing program for each host.

8. Write a high-level specification of an M and N pacing processing program in each host in a high-level language.

9. Suppose that the following set of operations is provided as the transport services:

OPEN
READ
WRITE
CLOSE

Write a high-level language specification of each of these operations.

10. Devise a mutual exclusion algorithm that passes a control token from node to node. A node can be in its critical section when it possesses the control token. Can you call this algorithm a distributed algorithm? Justify your answer.

11. Show that there exist a number of mutual exclusion algorithms that vary in the degree of decentralization.

12. How does the network topology affect the selection and performance of mutual exclusion algorithms?

13. The three mutual exclusion algorithms compared in Table 6.4 require that each node know the names of all other nodes and the total number of them. Show a detailed algorithm for a node insertion and for a node removal for each mutual exclusion algorithm. Assume that packets will never be lost and that the names of the nodes that can potentially be connected to the network are known a priori to any node.

14. For Maekawa's square-root algorithm, prove the following:
    a. Mutual exclusion is enforced.
    b. Deadlock is prevented.
    c. Starvation cannot occur.

References

Albert, A. A., and R. Sandler. (1968). *An Introduction to Finite Projective Planes.* Holt, Rinehart and Winston, N.Y.

Bertine, H. V. "Physical level protocols." (1980). *IEEE Transacations on Communications* COM-28, 4, pp. 433–444.

Burr, W. E. (August 1983). "An overview of the proposed American national standard for local distributed data interfaces." *Communications of the ACM* 26, 8, pp. 554–561.

Chang, E., and R. Roberts. (May 1979). "An improved algorithm for decentralized extrema-finding in circular configurations of processors." *Communications of the ACM* 22, 5, pp. 281–283.

Gifford, D. K. (December 1979). "Weighted voting for replicated data." *Proceedings of the 7th Symposium on Operating System Principles*, pp. 150–162.

Hirschberg, D. S., and J. B. Sinclair. (November 1980). "Decentralized extrema-finding in circular configurations of processors." *Communications of the ACM* 23, 11, pp. 627–678.

IEEE Computer Society. (May 1982). *IEEE Project 802: Local Network Standards, Draft C.*

International Standards Organization. (April 1981). "Data processing—open systems interconnection—basic reference model." *ISO/TC97/SC16 N719.* [Also *Computer Networks* 5, pp. 81–118.]

————. (1982a). "Reference model of open system interconnection." *ISO/TC 97/SC 16, Draft International Standard ISO/DIS 7498.*

————. (June 1982b). "Transport service definition." *ISO/TC 97/SC 16, Draft Proposal ISO/DP 8072.*

————. (June 1982c). "Transport protocol specification." *ISO/TC 97/SC 16, Draft Proposal ISO/DP 8073.*

Lamport, L. (July 1978). "Time, clocks and the ordering of events in a distributed system." *Communications of the ACM* 21, 7, pp. 558–564.

————. (1986a). "The mutual exclusion problem: part I—a theory of interprocess communication." *Journal of the ACM* 33, 2, pp. 313–326.

————. (1986b). "The mutual exclusion problem: Part II—statement and solutions." *Journal of the ACM* 33, 2, pp. 327–348.

Maekawa, M. (May 1985). "A $\sqrt{N}$ algorithm for mutual exclusion in decentralized systems." *ACM Transactions on Computer Systems* 3, 2, pp. 145–159.

Metcalfe, R. M., and D. R. Boggs. (July 1976). "ETHERNET: Distributed packet switching for local computer networks." *Communications of the ACM* 19, 7, pp. 395–404.

Meijer A., and P. Peters. 1982. *Computer Network Architectures.* Pitman, London, and Computer Science Press, Rockville, Md.

Myers, W. (August 1982). "Toward a local network standard." *IEEE MICRO* 2, 3, pp. 28–45.

National Bureau of Standards. (1983a). "Specification of a transport protocol for computer communications." *Vol. 1: Overview and Services, Proposed Federal Information Processing Standards, ICST/HLNP-83-1,* National Bureau of Standards.

————. (1983b). "Specification of a transport protocol for computer communications." *Vol. 2: Class 2 Protocol, Proposed Federal Information Processing Standards, ICST/HLNP-83-2,* National Bureau of Standards.

————. (1983c). "Specification of a transport protocol for computer communications." *Vol. 3: Class 4 Protocol, Proposed Federal Information Processing Standards, ICST/HLNP-83-3,* National Bureau of Standards.

———. (1983d). "Specification of a transport protocol for computer communications." *Vol. 4: Service Specification, Proposed Federal Information Processing Standards, ICST/HLNP-83-4,* National Bureau of Standards.

———. (1983e). "Specification of a transport protocol for computer communications." *Vol. 5: Guidance for the Implementor, Proposed Federal Information Processing Standards, ICST/HLNP-83-5,* National Bureau of Standards.

———. (1983f). "Specification of a transport protocol for computer communications." *Vol. 6: Guidance for Implementation Selection, Proposed Federal Information Processing Standards, ICST/HLNP-83-6,* National Bureau of Standards.

Ricart, G., and A. K. Agrawala. (1981). "An optimal algorithm for mutual exclusion." *Communications of the ACM* 24, pp. 9–17. [Corrigendum, *Communications of the ACM* 24, 9, p. 578.]

Rybczinski, A. M. (1980). "X.25 interface and end-to-end virtual circuit service characteristics." *IEEE Transactions on Communications* COM-28, 4, pp. 500–510.

Skeen, D. (February 1982). "A quorum-based commit protocol." *Proceedings of the 6th Berkeley Workshop on Distributed Data Management and Computer Networks,* pp. 69–80.

Tanenbaum, A. S. (December 1981). "Network protocols." *Computing Surveys* 13, 4, pp. 453–489.

Thomas, R. H. (June 1979). "A majority consensus approach to concurrency control for multiple copy databases." *ACM Transactions on Database Systems* 4, 2, pp. 180–209.

Tomlinson, R. S. (1975). "Selecting sequence numbers," *Proceedings of the ACM SIGCOMM/SIGOPS Interprocess Communication Workshop,* pp. 11–23.

Zimmermann, H. (1980). "OSI reference model—the ISO model of architecture for open system interconnection." *IEEE Transactions on Communications* COM-28, 4, pp. 425–432.

Suggested Readings

Burkhardt, H. J., and S. Schindler. (1981) "Structuring principles of the communication architecture of open systems—a systematic approach." *Computer Networks* 5, pp. 157–166.

Carlson, D. E. (1980). "Bit-oriented data link control procedures." *IEEE Transactions on Communications* COM-28, 4, pp. 455–467.

Carr, C. S., S. D. Crocker, and V. G. Cerf. (1970). "Host-host communication protocol in the ARPA network." *Proceedings of the AFIPS 1970 Spring Joint Computer Conference,* 36, pp. 589–597.

Carvalho, O. S. F., and G. Roucairol. (February 1983). "On mutual exclusion in computer networks." *Communications of the ACM* 26, 2, pp. 146–147.

Cerf, V. G., and P. T. Kirstein. (1978). "Issues in packet-network interconnection." *Proceedings of the IEEE* 66, 11, pp. 1386–1408.

Corr, F. P., and D. H. Neal. (1979). "SNA and emerging international standards." *IBM Systems Journal* 18, 2, pp. 244–262.

Cotton, I. W. (1980). "Technologies for local area computer networks." *Computer Networks* 4, 5, pp. 197–208.

Day, J. D. (1979). "Resource-sharing protocols." *IEEE Computer* 12, 9, pp. 47–56.

Donnelley, J. E. (1979). "Components of a network operating system." *Computer Networks* 3, pp. 389–399.

Ebihara, Y.; K. Ikeda; et al. (1983). "GAMMA-NET: a local computer network coupled by a high speed optical fiber ring bus—system concept and structure." *Computer Networks* 7, pp. 375–388.

Franta, W. R., and I. Chlamtac. (1981). *Local Networks: Motivation, Technology, and Performance*. Lexington Books, Lexington, Mass.

Green, P. E. (1979). "An introduction to network architectures and protocols." *IBM Systems Journal* 18, 2, pp. 202–222.

Halsey, J. R.; L. E. Hardy; and L. F. Powning. (1979). "Public data networks: their evolution, interfaces, and status." *IBM Systems Journal* 18, 2, pp. 223–243.

Kimbleton, S. R., and R. L. Mandell (1976). "A perspective on network operating systems." *Proceedings of the 1976 AFIPS National Computer Conference* 45, pp. 551–559.

Kobayashi, K. (1981). "Computer, communications and man: the integration of computer communications with man as an axis." *Computer Networks,* pp. 237–250.

Maekawa, M.; I. Yamezaki; et al. (April 1979). "Experimental polyprocessor system (EPOS)—architecture." *Proceedings of the 6th Annual Symposium on Computer Architecture,* pp. 188–195.

Rowe, L. A., and K. P. Birman. (1982). "A local network based on the UNIX operating system." *IEEE Transactions on Software Engineering* SE-8, 2, pp. 137–146.

Rybczynski, A. M., and J. D. Palframan. (1980). "A common X.25 interface to public data networks." *Computer Networks* 4, pp. 97–110.

Siewiorek, D. P., et al. (October 1978). "A case study of C.mmp, Cm* and C.vmp, Part I: Experience with fault-tolerance in microprocessor systems." *Proceedings of the IEEE* 66, 10, pp. 1178–1199.

———. (October 1978). "A case study of C.mmp, Cm* and C.vmp, Part II: Predicting and calibrating reliability of multiprocessor systems." *Proceedings of the IEEE* 66, 10, pp. 1200–1220.

Tanaka, H., and T. Moto-oka. (1981). "Distributed file management and job management of network-oriented operating system." *JIPS* 4, pp. 18–25.

Tanenbaum, A. S. (1981). *Computer Networks*. Prentice-Hall, Englewood Cliffs, N. J.

Thomas, R. H. (1973). "A resource-sharing executive for the ARPANET." *Proceedings of the 1973 AFIPS National Computer Conference* 42, pp. 155–163.

VAX Software Handbook. 1982. Digital Equipment Corporation.

Walden, D. (April 1972). "A system for interprocess communication in a resource sharing computer network." *Communications of the ACM* 15, 4, pp. 221–230.

Walden, D. C., and A. A. McKenzie. (September 1979). "The evolution of host-to-host protocol technology." *IEEE Computer* 12, 9, pp. 29–38.

Watson, R. W., and J. G. Fletcher. (1980). "An architecture for support of network operating system services." *Computer Networks* 4, pp. 33–49.

Wecker, S. (1979). "Computer network architecture." *IEEE Computer* 12, 9, pp. 58–72.

———. (1980). "DNA: the digital network architecture." *IEEE Transactions on Communications* COM-28, 4, pp. 510–526.

Wulf, W. A., et al. (June 1974). "Hydra: the kernel of a multiprocessor operating system." *Communications of the ACM* 17, 6, pp. 337–345.

———. 1981. *Hydra/C.mmp: An Experimental Computer System.* McGraw-Hill, New York.

Yakubaitis, E. A. 1983. *Network Architectures for Distributed Computing*, Allerton Press, N.Y.

Distributed Concurrency Control, Deadlock, and Recovery

7

7.1   Introduction

The merging of computer and communications technologies has made distributed processing both desirable and economically feasible. The design problems of centralized systems carry over to distributed systems, but different, and often more complex, solutions are required. This increased complexity is due to the fact that resources or data may be geographically distributed over a collection of remote sites. Communication by message passing among sites may involve arbitrary delay and, in many cases, there is no central controlling site.

This chapter addresses three major problems encountered in the design of distributed systems. The first problem, maintaining the consistency of distributed data, is the counterpart of controlling access to shared resources in centralized systems. Two techniques for dealing with this problem, locks and time stamps, are presented. If locks are used, the first problem gives rise to a second problem, namely, deadlock. Methods of distributed deadlock detection and prevention are discussed in various sections of this chapter. The third problem deals with recovery from failure. If a site or remote piece of software fails or if deadlock occurs, it should be possible to gracefully undo the effect of any computations in progress. Issues involving failure recovery are also discussed in this chapter. We begin by introducing some fundamental concepts.

7.2   Database Consistency

A database consists of a collection of objects (such as files or records), each viewed as a single-unit resource, on which a basic read or write *action* may be performed. A database computation can be viewed as a sequence of actions applied to some subset of objects in the database. The software that manages the accessing of objects is called a *database system*. Each database must satisfy a set of assertions called *consistency constraints.* For example, in a financial database, one assertion would be that the balance of each account is equal to the sum of the deposits minus the sum of the withdrawals. The state of a database is defined to be *consistent* if it satisfies all of its consistency constraints. These internal consistency constraints may be very complex, and the complete set of such constraints may be larger than the database itself. It is impractical and perhaps impossible to explicitly state all of the consistency constraints of a large database.

In order to deal with the problem of consistency, the concept of a *transaction* is introduced. A transaction is a sequence of actions of a computation, which constitutes a perceived logical unit of work on the database, and which takes the database from one consistent state to another. For increased performance it is desirable to allow for concurrent execution of transactions. However, arbitrary interleaving of the actions of concurrent transactions will often produce an inconsistent state and, as a consequence, controls are needed on concurrent access.

Figure 7.1 illustrates these concepts. One consistency constraint for this example is that the sum of the account balances must remain constant. If the transactions are executed in sequence, the consistency is preserved. If the transactions run concurrently, the individual actions may be interleaved to produce a final balance in account B of either \$250 or \$100. This phenomenon is referred to as the *lost update anomaly.* If transaction T_3 reads account A and account B during the execution of transaction T_1, then its printed results might indicate that money had "disappeared" (A debited but B not yet credited). This is referred to as the *inconsistent retrieval anomaly.*

Although T_1 and T_2 individually preserve consistency, they have the following properties [Eswaran, et al. 1976]:

Temporary inconsistency: After the first write of either T_1 or T_2, the database is inconsistent.

Conflict: If transaction T_2 is executed between the first and second write actions of T_1, then the final sum of the balances of accounts will equal \$800 rather than \$700, violating the consistency requirements.

Temporary inconsistency is an inherent property and, as a consequence, consistency is enforceable only upon completion of a transaction. Conflict is much more serious and must be avoided.

7.3   Assumptions and Requirements

A common approach to this is to keep all values of the objects used in a transaction invisible to other transactions until the transaction completes and a new consistent state is established. Prior to explaining the details of this approach, we state some assumptions and requirements for distributed systems.

7.3.1   Database Model

In this section, we present a conceptual model of a *distributed database system.* This *object-entity model,* along with corresponding notation, is similar to the model presented by Traiger, et al. [1982].

Figure 7.1 Three Concurrent Transactions.

Initial Balance in Accounts

A $400
B $200
C $100

Transactions

T_1
  begin
    read account A to obtain A's balance
    read account B to obtain B's balance
    write A's balance $-$ 50 to account A
    write B's balance $+$ 50 to account B
  end

T_2
  begin
    read account B to obtain B's balance
    read account C to obtain C's balance
    write B's balance $-$ 100 to account B
    write C's balance $+$ 100 to account C
  end

T_3
  begin
    read account A to obtain A's balance
    read account B to obtain B's balance
    print A's balance
    print B's balance
  end

A distributed database system is hosted by a collection of geographically separate computers called *sites*. Each site has a unique identifier, and the sites are interconnected by a common network. Sites communicate with each other by means of *messages* sent over the network. Messages may be arbitrarily delayed in the network, but it is assumed that all messages are eventually delivered. Furthermore, it is assumed that messages, sent from one site to another, are delivered in the order in which they were sent. Chapter 6 described how these conditions can be satisfied.

The database consists of a unique set of *entities*, such as records or files, that are uniquely named and that serve as indivisible units of access. An entity is realized as one or more *data objects,* each of which is uniquely identified by an <entity_name, site_identifier> pair. *Replication* of an entity occurs if it is represented by more than one object. Replication can result in improved performance if the cost of storing and maintaining (updating) copies is less than the cost of access. Also, replication can improve availability in the sense that if one site becomes inaccessible, then it

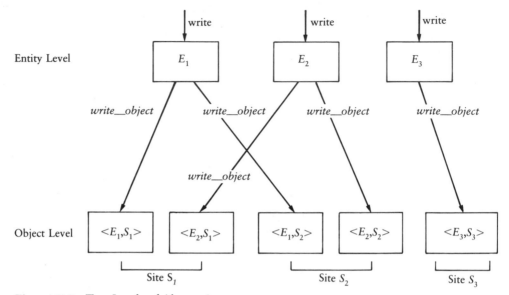

Figure 7.2 Two Levels of Abstraction.

may be possible to access the data at another site. Figure 7.2 illustrates the correspondence between entities and objects. An entity E, replicated at sites $S_1, \ldots, S_k$, is represented by the objects $<E, S_1>, \ldots, <E, S_k>$.

Each transaction T is supervised by a single *transaction manager (TM)*, which is in complete charge of overseeing the distributed computation. Four operations are defined at the transaction-TM interface:

read (E_i) returns the value of entity E_i.

write $(E_i,$ value) sets entity E_i to the specified value.

begin and *end* are used to bracket a transaction execution.

Each read request on an entity is translated by the TM into a *read* action, $(T, read\_object <E,S>,V)$, on some associated object. Each write request on an entity is translated into a collection of *write* actions of the form $(T, write\_object <E,S>,V)$, one for each associated object. In addition, the TM generates a $(T, commit\_object, <-,S>, -)$, one for each site S where any action was performed, to indicate successful completion of a transaction at site S.

Object managers (OMs) perform actions on their respective objects in response to requests from the TMs. In response to a request for a *read_object* action, the OM returns a value to the TM. A corresponding *commit_object* action has the effect of making permanent the effect of the last write on that object. As indicated in Figure 7.2, more than one OM may work for a single TM. TMs may communicate with both local and nonlocal OMs, but TMs do not communicate with other TMs. The execution of a TM is sequential: The TM waits for the completion of one action before requesting the next action.

In our model it is assumed that each entity is fully replicated or not replicated at all. This is not a major conceptual restriction, since a partially replicated entity can be treated as a collection of distinct entities with the global consistency constraint that these entities all have a consistent set of data (the same version of values). This global constraint, however, must be embodied in the structure of the transaction.

It is assumed that a write request for an entity results in the update of every copy while a read request needs to read only one copy. While this manner of dealing with replicated entities is a common approach, the model can be generalized to a weighted voting scheme [Gifford, 1979].

There are several models to describe how a transaction is represented and executed in a distributed system. A common approach is to assume that an agent process is created at each remote site involved in the execution of the transaction. On behalf of the transaction, a remote agent requests, acquires, and releases the required resources at the respective sites and may return a completion signal to the calling process when access has been completed. One model assumes that these processes are created when a remote access is required and cease to exist upon completion of the remote access [Menasce and Muntz, 1979]. A variation of the model [Gray, 1978] assumes that remote processes are established when a transaction is initiated and continue to exist until the transaction is completed. Yet another model [Rosenkrantz, et al. 1978] assumes that a transaction originates at a site and migrates from site to site as required to request the object operations. A transaction, at each site visited, is represented by an agent process. The flow of control through the network unwinds in a normal way, eliminating processes at each site. At various points in this chapter, we will use the model that seems most convenient. The developed results, however, are applicable to all the models either directly or with a straightforward extension.

7.3.2 Requirements of the Solution

The details of data distribution, replication, and concurrency should be transparent to the user. Four necessary types of transparency make a distributed system as easy to use as a centralized system [Traiger, et al. 1982].

1. *Location transparency:* Although data are geographically distributed and may move from site to site, the programmer need not be concerned with their location.
2. *Replication transparency:* The programmer may treat each entity as a single item, without knowledge of whether or not the entity is replicated.
3. *Concurrency transparency:* The programmer may view his transaction as being the only activity in the system.
4. *Failure transparency:* It must appear that either all or none of the actions of a transaction have successfully completed. Once a transaction completes, its effects should survive future hardware and software failures.

Subsequent sections of this chapter present methods for realizing these requirements.

7.4   Concurrency Control Based on Locking

In order to maintain consistency of distributed data, constraints must be placed on the structure of transactions and the manner in which concurrency may be realized. Although many algorithms have been used or proposed, most of them depend on the use of either *locks* or *timestamps*. This section is concerned with *locking techniques* while Section 7.11 deals with time stamping.

7.4.1   Lock Actions

Objects accessed by a transaction are locked in order to ensure their inaccessibility to other transactions while the database is temporarily in an inconsistent state. There are three *lock-related actions* on objects:

1. *(T, lock_X<E,S>)* denotes a request by transaction T for an exclusive lock on the object $<E,S>$. The request is granted only when no other transaction is holding a lock of any type on the object.

2. *(T, lock_S <E,S>)* denotes a request by transaction T for a shared lock on the object $<E,S>$. The request is granted only when no transaction is holding an exclusive lock on the object.

3. *(T, unlock <E,S>)* denotes the release of any lock by transaction T on the object $<E,S>$.

Two lock requests are said to *conflict* if they involve the same object and at least one of them is for an exclusive lock. A transaction is allowed to request a lock on the same object more than once and in different modes. However, once it has been granted an exclusive lock on an object, this locking mode persists until an unlock is requested. If a lock request cannot be granted, the transaction is blocked from further execution until the lock becomes available.

7.4.2   Structural Properties of Transactions

The following definitions [Eswaran, et al. 1976; Traiger, et al. 1982] place constraints on the manner in which transactions may be structured.

A transaction is said to be *well-formed* if it reads an object only while it is holding a shared or exclusive lock on the object and if it writes an object only while it is holding an exclusive lock on the object.

A transaction is *two-phase* if it does not issue a lock action after it has issued an unlock action. The first phase of the transaction, called the *growing phase*, begins with the first action and continues up to the first unlock action. The second phase of the transaction, called the *shrinking phase*, begins with the first unlock action and continues through the last action.

A transaction is *strong two-phase* if all unlock actions are issued at the very end of the transaction.

Figure 7.3(a) A Well-Formed Transaction.

$<$ $(T_1, lock\_S <A, S>, -),$
$(T_1, read\_object <A, S>, A\_balance),$
$(T_1, unlock <A, S>, -),$
$(T_1, lock\_S <B, S>, -),$
$(T_1, read\_object <B, S>, B\_balance),$
$(T_1, unlock <B, S>, -),$
$(T_1, lock\_X <A, S>, -),$
$(T_1, write\_object <A, S>, A\_balance - 50),$
$(T_1, unlock <A, S>, -),$
$(T_1, lock\_X <B, S>, -),$
$(T_1, write\_object <B, S>, B\_balance + 50),$
$(T_1, unlock <B, S>, -) >$

Figure 7.3 shows an example of (a) a well-formed transaction that is not two-phase and also an example of (b) a transaction that has both properties. For simplicity, the *commit_object* actions are not shown in this example. Eswaran, et al. [1976] has shown that necessary and sufficient conditions for consistency in a concurrent environment are that all transactions be well-formed and two-phase.

A later section will discuss the recoverability of a failed transaction; this places additional requirements on our system. Thus, in order to complete the model, we will assume that *all* transactions are strong two-phase and that all *commit_object* actions will immediately precede the unlock actions for the transaction.

It is not necessary to execute a lock action on every object associated with an entity. Some suggested implementation strategies are *primary site locking* and *primary copy locking* [Bernstein and Goodman, 1981]. In primary site locking, one site is designated the lock manager and all locks are requested from this site. After a lock has been granted, subsequent reads or writes may take place on any copy. Writing may be delayed, but all copies must be updated prior to releasing the lock. The primary copy locking technique is an extension of the previous method in that each entity in the database has some unique site designated as the lock manager. The use of several such sites tends to alleviate the bottleneck and vulnerability to

Figure 7.3(b) A Well-Formed Two-Phase Transaction.

$<$ $(T_1, lock\_X <A, S>, -),$
$(T_1, lock\_X <B, S>, -),$
$(T_1, read\_object <A, S>, A\_balance),$
$(T_1, write\_object <A, S>, A\_balance - 50),$
$(T_1, read\_object <B, S>, B\_balance),$
$(T_1, write\_object <B, S>, B\_balance + 50),$
$(T_1, unlock <A, S>, -),$
$(T_1, unlock <B, S> -) >$

failure of the primary site method. Under the assumption of strong two-phase transactions, lock and unlock actions need not be explicitly requested by a TM. A *read_
object* action could carry with it an implicit request for a shared lock, if the object
has not already been locked by the transaction. Similarly, a *write_object* action could
carry with it an implicit request for an exclusive lock. The OM may execute the
necessary unlock actions immediately after executing a *commit* action.

7.4.3   Schedules

The sequence of actions for a well-formed and strong two-phase transaction T, may
be represented as [Traiger, et al. 1982]

$$Q_T = <(T, A_1<O_1>, V_1), (T, A_2<O_2>, V_2), \ldots, (T, A_k<O_k>, V_k)>$$

where A_i, O_i, and V_i specify the ith action, ith object and ith value, respectively. A_1
must be a *lock_X* or *lock_S* action while A_i, $2 \leq i < k - \alpha$, is one of *read_object*,
write_object, lock_S, and *lock_X*. The last α actions must be a sequence of *unlock*
actions, preceded by a *commit_object*.

7.4.4   Serial and Legal Schedules

The concurrent execution of a set of transactions results in the execution of a sequence
of interleaved actions on objects at each involved site in the network. Each of these
sequences is called a *local schedule,* and the control of its structure is the fundamental
issue of *concurrency control.* To develop some important theoretical results, we first
restrict our attention to a single-site system with one centralized schedule. The results
will be extended later to include the general case. Given a set of transactions $T_1, \ldots, T_n$,
a schedule for a single-site system is an interleaving of their actions to form a global
sequence

$$Q = < \ldots, (T_i, A_{ij} <O_{ij}>, V_{ij}), \ldots >$$

with A_{ij} denoting the jth action of transaction T_i. From the definition of lock actions,
it is clear that not all schedules are realizable. As a consequence, we restrict our
attention to *legal schedules,* that is, schedules in which transactions do not simultaneously hold conflicting locks. A particularly important subset of legal schedules
is the set of *serial schedules,* in which one transaction completes all of its actions
before the next transaction begins. Figures 7.4 and 7.5 show a serial schedule and
a legal schedule, respectively, for the transactions given in Figure 7.1. A serial schedule has no concurrency, but it is of interest since it preserves database consistency.
We are interested in the larger class of legal schedules, which may exhibit concurrency
and which are equivalent to some serial schedule. Such schedules are said to be
serializable. The next section explains the concept of equivalence.

Figure 7.4 A Serial Schedule.

$< \ (T_1, \ lock\_X <A, S>, -),$
  $(T_1, \ read\_object <A, S>, A\_balance),$
  $(T_1, \ lock\_X <B, S>, -),$
  $(T_1, \ read\_object <B, S>, B\_balance),$
  $(T_1, \ write\_object <A, S>, A\_balance - 50),$
  $(T_1, \ write\_object <B, S>, B\_balance + 50),$
  $(T_1, \ commit\_object <-, S>, -),$
  $(T_1, \ unlock <A, S>, -),$
  $(T_1, \ unlock <B, S>, -),$
  $(T_2, \ lock\_X <B, S>, -),$
  $(T_2, \ read\_object <B, S>, B\_balance),$
  $(T_2, \ lock\_X <C, S>, -),$
  $(T_2, \ read\_object <C, S>, C\_balance),$
  $(T_2, \ write\_object <B, S>, B\_balance - 100),$
  $(T_2, \ write\_object <C, S>, C\_balance + 100),$
  $(T_2, \ commit\_object <-, S>, -),$
  $(T_2, \ unlock <B, S>, -),$
  $(T_2, \ unlock <C, S>, -),$
  $(T_3, \ lock\_S <A, S>, -),$
  $(T_3, \ read\_object <A, S>, A\_balance),$
  $(T_3, \ lock\_S <B, S>, -),$
  $(T_3, \ read\_object <B, S>, B\_balance),$
  $print \ A\_balance,$
  $print \ B\_balance,$
  $(T_3, \ commit\_object <-, S>, -),$
  $(T_3, \ unlock <A, S>, -),$
  $(T_3, \ unlock <B, S>, -) >$

7.4.5 Equivalent Schedules

The following definition is from Traiger, et al. [1982] and will be used to define the equivalence of two schedules. Given a schedule Q, the *dependency relation* DEP(Q) is a ternary relation such that for any distinct transactions T_1 and T_2 and any object O and value V, $(T_1, <O,V>, T_2) \in$ DEP(Q) if

1. $Q = < \ldots, (T_1, write\_object <O>, V_1), \ldots,$
   $(T_2, write\_object <O>, V_2), \ldots >$
   or

2. $Q = < \ldots, (T_1, write\_object <O>, V_1), \ldots,$
   $(T_2, read\_object <O>, V_2), \ldots >$
   or

3. $Q = < \ldots, (T_1, read\_object <O>, V_1), \ldots,$
   $(T_2, write\_object <O>, V_2), \ldots >$

where no actions of the form $(T_3, write\_object<O>, V_3)$ occur in the middle ellipsis. Informally, DEP(Q) identifies pairs of transactions T_i and T_j in the schedule Q, with

Figure 7.5   A Legal Schedule.

$<$ $(T_1, lock\_X <A, S>, -)$,
$(T_2, lock\_X <B, S>, -)$,
$(T_1, read\_object <A, S>, T_1's\ A\_balance)$,
$(T_2, read\_object <B, S>, T_2's\ B\_balance)$,
$(T_2, lock\_X <C, S>, -)$,
$(T_2, read\_object <C, S>, T_2's\ C\_balance)$,
$(T_2, write\_object <B, S>, T_2's\ B\_balance - 100)$,
$(T_2, write\_object <C, S>, T_2's\ C\_balance + 100)$,
$(T_2, commit\_object <-, S>, -)$,
$(T_2, unlock <B, S>, -)$,
$(T_1, lock\_X <B, S>, -)$,
$(T_1, read\_object <B, S>, T_1's\ B\_balance)$,
$(T_1, write\_object <A, S>, T_1's\ A\_balance - 50)$,
$(T_1, write\_object <B, S>, T_1's\ B\_balance + 50)$,
$(T_1, commit\_object <-, S>, -)$,
$(T_1, unlock <A, S>, -)$,
$(T_3, lock\_S <A, S>, -)$,
$(T_3, read\_object <A, S>, T_3's\ A\_balance)$,
$(T_1, unlock <B, S>, -)$,
$(T_3, lock\_S <B, S>, -)$,
$T_3, print\ T_3's\ A\_balance$,
$(T_3, read\_object <B, S>, T_3's\ B\_balance)$,
$T_3, print\ T_3's\ B\_balance$,
$(T_2, unlock <C, S>, -) >$,
$(T_3, commit\_object <-, S>, -)$,
$(T_3, unlock <A, S>, -)$,
$(T_3, unlock <B, S>, -) >$

T_j either directly dependent on a value that T_i has written or T_j the first transaction to overwrite a value that T_i has previously read or written. In order to establish similar dependencies for transactions that have first and last actions in Q, we introduce imaginary initial and final transactions, T_I and T_F, and augment DEP(Q) in the following manner:

1. If the first read or write action in Q on object O is a *write_object* by transaction T, then

   $(T_I, <O,V>, T) \in$ DEP(Q)

2. If the first read or write actions in Q on object O (preceding the first *write_object* on object O) are *read_object* actions by transactions T_1, T_2, $\ldots$, T_m, then

   $(T_I, <O,V>, T_i) \in$ DEP(Q)   for $1 \leq i \leq m$

3. If the last read or write action in Q on object O is a *write_object* by transaction T, then

$$(T, <O,V>, T_F) \in DEP(Q)$$

4. If the last read or write actions in Q on object O (after the last *write_object* on object O) are *read_object* actions by transactions $T_1, T_2, \ldots, T_m$, then

$$(T_i, <O,V>, T_F) \in DEP(Q) \quad \text{for } 1 \leq i \leq m$$

These dependency relations uniquely define the input and output values for each transaction T in a schedule Q. If the input and output values for each transaction are the same in two distinct schedules, then the schedules produce the same results. So we define two schedules to be *equivalent* if they have the same DEP relation. Furthermore, we define the class of schedules equivalent to some serial schedule to be the class of *consistent schedules,* since each member preserves database consistency.

7.5 Theorems on Consistency

This section presents three important theorems on concurrency control that establish a relationship between the structure of transactions and the structure of both global and local schedules. The first theorem holds in a centralized system.

THEOREM 7.1

[Eswaran, et al. 1976; Rosenkrantz, et al. 1978; Traiger, et al. 1982]: *If* $\{T_1, T_2, \ldots, T_k\}$ *is a set of well-formed and two-phase transactions, then any legal schedule* Q_0 *is consistent.*

PROOF

It suffices to show that Q_0 is equivalent to a serial schedule. Define HAPPEN(T) to be the index in Q_0 of the first unlock action of T. HAPPEN induces a total order on the transactions and, without loss of generality, we may assume $HAPPEN(T_i) < HAPPEN(T_{i+1})$ for all $0 \leq i < k$. The proof consists of constructing a set of partial schedules Q_i for $i = 1, \ldots, k - 1$, so that Q_i does not contain the actions of T_j for $j < i$ and Q_{i-1} is equivalent to $T_i Q_i$. This will establish that Q_0 is serializable. We will briefly outline the proof for $i = 1$. In Q_0, consider any two adjacent actions $(T_i, A_i < O_i >, V_i) (T_1, A_1 < O_1 >, V_1)$, with $T_i \neq T_1$. We will show that these two actions can be interchanged to form an equivalent schedule Q_0'. There are several cases to consider.

1. Suppose A_1 or A_i is a *commit_object* action. Since this action affects neither the locking status nor the values of objects, Q_0' is legal and $DEP(Q) = DEP(Q_0')$.

2. Suppose $O_i \neq O_1$. Then A_i and A_1 do not conflict because they access different objects. As a result, Q_0' is legal and $DEP(Q) = DEP(Q_0')$.

3. Suppose $O_i = O_1$. Neither A_i nor A_1 can be a *write_object* action or a *lock_X* action, because this would mean that both T_1 and T_i are concurrently holding exclusive locks on O_1. We conclude that A_i and A_1 must be *lock_S*, *unlock*, or *read_object* actions. There are two subcases to consider.

   a. Suppose $A_i \neq unlock$. Then A_i and A_1 may be interchanged without affecting either the legality of the schedule or the DEP relation.

   b. Suppose $A_i = unlock$. $DEP(Q_0) = DEP(Q_0')$ because DEP does not involve lock actions. To establish legality of Q_0', note that A_1 cannot be a *lock_S*, since this would violate the assumption that $HAPPEN(T_1) < HAPPEN(T_i)$. If A_1 is an *unlock* or *read_object* action, then legality is also clear.

   Thus, we can move all actions of T_1 to form the sequence $T_1 Q_1$, which is equivalent to Q_0. Continuing the process for $T_2, \ldots, T_n$, we end up with Q_0 equivalent to the serial schedule $T_1 \ldots T_n$.

At this point, it is not known if Theorem 7.1 will hold in a distributed system since each site performs its actions without knowledge of activities at other sites. The local schedule for site j may involve the actions of several transactions and can be represented by

$$Q_j = < \ldots, (T_i, A_{ij}<O_{ij}>, V_{ij}), \ldots >$$

The next theorem, from Traiger, et al. [1982], establishes the fact that the execution of actions in local site schedules may be modeled as the execution of a single schedule at some centralized site. The theorem relies heavily on our assumption that individual transactions are sequences of actions and may not be true if concurrency within a transaction were allowed.

THEOREM 7.2

Let $Q_1, \ldots, Q_n$ be the set of site schedules for the set of transactions $\{T_1, \ldots, T_m\}$. Then there is a global schedule Q such that (a) the action sequences of T_i and Q_i are subsequences of Q, and (b) if each Q_i is legal, then Q is legal.

PROOF

Each site j is assumed to have an imaginary local clock (implementable by a simple counter), whose value is denoted by C_j, similar to that described in Chapter 6. We will assume that the TM also maintains an imaginary transaction clock with value denoted by C_T. If the TM is at site i, $C_T = C_i$ at the outset. When the TM requests an action on a remote object at site j, it first increments C_i and then a request message

("*REQUEST*", C_i, T, $A < O >$, V)

is sent to site j. Upon receipt of the message, site j adjusts its clock

$C_j : = max(C_j, C_i)$

When site j executes action A on object O for transaction T, it increments C_j and sends an acknowledgement to the TM

("ACK", C_j, T, $A < O >$, V)

Upon receipt of the acknowledgment, the TM sets

$C_i := max(C_i, C_j)$ and
$C_T := C_i$

To form an equivalent global schedule, combine the site schedules and sort the actions in ascending order on (C_i, site number). This Q satisfies properties (a) and (b) of the theorem.

Although the technique used in the proof assumes that the TM resides at a single site, the method would also work in other models, such as where a transaction is assumed to move from site to site.

Theorem 7.3, also from Traiger, et al., restates the result of Theorem 7.1 for a multisite system. The proof is similar to Theorem 7.1 and is left to the reader.

THEOREM 7.3

If all transactions are well-formed and two-phase, then any legal execution of the transactions by a distributed system will be equivalent to the execution of some consistent schedule by a system consisting of a single site.

Figure 7.6 shows a set of possible schedules for the three transactions in Figure 7.1. It is assumed that accounts A, B, and C are each replicated at the two sites S_1 and S_2 and that the transaction managers for T_1 and T_3 are at S_1, while the transaction manager for T_2 is at S_2. Note that each transaction performs only one *read_object* action for an account, while two *write_object* actions are required to update an account. Also note that transaction T_1 defers updates on objects $<A, S_2>$ and $<B, S_2>$ until it commits. In this example, a lock on an entity results in a lock action on the associated object at each site. Adopting a primary site or primary copy implementation strategy would require only one lock per entity.

7.6 Deadlock Detection

The *deadlock* problem was studied extensively in Chapter 4, and the theory can be directly applied to database systems. Some simplification, however, is possible due to two characteristics of a database system. First, a database is viewed as a collection of "single-unit reusable" resources. Second, the states of the database system are expedient. As a consequence, each resource is either not in use or its single unit is associated with one or more current users (transactions). This leads to the observation that resource nodes are redundant and can be eliminated from the reusable resource graph.

Given a reusable resource graph representing the state of a database system, the transformation to a graph without resource nodes is straightforward: If R is a resource and P and Q are processes such that (P, R) and (R, Q) are edges in the graph, then

Figure 7.6 A Schedule for Three Transactions Working on Replicated Data in Two Sites.
(a) Schedule at Site S_1.

$<$ $(T_1, lock\_X <A, S_1>, -)$,
  $(T_2, lock\_X <B, S_1>, -)$,
  $(T_1, read\_object <A, S_1>, T_1's\ A\_balance)$,
  $(T_2, lock\_X <C, S_1>, -)$,
  $(T_2, write\_object <B, S_1>, T_2's\ B\_balance\ -100)$,
  $(T_2, write\_object <C, S_2>, T_2's\ C\_balance\ +100)$,
  $(T_2, commit\_object <-, S_1>, -)$,
  $(T_2, unlock <B, S_1>, -)$,
  $(T_1, lock\_X <B, S_1>, -)$,
  $(T_1, read\_object <B, S_1>, T_1's\ B\_balance)$,
  $(T_1, write\_object <A, S_1>, T_1's\ A\_balance\ -50)$,
  $(T_1, write\_object <B, S_1>, T_1's\ B\_balance\ +50)$,
  $(T_1, commit\_object <-, S_1>, -)$,
  $(T_1, unlock <A, S_1>, -)$,
  $(T_3, lock\_S <A, S_1>, -)$,
  $(T_3, read\_object <A, S_1>, T_3's\ A\_balance)$,
  $(T_1, unlock <B, S_1>, -)$,
  $(T_3, lock\_S <B, S_1>, -)$,
  $T_3, print\ T_3's\ A\_balance$,
  $(T_3, read\_object <B, S_1>, T_3's\ B\_balance)$,
  $T_3, print\ T_3's\ B\_balance$,
  $(T_2, unlock <C, S_1>, -)$,
  $(T_3, commit\_object <-, S_1>, -)$,
  $(T_3, unlock <A, S_1>, -)$,
  $(T_3, unlock <B, S_1>, -)$ $>$

the transformed graph will have an edge (P, Q). This latter graph is called a *transaction wait-for graph (TWFG)* since any edge represents one transaction waiting for another to release the resource. Since we have single-unit resources, a cycle is both a necessary and sufficient condition for a deadlock to exist, and deadlock detection algorithms are based on finding a cycle in the TWFG. Figure 7.7 gives an example of a TWFG. The "share" and "exclusive" labels on edges are for expository purposes only. The principal difficulty in implementing *deadlock detection* in a distributed system lies in the efficient construction of the TWFG. Local TWFGs can be easily constructed but, in order to detect *global deadlocks*, these TWFGs must be combined into a "global" TWFG.

In the discussion that follows, we adopt the model in which a transaction is represented by a collection of distributed processes, called *agents*. If the transaction requests access to resources at a remote site, a *remote* agent is created at the remote site to implement the actual request, access, and release of resources. The remote agent ceases to exist when the remote access is complete. The results are equally applicable, with slight modification, to any other models mentioned in Section 7.3.1.

Figure 7.6(b) Schedule at Site S_2.

$< \ (T_1, \ lock\_X <A, S_2>, \ -),$
$\quad (T_2, \ lock\_X <B, S_2>, \ -),$
$\quad (T_2, \ read\_object <B, S_2>, \ T_2's \ B\_balance),$
$\quad (T_2, \ lock\_X <C, S_2>, \ -),$
$\quad (T_2, \ read\_object <C, S_2>, \ T_2's \ C\_balance),$
$\quad (T_2, \ write\_object <B, S_2>, \ T_2's \ B\_balance \ -100),$
$\quad (T_2, \ write\_object <C, S_2>, \ T_2's \ C\_balance \ +100),$
$\quad (T_2, \ commit\_object <-, S_2>, \ -),$
$\quad (T_2, \ unlock <B, S_2>, \ -),$
$\quad (T_1, \ lock\_X <B, S_2>, \ -),$
$\quad (T_1, \ write\_object <A, S_2>, \ T_1's \ A\_balance \ -50),$
$\quad (T_1, \ write\_object <B, S_2>, \ T_1's \ B\_balance \ +50),$
$\quad (T_1, \ commit\_object <-, S_2>, \ -),$
$\quad (T_1, \ unlock <A, S_2>, \ -),$
$\quad (T_1, \ unlock <B, S_2>, \ -),$
$\quad (T_2, \ unlock <C, S_2>, \ -) \ >$

The transaction may simultaneously request resources at several remote sites, thereby creating several remote agents.

The original agent communicates with a remote agent via input and output ports, which connect the sites. Figure 7.8 illustrates a collection of local TWFGs and the use of remote agents, denoted by square nodes, in constructing a global TWFG. A communication link, represented by a dashed arc, connects an agent with its remote agent via *input* ports and *output* ports (diamond-shaped nodes labeled I and O, respectively). The presence of a local I/O path from an input port to an output port is a necessary but not sufficient condition for a site to be involved in a global deadlock. In the following subsections we describe both centralized and distributed algorithms for combining such I/O paths into a global TWFG.

This model of distributed processes is sufficient to model any distributed operating system for the purpose of deadlock analysis. In particular, it can be applied to both a system of transactions, in which transactions normally have short lives, and a system of normally long lived processes. The former is typically used to represent a database system, whereas the latter is used to model an operating system. As a consequence, the terms *transaction* and *process* are used interchangeably in this section.

7.6.1 Centralized Deadlock Detection

In centralized deadlock detection, one site, the *central detector,* is designated as being responsible for the detection of global deadlocks. There are two basic approaches. In *periodic* deadlock the central detector initiates action by periodically polling the various sites. Each site responds with its set of I/O paths or a message that states that no such paths exist. In *continuous* deadlock each local site initiates action by informing the central detector when an I/O path is formed and again when it disappears.

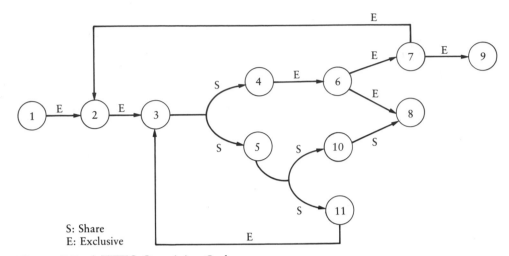

S: Share
E: Exclusive

Figure 7.7 A TWFG Containing Cycles.

Upon receiving information from the local sites, the central deadlock detector constructs the global TWFG and performs the deadlock analysis.

Although centralized deadlock detection is conceptually simple, there are several problems involved with its implementation. The first problem is one of *phantom (false) deadlocks*. For example, assume continuous deadlock detection and suppose the initial states of sites A and B to be those shown in Figure 7.9(a). The I/O path at site A is sent to the central deadlock detector and the global TWFG is constructed. At this point, suppose that transaction 3 releases the resource requested by transaction 2, which in turn releases the resource requested by transaction 1. When the release message from the remote agent at site B of transaction 2 has reached site A, the I/O path at site A disappears and this new information is sent to the central detector. While this latter information is in transit, suppose transaction 3 requests the resource held by transaction 4, and transaction 2 again requests the resource held by transaction 3, creating the state shown in Figure 7.9(b). The new I/O path at site B is reported to the central deadlock detector. If this latter message arrives before the previous message from site A arrives, the central deadlock detector will construct the TWFG shown in Figure 7.9(c) and will detect a phantom deadlock. Similar scenarios are possible if deadlock detection is periodic.

Note that the phantom deadlock in Figure 7.9 occurs because transactions 2 and 3 rerequest resources after having released them. A phantom deadlock cannot occur if two-phase locking is used, since this type of behavior by an individual transaction is prohibited. However, it is not always possible to apply two-phase locking in a distributed operating system. If they are allowed to occur, the issue is how to distinguish between real and phantom deadlocks. One approach would be to attempt no distinction between the two and always invoke a recovery technique. This provides for rapid detection of a real deadlock but also incurs unnecessary abortion and restart of processes in the case of phantom deadlock. A second approach

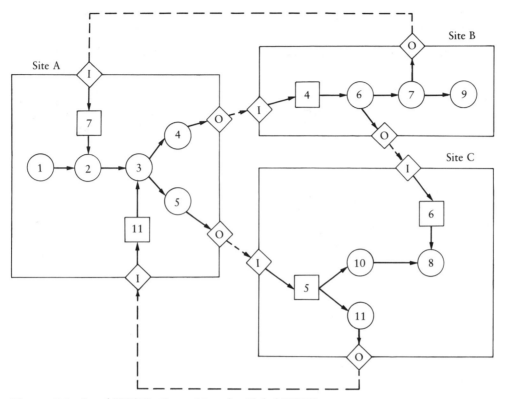

Figure 7.8 Local TWFGs Comprising the Global TWFG
of Figure 7.7.

is for the deadlock detector to delay invoking a recovery program until it determines
that the perceived deadlock is persistent. However, repeated detection of a deadlock
still does not guarantee that the deadlock is real because the same steps that created
the phantom deadlock might reoccur [Ho and Ramamoorthy, 1982; Jagannathan
and Vasuderan, 1983]. The usual approach taken in subsequent sections is to prevent the occurrence of phantom deadlocks by adopting a labeling scheme whereby
each newly created transaction is given a unique identification.

    A second problem with centralized deadlock detection is concerned with the
high volume of message traffic between the local sites and the central site. If continuous checking incurs too much overhead, periodic deadlock detection might prove
to be a better alternative. The tradeoff is between rapid detection of deadlocks and
reduced message traffic. There are several variations of periodic deadlock detection
that will reduce the number of required messages. First, when the central deadlock
detector requests a site to send I/O path information, the site need not respond if it
has no information to send. The deadlock detector interprets no response as no I/O
path. A further modification would be to totally eliminate requests from the deadlock detector. If no I/O path information is received within a given time interval, the
central detector assumes that none exists. Still another variation is for a site to report

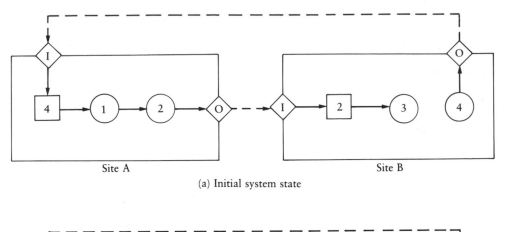

(a) Initial system state

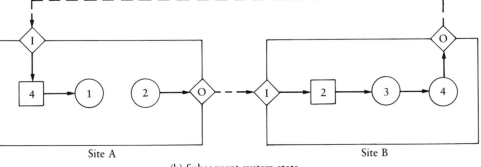

(b) Subsequent system state

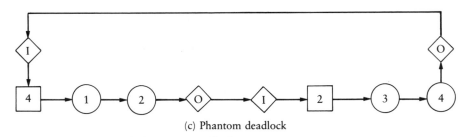

(c) Phantom deadlock

Figure 7.9   Formation of Phantom Deadlocks.

the creation of an I/O path only after it has persisted at its local site for more than some threshold [Menasce and Muntz, 1979]. While this further delays the detection of a deadlock, it also further reduces the message traffic and increases the probability that the I/O path is actually involved in a deadlock. Since the expiration of a time period is interpreted as information, these variations are feasible only if communication is reliable and the clocks at each site are closely synchronized. Careful experimentation would be needed to determine the length of an "optimal" time period.

A third problem with centralized deadlock detection is its vulnerability to failure. If the central site fails, the entire system fails. One approach to alleviating the failure problem is to provide a backup central site or to designate a group of such sites.

7.6.2   Hierarchical Deadlock Detection

The technique of centralized deadlock detection can be extended to form a logical hierarchy of deadlock detectors. The method is similar to the scheme of Menasce and Muntz [1979].

A local deadlock detector exists at each site that controls access to a portion of the database. Each such detector maintains a local TWFG, as previously described, and is in charge of detecting and resolving any local deadlocks. A local I/O path at a site is reported to a parent deadlock detector, perhaps residing at a remote site. Each parent detector is in charge of detecting and resolving any deadlock that is local to itself and the set of its descendent sites. Each parent detector, in turn, reports I/O paths to its parent, and so on. The process terminates at some designated central detector.

Hierarchical deadlock detection significantly eases the problems of the high cost of constructing the global TWFG. It also eases, but does not eliminate, the vulnerability to failure of central sites. However, phantom deadlocks remain as a potential problem.

7.6.3   Distributed Deadlock Detection

Distributed deadlock detection has been the subject of intensive research in recent years and a number of algorithms have been proposed [Isloor and Marsland, 1979; Menasce and Muntz, 1979; Obermarck, 1982; Chandy, et al. 1983; Maekawa, 1983]. Two algorithms from Maekawa, one for periodic detection and the other for continuous detection, are described in this section. These algorithms are interesting in that they avoid the detection of phantom deadlocks (except where a transaction may be aborted for resolving other deadlocks or for reasons other than deadlock). Only one site will attempt to resolve a distinct deadlock, and the algorithms require only an average of $n \log_2 n$ messages to detect deadlock (where n is the number of sites).

Assume that each transaction is assigned a unique network identification of the form (Q_S, S) when it is created. S is the site identification and Q_S is a unique local identification, generated as the next member of a nondecreasing sequence of integers. Note that a simple counter or a local clock could serve as the generator of this sequence. In a manner similar to the synchronization of a system of clocks, described in Chapter 6, assume that the generators of transaction identifiers remain loosely synchronized in the sense that if site S receives a message from site T, then site S updates its generator by

$$Q_S = \max (Q_S, Q_T) + 1$$

Since this network identification scheme serves to totally order the transactions in the system, the pair (Q_S, S) will be referred to as the *sequence* number of a transaction.

To describe the algorithms for distributed deadlock detection, some additional rules are required for creating input and output ports and remote agents, and for labeling nodes. Consider, for example, the three sites shown in Figure 7.10. The agent for a transaction at its original site (called the *original* agent) is represented by a circle node and denoted by $((i,A),0)$ where i is the local identification of the transaction, A is the site name, and the value "zero" in the second component indicates that this agent represents the transaction at its original site. A remote agent at site S, for transaction i at site A, is represented by a square node and denoted by $[(i,A),g,S]$, where g is the agent's sequence number for this transaction. Since the original agent for the transaction is given the sequence number $g = 0$, remote agents, created for the transaction, are given successive sequence numbers for their values of g. Thus, variable g uniquely identifies agents for a transaction. Since it is assumed that a remote agent ceases to exist upon the completion of the requested access, g uniquely identifies a wait-for relationship or an edge in the TWFG; that is, different requests directed to the same transaction result in an agent with a new g. If a different transaction model is used, g may have to be interpreted in a slightly different manner to serve this purpose. For example, if a remote agent continues to exist until the transaction is completed (or even longer), a new value of g should be generated for each request. Since the sole purpose of g is to avoid phantom deadlock, its existence is not necessary if two-phase locking is used.

When the original agent for transaction i at site A requests a resource at a remote site B, an output port node denoted by $<(i,A),g,A,B>$ is created at site A and an input port node denoted by $<(i,A),g,B,A>$ is created at site B, where g is the agent number for the newly created agent at site B. Edges are created from $((i,A),0)$ to $<(i,A),g,A,B>$, from $<(i,A),g,A,B>$ to $<(i,A),g,B,A>$, and from $<(i,A),g,B,A>$ to $[(i,A),g,B]$. When a signal is returned from a remote agent, indicating completion of work, the remote agent is deleted. If the transaction again requests a resource at the same remote site, a new remote agent is created with a new sequence number.

Each I/O path in the network has an associated sequence number determined by

$$highest \text{ (p)} = \text{the highest sequence number of any transaction contained in}$$
$$\text{I/O path } p \text{ (excluding agents for remote transactions)}.$$

Consider the example of Figure 7.10. If p is the path from $<(6,C),1,A,C>$ to $<(2,A),1,A,B>$, then $highest$ (p) $= (2, A)$. If p is the path from $<(4,B),1,C,B>$ to $<(6,C),1,C,A>$, then $highest$ (p) $= (6, C)$.

The local sites along a *global I/O path* communicate by *deadlock-detection messages* or simply *detection messages*. A detection message contains three items of information:

1. The identification of the site that originated the message
2. The message sequence number
3. A description of the global I/O path from the originating site to the current site

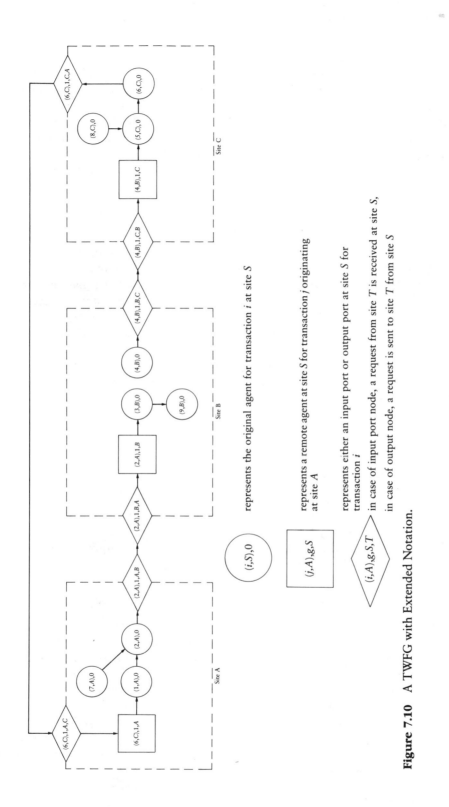

represents the original agent for transaction i at site S

represents a remote agent at site S for transaction j originating at site A

represents either an input port or output port at site S for transaction i

in case of input port node, a request from site T is received at site S,

in case of output node, a request is sent to site T from site S

$(i,S),0$

$(j,A),g,S$

$(i,A),g,S,T$

Figure 7.10 A TWFG with Extended Notation.

259

The message sequence number is computed when the detection message is initiated and is defined to be *highest* (corresponding local I/O path at the originating site). The description of the global I/O path is extended by each site before it is passed to another site. Note that any two detection messages are identical only when all three items match. Therefore, detection messages that traverse different paths will be different. There is actually some redundancy in the information carried by a detection message since the message sequence number contains the identification of the originating site. This redundancy is maintained in order to cope with a more general scheme in which the sequence number is determined by other than site number.

A Periodic Deadlock-Detection Algorithm

Periodically, each site determines if it has a local I/O path and, if it does, sends a detection message to the site named in the corresponding output port of the path. If the local I/O path persists, more than one detection message may be sent on its behalf. Thus, multiple messages involving the same I/O path could be present in the system. If a deadlock-detection message is received from another site, the receiving site extends the information, if possible, with local I/O paths and sends the information to the next involved site. Rules 1 and 2, given next, describe the precise protocol for the periodic global deadlock-detection algorithm. We assume that each rule is performed by the local deadlock detector without interference from any agents so that the state reflected by the local TWFG does not change while it is being analyzed.

ALGORITHM 7.1

Rule 1 Deadlock detection is initiated:

When deadlock detection is initiated at site *A,* the site first resolves any local deadlock. The site then checks for the existence of any local I/O path. For each existing I/O path p, the deadlock detector generates a detection message (A, $highest(p)$, p) and sends it to the site specified by the output port for p.

Rule 2 A detection message is received at site B:

Rule 2.1   Site B is not the originating site of the message:

Site *B* determines if it has already contributed to the I/O path in this message. If it has, the message is discarded. Otherwise, site *B* checks for the existence of any local I/O paths that will extend the global I/O path information of the message. If none exist, the message is discarded. Otherwise, for each such existing local I/O path p, site *B* compares $highest(p)$ with the message sequence number. If the message sequence number is higher, the global I/O path information of the message is extended with p and the message is passed to the next site identified by the output port of p. If there is no local I/O path p whose $highest(p)$ is lower than the message sequence number, the message is discarded.

Rule 2.2   Site B is the originating site of the message:

Site *B* determines if the local I/O path, which was used to originate the message, still exists. If it does not, the message is discarded. If it does, a global deadlock is detected. The local deadlock detector selects the transaction in the global I/O path with the highest sequence number as the victim. Note that the original agent for this transaction is at site B.

Theorems 7.4 and 7.5 establish that all real deadlocks are detected and any detected deadlock is real.

THEOREM 7.4

In distributed periodic deadlock detection, a global deadlock will be detected by some site.

PROOF

A site generates a deadlock-detection message for each local I/O path. Each detection message is passed to the next site if there exists an I/O path that can extend the global I/O path of the message. When the message is passed, its global I/O path information is extended with the I/O path at this site. The detection messages are totally ordered according to their unique sequence numbers. The message whose sequence number is equal to the highest sequence number of any transaction on the cycle will return to its originating site, whereas all others will be discarded. This returned message identifies the global cycle.

THEOREM 7.5

In distributed periodic deadlock detection, a detected global cycle identifies a real global deadlock.

PROOF

Assume the contrary; that is, some site *A* has detected a phantom deadlock. Then site *A* has initiated a deadlock-detection message m_A that is extended by one or more sites and returned to site *A*. Furthermore, if the deadlock is a phantom, then the detected cycle never actually existed and was never in the process of being formed. Hence, there must be at least one I/O path, over which m_A was passed, that no longer exists. Two cases are possible.

Case 1   A completion signal was returned, eliminating an I/O path:

The transmission of the completion signal occurs from some site *T* to some site *S* (backward), whereas a detection message is sent from *S* to *T* (forward). Three subcases are possible.

   a. Before the detection message is sent, the completion signal is received at site S.

In this case, since each rule is implemented as an indivisible local operation, the I/O path is broken at site S before the detection message is sent. Thus, the detection message would be discarded at site S.

b. Before the completion signal is sent, the detection message is received.

In this case the detection message would be discarded at site T.

c. The completion signal and the detection message are simultaneously in transit.

Suppose the completion signal is returned to agent $((i,S),0)$ from agent $((j,T),0)$. This means that remote agent $[(i,S),1,T]$ and input port $<(i,S),1,T,S>$ no longer exist. Thus, the detection message will be discarded at T. Note that if, in the meantime, agent $((i,S),0)$ initiates a new request for a resource held by $((j,T),0)$, a new remote agent and input ports are created with new sequence numbers. In this case, T will not be able to extend the I/O path information with a local I/O path.

In all subcases, the detection message is discarded, contradicting the hypothesis that a cycle was detected.

Case 2   The cycle is broken by the resolution of another deadlock:

This situation can arise if two distinct global cycles have a common transaction. The broken cycle is *transient* in that it existed only temporarily or would have really existed, but was in the meantime resolved due to a distinctly different deadlock. Note that a transient cycle is different from a phantom deadlock since the latter implies an imaginary cycle that could never have a real (past, present, or future) existence. The absence of a phantom deadlock contradicts the hypothesis, concluding the discussion of this case. Note that it is possible for the transient cycle, detected at some site A, to have a higher sequence number than the cycle that was detected and broken by some (possibly different) site B. Although B aborts one of its transactions, A might also (needlessly) abort one of its transactions.

For example, assume the system state shown in Figure 7.11 and suppose that each site generates a detection message at about the same time. The detection message m_A, originating at site A, has the sequence number $(4, A)$. Since this is less than the sequence number of the I/O path at site B, m_A is discarded at site B. The detection message m_B, originating at site B, has a higher sequence number than the sequence numbers of the I/O paths at both sites C and A. Therefore, m_B returns to its originating site, and site B detects a global deadlock. The detection message m_C, originating at site C, has a higher sequence number than the I/O path at site A, but a lower sequence number than the I/O path at site B. Therefore, it is discarded at site B.

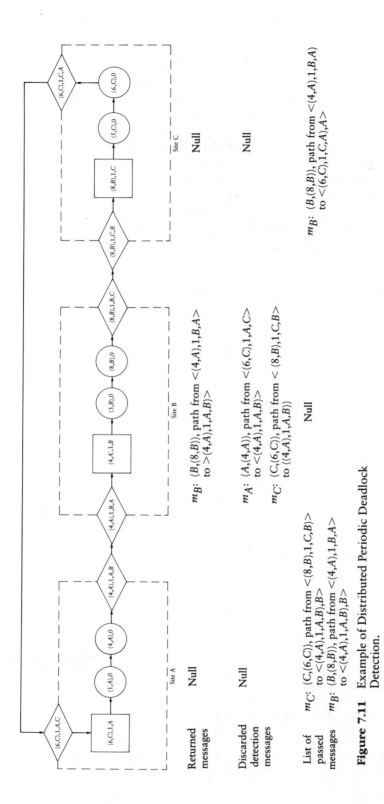

Figure 7.11 Example of Distributed Periodic Deadlock Detection.

A Continuous Deadlock-Detection Algorithm

In the continuous algorithm, a detection message is generated by a site when an I/O path is formed and is sent to the next site, indicated by the output port. Upon receipt of a detection message, a site will either discard the message, if no local I/O paths exist, or it will propagate a detection message to *all* sites, determined by the output ports of the local I/O paths that will extend the I/O path in the message. The site that detects a global deadlock does not necessarily contain the transaction with the highest sequence number. Therefore an *abort* message is sent from the detecting site to the site where the abortion is to take place. If the aborted transaction at some site A has an agent at site B, an *abort_agent (transaction number, agent_number)* message is further sent to site B to abort the remote agent.

ALGORITHM 7.2

Rules 1 through *8* describe the continuous global deadlock-detection protocol. As in the previous algorithm, we assume that each rule is performed by the local deadlock detector without interference from any agents so that the state reflected by the local TWFG does not change while it is being analyzed.

Rule 1   Request for a local resource:

When an agent for transaction T_i requests a local resource held by an agent for transaction T_j and the resource cannot be granted, then an edge between the agents is added to the local TWFG.

> *Rule 1.1*
>
> First, any local deadlocks are resolved by aborting one or more transactions having the highest sequence numbers.
>
> *Rule 1.2*
>
> For any I/O path p created by the request, the local deadlock detector generates a detection message $(A, highest(p), p)$ and passes it to the next site.

Rule 2   Request for a nonlocal resource:

When transaction T_i at site A requests a resource at site B, a request message is sent to site B. The deadlock detector creates an output port node $<(i,A),g,A,B>$ and adds an edge from node $((i, A),0)$ to node $<(i,A),g,A,B>$ in the TWFG of site A, and then applies *Rule 1.2*.

Rule 3   A request message is received at a site:

When a request message from transaction T_i at site A is received at site B requesting a resource at site B, a remote agent $[(i,A),g,B]$ for transaction T_i and input port $<(i,A),g,B,A>$ are created at site B along with an associated request edge from the input port to the remote agent. *Rule 1* is then applied to handle the request by the remote agent for the local resource.

Rule 4   A detection message is received at site A:

Rule 4.1   Site A is not the originating site and there exist I/O paths that extend the global I/O path of the message:

For each such I/O path p, the global I/O path information of the message is extended with p and sent to the next site as determined by the output port of p.

Rule 4.2   Site A is not the originating site and there exist no I/O paths that extend the global I/O path of the message:

The message is simply discarded.

Rule 4.3   Site A is the originating site of the message, and it still has the local I/O path as indicated in the global I/O path information of the message:

In this case a global deadlock is detected. The deadlock detector selects, as the victim, the transaction in the global I/O path with the highest sequence number and sends an abort message to the site that contains the victim.

Rule 4.4   Site A is the originating site of the message but the local I/O path, contained in the I/O path information of the message, no longer exists:

A transaction at site A was aborted to resolve another deadlock. Thus, the message is simply discarded.

Rule 5   An abort message is received at a site:

The deadlock detector checks whether the victim is still in this site. If not, the abort message is discarded. (This case may occur because more than one detection message may detect the same deadlock.) Otherwise, the victim is aborted and the corresponding node is deleted from the TWFG. If the aborted transaction has an agent at another site, then an *abort_agent* request is sent to the site.

Rule 6   An abort_agent message is received at a site:

The specified agent is deleted and the corresponding node is removed from the local TWFG.

Rule 7   Site B returns a completion signal to site A:

When a remote agent at site B for transaction T_i at site A has completed its task and is to return a completion signal to site A, the deadlock detector is informed of this. It then deletes nodes $<(i, A),g,B,A>$ and $[(i, A),g,B]$, and the edge connecting them.

Rule 8   Site A has received a completion signal for transaction (i, A) from site B:

The deadlock detector at site A removes node $<(i, A),g,A,B>$ and edge from $((i,A),0)$ to $<(i,A),g,A,B>$.

Theorem 7.6 establishes the validity of continuous deadlock detection.

THEOREM 7.6
Assume distributed continuous deadlock detection.

a. *If there is a global deadlock, then it is detected by some site.*
b. *If a site detects a global cycle, there actually is a global deadlock (may be transient).*

The proof is similar to the proofs of Theorem 7.1 and Theorem 7.2.

To exemplify this algorithm, assume the system state shown in Figure 7.12. If transactions $(1, A)$, $(3, B)$, and $(5, C)$ request resources held by transactions $(4, A)$, $(8, B)$, and $(6, C)$, respectively, an I/O path is created at each site. Each detection message will return to its original site, which detects a global deadlock. All three sites then send an abort message to site B, which contains the highest sequence numbered transaction, $(8, B)$. The first abort message received causes site B to abort transaction $(8, B)$ and modify the TWFG accordingly. Two subsequent abort messages are simply discarded.

To see that phantom deadlocks are not reported, assume the system state shown in Figure 7.13(a) and suppose that detection messages, originating at site B and C, are in transit to site A. In the meantime, transaction $(1, A)$ releases its resource, which leads to the completion of the agent for transaction $(6, C)$ at site A and the release by $(6, C)$ of the resource requested by transaction $(5, C)$. Transaction $(6, C)$ then requests a resource held by transaction $(1, A)$, which in turn requests a resource held by transaction $(4, A)$. This state is shown in Figure 7.13(b). Site A will subsequently discard the detection messages from sites B and C.

The two algorithms presented in this subsection allow for a process or transaction to hold multiple locks and wait for multiple processes or transactions. Chandy, et al. has also investigated this wait-for-all (AND) model [1983], as well as the wait-for-any (OR) model [Chandy and Misra, 1982]. In a wait-for-all model, deadlock arises when there is a cycle whereas in a wait-for-any model, deadlock arises only if a knot exists. A wait-for-any model is useful in systems such as CSP or Ada, as described in Chapter 3. The algorithms presented in this chapter can be extended to a wait-for-any model in a rather straightforward way to detect the existence of a knot (see Problem 12). The properties that phantom deadlocks are not detected and that only one site will attempt to resolve deadlock are preserved. A general model with both wait-for-all and wait-for-any relationships can be treated with some further extensions.

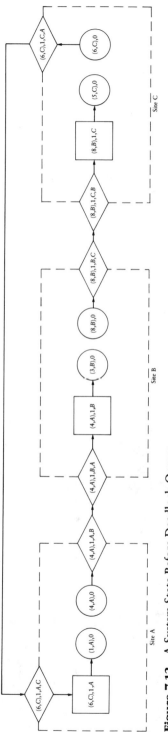

Figure 7.12 A System State Before Deadlock Occurs.

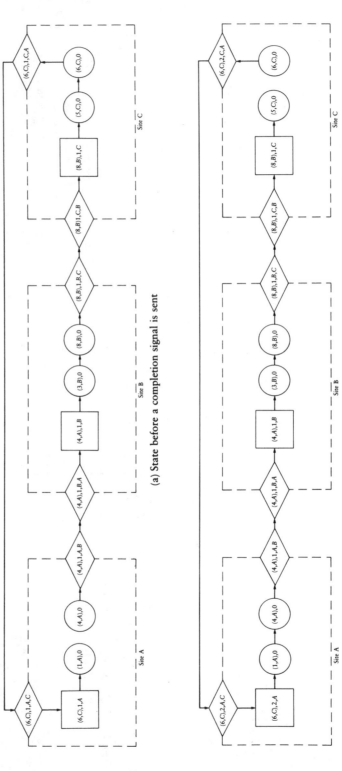

(a) State before a completion signal is sent

(b) State after a completion signal is sent and a new request for a nonlocal resource is issued

Figure 7.13 Nondetection of Phantom Deadlock.

7.6.4 Performance

Suppose that n sites are involved in a deadlock forming a cycle. Then the proposed algorithms, either periodic or continuous, require the same number of messages as the algorithm proposed by Chang and Roberts [1979] to find the highest (or lowest) numbered site. It is shown that the number of required messages in the best case is $2n - 1$ and in the worst case $n(n + 1)/2$. Also, the average number of required messages is

$$E[k] = n\left(1 + \frac{1}{2} + \frac{1}{3} + \cdots + \frac{1}{n}\right)$$

Since $E[k]$ is less than $n \log_2(n + 1)$, the algorithms are reasonably efficient. Furthermore, Obermarck [1982] has observed that the average number of sites involved in a global cycle is quite small (almost all cycles are of length 2), and the average number of I/O paths per site is much less than 2. Therefore, the proposed algorithms perform better in practice than any centralized algorithm, which requires two messages per site: one message to request the TWFG information from a site and another message for the reply.

If large cycles are expected for a database application, the message-passing mechanism can be modified in a manner similar to the Hirschberg and Sinclair algorithm [Hirschberg and Sinclair, 1980]. This algorithm requires $O(n \log n)$ messages even in the worst case. However, because of its rather large constant multiplier, the algorithms here are more efficient if the length of cycles is reasonable (less than approximately 16).

The distributed deadlock-detection algorithms presented in this chapter have advantages over centralized algorithms in that they are not vulnerable to the failure of a central site and they do not detect phantom deadlocks. Two advantages of continuous detection over periodic detection are the early detection of deadlocks and the potential for requiring only one detection message for each generated I/O path (since periodic detection may repeatedly generate detection messages as long as an I/O path persists). If periodic detection is used, then the determination of a "reasonable" or "optimal" time period becomes an issue. Also, it should be noted that the criteria for selecting a victim may be changed to any other scheme that assigns some cost to each transaction. The sequence number used in the algorithms is just one of the convenient schemes. Finally, it should be noted that to simply detect deadlock, it is not necessary for the information in the detection message to be extended by each site along the cycle. The fact that a detection message returns to its originating site is enough to declare the existence of deadlock.

7.7 Deadlock Prevention and Avoidance

As stated in Chapter 4, there are three basic approaches to the prevention of deadlock: ordered requests, collective requests, and preemption. The advantage of the first two approaches is that, with them, it is never necessary to abort and restart transactions. The disadvantages are limited concurrency and inapplicability in distributed database systems. A potentially attractive approach to using the method of ordered resources in database systems is presented in Section 7.9. This method will depend on Section 7.8, which develops the idea of a database as a collection of more finely grained lockable objects.

The third approach, preemption, has more applicability in distributed systems and is integrally tied to synchronization techniques for maintaining consistency. Typically, preemption is based on some priority ordering of the transactions in the system. Suppose T_i requests access to a resource held by T_j. If transaction T_i has a lower or equal priority, then T_i waits for T_j to release the resource. If T_i has a higher priority, then the resource is preempted by aborting T_j. To avoid the possibility of continuous abortion and restarting of the same transaction, time stamps can be used as priorities. Section 7.11 will be concerned with the use of time stamps for synchronization of access to maintain consistency. Preemption to prevent deadlock is a natural byproduct of this development.

Deadlock avoidance is limited to those cases in which future resource needs are known in advance. For database systems, the method is too conservative, resulting in the unnecessary abortion of an excessive number of transactions.

7.8 Lock Granularity

The choice of *lockable object,* or *granularity* of the database, presents a tradeoff between increased concurrency and system overhead. Finer granularity, at the record or field level, provides more opportunity for concurrency, but more locks must be managed by the database system. Thus, it may be desirable to allow lockable objects of different levels of granularity to coexist in a database system. In this section we discuss the management of two such systems: a hierarchical system of locks and a system based on a directed acyclic graph of locks.

7.8.1 Hierarchical Locks

The discussion of hierarchical locks follows the development in Gray [1978]. Hierarchical locks assume that the granularity of the resources is organized as a tree structure, as seen in Figure 7.14(a). Each level is identified by a generic name representing all resources which are instances of that type. Figure 7.14(b) shows an example of actual resources in such a hierarchy.

If a transaction has exclusive access (denoted by X) or shared access (denoted by S) to a component, then it has implicit X or S access, respectively, to all of its descendent components. Some control is required to prevent transactions from acquiring conflicting locks. In particular, a transaction should not be allowed to lock a component of an object if any one of the higher level components is already locked. For this purpose, we define the notions of *compatible* locking modes and *intention* modes.

Two locking modes are defined to be *compatible* if they can be concurrently granted to the same object. A new type of locking mode, the intention mode (denoted by I), has the intuitive purpose of announcing the intention to lock components at

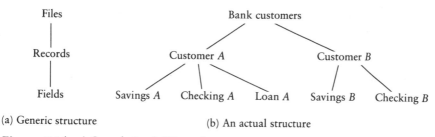

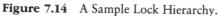

(a) Generic structure   (b) An actual structure

Figure 7.14 A Sample Lock Hierarchy.

a lower level. To lock a particular object at some level, intention access must first be obtained to all the higher level components. If object A is tagged *I*, then a request to lock A in *S* or *X* mode must be denied since it may already have a lower component locked in *X* mode. Thus, the locking modes *X*, *S*, and *I* are incompatible with each other. However, two transactions may hold *I* locks on the same component since lower level components will be explicitly locked in, *X*, *S*, or *I* modes.

To allow for greater concurrency, three different modes of intention are defined: *intention share* (denoted by *IS*), *intention exclusive* (denoted by *IX*), and *share mode* (denoted by *SIX*). The resulting six lock modes can be summarized as follows:

NL: Allows no access to the component.

IS: Provides the requesting transaction with *intention share* access to the component and allows the requesting transaction to explicitly lock lower level components in either *S* or *IS* mode.

IX: Provides the requesting transaction with *intention exclusive* access to the component and allows the requesting transaction to explicitly lock lower level components in *X*, *S*, *SIX*, *IX*, or *IS* mode.

S: Provides the requesting transaction with *share* access to the component and (implicit) share access to all lower level components.

SIX: Provides the requesting transaction with *share* and *intention exclusive* access to the component and (implicit) share access to all of its lower level components, and allows the requesting transaction to explicitly lock descendent components in *X*, *SIX*, and *IX* mode.

X: Provides the requesting transaction with exclusive access to the component and (implicit) exclusive access to all lower level components.

The *SIX* mode is introduced to allow a transaction to read all components and write some components in a subtree. The transaction locks the component in *SIX* mode to obtain share access to the entire subtree. It sets *X* locks on those lower components in the subtree to obtain exclusive access when it updates them. *SIX* mode is compatible with *IS* mode since other transactions requesting *IS* mode will explicitly lock lower components in *IS* or *S* mode, thereby preventing their simultaneous update. However, *SIX* mode is not compatible with *IX*, *S*, *SIX*, or *X* mode requests.

Table 7.1 shows the compatibility of the six request modes. Figure 7.15 is a lattice that shows the partial ordering of the request modes, with *NL* serving as the

Table 7.1   Compatibility Relations [Gray, 1978. Copyright © 1978 by Springer-Verlag, Heidelberg. Reprinted by permission].

	NL	IS	IX	S	SIX	X
NL	YES	YES	YES	YES	YES	YES
IS	YES	YES	YES	YES	YES	NO
IX	YES	YES	YES	NO	NO	NO
S	YES	YES	NO	YES	NO	NO
SIX	YES	YES	NO	NO	NO	NO
X	YES	NO	NO	NO	NO	NO

YES: Compatible; NO: Not compatible.

greatest lower bound (least exclusive mode) and X being the least upper bound (most exclusive mode). A transaction may rerequest the same resource for two reasons. First, it may be more efficient to simply request access to the resource than to check to see if it already has access. Second, it may need to strengthen its current access mode. A request for a resource component already held by the requesting transaction is called a *conversion*. The lattice in Figure 7.15 specifies the rules for computing the new mode. If a transaction holds an x-lock and requests a y-lock on a component, then the request is changed to a request for the least upper bound of x and y. Thus, the lock mode held by a transaction on a component never decreases. If the new mode is incompatible with the mode of a lock held by some other transaction, then the requesting transaction must wait and, of course, deadlock may result. Table 7.2 shows all possible conversions for the lattice in Figure 7.15.

In order to prevent the acquisition of access to a resource component without prior acquisition of the proper access to an *ancestor* component, each transaction must obey the following locking protocol. These rules follow directly from the description of the lock modes:

- Prior to requesting an *S* or *IS* lock on a resource component, the requesting transaction must hold an *IS* or *IX* lock on all the ancestor components.

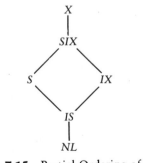

Figure 7.15   Partial Ordering of Request Modes [Gray, 1978].

Table 7.2 New Modes for a Conversion [Gray, 1978. Copyright © 1978 by Springer-Verlag, Heidelberg. Reprinted by permission].

Current Mode	Requested Mode				
	IS	**IX**	**S**	**SIX**	**X**
IS	IS	IX	S	SIX	X
IX	IX	IX	SIX	SIX	X
S	S	SIX	S	SIX	X
SIX	SIX	SIX	SIX	SIX	X
X	X	X	X	X	X

- Prior to requesting an *X*, *SIX*, or *IX* lock on a resource component, the requesting transaction must hold an *SIX* or *IX* mode on all the ancestor components.

- When a transaction terminates, locks can be released in any order. Otherwise, they must be released in leaf-to-root order.

We exemplify the use of these rules using Figure 7.14. In order to update the record "Savings *B*," a transaction performs the following sequence of lock and unlock operations:

lock file "Bank customers" in mode *IX*

lock record "Customer *B*" in mode *IX*

lock field "Savings *B*" in mode *X*

update

unlock field "Savings *B*"

unlock record "Customer *B*"

unlock file "Bank customers"

7.8.2 Directed Acyclic Graph of Locks

The concept of hierarchical locks can be extended to a set of resources that is organized as a directed acyclic graph (DAG), in which a resource component may have more than one parent. An example is shown in Figure 7.16. We extend the protocols for acquiring locks to resource components:

- A transaction is "implicitly" granted an *S* lock to a resource component if it has been "implicitly" or "explicitly" granted an *S*, *SIX*, or *X* lock to at least one of the parents of the component. Note that this implies that the transaction has been "explicitly" granted an *S*, *SIX*, or *X* access to one of the ancestors.

- A transaction is "implicitly" granted an *X* lock to a resource component *C* if it has been "implicitly" granted an *X* lock to all of the parents. This means that one component in each path leading to component *C* is explicitly granted in *X* mode and all its ancestors are explicitly granted in *IX* or *SIX* mode.

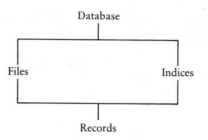

Figure 7.16   A Directed Acyclic Graph (DAG).

Each transaction must obey the following DAG *lock protocol:*

- Prior to requesting an *S* or *IS* lock on a resource component, the requesting transaction must hold an *IS* (or greater mode) lock to at least one parent and to all ancestors on one of its paths to a root (a source node in the DAG).

- Prior to requesting an *IX, SIX,* or *X* lock to a resource component, a requesting transaction must hold an *IX* (or greater mode) lock to all of its parents. This implies that the transaction will hold *IX* (or greater mode) locks to all ancestor components, and no other transaction will hold a lock on an ancestor component that is incompatible with *IX.*

- When a transaction terminates, locks can be released in any order. Otherwise, they must be released in leaf-to-root order.

For example, assume the lock structure shown in Figure 7.16. In order to gain implicit *S* access to records in a file *F* via the index *I,* a transaction performs the following lock operations:

lock database with mode *IS*
lock index *I* with mode *S*

7.8.3   Equivalence of the DAG Lock Protocol and Conventional Lock Protocol

In this section we show that a DAG lock protocol can be expressed in terms of an equivalent conventional protocol (one that uses two conventional lock modes, *S* and *X*) to lock unit resource items (components that are sinks of the DAG) in the database. The reader may refer to Section 4.3 for a review of the basic terminology of directed graphs. Some additional notation and terminology will be useful in our discussion. Let $G = (N,A)$ denote a DAG consisting of a set of resource components *N* and a set of directed arcs *A*. Note that a DAG may have more than one root (source). A *node-slice* of a sink *n*, denoted by NS_n, is a subset of *N* so that each path from a source to *n* contains a member of the slice. Let $M = \{NL, IS, IX, S, SIX, X\}$ and $m = \{NL, S, X\}$ denote the DAG and conventional sets of lock modes, respectively. Define the compatibility matrix *C* to be a mapping function $M \times M \rightarrow \{YES, NO\}$, as defined in Table 7.1, and define the restricted compatibility matrix R to be the submap function $R: m \times m \rightarrow \{YES, NO\}$. A lock graph G_T, for a transaction T, is a DAG in which all "explicit" locks held by the transaction T label its nodes. In other words, $G_T: N \rightarrow M$ is a mapping in which $G_T(n)$ denotes the explicit lock held by transaction T on node n. The set of implicit locks on the sinks of the DAG can be described by introducing the notion of a projection mapping. The *projection* of a lock graph G_T is the mapping $g_T: sinks \rightarrow m$ such that for any sink n,

1. $g_T(n) = X$ if there exists a node-slice NS_n of n such that $G_T(k) = X$ for all $k \in NS_n$;
2. $g_T(n) = S$ if (1) is not true and $G_T(a) \in \{S, SIX, X\}$ for some ancestor a of n; or
3. $g_T(n) = NL$ if (1) and (2) are not satisfied.

Given two transactions T_1 and T_2, two lock graphs G_{T_1} and G_{T_2} are compatible if for all $n \in N$, $C[G_{T_1}(n), G_{T_2}(n)] = YES$. Also, two projections are compatible if for all sinks n, $R[G_{T_1}(n), G_{T_2}(n)] = YES$. The following theorem, the major goal of this section, states that if the locks (selected from M) set by two transactions are compatible, then the locks (selected from m) implicitly required for the conventional lock protocol are compatible.

THEOREM 7.7

[Gray, 1978] *If two lock graphs G_{T_1} and G_{T_2} are compatible, then their projections g_{T_1} and g_{T_2} are compatible.*

PROOF

Suppose g_{T_1} and g_{T_2} are incompatible. Then there must exist a sink n with $g_{T_1}(n) = X$ and $g_{T_2}(n) \in \{S, X\}$ (or vice versa). We will assume the former. It follows from the definition of projection that there exists a node-slice NS_n such that for all $k \in NS_n$, $G_{T_1}(k) = X$. Also, for some ancestor n_0 of n, it must be true that $G_{T_2}(n_0) \in \{S, SIX, X\}$. This implies that there is a path P from a source to n_0 on which G_{T_2} does not take the value NL. There are two cases:

Case 1   P intersects the node-slice at n_i:

Then G_{T_1} and G_{T_2} are incompatible since $G_{T_1}(n_i) = X$, which is incompatible with the nonnull value of $G_{T_2}(n_i)$.

Case 2   The path from n_0 to the sink n intersects the node-slice at n_i:

For each ancestor a of n_i, $G_{T_1}(a) \in \{IX, SIX, X\}$. Note that n_0 is such an ancestor. Since $G_{T_2}(n_0) \in \{S, SIX, X\}$ we have $C[G_{T_1}(n_0), G_{T_2}(n_0)] = NO$. This contradicts the assumption.

Theorem 7.7 is actually a special case of the more general theorem proved by Korth [1982].

To exemplify this result, consider Figure 7.14. A legal schedule, corresponding to the one shown in Figure 7.6, can be obtained by simply replacing a *lock_X* $<A,S>$ by a sequence of *lock_IX* $<F,S>$ and *lock_X* $<A,S>$ operations. Similarly an *unlock* $<A,S>$ is replaced with a sequence of *unlock* $<A,S>$ and *unlock* $<F,S>$ operations.

7.9   Deadlock Freedom Using Edge Locks

When multiple levels of granularity are used to identify lockable objects in a database, and a DAG locking protocol is used, it is possible to use an ordered request approach to prevent deadlocks. The order of requests is determined by the levels of granularity and the structure of the DAG. Korth has devised a series of locking protocols that are free from deadlocks [Korth, 1982] and are generalizations of the protocol described in Section 7.8.

Deadlock freedom is achieved by the use of *edge* locks, which prevent a transaction U, following transaction T, from bypassing T in the process of locking nodes of the DAG. Suppose (A,B) is an edge in a DAG G. The intuitive purpose of locking (A,B) is to serialize all access to descendents of B as long as a deadlock involving those nodes is possible. An edge lock must be obtained on (A,B) as a precondition for obtaining a node lock on B. Similarly, a node lock on A must be obtained prior to obtaining the edge lock on (A,B). EX and ES denote exclusive and shared locking modes for edges. To enforce the ordered resource usage policy, a transaction must obey the following protocol from Korth [1982].

Leaf-to-Root Node Release Rule:

> For each node n of G,
>
> 1. T must be two-phase with respect to n, and
> 2. T cannot release a lock on n while holding a lock on a child of n. (This requirement imposes a downward-moving phase and an upward-moving phase on every path of G.)

Majority Parent Rule (with respect to an access mode):

> A transaction T can request a lock on a nonroot node n in access mode Z or *intention Z* only if T already holds a lock in mode *intention Z* (or a more exclusive mode) on a majority of all parents of n.

Majority-In-Edge Rule (with respect to access mode Z):

> A transaction T can request a lock on a nonroot node n in access mode Z only if T already holds a lock in mode EZ (or a more exclusive mode) on a majority of the edges leading into node n.

Overall Protocol:

> A transaction T must
>
> 1. Obey the *Majority Parent Rule* and *Majority-In-Edge Rule*.
> 2. Obey the *Leaf-to-Node Release Rule*.
> 3. Obtain a lock on node n in mode *intention Z* prior to obtaining an EZ lock on edge (n, m). The locks on n and all needed out-edges from n must be simultaneously requested.

Furthermore, the compatibility of locks must be observed and the transactions waiting on a particular node must be serviced in FIFO order. In the interest of efficiency, an edge lock on (n, m) should be released as soon as the desired node lock on m is acquired.

As an example, consider the DAG (actually a tree) shown in Figure 7.17(a). If a transaction T wishes to write leaves D and E, it performs the steps shown in Figure 7.17(b). Each numbered step must be implemented as an atomic request for locks. The ordering of lock and unlock statements within a step is not important. The steps shown in the figure ensure that no transaction U, following a transaction T, will bypass the locks held by T.

If the DAG happens to be a tree, the locking protocol can be weakened so that the edge lock rules need be observed only in the subtree of the tree in which sibling nodes are locked. The result is an increase in exploitable concurrency.

7.10   Recovery

Recovery is defined to mean the restoration of a previous consistent database state in the event of transaction or system failure. The traditional centralized approach of taking periodic checkpoints and recovering from failure by rolling back transactions to the most recent checkpoint, is complicated by the consistency problem in a distributed database and the need to recover from any combination of communication failures, site failures, and transaction failures, including such failures during the recovery process itself.

It is assumed that a *recovery management* system is in place. This system maintains a history of all recoverable actions of a transaction, oversees the abortion or

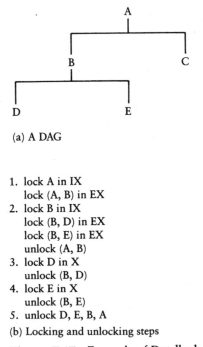

(a) A DAG

1. lock A in IX
   lock (A, B) in EX
2. lock B in IX
   lock (B, D) in EX
   lock (B, E) in EX
   unlock (A, B)
3. lock D in X
   unlock (B, D)
4. lock E in X
   unlock (B, E)
5. unlock D, E, B, A

(b) Locking and unlocking steps

Figure 7.17   Example of Deadlock-Free Locking Protocol.

commitment of transactions, and periodically records the state of the system (check-point) to allow restart of individual sites. The discussion on recovery follows the work in Gray [1978] and Kohler [1981].

7.10.1   Atomic Actions

Many researchers have proposed the concept of an *atomic action* as central to the structuring of fault-tolerant systems for multiple interacting processes [Lomet, 1977; Eswaran, et al., 1976; Lampson and Sturgis, 1976; Randell, 1979; Reed, 1983]. This concept is important because it provides a simple conceptual framework for dealing with error detection and recovery. Atomic actions can be characterized in the following four equivalent ways [Randell, 1979]:

1. Processes performing an atomic action are unaware of the existence of processes not involved in the atomic action and vice versa.
2. Processes performing an atomic action do not communicate with other processes while the action is being performed.
3. Processes performing an atomic action cannot detect any state change other than their own and reveal no state changes until the action is complete.
4. An atomic action is indivisible and instantaneous in the sense that its effect on the database is the same as if it were executed with uninvolved processes as opposed to being executed concurrently.

An atomic action is actually a generalization of the concept of a transaction. In this chapter, the two terms are used interchangeably.

If a failure occurs that prevents the successful completion of an atomic action, then the state of all objects modified by this action must be restored to the state that existed at the beginning of the action. This is called *backward error recovery* [Randell, 1979], and a transaction whose updates can be performed without undoing the updates of other transactions is said to be *recoverable*. Recoverability can be realized by imposing the following two requirements on the implementation of an atomic action:

1. Updated objects are not released until the action is completed.
2. The initial state of all objects modified by the action can be reconstructed.

The first requirement can be satisfied by the use of an *atomic commitment* and the second can be satisfied by the use of history logs and a DO_UNDO_REDO paradigm. Both of these techniques will be discussed in the next section.

7.10.2   Implementation of Atomic Actions

Figure 7.18 shows the three possible outcomes of a transaction. If the transaction successfully completes, it issues a *commit* action to effect permanent changes to the database. If the transaction detects conditions under which it cannot successfully complete (e.g., erroneous input or violations of other conditions for correct execution), then it aborts itself. It may also be aborted by the system due to external events

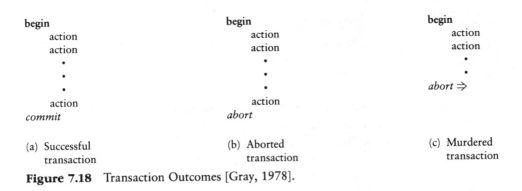

Figure 7.18 Transaction Outcomes [Gray, 1978].

(e.g., deadlock resolution, time-out, protection violation, system crash, user signal to kill the transaction).

Lock Requirements

If a transaction is aborted, but its updates were visible to other concurrent transactions, then other transactions may also have to be rerun. This is called the *domino effect* or *cascading aborts*. To prevent the need to rerun already completed transactions, all exclusive mode locks must be held until the transaction has committed. If it is necessary for a restarted transaction to produce precisely the same result, then it is also necessary for the transaction to hold all share mode locks. Figure 7.19 illustrates the problem if locks are not held. Suppose a system crash occurs at time S. Prior to the crash, T_3 updates an object A and releases its lock, after which T_4 reads the value of A, writes the value of B and terminates. T_3 can be undone and restarted but T_4 is not undone even though its output was dependent on T_3's update.

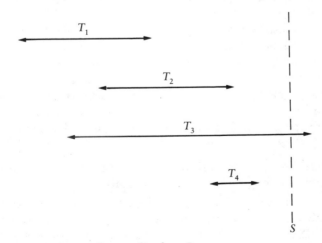
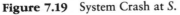

Figure 7.19 System Crash at S.

Storage Management for Atomic Actions

There are two approaches to the management of storage for effecting updates to a database: use of private workspace and updating in place. We will describe the protocol associated with each approach.

USE OF PRIVATE WORKSPACE   The use of *private workspace* as a storage management technique is described within the context of the object-entity model presented in Section 7.3. The description is first given for a centralized system and then modified for a distributed system. In a centralized system (with single site S), the actions of a transaction T have the following effects on the private workspace [Bernstein and Goodman, 1981, Lampson, 1981]:

begin: The TM establishes a private workspace to temporarily hold relevant database values.

read(E):   If a copy of E exists in T's private workspace, its value is returned. Otherwise, the TM issues a $(T, read\_object <E,S,>,V)$ to the OM to retrieve a copy of E and puts it into T's private workspace.

write(E, new-value):

   If a copy of E exist in T's private workspace, its value is changed to new-value. Otherwise, a copy of E with new-value is created in T's private workspace.

end: The TM issues $(T, write\_object <E,S>)$, the value of E in T's private workspace) for each entity E that has been updated by T. When all *write_object* operations are processed, T's private workspace is discarded and $(T, commit\_object <-,S> -)$ is issued.

T may be aborted at any time prior to processing a *write_object*. However, once a *write_object* has been performed, T cannot be aborted in order to avoid the possibility of forming an inconsistent database state. In other words, an atomic commitment is required of all updates to permanent storage. The concept of atomic commitment will be explored later.

Storage management for a distributed system differs from that for a centralized system. Since the movement of data among sites is expensive, the private workspace is distributed and the flow of data is regulated by query optimization procedures to reduce the data traffic. The details of distribution and query optimization have no direct effect on recovery management. We assume for this discussion, however, that the private workspace is only partitioned among sites but not replicated. The effects of the transaction steps are as follows [Bernstein and Goodman, 1981, Lampson, 1981]:

begin: The TM creates a private workspace for T. The private workspace is partitioned among sites to reduce the traffic.

read(E):   If a copy of E exists in T's private workspace, its value is returned. Otherwise, the TM selects an object $<E,S_j>$ and issues a $(T, read\_object <E,S_j>,V)$ to the OM at site S_j. The OM places the obtained value V in the private workspace. The TM returns this value to T.

write(E, new-value):

> If a copy of *E* exists in *T*'s private workspace, its value is updated to new-value. Otherwise a copy of *E* with new-value is created in the private workspace.

end: Two-phase commit is performed.

An atomic commitment is performed by a so-called *two-phase commit,* which will be described in detail in the next section.

UPDATING IN PLACE   The *updating in place* storage management technique uses the *DO-UNDO-REDO log protocol* and *write-ahead log protocol.* We first describe the DO-UNDO-REDO log protocol, which uses an incremental log of changes to recover both committed and uncommitted actions. For each *write_object* action, a *log record* is written that records both the old and new value of the object. This information will be used later if the operation must be undone or redone. These records are aggregated by transaction and collected in a common system log stored in nonvolatile storage (such as disk storage made reliable by duplexing or triplexing). Every recoverable database action must be implemented as a collection of operations [Gray, 1978]:

1. A *do* operation that does that action and records a log record
2. An *undo* operation that, on the basis of a log record, undoes the action
3. A *redo* operation that, on the basis of a log record, redoes the action
4. An optional *display* operation that displays the log

The *undo* and *redo* operations must function correctly, even if another crash occurs during crash recovery. For example, suppose that a *write_object* action is effected in the database storage before the log record for the object is recorded in the nonvolatile storage. If a system crash occurs before the log record is written, then the update cannot be undone. Similar problems exist if the system crashes in the middle of committing a collection of updates, leaving an inconsistent database state. The *write-ahead log protocol* is used to record the action in the log, prior to effecting the actual update of the database [Gray, 1978]:

1. The undo log is written to the nonvolatile storage prior to performing uncommitted updates of recoverable objects to the permanent database storage.
2. The redo and undo log records are written to the nonvolatile storage, prior to committing an update of a recoverable object. (This allows the transaction manager to go either way on the transaction commit.)

The Two-Phase Commit Protocol

The problem of committing objects in a distributed database is the same as the problem encountered in Chapter 6 in attempting to close a connection over an unreliable communication line. This problem may be paraphrased as the *generals paradox* [Gray, 1978], which may be stated as follows.

Two armies must cooperate to capture a hill from the enemy. If they simultaneously attack, they are assured of success. If only one army attacks, it will be defeated. The generals of each army communicate by messengers in order to agree on a time when they will launch their attack. These messengers are not completely reliable because there is some chance that they will be captured by the enemy. The problem is to find some communication protocol that allows the generals to agree on a common time to attack and assures the armies of victory. To prove that there exists no fixed-length protocol, suppose the contrary, and let L denote the shortest such protocol. In this protocol, suppose that the last (Lth) messenger is lost. Since L is the minimum length, it must contain useful information and the general waiting for it will not order an attack. This contradicts the assumption that a fixed-length protocol exists.

This (purported) paradox is the same problem encountered in committing objects at different database sites. For example, suppose funds are transferred from an account in Tokyo to an account in New York. Both the debit in Tokyo and the credit in New York must be either both processed (committed) or both rejected (aborted).

By relaxing the constraint that the protocol be finite in length, a practical solution can be found to the problem of implementing an atomic commitment in a distributed system. The two-phase commit protocol assumes a *commit coordinator* that oversees the distributed commitment and communicates with all remote agents *(cohorts)* of a transaction. The actual length of protocol is arbitrary, depending on the reliability of the system at the time the commitment of permanent updates to the database is attempted. Given a request for a commit from a cohort, the following protocol is followed [Gray, 1978; Kohler, 1981]:

COMMIT COORDINATOR

PHASE 1

1. Send a PREPARE message to each cohort and wait for a reply from each cohort.
2. a. If any cohort sends an ABORTED reply or fails to respond within a predetermined time period, then undo the transaction: Broadcast an ABORT message to all cohorts, write an ABORT record in the log, wait for acknowledgments (ACK_ABORTs) from each cohort, and terminate.
   b. If all cohorts send a PREPARED reply, then start Phase 2.

PHASE 2

1. Write a COMMIT record in the log, send a COMMIT message to each cohort, and wait for an ACK_COMMIT reply message from each cohort.
2. Upon receiving all ACK_COMMIT messages, write a COMPLETE record in the log and terminate.

COHORT

PHASE 1

1. Wait for the coordinator to send a PREPARE message.
2. After completing part of the transaction, write an UNDO-REDO log in the nonvolatile storage as described in step 2 of the write-ahead log protocol.

3. If step 2 was successfully completed, write a COMPLETE record in the log and send a PREPARED message to the coordinator. Otherwise, send an ABORTED message to the coordinator.

PHASE 2

Wait for a message from the coordinator stating the final disposition of the transaction.

1. If an ABORT message is received, then undo the transaction, release locks, and send an ACK_ABORT to the coordinator.
2. If a COMMIT message is received, then release locks and send an ACK_ COMMIT message to the coordinator.

The two-phase commit protocol is summarized in Figure 7.20. In the event of system crash and restart, the recovery manager obeys the following rules [Kohler, 1981]:

1. If the commit coordinator crashes before it writes a COMMIT record in its log (step 1 of Phase 2), then an ABORT message is sent to each cohort.
2. If the commit coordinator successfully writes a COMMIT record but crashes before writing a COMPLETE record (step 2 of Phase 2), then send a COMMIT message to each cohort.
3. If the commit coordinator crashes after writing the COMPLETE record, then the job of the commit coordinator is complete and restart can be ignored.

This protocol is called *two-phase* because if any cohort aborts or crashes in its Phase 1, then the entire transaction will be aborted, whereas if any cohort crashes in its Phase 2, then the recovery manager of that participant will ask the coordinator whether or not it should redo or undo its part of the transaction. Since the cohort recorded enough information for this in the log during Phase 1, the recovery manager can go either way with the cohort. Also, since restart may be required any number of times, the *redo* and *undo* operations must be *idempotent,* that is, repeatable any number of times. If the coordinator crashes before it writes the log record, then restart will broadcast ABORT to all cohorts. No cohort will commit prior to receiving a COMMIT message. On the other hand, if the restart finds COMMIT in the coordinator's log, then the recovery manager broadcasts COMMIT to all participants. The net effect is that either all the cohorts commit or that none of them commit (all are undone).

The above two-phase commit protocol is based on the use of logs. It can, however, be readily modified to one based on the use of private workspaces. By keeping both original and updated data available, actions can be repeated. Also, records of ABORT, COMMIT, and COMPLETE can be simply maintained by local variables in the private workspace.

It can be shown that the protocol requires $4n$ messages if there are n participants. This number can be reduced to $2n$ if messages are circularly passed from one site to another, one message in each phase. This is called the *nested two-phase commit protocol.* It is appropriate for a system with the following characteristics:

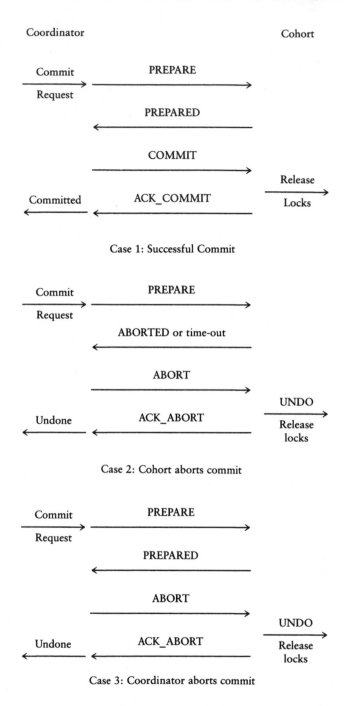

Figure 7.20 Possible Coordinator–Cohort Interactions [Kohler, 1981. Copyright © 1981 by Association for Computing Machinery, Inc. Reprinted by permission].

1. There is a high cost associated with message passing and a broadcast facility is not available.
2. The demand for concurrency is low.
3. The cohort structure of the transaction is static or universally known.

The general two-phase commit protocol is appropriate if a broadcast facility is available and parallelism among participants is desirable.

7.10.3 Structure of Recovery Management System

Recovery management, as outlined by Gray [1978], is shown in Figure 7.21 and consists of two components:

1. A recovery manager responsible for the tracking of transactions, the coordination of transaction commits and aborts, and system checkpoints and restart
2. A log manager used by the recovery manager and other components to write records in the system log for the transaction or system

7.11 Synchronization Techniques Based on Timestamp Ordering

In the timestamp ordering approach to synchronization, a unique timestamp is affixed to each transaction, and all conflicting actions must be processed in timestamp order. Any action that arrives late is rejected, causing the issuing transaction to be aborted and restarted. The timestamp ordering mechanism guarantees that all edges in the TWFG are in timestamp order. Since all transactions have unique time-

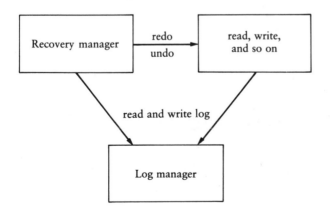

Figure 7.21 Relationship Between Log Components of Recovery Management [Gray, 1978].

stamps, no cycles are possible in the graph (preemption using timestamp priority is used to prevent their occurrence). Thus, timestamp ordering is deadlock-free. In addition, the timestamp order defines the precise equivalent serial schedule and so consistency is preserved. The discussion in subsequent sections follows portions of the development by Bernstein [1981].

7.11.1 Basic Timestamp Ordering Implementation

We first outline the steps for a basic implementation, ignoring two-phase commit:

1. A *TM* assigns a unique timestamp to a new transaction *T*.

2. The *TM* attaches the timestamp to all actions issued to *OMs* on behalf of the transaction.

3. Each *OM* has a *timestamp ordering scheduler* that schedules local actions according to their timestamp ordering. For each object *O*, the scheduler at an *OM* records the largest timestamp of all completed *read_object* actions and all completed *write_object* actions. These timestamps will be denoted by TS_R and TS_W, respectively.

4. For a requested *read_object* action, the scheduler compares the timestamp *TS* with TS_W. If $TS < TS_W$, the scheduler rejects the action and the *TM* aborts the issuing transaction. Otherwise, the scheduler places the action in a strict FIFO queue for pending actions on object *O* and sets TS_R to $max(TS_R, TS)$.

5. For a requested *write_object* action, the scheduler compares the timestamp *TS* with the maximum of TS_R and TS_W. The scheduler rejects the action if *TS* is smaller; otherwise, it places the action in the queue and sets TS_W to *TS*.

6. If it is necessary to abort a transaction, it will be assigned a new (larger) timestamp by the *TM* and restarted.

Figure 7.22 illustrates the procedure for basic timestamp ordering. The values of TS_R and TS_W reflect the completion of processing of the actions by the scheduler.

This basic approach suffers from three specific problems: cyclic restarts, unnecessary restarts, and infinite restarts. To illustrate the problem of cyclic restarts, suppose that two transactions T_1 and T_2 each consist of a *read_object(O)* followed by a *write_object(O)* for the same object *O*, and suppose an attempt is made to form the following (unrealizable) schedule:

$$< \cdots (T_1, read\_object <O>, V_1), \ldots, (T_2, read\_object <O>, V_2),$$
$$(T_1, write\_object <O>, U_1), (T_2, write\_object <O>, U_2) \cdots >.$$

If the timestamp order of T_1 is less than that of T_2, then $(T_1, write\_object <O>, U_1)$ fails (is rejected) and so T_1 is given a new larger timestamp and is restarted. If this new T_1 immediately requests a *read_object<O>* action, then $(T_2, write\_object <O>, U_2)$ fails and T_2 must be restarted. An endless sequence of restarts of T_1 and T_2 is possible.

An unnecessary restart occurs if the actual execution sequence is in the reverse order of timestamp. A simple example is one in which the timestamp of T_2 is greater

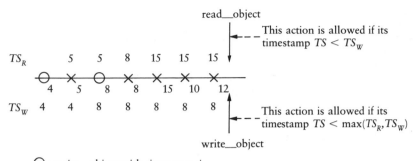

O_i: write_object with timestamp i

$\times_i$: read_object with timestamp i

Figure 7.22   Basic Time-stamp Ordering.

than that of T_1, but all actions of T_2 are completed before any action of T_1. T_1 will be rejected even though the serial schedule T_2 followed by T_1 is perfectly acceptable.

Infinite wait can occur if an older transaction, each time it restarts, finds it has to wait for a younger conflicting transaction. This is a starvation-related problem.

7.11.2   Two-Phase Commit

In timestamp approaches to synchronization, two-phase commit is implemented by introducing a *prewrite* action. This *prewrite* must be requested by the TM prior to the subsequent *write_object* action and both must carry the same timestamp. The operation has the logical effect of setting a write-lock on object O for the duration of the two-phase commit. Once a *prewrite* has been accepted by the scheduler, the corresponding *write_object* will not be rejected. Any other *read_object* or *write_object* action that arrives in the interim and has a timestamp greater than TS is buffered until the corresponding *write_object* is performed (sent to the OM for object O). If a *prewrite* arrives out of order, it is rejected and the transaction is given a new (larger) timestamp and restarted. Consider the sequence shown in Figure 7.23. P_j is an interval from $(T_1,$ *write_object* $<O>, V_1)$ to $(T_2,$*prewrite* $<O>, -)$, where T_1 and T_2 have timestamps i and j, respectively, with $i < j$. W_j is an interval from $(T_2,$*prewrite* $<O>, -)$ to $(T_2,$*write_object* $<O>, V_2)$. In the interval P_j (prewrite phase), the next *prewrite* has not been issued, and any *read_object* actions are allowed. In interval W_j (write phase), any *read_object* and *write_object* with timestamp greater than j must be buffered. Also, any subsequent *prewrites* must also be buffered.

We now describe the method of basic timestamp ordering with two-phase commit. Define the following variables:

TS_R :   the maximum timestamp of any *read_object* that has been processed

TS_W :   the maximum timestamp of any *write_object* that has been processed

min_TS_R :   the minimum timestamp of any buffered *read_object*

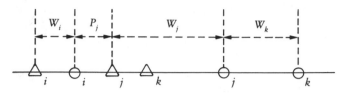

$\triangle_i$: prewrite with timestamp i

$\bigcirc_i$: write__object with timestamp i

$i < j < k$

Figure 7.23   Prewrite Intervals and Write Intervals.

min_TS_W :   the minimum timestamp of any buffered *write__object*

min_TS_P :   the minimum timestamp of any buffered *prewrite*

It is assumed that the all TM timestamps as well as these variables, are initialized to zero and that min_TS_R, min_TS_W, and min_TS_P retain their values when the corresponding buffers become empty. We also assume that each *read__object, write__object,* and *prewrite* action is an indivisible operation with respect to the local scheduler.

ALGORITHM 7.3

1. A *read__object* with timestamp *TS* is

    a. Rejected if $TS < TS_W$

    b. Output to be performed by the OM if $TS_W = min\_TS_P$ (prewrite phase)

    c. Output if $TS_W < min\_TS_P$ (write phase) and $TS = min\_TS_P$

    d. Buffered if $TS_W < min\_TS_P$ and $TS > min\_TS_P$

2. A *prewrite* with timestamp *TS* is rejected if $TS < max(TS_R, TS_W)$. Otherwise, it is buffered.

3. A *write__object* is never rejected provided that the corresponding *prewrite* has been accepted. If its timestamp $TS > min\_TS_P$, the request is buffered; else it is output. When the *write__object* request is output the corresponding *prewrite* is deleted from the buffer. If this causes min_TS_P to increase, the buffered *read__objects* and *write__objects* are retested to see if any of them can be output.

Figure 7.24 shows a sample trace of the execution of the algorithm. The values or actions of *Buffer, Output,* and TS_R are reflected upon completion of processing of an action by the scheduler. Finally, it should be noted that, although the algorithm

Requests: x_0 $\triangle_0$ $\bigcirc_0$ x_1 $\triangle_1$ x_2 $\bigcirc_1$ x_3 $\triangle_2$ $\triangle_3$ x_4 $\bigcirc_2$ x_4 $\triangle_4$ x_5 $\triangle_5$ $\bigcirc_5$ $\bigcirc_3$ $\bigcirc_4$

Buffer: $\triangle_0$ $\triangle_1$ $\triangle_1$ $\triangle_3$ $\triangle_3$ $\triangle_3$ $\triangle_3$ $\triangle_3$ $\triangle_3$ $\triangle_3$ $\triangle_3$ $\triangle_4$

x_2 x_4 x_4 x_4 x_4 x_4 x_4 x_4 x_5

x_4 x_4 x_4 x_4 x_4 $\triangle_5$

$\triangle_4$ $\triangle_4$ $\triangle_4$ $\triangle_4$ $\bigcirc_5$

x_5 x_5 x_5

$\triangle_5$ $\triangle_5$

$\bigcirc_5$

$\bigcirc_3$ $\bigcirc_4$

Output: x_0 $\bigcirc_0$ x_1 $\bigcirc_1$ x_3 x_4 x_5

x_2 x_4 $\bigcirc_5$

TS_R	0	0	0	1	1	1	2	3	3	3	3	3	3	3	3	3	3	4	5
min-TS_R	0	0	0	0	0	2	2	2	2	2	4	4	4	4	4	4	4	5	5
min-TS_P	0	0	0	0	1	1	1	1	1	3	3	3	3	3	3	3	3	4	5
TS_W	0	0	0	0	0	0	1	1	1	1	1	1	1	1	1	1	1	3	5
min-TS_W	0	0	0	0	0	0	0	0	0	0	0	0	0	0	0	0	5	5	5
O/B/R	O	B	O	O	B	B	O	B	R	B	B	R	B	B	B	B	B	O	O

x_i: read_object with timestamp i

$\triangle_i$: prewrite with timestamp i

$\bigcirc_i$: write_object with timestamp i

O/B/R: output/buffered/rejected

Figure 7.24   Time-stamp Ordering with Two-Phase Commit.

is stated for an individual object, a transaction actually issues a series of *prewrites*, one for each object to be updated, prior to committing.

7.11.3 Improvements on the Method of Basic Timestamp Ordering

In an attempt to alleviate some of the problems associated with the basic approach to using timestamps, four techniques for improvements have been developed and will be described here.

The Thomas Write Rule

If two consecutive *write_objects* conflict with each other and the newer request has timestamp smaller than the older one, the newer one can simply be ignored, eliminating unnecessary *write_object* actions [Thomas, 1979]. This is known as the Thomas Write Rule.

Multiversion Timestamp Ordering

At the expense of storage space, the multiversion timestamp ordering technique will avoid rejecting *read_object* actions [Reed, 1983]. An object O consists of a sequence of *versions,* each of the form (TS_W, value) that record the timestamps and values of all processed *write_object* $<O>$ actions and a sequence of timestamps TS_R's of all processed *read_object* $<O>$ actions. A multiversion object is illustrated in Figure 7.25. In practice, older versions are discarded in order to reduce memory requirements. Ignoring two-phase commit, multiversion timestamp ordering is implemented by the following rules:

1. A *read_object* action with timestamp TS is processed by reading the version of O with largest timestamp less than TS and adding TS to the set of TS_R's.

2. A *write_object* action with timestamp TS is allowed if there is no TS_R in the semiopen interval [TS, smallest $TS_W > TS$). A new version of O with timestamp TS is created.

Wait_Die and Wound_Wait

The two protocols described in this section are used in conjunction with locks to produce consistent schedules [Rosenkrantz, et al., 1978]. In the *wait_die* protocol, T_i can wait for T_j if T_i is older (has a smaller timestamp) than T_j. Otherwise, it is restarted (dies). In the *wound_wait* protocol, T_i can wait for T_j if T_i is younger (has a larger timestamp). Otherwise, T_j is aborted (wounded). Restarted transactions maintain their original timestamps. Both protocols have some advantages over basic timestamp ordering. Priority is given to older transactions and neither cyclic restarts nor infinite restarts are possible since, by retaining their timestamp, young aborted transactions eventually become old transactions. Unnecessary restarts are avoided since two transactions can be executed serially but in the reverse order of timestamp. On the other hand, younger transactions may have to be restarted many times, thus introducing significant system overhead. Rosenkrantz, et al. [1978] have proposed several other alternatives (to increase concurrency) that compute both global and local "CAN_WAIT_FOR" relations and use separate restart protocols for local and global (distributed) transactions.

Conservative Timestamp Ordering

Conservative timestamp ordering totally eliminates restarts during timestamp ordered scheduling [Bernstein and Shipman, 1980]. Prior to outputting the operation with

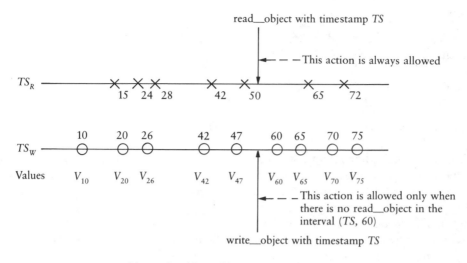

X_i: read_object with timestamp i

O_i: write_object with timestamp i

Figure 7.25 Multiversion Time-stamp Ordering.

smallest timestamp TS, the scheduler waits until it has received an operation from every TM with a timestamp larger than TS. It is assumed that each TM sends action requests in timestamp order and that the network delivers the requests from a TM in the order in which they were sent. Conservative timestamp ordering processes all operations in timestamp order whether they conflict or not. Three major problems must be overcome, however, if the method is to be practical.

First, if some TM never sends an operation, the scheduler is unable to function. To solve this problem, each TM must periodically send a timestamped null operation to every scheduler. If a TM rarely needs to request an action, it can send a null operation with very large timestamp to signal its intent to not communicate for some extended period of time.

Second, the solution to the first problem may introduce extensive traffic. In order to reduce traffic, the concept of *transaction class* is introduced. A class is defined by a readset (a set of objects to be read) and a writeset (a set of objects to be written). A transaction belongs to a class if its readset and writeset are subsets of the readset and writeset, respectively, of the class. Every class is associated with exactly one TM. Since the scheduler need only wait for action requests from those TMs whose class contains the object concerned, traffic can be substantially reduced. Class definitions are static.

Third, conservative timestamp ordering is overly conservative in the sense that actions are processed in timestamp order regardless of whether or not they conflict. To ease this problem, *conflict graph analysis* may be used. A *conflict graph* is an undirected graph that depicts potential conflicts between transactions in different classes. Actions of two transactions from classes C_i and C_j need not be synchronized if C_i and C_j are not involved in a cycle in the conflict graph. Since the classes are static, the conflict graph may be preanalyzed and the conflict knowledge stored at each *OM* for the scheduler.

7.12   Summary

One of the most important issues of distributed systems is the distribution of data. Operating systems and database management systems must cooperatively provide efficient, correct, and reliable methods to control concurrency, deadlock, and recovery. When it comes to actual implementation, the question may arise as to how the work should be distributed between the operating system and the database management system. Clearly, more common and basic work should be performed by the operating system and more application-oriented work should be done by the database management system. The actual boundary between the divisions may vary from system to system.

The algorithms, theories, and methods described in this chapter are nothing more than efforts to make the complexities and restrictions transparent to users. Users should be free from worries about data location, replication, concurrency, and failure in distributed systems. This is yet another step of virtualization of computer systems.

Key Words

abort	conservative time-stamp ordering	idempotent
abort_agent	consistent schedules	inconsistent retrieval anomaly
ancestor	continuous dead-lock detection	intention exclusive
atomic action	deadlock	intention share mode
atomic commitment	deadlock detection	I/O path
audit trails	distributed database	leaf-to-root node release rule
backward error recovery	DO-UNDO-REDO log protocol	legal schedule
cohort	edge mode	location transparency
commit	failure transparency	lock actions
commit coordinator	generals paradox	lockable objects
commit_object	global I/O path	locking techniques
compatible mode	global deadlock	lost update anomaly
concurrency control	granularity	nested two-phase
concurrency transparency		

commit protocol

object managers (OMs)

periodic deadlock detection

phantom deadlock

prewrite

private workspace

read_object

recovery manager

redo

replication

transparency

serial schedule

serializability

share mode

starvation

strong two-phase transaction

transaction managers (TMs)

transaction wait-for graph (TWFG)

two-phase

two-phase commit

undo

unlock

updating in place

wait-die protocol

well-formed

wound-wait protocol

write-ahead log protocol

write_object

Questions

1. Enumerate all possible values of the final balances of accounts A, B, and C after the three transactions shown in Figure 7.1 have completed.

2. Illustrate how the well-formed transaction in Figure 7.3(a) can see an inconsistent state.

3. Follow the steps of each schedule in Figures 7.5 and 7.6, and show that both in fact produce the same and correct results.

4. Enumerate all legal schedules of the three transactions shown in Figure 7.1.

5. Suppose the three accounts A, B, and C shown in Figure 7.1 are placed in three different sites S_1, S_2, and S_3. Write a legal schedule for three transactions T_1, T_2, and T_3, and verify that the schedule in fact produces the correct results.

6. Suppose the three accounts A, B, and C in Figure 7.1 are fully replicated at all sites, but S_1 is the primary copy site for A and B while S_2 is the primary copy site for C. Write a legal schedule for the three transactions and verify that the schedule produces the correct results.

7. Give a precise description of how centralized periodic deadlock detection may detect a phantom deadlock.

8. Consider the lock hierarchy in Figure 7.14. Show a sequence of lock operations to access Checking A in exclusive mode. Also show a sequence of lock releases.

9. Assume the lock hierarchy in Figure 7.14. Show a sequence of lock operations and a sequence of lock release operations for the following cases:

   a. Checking A is currently locked in S mode for a transaction and a new request by the transaction is made in mode X.

   b. Checking A is currently locked in S mode for a transaction and a new request by the transaction is made in mode S.

    c. Checking A is currently locked in X mode for a transaction and a new request by the transaction is made in mode S.

10. Illustrate, using Figure 7.19, how a crash at time S may leave an inconsistent system state. Use three bank accounts that are updated by T_2, T_3, and T_4.

11. Illustrate the steps of the DO-UNDO-REDO and write-ahead log protocol for a write operation.

12. Explain each of the three cases shown in Figure 7.20 and show that the consistency of the database is maintained.

13. State a sequence of actions in the event of:

    a. Commit coordinator crash

    b. Cohort crash

    c. Commit coordinator crash during a recovery from a cohort crash

    d. Two crashes of the commit coordinator and a cohort.

14. Show that timestamp ordering is a valid serialization order and is deadlock-free.

15. Assume two transactions. Illustrate how each of the following circumstances may occur if basic timestamp ordering is used: (1) no transaction is aborted; (2) one transaction is aborted, restarted, and successfully completed; (3) one transaction is unnecessarily aborted; and (4) a couple of transactions are repeatedly restarted.

16. Describe what has happened at each step of the execution trace shown in Figure 7.24.

17. Construct examples to show how performance can be improved by the Thomas Write Rule and multiversion timestamp ordering.

18. Construct a request action sequence for which the basic timestamp ordering method has an advantage over the wait_die protocol. Similarly, illustrate the converse.

19. Repeat Question 18 using the wound_wait protocol.

20. Construct a request action sequence for which the performance of the conservative timestamp ordering method is as good as that of the basic timestamp ordering method. Also, illustrate a case where the performance is worse.

21. Why does conservative timestamp ordering avoid restarts?

Problems

1. Define a suitable data structure and other necessary variables to maintain a TWFG. Write a formula for computing the memory requirements.

2. Suppose that an I/O path is created every t seconds in a system of N sites. Compute the number of messages for each of the following deadlock-detection algorithms:

   a. Centralized periodic detection with period p

   b. Centralized continuous detection

   c. Distributed periodic detection where every deadlock cycle involves n sites

   d. Distributed continuous detection where every deadlock cycle involves n sites

3. In timestamp ordering with two-phase commit, is it really advantageous to allow *read_object* operations for transactions with larger timestamps in the prewrite phase? In particular, compare the performance of the following three approaches:

   a. All nonconflicting *read_object* operations are permitted (output).

   b. All *read_object* operations are buffered until a prewrite is issued.

   c. Only the first *read_object* operation is permitted; all others are buffered.

4. Prove that multiversion timestamp ordering is correct. You must show that every schedule is equivalent to a serial schedule in timestamp order. (*Hint:* Let R be a *read_object* action that is processed "out of order"; that is, suppose R is executed after a *write_object* action whose timestamp exceeds the timestamp of R. Show that R would read the value that it would have read had it been processed in timestamp order. Similarly, deal with *write_object* actions.)

5. Implement *write* and *read* operations at the entity level using the transport/session services described in Chapter 6.

6. Explain how *write_object* and *read_object* operations are translated into sequences of file operations.

7. Write a simulator that can compute the amount of concurrency for the locking approach, hierarchical locking approach, basic timestamp ordering, multiversion timestamp ordering, and others. Run it for random sequences of requests and compare the results.

8. Can you prove that either the locking approach or the basic timestamp ordering allows more concurrency? How about the concurrency of the lock approach and other improved timestamp orderings?

9. Devise the most efficient algorithm to determine whether a given TWFG contains a deadlock.

10. Propose several data structures suitable to represent TWFGs and evaluate them.

11. Can you extend or modify the continuous deadlock-detection algorithm so that a deadlock-detection message, originating at the site that contains the transaction with the highest timestamp, will always detect deadlock?

12. Extend the distributed continuous deadlock-detection algorithm in Section 7.6.3 to a wait-for-any model. [*Hint:* (a) Find an efficient algorithm to detect a knot, (b) a blocked transaction waits until either all detection messages originating at this transaction have returned and deadlock is detected, or until the transaction is activated, and (c) an active or activated transaction discards all the detection messages that it receives, including those originating at this transaction.]

13. Modify the distributed continuous deadlock-detection algorithm presented in Section 7.6.3 to a system of distributed processes that communicate by message

passing. Do not assume any centralized control. You may assume that an agent for a blocked process will process deadlock-detection messages.

14. Why is the applicability of the collective requests and ordered requests deadlock prevention approaches limited in database systems?

15. Can you extend timestamp ordering to hierarchically organized objects?

16. Which concurrency control method can you extend to include user-defined objects?

17. Implement the two-phase commit protocol using the transport/session services described in Chapter 6.

18. Incorporate a two-phase commit using *prewrites* into multiversion timestamp ordering.

19. Compare the performance of various approaches for concurrency control. State their applicability.

References

Bernstein, P. A., and N. Goodman. (June 1981). "Concurrency control in distributed database systems." *ACM Computing Surveys* 13, 2, pp. 185–221.

Bernstein, P. A., and D. W. Shipman. (March 1980). "The correctness of concurrency control mechanisms in a system for distributed databases (SDD-1)." *ACM Transactions on Database Systems* 5, 1, pp. 52–68.

Chandy, K. M., and J. Misra. (May 1983). "Distributed deadlock detection," *ACM Transactions on Computer Systems* 1, 2, pp. 144–156.

Chandy, K. M.; J. Misra; and L. M. Haas. (May 1983). "Distributed deadlock detection." *ACM Transactions on Computer Systems* 1, 2, pp. 144–156.

Chang, E., and R. Roberts. (May 1979). "An improved algorithm for decentralized extrema-finding in circular configurations of processes." *Communications of the ACM* 22, 5, pp. 281–283.

Eswaran, K. P.; J. N. Gray; et al. (November 1976). "The notions of consistency and predicate locks in a database system." *Communications of the ACM* 19, 11, pp. 624–633.

Gifford, D. K. (1979). "Weighted voting for replicated data." *Proceedings of the Seventh Symposium on Operating Systems Principles*, pp. 150–162.

Gray, J. N. (1978). "Notes on database operating systems." In *Operating Systems: An Advanced Course, Lecture Notes in Computer Science* 60, Springer-Verlag, N.Y. pp. 393–481.

Hirschberg, D. S., and J. B. Sinclair. (November 1980). "Decentralized extrema-finding in circular configurations of processors." *Communications of the ACM* 23, 11, pp. 627–628.

Ho, G. S., and C. V. Ramamoorthy. (November 1982). "Protocols for deadlock detection in distributed database systems." *IEEE Transactions on Software Engineering* SE-8, 6, pp. 554–557.

Isloor, S. S., and T. A. Marsland. (1979). "System recovery in distributed databases." *Proceedings of IEEE COMPSAC 79*, pp. 421–426.

Jagannathan, J. R., and R. Vasudevan. (May 1983). "Comments on 'Protocols for deadlock detection in distributed database systems.'" *IEEE Transactions on Software Engineering* SE-9, 3, p. 371.

Kohler, W. H. (June 1981). "A survey of techniques for synchronization and recovery in decentralized computer systems." *ACM Computing Surveys* 13, 2, pp. 149–183.

Korth, H. F. (December 1982). "Deadlock freedom using edge locks." *ACM Transactions on Database Systems* 7, 4, pp. 632–562.

Lampson, B. W. "Atomic Transactions." (1981). In *Distributed Systems—Architecture and Implementation, Lecture Notes in Computer Science* 105, Springer-Verlag, N.Y., pp. 246–264.

Lampson, B. W., and H. E. Sturgis. (1976). "Crash recovery in a distributed storage system." Unpublished paper, Computer Science Laboratory, Xerox Palo Alto Research Center, Palo Alto, Calif.

Lomet, D. B. (March 1977). "Process structuring, synchronization, and recovery using atomic actions." *ACM SIGPLAN Notices* 12, 3, pp. 128–139.

Maekawa, M. 1983. "Distributed deadlock detection algorithms without phantom deadlocks." Technical Report 83-11, Department of Information Science, University of Tokyo, Tokyo, Japan.

Menasce, D. A., and R. R. Muntz. (May 1979). "Locking and deadlock detection in distributed data bases." *IEEE Transactions on Software Engineering* SE-5, 3, pp. 195–202.

Obermarck, R. (June 1982). "Distributed deadlock detection algorithm." *ACM Transactions on Database Systems* 7, 2, pp. 187–208.

Randell, B. (1979). "Reliable computing systems." In *Operating Systems: An Advanced Course, Lecture Notes in Computer Science* 60, Springer-Verlag, N.Y., pp. 283–391.

Reed, D. P. (February 1983). "Implementing atomic actions on decentralized data." *ACM Transactions on Computer Systems* 1, 1, pp. 3–23.

Rosenkrantz, D. J.; R. E. Stearns; and P. M. Lewis. (June 1978). "System level concurrency control for distributed database systems." *ACM Transactions on Database Systems* 3, 2, pp. 178–198.

Thomas, R. H. (June 1979). "A majority consensus approach to concurrency control for multiple copy databases." *ACM Transactions on Database Systems* 4, 2, pp. 180–209.

Traiger, I. L.; J. Gray; et al. (September 1982). "Transactions and consistency in distributed database systems." *ACM Transactions on Database Systems* 7, 3, pp. 323–342.

Suggested Readings

Bayer, R.; H. Heller; and A. Reiser. (June 1980). "Parallelism and recovery in database systems." *ACM Transactions on Database Systems,* 5, 2, pp. 139–156.

Bernstein, P.A.; N. Goodman; et al. (May 1978). "The concurrency control mechanism of SDD-1: a system for distributed databases (the fully redundant case)." *IEEE Transactions on Software Engineering,* SE-4, 3, pp. 154–168.

Bernstein, P.A.; N. Goodman; et al. (December 1981). "Query processing in a system for distributed databases (SDD-1)." *ACM Transactions on Database Systems,* 6, 4, pp. 602–625.

Bernstein, P. A.; D. W. Shipman; and J. B. Rothnie. (March 1980). "Concurrency control in a system for distributed databases (SDD-1)." *ACM Transactions on Database Systems, 5,* 1, pp. 18–51.

Bernstein, P.A.; D. W. Shipman; and W. S. Wong. (May 1979). "Formal aspects of serializability in database concurrency control." *IEEE Transactions on Software Engineering,* SE-5, 3, pp. 203–215.

Chamberlin, D. D.; R. F. Boyce; and I. L. Traiger. (1974). "A deadlock-free scheme for resource locking in a database environment." *Information Processing 74,* North-Holland Publishing, pp. 340–343.

Chang, E., and R. Roberts. (May 1979). "An improved algorithm for decentralized extrema-finding in circular configurations of processes." *Communications of the ACM, 22,* 5, pp. 281–283.

Chandy, K. M., and J. Misra. (November 1982). "Distributed computation on graphs: shortest path algorithms." *Communications of the ACM, 25,* 11, pp. 833–847.

Chandy, K. M.; J. C. Browne; et al. (March 1975). "Analytic models for rollback and recovery strategies in database systems." *IEEE Transactions on Software Engineering,* 1, 1, pp. 100–110.

Coffman, E. G.; E. Gelenbe; and B. Plateau. (January 1981). "Organization of the number of copies in a distributed database." *IEEE Transactions on Software Engineering,* 7, 1, pp. 78–84.

Garcia-Molina, H., and G. Wiederhold. (June 1982). "Read-only transactions in a distributed database." *ACM Transactions on Database Systems, 7,* 2, pp. 209–234.

Gligor, V. D., and S. H. Shattuck. (September 1980). "On deadlock detection in distributed systems." *IEEE Transactions on Software Engineering,* SE-6, 5, pp. 435–440.

Hammer, M. M., and D. W. Shipman. (December 1980). "Reliability mechanism for SDD-1: a system for distributed databases." *ACM Transactions on Database Systems, 5,* 4, pp. 431–466.

Kung, H. T., and J. T. Robinson. (June 1981). "On optimistic methods for concurrency control." *ACM Transactions on Database Systems, 6,* 2, pp. 213–226.

Langer, A. M., and A. W. Shum. (November 1982). "The distribution of granule accesses made by database transactions." *Communications of the ACM, 25,* 11, pp. 831–832.

Lehman, P. L., and S. B. Yao. (December 1981). "Efficient locking for concurrent operations on B-trees." *ACM Transactions on Database Systems, 6,* 4, pp. 650–670.

Menasce, D. A.; G. J. Popek; and R. R. Muntz. (June 1980). "A locking protocol for resource coordination in distributed databases." *ACM Transactions on Database Systems, 5,* 2, pp. 103–138.

Merlin, P. M., and P. J. Schweitzer. (March 1980). "Deadlock avoidance in store-and-forward networks—II: other deadlock types." *IEEE Transactions on Communications,* COM-28, 3, pp. 355–360.

Oppen, D. C., and Y. K. Dalal. (July 1983). "The clearinghouse: a decentralized agent for locating named objects in a distributed environment." *ACM Transactions on Office Information Systems,* 1, 3, pp. 230–253.

Randell, B. (June 1975). "System structure for software fault tolerance." *IEEE Transactions on Software Engineering,* 1, 2, pp. 220–232.

Russell, D. L. (March 1980). "State restoration in systems of communicating processes." *IEEE Transactions on Software Engineering,* 6, 2, pp. 183–194.

Schlageter, G. (September 1978). "Process synchronization in database systems." *ACM Transactions on Database Systems,* 3, 3, pp. 248–271.

Sekino, A.; K. Moritani; et al. (1984). "The DCS—a new approach to multisystem data-sharing." *Proceedings of National Computer Conference,* pp. 59–68.

Silberschatz, A., and Z. Kedem. (January 1980). "Consistency in hierarchical database systems." *Journal of the ACM,* 27, 1, pp. 72–80.

Smith, J. M., and D. C. P. Smith. (June 1977). "Database abstractions: aggregation." *Communications of the ACM,* 20, 6, pp. 405–413.

Stonebraker, M. (May 1979). "Concurrency control and consistency of multiple copies of data in distributed INGRES." *IEEE Transactions on Software Engineering,* SE-5, 3, pp. 188–194.

Tanenbaum, A. S. 1981. *Computer Networks.* Prentice-Hall, Englewood Cliffs, N.J.

Verhofstad, J. S. M. (June 1978). "Recovery techniques for database systems." *Computing Surveys,* 10, 2, pp. 168–195.

Computer
Security

8.1   Introduction

Computer security has been the subject of intensive research for more than a decade, and still remains one of the major research issues of the day. Its importance continues to grow as more sensitive information is stored and processed by computers and transmitted over computer communication networks. The security requirements of current systems vary with the type of information being processed. First and foremost, military information processing systems have perhaps the most stringent requirements. These are followed by information systems maintained by banks, law enforcement agencies, time-sharing service bureaus, hospitals, credit bureaus, government social service agencies, and corporations. As more small business and even personal home computer systems become part of larger networks, the security of individual data becomes a growing issue.

In order to design a secure information system or evaluate the security of any given information system, we must first define a formal model of security. The access matrix model, described in Section 8.2, focuses on the control of direct access to stored information. Because access control is unable to regulate the creation and dissemination of private copies of information, Section 8.3 introduces the concept of controlling access to information through classification of users and information. This concept is developed further in Section 8.4 by introducing the *information flow control* model. Section 8.5 deals with approaches to implementing access controls. Since information may be inadvertently left in unprotected form or surreptitiously observed or modified as it passes through a communication channel, the encryption techniques discussed in Section 8.6 become a necessary part of overall security. Finally, Section 8.7 briefly discusses the problem of user authentication.

8.2   Definition of Security and Common Violations

The general concept of *security* is broad and entails such things as moral issues, imposed by society, and legal issues, where control is legislated over the collection and dissemination of information, subject rights, and penalties for abuse. It also involves more technical issues such as control over the access and modification of stored or transmitted information.

Apart from societal and legislative controls, computer security can be generally divided into three areas: external security, interface security, and internal security. *External security* is concerned with physical access to the overall computer facility. This includes the control of access to communications lines, removable memory media such as tapes and disks, and terminals such as automated teller machines. It also is concerned with safeguarding information from natural disasters such as fire, floods, earthquakes, and sabotage efforts, which would affect the entire facility. *Interface security* is concerned with the authentication (identification) of a user once physical access to the computer becomes feasible. *Internal security* deals with three major controls: control of access within computer systems (*protection*), safeguarding of information transmitted over communication lines between computer systems (*communication security*), and safeguarding of stored information that is inadvertently or maliciously disclosed (*file security*).

Many aspects of external security do not have a technical solution but rely instead on proper managerial control and stringent guidelines and procedures for accountability and levels of control, and preventive measures against accidental or malicious loss or disclosure of information. As such, external security is beyond the scope of this book and will be mentioned only when necessary to clarify the context for internal and interface security. The focus of attention in this chapter, as depicted in Figure 8.1, is internal security. A brief discussion of a conventional approach to interface security is also included.

The security flaws of computer systems and approaches to penetration have been enumerated in the literature [Linde, 1975, Filipski and Hanko, 1986]. Following are a few of the more common flaws:

- *The system does not authenticate itself to the user:* A common way to steal passwords is for an intruder to leave a running process, which masquerades as the standard system logon process. After an unsuspecting user enters an identification and password, the process records the password, gives an error message (identical to the one standardly provided by the logon process in case of mistyped information), and aborts, leaving the true logon process in place to take care of any retry.

- *Improper handling of passwords:* Passwords may not be encrypted, or the table of encrypted passwords may be exposed to the general public, or a weak encryption algorithm may be used. If passwords are not encrypted, then penetration involves gaining unauthorized access to the password table. If encryption is used, but the algorithm is weak and the password file is available, then penetration amounts to performing inverse encryption. Even if a strong encryption algorithm is used, knowledge of the algorithm and encrypted passwords (along with user identification) allows the penetrator to take advantage of users who make poor password selections (too short or obvious choices such as a nickname, spouse or children's names, street name, and so on).

- *Improper implementation:* A security mechanism may be well thought out but improperly implemented. Erroneous code (e.g., improper testing of condition

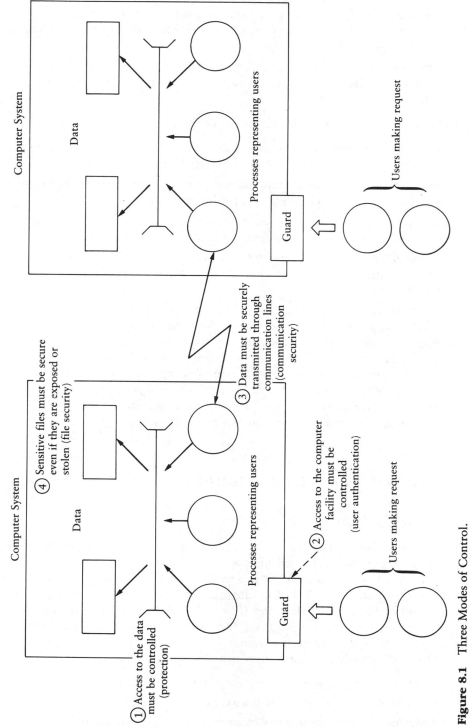

Figure 8.1 Three Modes of Control.

codes) may allow a penetrator to exercise certain branches of the code and gain unauthorized access. For example, timely abortion of a process that has called a system routine may leave the penetrator with system administrator access rights to files.

- *Parameter passing by reference:* The parameters are still in the user's address space after their legality is checked. The user could modify them just before the system uses them.

Some of the more successful penetration methods are:

Asynchronism: If multiple processes are simultaneously executed, one process can alter parameters that the other has tested but not as yet used.

Browsing: A penetrator circumvents the protection and searches the computer system, attempting to locate privileged information.

Clandestine code: Under the guise of correcting an error in the operating system, code is embedded to allow subsequent unauthorized entry to the system.

Masquerade: A penetrator assumes the identity of a legitimate user after he or she has obtained the proper password or circumvented the authentication mechanism.

Trojan horse: A borrowed program may surreptitiously access information that belongs to the borrower. It may also allow unauthorized access to the system (similar to clandestine code). A highly sophisticated Trojan horse may erase itself, making it difficult to detect its previous existence. Or, it may be present only in the binary version of a software package but not in the source code, and any recompilation of the source code will always reinstall it in the binary code [Thompson, 1984]. Subsequent sections describe a systematic approach to solving many aspects of the protection problem.

8.3   A Model for Access Control

8.3.1   Access Matrix Model

This section deals with methods of restricting access to objects based on the identity of the accessing entities. In particular, we present the *access matrix model,* which will provide a basic framework for describing protection systems. The model was formulated by Lampson [1971] and subsequently refined by Graham and Denning [1972] and by Harrison, Ruzzo, and Ullman [1976]. The model presented here is basically the same as that of Graham and Denning, and our presentation of the model generally follows their discussion.

The model consists of three components:

1. *Objects*—Entities to which access must be controlled
2. *Subjects*—Active entities that access objects
3. *Rules*—Govern the manner in which subjects may access objects

Each object is given a unique unforgeable system identification at the time of its creation. Common examples of objects are files, pages of main memory, programs, and auxiliary memory devices. Subjects are also objects since they too must be protected. A subject may be regarded as a (process, domain) pair where a *domain* is the protection environment (context) in which the *process* is executing. A process may change domains during the course of its execution, thereby playing a role in more than one subject.

The system maintains, in a *protection state,* all information that specifies the types of access that subjects have to objects. Three issues need to be addressed:

1. Representation of the protection state
2. Enforcement of access constraints (as specified by the protection state) for every attempted access by a subject to an object
3. A controlled way for subjects to alter the protection state, thereby effecting a state transition.

Representation of the Protection State

The protection state in this model is represented by an access matrix A, in which the rows denote subjects and the columns denote objects. The entry $A[S,X]$ defines the access rights (privileges, attributes) held by subject S to object X. Figure 8.2 shows an access matrix. In this protection state, S_1 has access privileges *wait and signal* to object S_2, *terminate* to object S_4, *read* to object X_1, and *read and execute* to object X_2. Similar privileges exist for subjects S_2, S_3, and S_4. The use of a *directed graph* is an alternative way to represent a protection state. For example, the protection state in Figure 8.2 is depicted in graph form in Figure 8.3.

Access attributes are names of operations on abstract data types, of which objects are specific instances. *Read, write, execute, open* and *close* are common attributes for files. For processes, *wait, signal, send,* and *receive* are common attributes. Some access attributes such as *read, write,* and *execute* may be *generic,* applying to more than one type of object.

Figure 8.2   Access Matrix.

Objects

	S_1	S_2	S_3	S_4	X_1	X_2
S_1		wait, signal		terminate	read	read, execute
S_2	wait, signal		wait, signal, send, terminate		append	write
S_3		wait, signal, receive		wait, signal, terminate	execute	
S_4			wait, signal	control		

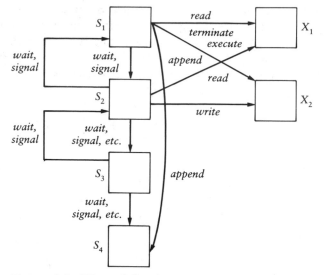

Figure 8.3   Directed Graph.

Enforcement of Access Constraints

An *object monitor* is associated with each type of object, and each access to an object is validated in the following manner:

1. A subject *S* attempts to perform an operation α on object *X*.
2. The triple (S, α, X) is formed by the system and passed to the object monitor of *X*.
3. The object monitor looks for the attribute α in $A[S,X]$. If present, access is permitted and the operation is allowed to proceed; otherwise, a protection violation occurs.

Since the identification of a subject is assumed to be unforgeable, the correctness of the system is determined by the correctness of the object monitors.

Protection State Transitions

The access matrix is itself a protected object, controlled by a distinguished monitor called the *access matrix monitor*. The access matrix monitor may transfer, grant, read, or delete access attributes upon authorized requests from subjects. It may create and destroy subjects and objects. In order to establish appropriate authorization for changing the access matrix, the attributes *owner* (of an object) and *control* (of a subordinate subject) are defined. In addition, the concept of a *copy flag* is defined as an extension to an attribute (denoted by "*") to allow controlled replication of the attribute.

Changes to the protection state are modeled by a set of commands that is specified by a sequence of actions that change the access matrix. The design of

Table 8.1   Protection System Commands [Graham and Denning, 1972. Reprinted by permission of AFIPS, Inc.]

Rule	Command (by S_o)	Conditions	Operation
R_1	transfer $\{{\alpha* \atop \alpha}\}$ to S,X	$\alpha*$ in $A[S_0,X]$	store $\{{\alpha* \atop \alpha}\}$ in $A[S,X]$
R_2	grant $\{{\alpha* \atop \alpha}\}$ to S,X	*owner* in $A[S_0,X]$	store $\{{\alpha* \atop \alpha}\}$ in $A[S,X]$
R_3	delete α from S,X	*control* in $A[S_0,S]$ or *owner* in $A[S_0,X]$	delete α from $A[S,X]$
R_4	$w := $ read S,X	*control* in $A[S_0,S]$ or *owner* in $A[S_0,X]$	copy $A[S,X]$ into w
R_5	create object X		add column for X to A; place *owner* in $A[S,X]$
R_6	destroy object X	*owner* in $A[S_0,X]$	delete column for X from A
R_7	create subject S		add row for S to A; execute create object S; place *control* in $A[S,S]$
R_8	destroy subject S	*owner* in $A[S_0,S]$	delete row for S from A; execute destroy object S

commands is an important issue in the access matrix model. Table 8.1 shows the commands proposed by Graham and Denning [1972].[1] A brief description of each command is presented here along with some examples. The examples assume the protection state shown in Figure 8.4.

R1: *transfer*—A subject that has $\alpha*$ access to an object may transfer a copy of the attribute to another subject. For example, S_1 can transfer to subject S_3 either *read* or *read** access to object F_1. If *read** is transferred, then S_3 may further propagate the attribute.

R2: *grant*—This command allows the owner of an object to grant any attributes (with exception of the *owner* attribute) to other subjects. S_3, for instance, can grant any operation on F_2 to S_1 and S_2.

R3: *delete*—This command allows subject S_0 to delete access attributes to object X by another subject S provided that either subject S is under *control* of S_0 or object X is owned by S_0.

R4: *read*—This allows a subject to read the contents of the access matrix. The authorization condition is the same as R3 and the operation is useful for determining current access to an object or by a subordinate subject.

---

[1]Harrison, Ruzzo, and Ullman [1976] have defined a different set of primitive actions. Depending on the choice of commands, different protection systems can be developed.

Figure 8.4   A Protection State [Graham and Denning, 1972. Reprinted by permission of AFIPS, Inc.].

Files

	S_1	S_2	S_3	F_1	F_2	D_1	D_2
S_1	control	owner block unblock	owner control	read* write*	read write	seek	owner
S_2	block unblock	control	switch	owner	update	owner	seek*
S_3			control	delete	owner execute		

R5: *create object*—This command allows any subject to create a nonsubject object.

R6: *delete object*—This command allows the deletion of an object by its owner.

R7: *create subject*—This command allows any subject to create a subordinate subject. The creating subject becomes the *owner* (by virtue of R5) and the new subject is in *control* of itself.

R8: *delete subject*—This command allows deletion of a subject by its owner.

As an example of the use of these commands, suppose a subject S wishes to create a subordinate process Q having memory segment M. S executes the command *create subject Q*. Subject S subsequently executes the sequence of commands: *create object M; grant write* to Q,M; and *grant read* to Q,M. As another example, suppose subject S wishes to delete the access rights of subordinate Q to object X. S executes command: $w := read\ (Q,X)$, followed by *delete w* from Q,X. There is a distinct difference between the control and owner attributes for subjects since a controller can only read and/or delete the attributes possessed by a subject.

It is assumed that subjects have a single owner. In addition to simple rules governing the creation, deletion, and modification of objects, single ownership provides a hierarchical relationship among subjects and avoids the political controversy that naturally arises in multiple ownership. If necessary for the model, we will assume that ownership is transfer-only; that is, the transferring subject loses the owner attribute. However, subjects may have multiple controllers. Note also that no subject is the owner of itself and a subject cannot acquire for itself an access attribute from a subordinate.

8.3.2   Levels of Sharing

The access matrix model defined in this chapter permits the following levels of sharing:

1. No sharing at all (complete isolation)
2. Sharing copies of data objects

3. Sharing originals of data objects
4. Sharing untrusted programs
5. Sharing between untrustworthy subsystems

It is apparent that level 1 sharing may be accomplished with the model. Level 2 sharing is similarly accomplished because different subjects may be allowed to access different copies of the same object. For level 3 sharing, suppose a subject S_1 wishes to share an object X with subject S_2. This can be accomplished by S_1 executing the command *transfer* α to S_2,X or *grant* α to S_2,X. It is clear that S_2 cannot obtain access to any other objects accessible by S_1, and the owner of S_2 cannot obtain access to X.

Sharing at levels 4 and 5 places severe demands on the protection systems. Suppose S_1 wishes to share the services of a program or subsystem S with S_2. S can access an object X and S_2 requires the same access to X. Both S_1 and S_2 are considered trustworthy. However, S_2 does not trust S, and it consequently needs a guarantee that S will not make an unauthorized access to any of S_2's objects. Furthermore, S_1 may wish at any time to revoke S_2's privilege to share S. One way to solve this problem is to define the concept of an *indirect* access attribute, as depicted in Figure 8.5. The following characteristics of indirect access are precisely those needed to solve the problem:

- An indirect attribute applies only to subjects and may be granted by the owner of a subject.

- If S_2 has indirect access to S, then it is able to access objects accessible to S in the same manner as they would be accessed by S. However, S_2 may not acquire for itself direct access to the objects. Also, S_2 may read (but not acquire) access attributes possessed by S.

- S_1, who is the owner of S, may at any time revoke S_2's indirect access to S.

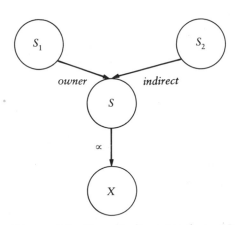

Figure 8.5   Use of Indirect Attributes [Graham and Denning, 1972. Reprinted by permission of AFIPS, Inc.].

The monitors for objects need only minor adjustment to incorporate the concept of *indirect* access:

1. S_2 requests *indirect* α access to X through S.
2. The system passes to the monitor of X the triple $(S_2, \alpha$ *indirect* $S, X)$.
3. The monitor of X looks to determine if *indirect* is in $A[S_2,S]$ and α is in $A[S,X]$. If found, α access of X is allowed to proceed; otherwise, a protection violation occurs.

As a more concrete example, indirect attributes may be used to allow a debugging program S_2 to obtain information during a debugging run of a program S.

The previous example illustrated the sharing of an untrustworthy subject among trustworthy subjects. A similar approach can be used in level 5 sharing, where untrustworthy subsystems share each other's objects (Figure 8.6(a)). Although T_1 and T_2 are both untrustworthy and mutually suspicious of each other, the indirect attribute allows them to share each others objects. A solution is shown in Figure 8.6(b).

Another approach to resolving the problem of sharing between untrustworthy subjects is to provide a facility that allows one subject to *switch* to another subject. Suppose a process P_1 is created to execute in a domain D_1, thus giving rise to the subject $S_1 = (P_1 D_1)$. A switch may be made to subject $S_2 = (P_2, D_2)$ if there is a switch attribute in $A[S_1,S_2]$. Upon switching domains, one may view the first as inactive and the second as active, with execution semantics similar to that of

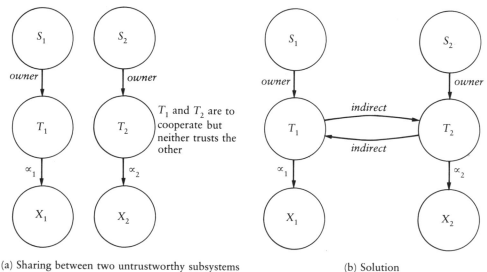

(a) Sharing between two untrustworthy subsystems   (b) Solution

Figure 8.6   Sharing Between Untrustworthy Subsystems.
[Graham and Denning, 1972. Reprinted by
permission of AFIPS, Inc.]

coroutines. The ability to switch from one domain to another provides the basis for implementation of *protected subsystems,* along with the ability to pass objects (with controlled access) as parameters when a switch is made (see Problem 6). This approach eliminates some of the awkwardness of the indirect attribute.

8.3.3   The General Issue of Trust

The access control system is correct only if trustworthy subjects are involved or, as illustrated in the previous section, some control can be placed on untrustworthy programs. However, the presence of untrustworthy subjects presents some problems that cannot be solved by the model. Several examples will illustrate some of the problems.

Passing an α^* attribute from one subject to another implies that the second subject is trusted to selectively further pass α or α^* in keeping with the wishes of the first subject.

The *read* attribute is all-powerful in the sense that it does not prevent the reader from making a copy of the resource and granting to others *read* access to this private copy. S_0 grants a *read* attribute (without copy flag) to S_1 only, with the intention that no other subject be able to obtain the contents of object X. This is correct only if S_1 is trustworthy, since S_1 can read X, write its own private copy, and then distribute the copy to other subjects.

More generally, if two untrustworthy subjects conspire, then the first may execute its rights on behalf of the second. Assume a *write* (or any other) attribute to object X is possessed by subject S_1. If S_1 and S_2 conspire, S_2 can write to X through S_1.

If subjects are shared, the owner of a subject can gain illegal access to the subject's indirect attributes, which might have been granted by yet a third subject. This is depicted in Figure 8.7 [Graham and Denning, 1972]. Suppose S_1, who is the owner of S, allows S_2 to execute S. S_2 grants to S α access to object X. The untrustworthy owner may illegally gain access to X by granting to itself indirect access to S.

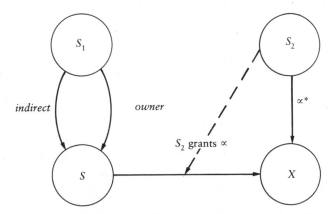

Figure 8.7   Indirect Attribute by an Untrustworthy Subject [Graham and Denning, 1972].

Problems of this nature deal with flow of information and will be addressed in the discussion of the information flow model.

8.3.4   The Confinement Problem

Section 8.3.3 illustrated why the element of trust is necessary in this model. If programs are shared, the protection problem is considerably more complex than if only data objects are shared. This difficulty is exemplified by the possible presence of a *Trojan horse*. A Trojan horse is a piece of code that is surreptitiously placed in a program in order to perform functions not advertised by the program specifications. Typically, it takes advantage of access rights belonging to an executing process in order to copy or misuse information in a way not relevant to its stated purpose. For example, a text editor or a compiler might be modified to copy confidential information or proprietary programs to a file accessible to another user. The term *Trojan horse* has also often been used to refer to a "trapdoor" planted in a system program which, on behalf of a specific user or parameter, allows unauthorized entry to other system functions or objects [Andler and Anderson, 1972; Linde, 1975]. To provide protection against a Trojan horse, it is necessary to encapsulate shared or borrowed programs in small protection domains with minimum access rights. In order to prevent illegal leakage of information, such a subsystem must be constrained to communicate only through its formal parameters, and it must not retain information from one call to the next. The facility for communication by means of formal parameters requires extension to the access control matrix (see Problem 7).

In general, a program that cannot retain or leak information is said to be *memoryless* or *confined,* and the prevention of such leakage is called the *confinement problem* [Lampson, 1973]. If a borrowed program does not retain information or output any information other than by its formal parameters, confinement can be ensured by restricting the access rights of the program. However, if a program retains or outputs information through other channels, access control alone is insufficient to ensure protection. Ensuring that a program does not retain information at or above some level of sensitivity is called the *selective confinement problem.*

Three types of channels have been identified that can be used to leak information [Lampson, 1973]: legitimate channels, storage channels, and covert channels. *Legitimate channels* are those that a process normally uses to convey information (e.g., messages, parameters, printed output). By covert use of a legitimate channel, it is possible to leak confidential information (e.g., by varying line spacing or by some form of encodement).

Storage channels are objects that are shared among processes. To illustrate the subtlety of how storage channels may be used, the following example shows a way to leak information by covert use of the file system (without reading or writing files). In this example, the assumed nature of the file system is one in which files are opened in a mutually exclusive mode, and a file that is opened by one process may be closed by another. Assume that two subjects S_1 and S_2 concurrently execute. Both will OPEN and CLOSE three files to convey one "bit" of information. Figure 8.8 illustrates how this can be done. The OPEN(file, error return) procedure returns control to "error return" if the file is already OPEN. The file *value* is used to convey the bit of

Figure 8.8 Leakage of Information over a Storage Channel.

value, set, reset: FILE;
data, received: INTEGER **range** 0..1

<table>
<tr><td align="center">S_1
(sender)</td><td align="center">S_2
(receiver)</td></tr>
<tr>
<td valign="top">

loop
    data : = the next sending bit;
    if data = 0 **then**
    end if;
L1 : OPEN (value, L1);
L2 : OPEN (set, L2);
L7 : OPEN (reset, L8);
    CLOSE (reset);
    goto L7;

L8 : CLOSE (reset);
end loop;

</td>
<td valign="top">

loop
    received : = 0;
L3 : OPEN (set, L4);
    CLOSE (set);
    goto L3;
L4 : OPEN (value, L5);
    received : = 1;
L5 : CLOSE (value);
    CLOSE (set);
L6 : OPEN (reset, L6);
    the next received bit : = received;
end loop;

</td>
</tr>
</table>

information; the file *set* is used to signal that one bit of information has been set by S_1; and file *reset* is used to signal that S_2 has received the information.[2]

Covert channels are those normally not intended for information transfer. For example, a program might vary its paging rate or otherwise control its execution time to send an observing process secret information. Generally, information sent over covert channels is based on time-dependent behavior.

Some protection problems involving conspiracies by untrustworthy subjects and general leakage can be eliminated if control is exercised over the *right to disseminate information*. In the next two sections, we will be primarily concerned with the set of operations that causes flows along legitimate and storage channels. Information flows along covert channels are not considered in this chapter since practical controls are not available.

8.4 Flow-Secure Access Controls

The method described in this section is an extension to the method of access control in the sense that the protection state, depicted by the access matrix, is determined by a definition of the secure flow of information. It is premised on the ability to impose a classification scheme on both objects and subjects and is motivated by a general security policy similar to that found in military organizations.

---

[2]Under certain timing conditions, both processes in Figure 8.8 may become involved in an infinite loop of busy waiting. For example, suppose statement L2 of S_1 is always executed immediately after L3 of S_2. This anomaly does not detract from the point of the example and could be corrected.

It is assumed that each object is assigned a *classification* (such as unclassified, confidential, secret, top secret) that denotes the security (or sensitivity) level of the information content. Also, each subject is assigned a *clearance* to access certain classes of information. We will use the term *security level* to denote the clearance of a subject or classification of an object. Furthermore, each object and each subject may be affiliated with a *compartment* (such as Middle East, Europe, Latin America, and so on) that categorizes the information content for the object and represents a need-to-know classification for a subject. The *security class SC* of an object or subject is specified by a pair (A, B), where A is the clearance or security level and B is a compartment designation.

In order to define a secure flow of information, a partial order must be imposed on the set of security classes. For this purpose, it is assumed that the set of security levels and the set of compartments each forms a *lattice*.[3] Figure 8.9 shows examples of these two types of lattice structures [Denning, 1976]. The collection of all possible security classes also forms a lattice that is the cross-product of the security level lattice and the compartment lattice. As such, it has a unique greatest lower bound and a unique least upper bound—for example, (unclassified, no compartments) and (top secret, all compartments).

Access controls are governed by the ordering of security classes. In particular, a subject S is allowed access to an object X if and only if two conditions are satisfied:

1. S has the appropriate clearance relative to the class of the object X.
2. The compartment designation for S is contained in the compartment designation for X.

The second condition is an application of the principle of *least privilege* or *need-to-know*.

Perhaps the best known use of flow control to implement access control is the Bell and LaPadula model [1973], which is a formalization and specialization of the military security policy. The description given here is similar to that given by Landwehr [1981].

In this model, each subject and object is assigned a security class and these classes are used to control the manner in which the access control matrix may be modified.

The access matrix defines four modes by which a subject may access an object:

1. *read-only:* The subject is allowed only read access to the object.
2. *append:* The subject is allowed only write access to the object.
3. *execute:* The subject is allowed only execute access to the object.
4. *read-write:* The subject is allowed only read or write access to the object.

In addition, there is a *control* attribute that allows a subject to pass to other subjects some or all of the access modes it possesses. The control attribute itself cannot be passed to another subject.

---

[3] A lattice is a partial ordered set in which any two elements have a unique least upper bound and a unique greatest lower bound.

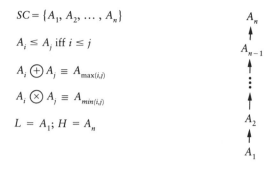

$$SC = \{A_1, A_2, \ldots, A_n\}$$

$$A_i \leq A_j \text{ iff } i \leq j$$

$$A_i \oplus A_j \equiv A_{max(i,j)}$$

$$A_i \otimes A_j \equiv A_{min(i,j)}$$

$$L = A_1; H = A_n$$

Description   Representation

(a) Linearly ordered lattice [Denning 1976, p. 238]

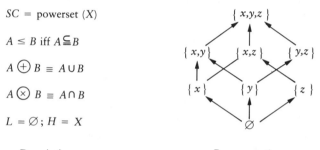

$$SC = \text{powerset } (X)$$

$$A \leq B \text{ iff } A \subseteq B$$

$$A \oplus B \equiv A \cup B$$

$$A \otimes B \equiv A \cap B$$

$$L = \varnothing; H = X$$

Description   Representation

(b) Lattice of subsets of $X = \{x,y,z\}$

Figure 8.9 Examples of Lattices [Denning, 1976. Copyright © 1976 by Association for Computing Machinery, Inc. Reprinted by permission].

The security of the method is based on two fundamental axioms:

The simple security property: Reading information from an object X by a subject S requires $SC(S) \geq SC(X)$.

*The * − property ("star-property"):* Appending information to an object X by subject S requires $SC(S) \leq SC(X)$, and both reading and writing of an object X requires $SC(S) = SC(X)$.[4]

If both properties hold, the protection state is considered secure. For example, in a system with the security levels unclassified, classified, secret, and top secret, a subject with a secret security level is able to acquire read access to an object with a classi-

---

[4]This is actually a simplification of the original rule.

fication that is not greater than secret and is able to acquire write access to an object with a classification that is not less than secret. More formally, if SC denotes the security class of an object or the current security class of a subject, then a subject S can read an object X and write an object Y only if $SC(X) \leq SC(S) \leq SC(Y)$.

With this type of regulation on access control, the focus of attention is on the rules defined to change or access the protection state (access control matrix):

1. *get (read, append, execute, read-write) access:* Used by a subject to initiate access to an object in the prescribed mode

2. *release (read, append, execute, read-write) access:* Used to release previously initiated access

3. *give (read, append, execute, read-write) access:* Used by a subject to grant access to a specified object to another subject

4. *rescind (read, append, execute, read-write) access:* Used by a subject to reduce the allowed access that some other subject has to a specified object

5. *create object:* Used by a subject to activate an inactive object (if the object does not exist, then it must first be created)

6. *delete object:* Used by a subject to deactivate an object

7. *change security level:* Used by a subject to alter the current security level of the specified object

Each rule has an associated set of restrictions to ensure that the *simple security policy* and ** — property* are satisfied. As examples, in Rule 1 a subject cannot initiate read access unless its security class is at least as great as the security class of the object; in Rule 3 the subject must have the control attribute for the object and the recipient subject must have the proper clearance; in Rule 4 the subject must have control of the object; and in Rule 7 a subject must have control and it cannot establish a security level for an object that exceeds the original clearance of the subject.

Designated *trusted subjects* are allowed to declassify information. A trusted subject is one that can be relied on not to compromise real-world security even if the simple security or ** —property* is violated.

Extensions to the Bell and LaPadula model include:

Hierarchies: Introduction of hierarchies of objects such as file directories

Integrity policy [Biba, 1977]: Allows control of unauthorized "upgrading" of information.

Database management systems [Hinke and Schaefer, 1975; Grohn, 1976]: Extends the concept of classification to elements of a relational database; develops the concept of integrity as a formal dual to security; develops a directory structure that partitions objects according to level of classification.

Development of automated program verifiers: These extensions typically embody the concept of information flow control (which is developed in the next section).

While numerous extensions exist, the Bell and LaPadula model has several restrictions. The security levels of subjects and objects are static; the granularity of access control is at the file level, which may be too large; and for a subject S that reads X

and writes Y, the condition $SC(X) \leq SC(S) \leq SC(Y)$ may be too strong since the information written to Y may not depend on the information from X. Thus, some operations may be disallowed by the model even though they are secure.

8.5 Information Flow Control

The information flow models presented in this section are concerned with controlling the flow of information from one object to another. The major advantages of this pure approach are added flexibility in analyzing flow over storage channels and the ability to analyze flow at a fine-grained level (such as at the program variable level). These methods are intended to be used in conjunction with access control techniques and, depending on the method, the clearance of a subject may or may not be considered. The discussion in this section is derived from Denning [1976, 1982] and Landwehr [1981].

8.5.1 The Lattice Model and Security Requirements

An information flow model is denoted by $FM = <N, P, SC, \leq, \oplus, \otimes>$, where

1. N is a set of storage objects.
2. P is a set of processes.
3. SC is a set of security classes. For notational convenience, if X is a storage object, then $SC(X)$ will be denoted by $\underline{X}$.
4. The relation $\leq$ is a partial order on security classes and determines whether information is allowed to flow from one object to another.
5. $\oplus$ is an associative and commutative binary operator on SC, denoting the *least upper bound;* for example, $A \oplus B$ is the least upper bound of classes A and B. Furthermore, for all $A, B, C \in SC$:

   a. $A \leq A \oplus B$ and $B \leq A \oplus B$, and
   b. $A \leq C$ and $B \leq C$ implies $A \oplus B \leq C$.

6. $\otimes$ is an associative and commutative binary operator on SC, denoting the *greatest lower bound;* for example, $A \otimes B$ is the greatest lower bound of classes A and B. Furthermore, for all $A, B, C \in SC$:

   a. $A \otimes B \leq A$ and $A \otimes B \leq B$, and
   b. $C \leq A$ and $C \leq B$ imply $C \leq A \otimes B$.

$(SC, \leq, \oplus, \otimes)$ forms a lattice, with lowest and highest classes formed by $\otimes SC$ and $\oplus SC$, respectively.

The system is defined to be secure, according to the lattice model *FM*, if and only if the execution of a sequence of operations by processes cannot give rise to an information flow that violates the $\leq$ relation.

8.5.2 Types of Information Flow

There are two types of information flow in programs: *explicit* and *implicit*. An explicit flow to an object Y occurs as the result of direct transfer of information from one storage object (variable) to another. Such statements have the general form $Y = f(X_1, \ldots, X_n)$ and the resulting information flow is denoted by $Y \leftarrow X_1, \ldots, Y \leftarrow X_n$. An implicit flow of information occurs as the result of a *conditioned* transfer of information. For example, a statement **if** $X = 0$ **then** $Y : = Z$ causes an implicit flow of information $Y \leftarrow X$ because, by testing the value of Y, it may be possible to determine the value of X (in this example, if the value of Y is Z, we know that the value of X is 0). In general, the variables in the boolean part of conditional and iterative statements cause an implicit flow to each variable assigned in the body of the construct.

The security requirements for any program can then be stated as:

1. An elementary statement S (e.g., assignment or I/O) is secure if any explicit flow caused by S is secure. Specifically, if $Y \leftarrow X_1, \ldots, Y \leftarrow X_n$, security requires that $\underline{X_1} \oplus \cdots \oplus \underline{X_n} \leq \underline{Y}$ holds (that is, to be certified, this flow must be allowed by the security lattice) after the execution of S. Here $\underline{X_i}$ or $\underline{Y}$ denotes the security level of object X_i or Y. The requirement can be more compactly stated as $\oplus \underline{X_i} \leq \underline{Y}$.

2. A conditioned statement $S = C : S_1, S_2, \ldots, S_m$, where the S_i are statements to be executed depending on the value of C, is secure if each S_i is secure and all implicit flows from C are secure. Specifically, all implicit flows are secure if a flow is allowed from all variables in C to all variables $Y_1, \ldots, Y_k$, which are assigned a value in some S_i. This condition is compactly stated as $\underline{C} \leq \otimes \underline{Y_i}$.

3. A program is secure if each statement is individually secure.

These security requirements have been implemented in varying degrees with static or dynamic binding of security classes to objects, and enforcement taking place at some combination of compile time, link time, and run time.

8.5.3 Compile-Time Certification with Static Binding

The method presented here is from Denning [1977]. Static binding means that objects and subjects are assigned a fixed security class. If external objects (such as files) are bound to the program, then it is assumed that the linker program will certify the legality of information flow from actual object to formally declared object. We assume static binding of security classes to all internally declared objects. Compile-time certification analyzes the flow of data through a program and compares this flow with the flow relation allowed by the security lattice.

The advantages are: (1) The certification does not impair run-time performance, (2) the certification process can be specified in a higher level language, and (3) once certified to be secure, the program cannot purposely leak information at run time (for example, it is not possible for a certified program to convey a value of a variable X by causing X security violations (and abortions) observable from the outside). The disadvantages are: (1) flows not specified by a program (for example, illegal flows caused by dangling pointers or illegal array subscripts) cannot be checked and (2) there is no accounting for flows caused by malfunctioning hardware at run time.

A program is certified *secure* if and only if, for any execution, the incurred flows are permissible by the information flow lattice. Unfortunately, this property is undecidable [Denning, 1977], and, as a result, the following *weak security* condition is adopted:

$X \rightarrow Y$ can be syntactically specified by a program only if $\underline{X} \leq \underline{Y}$

One result of this weaker condition is that secure programs might not be certified. For example, the statement

if $C = 0$ **then if** $C \neq 0$ **then** $S := T$

will never result in an information flow during execution. The statement, however, does specify the flows $T \rightarrow S$ and $C \rightarrow S$ and may not certify depending on the values of $\underline{C}$, $\underline{S}$ and $\underline{T}$.

The Certification Process for Elementary Programs

The least upper bound and greatest lower bound properties (5) and (6) of the flow lattice model allow certain efficiencies in the compile-time certification process. In particular, if $Y \leftarrow X_1, \ldots, Y \leftarrow X_n$, then it suffices to certify that $\underline{Y} \geq \oplus \underline{X}_i$. If $Y \rightarrow X_i$ for $1 \leq i \leq n$, then it suffices to certify that $\underline{Y} \leq \otimes \underline{X}_i$. Table 8.2 summarizes the certification function of a compiler for a language involving assignment, conditional, and iterative statements.

Figure 8.10 is an example (adapted from Denning, 1977) of a program and the corresponding compile-time certification. Note that all constants are bound to the lowest class. In this example, there are only two classes H (high) and L (low). Since all specified flows are certified, the program is certified.

Table 8.2 Certification Function of a Compiler

Statement Type	Flow Certification
$Y: = f(X_1, \ldots, X_n)$	$\oplus \underline{X}_i \leq \underline{Y}$
output $X_1, \ldots, X_n$ **to** f	$\oplus \underline{X}_i \leq \underline{f}$
input $X_1, \ldots, X_n$ **from** f	$\underline{f} \leq \otimes \underline{X}_i$
if $C(X_1 \ldots X_n)$	$\oplus \underline{X}_i \leq \otimes \underline{Y}_i \{\otimes \underline{Z}_i\}$
then B_1	where Y_i are assigned in B_1
$\{$**else** $B_2\}$	and Z_i are assigned in B_2
while $C(X_1 \ldots X_n)$ **do** B	$\oplus \underline{X}_i \leq \otimes \underline{Y}_i$
	where Y_i are assigned in B

Figure 8.10   Compile-Time Certification of an Elementary
Program [Adapted from Denning, 1977.
Copyright © 1977 by Association for
Computing Machinery, Inc. Reprinted by
permission].

```
 1. program sumval(f1,f2,f3,f4);
 2. var i,n: integer class L;
 3.      flag: boolean class L;
 4.        x,tot: integer class H;
 5.      f1,f2: file class L;
 6.      f3,f4: file class H;
 7. begin
 8.   i := 1;
 9.   n := 0;
10.   tot := 0;
11.   while i < 100 do
12.     begin
13.       input flag from f1;
14.       output flag to f2;
15.       input x from f3;
16.       if flag then
17.         begin
18.           n := n + 1;
19.           tot := tot + x
20.         end
21.       i := i + 1;
22.     end;

23.   output n, tot, tot/n to f4;

24. end.
```

Certification conditions (right column):

- Line 8: $\underline{1} \leq \underline{i} \ (L \leq L)$
- Line 9: $\underline{0} \leq \underline{n} \ (L \leq L)$
- Line 10: $\underline{0} \leq \underline{tot} \ (L \leq H)$
- Line 13: $\underline{f1} \leq \underline{flag} \ (L \leq L)$
- Line 14: $\underline{flag} \leq \underline{f2} \ (L \leq L)$
- Line 15: $\underline{f3} \leq \underline{x} \ (H \leq H)$
- Line 18: $\underline{n} \oplus \underline{1} \leq \underline{n} \ (L \leq L)$
- Line 19: $\underline{tot} \oplus \underline{x} \leq \underline{tot} \ (H \leq H)$
- Line 20: $\underline{flag} \leq \underline{n} \otimes \underline{tot} \ (L \leq L)$
- Line 21: $\underline{i} \oplus \underline{1} \leq \underline{i} \ (L \leq L)$
- Line 22: $\underline{i} \oplus \underline{100} \leq \underline{flag} \otimes \underline{f2} \otimes \underline{x}$
- Line 23: $\underline{n} \oplus \underline{tot} \oplus \underline{tot} \oplus \underline{n}$

Handling Array and Record Objects

The process of flow certification can be readily extended to structures where access
or assignment is allowed on individual components. Consider a read access reference
to an array element

$$X := A[E_1, \ldots, E_n]$$

Certification requires combining the classes of the subscripts with the class of the
array in calculating the flow

$$\underline{X} \leftarrow \underline{A} \oplus \underline{E_1} \oplus \cdots \oplus \underline{E_n}$$

If a write access reference is made to an array element

$$A[E_1, \ldots, E_n] := X$$

then the information flow is given by

$$\underline{A} \leftarrow \underline{X} \oplus \underline{E}_1 \oplus \cdots \oplus \underline{E}_n$$

The need for verification of flows from the subscripts to the array is illustrated by the following example. Suppose all elements of the array are zero and some element is assigned a nonzero value. By inspecting the elements of the array, it is possible to deduce the value of the subscripts, thereby illustrating the flow of information. The compiler must check for out-of-range subscripts to avoid the possibility of undetected run-time security violations.

Suppose a record R has fields $F_1, \ldots, F_n$. The flow under assignment ($R.F_j := x$ or vice versa) is handled as a normal assignment since each field has its own security class. However, writing R to a file G requires certification of the information flow

$$\oplus \underline{F}_i \rightarrow \underline{G}$$

and reading R from F requires certification of the flow

$$\underline{G} \rightarrow \otimes \underline{F}_i$$

Flow Analysis of Procedure Calls

A program that calls procedures is secure if and only if the main procedure and all called procedures are secure and the parameter flow is secure. Let f be a procedure with formal input parameters X_i, $1 \le i \le m$ and formal output parameters Y_j, $1 \le j \le n$. Suppose f is called by p with actual input and output parameters A_i and B_j, respectively. The call statement is secure if (1) f is secure, (2) $\underline{A}_i \le \underline{X}_i$ for all i, and (3) $\underline{Y}_j \le \underline{B}_j$ for all j. The procedure f is secure if all flows of f can be certified. If the call is conditioned on the set $\{E_1, \ldots, E_r\}$, with $\underline{E} = \oplus \underline{E}_i$, then an implicit flow occurs and we must have $\underline{E} \le \otimes \underline{B}_j$. Also, if $Z_1, \ldots, Z_k$ are other output objects of f, then $\underline{E} \le \otimes \underline{Z}_j$ must hold.

If p and f are compiled together, they can be certified together. Otherwise the linker can certify the call statement. In this latter case, the compiler must output for p the classes of all actual input and output parameters, along with the class $\underline{E}$ on which the call is conditioned. It must output for f the classes of all formal parameters, along with the classes of any other objects that may be written. The link-time certification is then carried out in the same manner as compile-time certification.

This method leads to serious problems in the case of library routines. To be callable by any program, the formal input and output parameters of a library routine must be declared at the highest class in the system. This, in effect, restricts their usefulness since calls with lower level inputs will have overclassified output values. One possible solution is to prepare and certify a separate version for each possible combination of input classes. A somewhat more attractive approach is to restrict f so that all output objects are declared as formal output parameters, each of which is a function of the input parameters. In this case, the security of the call is certified if $(\oplus \underline{A}_i) \oplus (\oplus \underline{E}_i) \le \otimes \underline{B}_j$. This latter approach, however, could result in failure to certify a secure procedure since an output value may not be a function of all input values.

Exception Handling

Exceptional conditions arising during the execution of a program may be regarded as unscheduled procedure calls. Since this involves the execution of potentially uncertified code, security violations may occur. The following section of program code (derived from Denning [1977]) would be certified by the compile-time mechanism:

```
1.    var count: integer class L;
2.        cond: boolean class L;
3.        f: file class L;
5.        val,sum: integer class H;
6.    begin
7.        count := 1;
8.        sum := 0;
9.        cond := true;
10.   while cond do
11.       begin
12.           sum := sum + val;
12.           count := count + 1
12.           output count to f
15.       end;
16.   end.
```

Suppose *MAX* denotes the maximum integer possible on the underlying machine and suppose *LAST* is the last value of count that is written to f prior to overflow of the value of sum (assuming that the file is available upon program completion or abortion). Then the value of val may be closely approximated from information on f since $(LAST - 1) * \text{val} \leq MAX \leq LAST * \text{val}$. A solution to this problem is to require the programmer to supply interrupt handlers. A PL/1-like handler for this example would be the code:

on *overflow* sum **do** cond := false

With this additional code, the program would fail to certify, thereby avoiding the previously undetected run-time violation. In general, other exceptions such as underflow, endfile, and so on must also be handled by appropriate extensions to the language.

The Confinement Problem Revisited

As discussed in Section 8.3, access control techniques are unable to deal adequately with the confinement problem. The concept of information flow can be used to certify that a procedure is confined—that is, that it does not retain classified information and it does not encode such information into storage objects. Let P denote a procedure with input parameters $X_1, \ldots, X_m$ and output parameters $Y_1, \ldots, Y_n$. The certification mechanism can be used to validate the following:

1. The procedure is internally secure (all called procedures must undergo certification).

2. Illegal flows do not occur to external objects.

3. Illegal flows do not occur to objects that are maintained between calls.

Property (3) implies that all externally referenced objects have known security classes, so they can be included in the flow analysis. This must include system calls to operate on objects managed by the execution environment (operating system). For example, the flow of a value n can be detected through n calls to lock nonconfidential files $F_1, \ldots, F_n$. In general, information flow control may be used to secure legitimate and storage channels but not covert channels.

8.5.4 Run-Time Certification with Static Binding

The method presented here is the one proposed by Fenton [1974]. Fenton's Data Mark Machine extends the program counter PC to include the security level of the executing process (initialized to *LOW*). Immediately prior to the execution of a conditional statement S, the security level in the program status word is replaced with $\underline{PC} \oplus \underline{C}$, where $\underline{C}$ is the security level of the boolean expression. If a statement S specifies an explicit flow from objects $X_1, X_2, \ldots, X_n$ to object Y, the run-time mechanism allows the execution of S if $\underline{PC} \oplus \underline{X}_1 \oplus \cdots \oplus \underline{X}_n \leq \underline{Y}$. Otherwise, execution of the statement is inhibited, and $\underline{PC}$ is restored to its previous value. Even if the body of S is not executed, implicit flow of PC to Y occurs and code must be inserted by the compiler to check for a potential flow violation. Using a stack mechanism, the machine allows for nested conditional statements. Upon leaving a conditional, the stack is popped and the program counter is replaced with its previous security level.

8.5.5 Certification with Dynamic Binding

Dynamic binding means that the class of an object changes with the class of the information that is stored in it. Instead of verifying that the flow relation $\leq$ holds, the system dynamically updates the security level of the object to which information flows in order to force the relation to hold. Certification systems based totally on dynamic binding are considered impractical since they do not tend to model the real world. The reader is referred to the literature for proposed architectures [Denning, 1975; Fenton, 1974].

8.6 Implementation of Access Controls

In this section, we will investigate several ways to implement access controls. We first look at some basic issues involved in selecting a design. This is followed by a description of actual implementations.

8.6.1   Implementation Issues

Each implementation is closely tied to the choice for representing and managing the access matrix. Overriding issues are adherence to fundamental design principles and the ability to enforce specific security policies.

Design Principles

Saltzer and Schroeder [1975] have identified numerous design principles for protection systems. Several of these are listed here:

Least privilege: Every subject should be given only those access rights necessary to complete its task. If the access requirements change, the process should switch domains. Furthermore, access rights should be acquired by explicit permission only; the default should be "no access."

Economy of mechanisms: Protection mechanisms should be small, so that they can be completely verified and correctly implemented. Security must be an integral part of the system design. Attempting to augment an existing system with security mechanisms is likely to result in a proliferation of complex mechanisms.

Acceptability: If the protection mechanisms are not easy to use, they are likely to be unused or incorrectly used.

Complete mediation: Every access to every object must be checked for authority.

Open design: The security of the system must not depend on keeping the design of the protection mechanism or its algorithms a secret.

Enforcement of Specific Security Policies

The concept of an *object monitor,* introduced in Section 8.3, allows control of direct access to objects. Many general-purpose operating systems simply implement some variation of the object monitor. However, object monitors, in their fundamental form, have no provision for incorporating security policies, such as information flow control as described in Section 8.4, which are peculiar to the organization that uses the computer system. For example, in the Bell and LaPadula model, the clearances of subjects must be compared with the classification of involved objects when changes are made to the access control matrix. In an information flow model with static binding and run-time certification, a scheme for integrating access and flow control might be to perform the following for each attempted access of an object:

```
if flow violation
   then
        if subject is not trusted
           then quit
if access violation
   then quit
```

Note that the classification of a subject is not needed in this algorithm although such a classification would be useful to establish the class of the standard output file (terminal, printer, and so on). A generalization of an object monitor is the *reference monitor* [Andler and Anderson, 1972], which allows for the incorporation of a specific set of security policies (defined in the reference monitor database). This idea is illustrated in Figure 8.11. The hardware and software that implement security-relevant functions will be referred to as the *security kernel*.

Representation and Management of the Access Matrix

Direct implementation of the access matrix as a two-dimensional structure is generally impractical due to the sparseness of the matrix. There are four traditional approaches to implementation:

1. *Table of triples:* The nonempty entries of A are maintained in a table, with each entry having the form $(S, X, A[S,X])$. This method has the advantage that only entries of active subjects and objects need to be stored. Although this method conserves space, a search for either objects that a subject can access or subjects that can access a given object can be inefficient. The method implies that the triples are stored in a central location and administered by a central object monitor.

2. *Capabilities:* Stored with each subject S is a list of pairs $(X, A[S,X])$, called *capabilities,* that represent the set of accessible objects and corresponding access privileges. The list, called a *capability list,* corresponds to a single row of the access matrix. This method has the following advantages:

   a. Only the entries of active subjects need to be maintained in main store.

   b. For a given subject, it is possible to efficiently determine the set of objects that can be accessed.

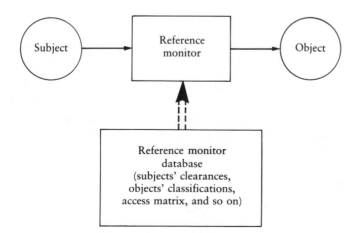

Figure 8.11   Reference Monitor Concept.

The disadvantages are:

a. For a given object, it may be inefficient to determine which subjects (or users) have access privileges.

b. Revocation may leave numerous copies of obsolete capabilities in the system, especially if the recipient of a capability chooses to transfer copies of the capability to other subjects.

The work of an object monitor is to administer capabilities to the various subjects, thus implying the existence of a centralized monitor. Segment tables and page tables are typical examples of the use of capabilities.

3. *Access control list:* Stored with each object X is a list of pairs $(S, A[S,X])$, one for each subject S that is allowed to access the object. The list corresponds to a single column in the access control matrix. The advantages of this method are:

a. For a given object, it is possible to efficiently determine which subjects (or users) have access privileges.

b. Revocation of privileges is inexpensive.

One disadvantage is that it may be expensive to determine the privileges of a given subject. In this method, a monitor is associated with each object. File directories are typical examples of the use of access control lists.

4. *Lock/key mechanism:* This method attempts to capture the advantages of both capabilities and access control lists. Stored with each subject S is a capability list, consisting of pairs of the form (X,K), where X denotes an object that can be accessed by S, using the *key K*. Stored with each object is an access control list (called a *lock list*), consisting of pairs of the form (L,α), where L denotes a *lock* and α denotes an access attribute. An attempted β access by subject S to object X results in the following actions by the protection system:

a. The system finds the pair (X,K) from the capability list of the subject S and passes it to the monitor of X.

b. The monitor permits the access only if it finds a pair (L,α) on the lock list with $K = L$ and β a subset of α.

The owner of X grants access by granting (X, K) pairs to subjects and placing (K, α) in the lock list. Revocation by the owner is accomplished by deleting (K, α) from the lock list (that is, by changing the lock). In this method, a centralized monitor is needed to dispense capabilities to subjects, while individual monitors are also associated with each object.

8.6.2   Access Hierarchies

Many computer systems provide hardware support for a *supervisor–user* mode hierarchy. While it is simple and inexpensive, it provides only for a two-level classification of subjects and no classification of objects; it is a degenerate implementation of the model. Some computer systems allow for more modes—an example is the four-level kernel/executive/supervisor/user hierarchy of the DEC VAX-11 family of computers.

The *protection rings* in MULTICS are a broad generalization of the hierarchy concept [Schroeder, et al., 1977]. Each ring defines a domain of access. Higher numbered rings imply access privileges that are a subset of privileges of lower numbered rings. The ring concept is illustrated in Figure 8.12. Each segment (code and data) has associated ranges of rings that specify the domains of subjects that are allowed to read, write, and execute. The state word of a process p specifies a ring number (its domain). A process requesting direct access to a segment in ring α must be executing in the $p \leq \alpha$ access range specified by the segment. A process that needs to perform a function that is not in its domain of access must switch to the appropriate *gate* of the required program in a lower ring. While protection rings have been successfully used to provide a powerful protection facility, their linear hierarchy is inconsistent with the principle of least privilege. Extensive damage can be done by a program error or Trojan horse in the lowered-numbered rings. Also, any specific security policy must be enforced by a security kernel constructed above the basic protection afforded by the ring mechanism.

8.6.3 Capability Systems

The term *capability,* introduced by Dennis and Van Horn [1966], has its conceptual origins in "codewords" [Illife and Jodeit, 1962] implemented in the Rice University Computer, and in "descriptors," implemented in the Burroughs B5000 computer. Capabilities have been subsequently used to form the protection basis of several computer systems.

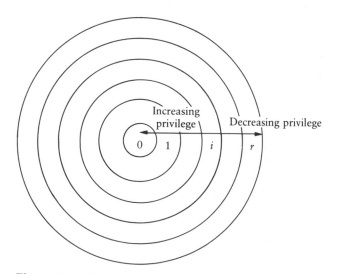

Figure 8.12 Protection Rings.

Each object is protected by a guard (monitor), which holds the description of the single identifier of the object. A subject has a collection of capabilities, one for each object, to which it has authorized access. When a subject presents a capability that matches the description of the identifier held by the guard, access is allowed to take place.

Implementation of a pure capability-based system, along with the unforgeability requirement, requires that the concept be embedded in hardware (for example, in a tagged architecture). Figure 8.13 shows a model of a descriptor-based capability system, enhanced by an authentication mechanism [Saltzer and Schroder, 1975]. An execution domain is established for a user process in the following way:

1. A user presents an identification and password to the computer system.
2. The system authenticates the user (for example, if the user proclaims "Smith" for an identity, the system verifies the password from the *user authentication* table).
3. The system creates a process *S* and assigns to it the capabilities pointed to by the entry in the user identification table (for example, the catalog for Smith).
4. The process *S* can access any segment for which a capability exists in its catalog.

The efficiency of the system is vested in the fact that authentication is done only once, after which the possession of a capability is considered incontestable proof that access should be allowed.

This mechanism controls direct access to objects and is therefore an implementation of an object monitor. In order to implement a monitor for the access matrix, a mechanism is needed to dynamically transfer capabilities between subjects. Such a mechanism must be embedded in the security kernel. There are several requirements for correct and efficient implementation:

1. The capabilities of each active subject must be stored in an area accessible only to the security kernel. Fast access is required.
2. The capabilities of all inactive subjects must be maintained in an easy-to-access area, accessible only to the security kernel. Consistency must be maintained between this latter set of capabilities and the capabilities of active subjects.
3. The clearances and classifications of all subjects and objects must be maintained in order to decide the legality of each command. In pure capability systems clearances are easily maintained but classifications of objects are difficult to maintain, particularly for dynamically bounded security systems.
4. The capabilities of an active subject generally do not need to contain the clearance of the subject. However, the clearance of the subject that is being granted an access right to an object, and the classification of the object are required. They should be maintained in an easily accessible place.

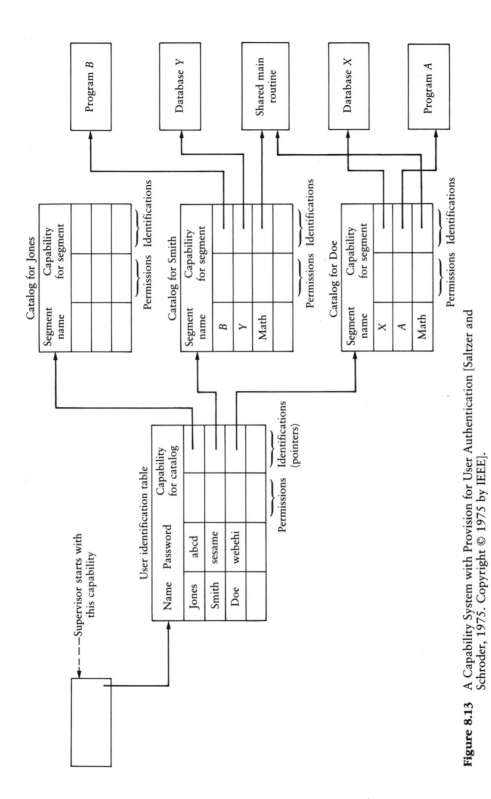

Figure 8.13 A Capability System with Provision for User Authentication [Saltzer and Schroder, 1975. Copyright © 1975 by IEEE].

329

5. Capabilities may contain attributes such as *owner* and *control,* which allow a subject to grant or delete access attributes or capabilities to or from another subject.

While the implementation of such an access matrix monitor is reasonably straightforward, it may require sizable code and data storage, which must be separated and protected from user processes.

A process may dynamically acquire or lose capabilities, thereby changing its domain of execution. Capability passing among processes is usually performed through interprocess communication. Within the context of the access matrix model, this means that new subjects come into existence. However, a single process may need to abruptly switch from one set of capabilities (domain) to another set (domain) in order to perform a certain task. An execution of a borrowed program is a typical example of such domain switching. This switching could be done as interprocess communication if the two instances of the process in different domains are recognized as distinct subjects. Theoretically, this causes no problems. However, it is more natural to view this switching as if the process simply switched domains, suspending one subject and activating another. The approach proposed by Dennis and Van Horn [1966] is based on an *enter* capability, which points to a capability list for a procedure to be called, thereby providing the right to transfer into the new domain. Domain switching, using the *enter* capability, is illustrated in Figure 8.14. Enter capabilities are used to implement entry points in *protected subsystems*. When an entry point is called, the domain is switched to that of the called procedure. It is restored when control is returned. The concept of protected subsystems supports the principle of least privilege, allows the construction of firewalls around untrusted programs, and provides a basic protection mechanism for abstract data types (see Problems 6, 8, and 15).

Implementation of Abstract Data Types

Abstract data types are an integral part of object-oriented languages such as CLU [Liskov, et al., 1977], Alphard [Wulf, et al., 1976], and Ada. An abstract data type is defined to be a collection of objects along with operations on the objects. The collection of procedures that are externally visible and accessible provide an interface of protected entry points to the domain defined by the data type.

In the HYDRA operating system [Wulf, et al., 1974], an external procedure is represented by a capability list that contains capabilities for the code of the procedure and local objects and also templates for parameters that are passed to the procedure. A template allows for the *amplification* of the rights to a parameter object. This concept of amplification is illustrated in Figure 8.15. Procedure P is called with parameter D, and a capability (D, RW) is formed for the procedure. Many of HYDRA's mechanisms are implemented in hardware in the INTEL iAPX 432 [Kahn, et al., 1981]. Ada is the principal programming language supported by the INTEL iAPX 432; Ada was also used to construct the operating system. An Ada package is represented by a capability list for procedures and data objects. Parameter objects (called *descriptor control objects*) are represented by templates, and access rights amplification is

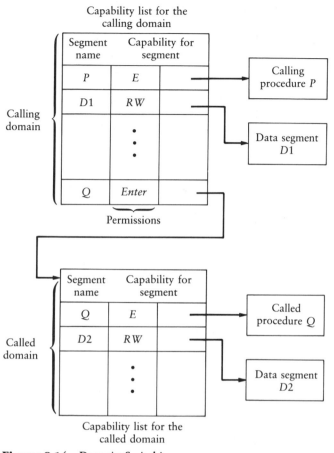

Figure 8.14 Domain Switching.

implemented. Extensions of the HYDRA mechanism that allow for finer control have been proposed [Jones and Liskov, 1976].

Capability-Based Addressing

As illustrated by Fabry [1974], capabilities can be efficiently integrated with main memory addressing mechanisms. Figure 8.16 illustrates this concept of *capability-based addressing*. An effective address consists of two parts: a capability for an object (memory segment) and the relative position within the object. The capability part contains a unique capability identifier, a specification of access rights, and a unique object identifier. The object monitor (memory addressing hardware) locates the named capability in the capability list and checks the access rights against the requested access type. The entry in the descriptor table is determined from the object identifier (possibly through hashing). The descriptor table contains the description of physical properties of the object: the base and the length of the object.

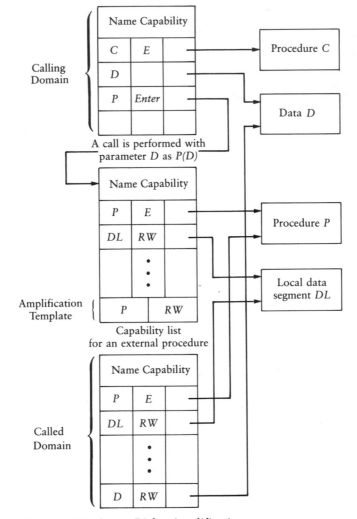

Figure 8.15 Access Rights Amplification.

This method of capability-based addressing allows for relocation of the object without changing the capability. The separation of capability information from object location provides a simple solution for the simultaneous accessing of shared programs. In particular, different subjects may have different names and access rights for the same shared object without regard for its location in main store.[5]

Address translation can be as efficient as segmentation since associative registers can be similarly used and because object names can be chosen so that they are hashed to unique entries in the descriptor table. In the SWARD system [Myers and Buck-

---

[5] For further discussion on the problems of sharing in paged and segmented systems, the reader is referred to Peterson and Silberschatz [1985].

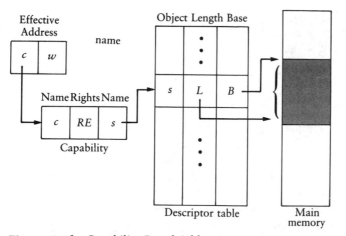

Figure 8.16 Capability-Based Addressing.

ingham, 1980], this is accomplished by incrementing a counter until the value hashes to an empty entry.

The IBM System/38 is an example of a recent high-level capability-based architecture. Many operating system functions, generally found in software in other systems, are implemented in the hardware. The system has a very large, uniformly addressable storage to which a single device-independent addressing mechanism allows access. Data is stored in object form and manipulated by object-oriented commands. Security is rigidly enforced; every reference to an object is checked.

Revocation

Capabilities are granted to subjects, which can disseminate copies to other subjects. The revocation problem of multiple copies is solved by use of indirect addressing [Redell and Fabry, 1974], as illustrated in Figure 8.17. The owner of an object X

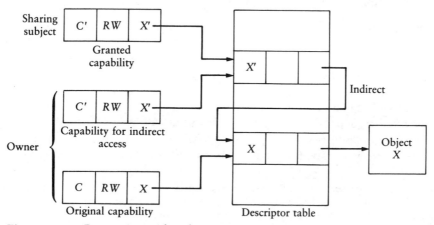

Figure 8.17 Revocation with Indirection.

creates a capability C' that points indirectly to the descriptor for X and grants the capability C' to other subjects. In turn, these subjects may pass capabilities to more subjects. Revocation is accomplished by deactivating or removing the indirect entry in the descriptor table.

8.6.4   Access Control List Systems

In access control list systems, the guard of an object maintains a list of identifiers of authorized users, along with their approved manner of access. In addition, each user has a unique, unforgeable identifier. When a subject S, executing on behalf of user U, attempts β access, the pair (U,β) is presented to the guard. Access is allowed if the guard finds in its list a pair (U,α) with β a subset of α.

Access control list implementations differ in several ways from the implementation of capability-based systems:

1. The access control list is, in theory, consulted on every access whereas, in capability systems verification is checked only once to decide if a capability can be granted. If the access control list is long, substantial overhead can be incurred on each access.

2. Revocation of access for user is simply performed by removing the corresponding entry from the list. In capability systems, even if indirection is used, a search of all capability lists is required to eliminate obsolete capabilities.

3. The design allows straightforward determination of who may access a particular object.

4. Since each object carries its own protection data, any grouping of objects for the purpose of naming, searching, and archiving is independent of any desired grouping for protection.

5. Attributes such as *ownership* and *control* are easily maintained in access control lists.

6. Domain switching requires separate processes for two instances of a process executing in different domains.

One apparent major difficulty with the implementation of access control lists is low efficiency. At some expense, the efficiency can be substantially improved by associative searches or the use of a cache store to maintain access control list entries for only the active users. Because the appeal of access control lists is offset, in conventional systems, by run-time overhead, many systems use a combined approach. An access control list is used to establish authorization, resulting in the issuance of a capability. Subsequent accesses are made via the capability. Figure 8.18 shows such an arrangement. Upon first access, a capability register (*shadow register*) is loaded. Subsequent references can proceed directly using the shadow register.[6] Since shadow

---

[6] The protection mechanisms of many file systems are based on a similar philosophy. A file is first opened and, after authorization is checked, a file descriptor to an in-core file control block is established. Subsequent accesses to the file by the process are made via the file descriptor.

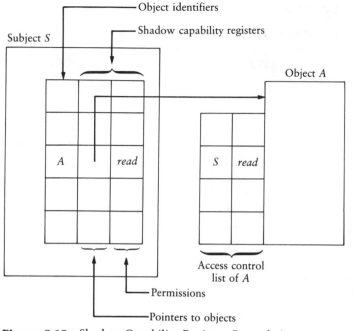

Figure 8.18   Shadow Capability Registers Beneath Access
Control List System.

registers are maintained only for active subjects, revocation is readily accomplished
by searching and removing the capability from all shadow registers and removing
the entry from the access control list.

Access control list systems directly implement the concept of object monitors
in the access matrix model. In order to implement an access matrix monitor, software
must be provided in the security kernel which a subject can call, requesting a change
in an access control list. In a typical application, only the owner of an object would
be allowed to change the access control list associated with the object.

The following are several examples of use of access control lists for file systems:

- MULTICS allows the full use of access control lists to protect files [Organick,
  1972]. The principle of least privilege is enforceable.

- In UNIX, the access control list for each file consists of three generic entries:
  owner, group, and *other* [Ritchie and Thompson, 1974]. The access rights for
  each entry consist of three bits to indicate *read, write,* and *execute* privileges.
  For directory type files, *execute* is interpreted as privilege to search a directory.
  VAX VMS uses a similar scheme. The principle of least privilege is not completely
  enforceable, even though the method may be satisfactory for most applications.

- In many systems, only two generic entries exist in the access control lists:
  owner and other. There is a questionable tradeoff between the principle of
  least privilege and the desire for simplicity and efficiency.

8.6.5   Lock/Key Systems

Lock/key systems combine aspects of capability systems and access control list systems. Examples of their use are the storage keys of IBM System 360/370, the file system of ASAP [Conway, et al., 1972], and the lock/key cryptographic sealing mechanism of Gifford [1982].

8.6.6   Security Kernels

Recent work in operating system security has been concerned with the development of security kernels. The objective of this approach is to isolate all security mechanisms in a small, distinct layer that resides between the hardware and the traditional operating system layer. Embedded in this layer are the functions of reference monitors along with the supporting database and security policies. This is a distinct departure from traditional approaches, which tend to strive for general-purpose protection and, as an afterthought, may be augmented to enforce specific policies. In addition to providing a high degree of protection for the security functions themselves, this isolation is a useful aid in the verification of system security. The concept is founded on three principles:

1. *Completeness:* Every access to an object must be mediated by the kernel.
2. *Isolation:* The kernel must be tamper-proof.
3. *Verifiability:* It must be possible to verify that the security kernel implements the security policy.

The impetus for research on the concept of a security kernel has come primarily from the military establishment. As a result of this, several kernel-based systems have been developed: MITRE security kernel [Schiller, 1975; Millen, 1976], MULTICS-based kernel designed at Case Western Reserve [Walter, et al., 1975], MULTICS with AIM [Schroeder, et al., 1977], UCLA Data Secure UNIX [Popek, et al., 1979], UNIX-based kernelized Secure Operating System (KSOS-11) for the PDP-11/70 at Ford Aerospace [McCauley and Drongowski, 1979; Berson and Barksdale, 1979], KSOS-6 for a Honeywell Level 6 machine [Broadbridge and Mekota, 1976] and Kernelized VM/370 (KVM/370) at SDC [Gold, et al., 1979].

At present, two major problems of the security kernel approach are their tendency to be large, thus making verification more difficult, and their poor performance. Since the idea seems fundamentally sound, research is continuing in this area. A few security kernel–based systems are commercially available, including the Honeywell Secure Communications Processor.

8.6.7   Extensions to Database Management Systems

Database management systems require more elaborate and finer access control. For a database, $A[S,X]$ specifies a set of *decision rules,* that define the conditions under which a subject S may access an object X, as well as what operations may be performed. The rules may define both data-independent and data-dependent conditions. Allowing a user to read only those student records for which the "department" field is "computer science" is an example of a data-dependent condition. This concept of dependency can also be extended to include *time-dependent* conditions (functions of system clock value) and *context-dependent* conditions (functions of combinations of data). For example, a subject may be allowed to read student names and identification numbers, but not pairs of names and grades nor pairs of identification numbers and grades. Access attributes may also specify *history-dependent* conditions (functions of previous states of the system). For example, a user who has previously processed certain classified data might not be permitted to write. In general, a decision rule may state any condition based on available information.

An example of such a database system is the *query modification* system proposed by Stonebraker and Wong [1974]. In their system, an access right is a call to a library procedure that tests access permission for each retrieved record.

8.6.8   Test and Verification

The access matrix model introduced in this chapter provides a theoretical basis for the study of access control. However, correctness of the algorithm does not imply correctness of the code that implements it and, as a consequence, some attention has been given to developing methods for *penetration analysis* (or *penetration studies*). The intent of such methods is to test the code and locate security weaknesses. An early approach for locating security flaws was developed by Linde [1975]. The method is called *flaw hypothesis methodology* and involves the following:

1. *Flaw hypothesis generation:* A study team examines well-known system weaknesses and uses this knowledge to list suspected flaws of the target system.

2. *Flaw hypothesis confirmation:* The suspected flaws are tested to determine if, in fact, they are real flaws.

3. *Flaw generalization:* Any confirmed flaws are analyzed to determine if they imply other flaws. The cycle is repeated with flaw hypothesis generation for any newly suspected flaws.

This technique was applied by Hebbard, et al. [1980] to the system subroutines of the Michigan Terminal System (MTS) operating system. It was discovered that a user could modify parameters after they were checked by the system but before they were used. Exploiting this flaw, the penetration team was able to modify the user's privilege level, disable the protection mechanism, and modify the system data (in particular, accounting information). The penetration could also cause the system to store sensitive information (such as passwords) in user-accessible segments. Obtaining free computer time and crashing the system was a natural byproduct of their penetration efforts. In particular, it was discovered that the correct operation of one security mechanism may depend on the correct operation of another. Once one mechanism was compromised, it was relatively easy to compromise other security mechanisms.

Harrison, Ruzzo, and Ullman [1976] considered the feasibility of proving *safeness* of a protection system modeled by an access matrix model. A system state P is defined to be *safe* for a generic right α if, from the state *P*, it is impossible to derive a state *Q* in which α could be *leaked*. A command *C* leaks α if it places α in some entry of the access matrix that did not previously contain it. With trustworthy subjects removed from the system, the question is whether a leak of a right α violates the security policies of the system. For an arbitrary protection system, it was shown that safety is undecidable. It is, however, decidable if no new subjects or objects can be created. Snyder [1981] introduced a *take-grant* graph model, which can be used to describe a restricted class of protection systems for which safety is decidable even if subjects are created.

8.7   Cryptography

8.7.1   Application of Cryptography to Secure Computer Systems

The access control and flow control methods described in previous sections provide substantial protection. However, there is still a need to prevent accidental or malicious disclosure of information in circumstances where these methods do not apply. In particular, there is a need to secure physical channels against illegal wiretaps and to remove the content of information files from the purview of individuals who bypass authentication mechanisms.

Figure 8.19 depicts some conceivable attacks in a distributed system. Security violations can be generally categorized as *passive wiretapping,* which refers to the unauthorized interception of messages (or reading of information), and *active wiretapping,* which includes such things as the following:

- *Modification*—Portions of the message are changed.
- *The introduction of spurious messages*—If the invalid messages carry valid address(es) and satisfy other consistency tests by the network layers, considerable disruption may occur.
- *Site impersonation*—A computer system that impersonates another legal network site is connected to a communication line.
- *Replay of previously transmitted information*—Previous valid transactions (e.g., authorization of cash withdrawal) can be repeated.
- *Disruption*—Selected messages may be prevented from delivery, or communications paths may be totally blocked.

The use of cryptography, discussed in this section, is the only known practical technique for guarding against security violations of this nature. Cryptography can also be used for digital signatures to authenticate the source of a message. In addition, it is the only known method of protecting stored information once the physical security is broken or logon authentication mechanisms are bypassed. The material presented in this section is derived from many sources. Principal references are [Popek and Kline, 1979; Denning, 1982; Meyer and Matyas, 1982; NBS, 1977; Diffie and Hellman, 1979].

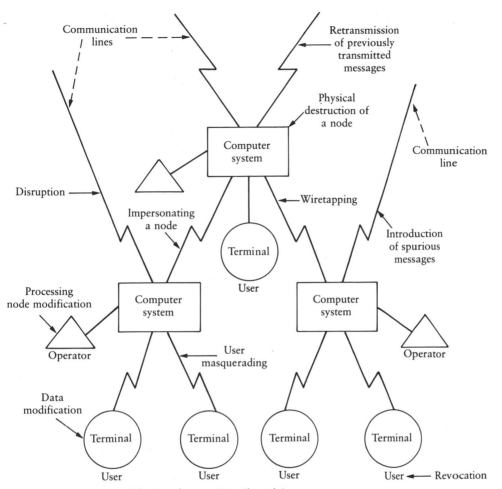

Figure 8.19 Conceivable Attacks to a Distributed System.

8.7.2 Cryptosystems and Security Requirements

Encryption (or *encipherment*) refers to the transformation of intelligible information into an unintelligible form for the express purpose of rendering it useless to a would-be perpetrator. This transformation process is represented by a mathematical function (enciphering algorithm)

$$C = E(M, K_E)$$

where M is *plaintext* information to be encrypted, K_E is an *encryption key,* and C is the resulting *ciphertext. Decryption* (or *decipherment*) is represented by a matching decryption function (deciphering algorithm)

$$M = D(C, K_D)$$

where K_D is a *decryption key.*

Cryptosystems fall into two categories: *conventional* and *public key*. A conventional cryptosystem is *symmetric* in that $K_E = K_D$ (or one key is easily derived from the other). The key is secret in that it is known only by authorized individuals. The underlying mathematical equations of modern conventional cryptosystems are typically easy to describe but so complex that they cannot be solved analytically. Public-key cryptosystems, proposed by Diffie and Hellman [1976], are *asymmetric* in that $K_D \neq K_E$. K_E is publicly known while K_D is known only to those who are authorized to decrypt messages. To be useful, it must be impractical to derive the decryption key from the encryption key. All proposed public-key cryptosystems are based on known mathematical problems that are currently difficult to solve but are easily described in mathematical terms.

The general structure of a cryptosystem is shown in Figure 8.20 [Lempel, 1979]. The function of an attacker (or *cryptanalyst*) *CA* is to produce the best estimate $\overline{M}$ of plaintext M given the functions E and D, the ciphertext C, possibly some side information *SI*, and K_E (in the case of a public-key system). The cryptanalyst does not know K_D. Although it may, in certain cases, be possible for the cryptanalyst to produce the correct M without having first found K_D, breaking an encryption system generally requires finding a scheme that is capable of producing K_D. The underlying assumption, in the case of conventional cryptosystems, is that K_D is kept secret by passing it to authorized individuals over a known secure channel.

The strength of a cryptosystem is measured by its resistance to attack, that is, how difficult it is to determine K_D. Based on increasing amounts and types of available *SI*, attacks can be classified, in order of increasing intensity, as follows:

1. *Ciphertext only*—The cryptanalyst has intercepted ciphertext material and has general knowledge of an opponent's message and statistical properties of the language (e.g., frequency of letters or words).

2. *Known plaintext*—The cryptanalyst has, in addition, substantial amounts of plaintext and corresponding ciphertext.

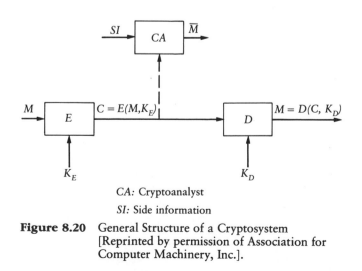

CA: Cryptoanalyst

SI: Side information

Figure 8.20   General Structure of a Cryptosystem [Reprinted by permission of Association for Computer Machinery, Inc.].

3. *Chosen plaintext*—The cryptanalyst can see, in addition, ciphertext for any plaintext.

4. *Chosen text*—The cryptanalyst can see, in addition, any plaintext for any ciphertext.

The requirement of most present-day commercial and government agencies is that the cryptosystem be able to withstand a chosen plaintext attack.

Security against attack can be classified as:

1. *Unconditionally secure*—K_D cannot be determined regardless of the available computing power.

2. *Computationally secure*—Determination of K_D is economically infeasible (that is, it would overwhelm all available computing resources).

The only known unconditionally secure cryptosystem in common use involves the use of a random key that has the same length as the plaintext to be encrypted. The key is used once and then discarded. The key is exclusively OR'd with the message to produce the ciphertext. Given the key and the ciphertext, the receiver uses the same method to reproduce the plaintext. The cryptanalyst is then faced with the task of inspecting 2^n messages, a great number of which will be valid.

In our treatment of this subject, we assume that the security of the system depends only on the secrecy of the keys and not on the secrecy of the algorithms. Furthermore, we assume that the general requirements of a cryptosystem are that it is computationally secure against a chosen plaintext attack and that the substitution of false ciphertext for original ciphertext does not escape detection. For pragmatic reasons, it is also assumed that the cryptosystem is efficient and easy to use.

8.7.3 Conventional Cryptosystems

The principal design criterion for secure cryptosystems is that *diffusion* and *confusion* is introduced into the stream of plaintext bits. Diffusion reduces the correlation among the string components by spreading it over long substrings. Confusion increases the complexity of functional dependencies, making them more difficult to detect. Most conventional algorithms rely to some extent on two basic enciphering techniques: transposition (permutation) and substitution. Transposition ciphers rearrange units (bits, characters, blocks) according to some fixed scheme. Many transposition ciphers rearrange the characters of plaintext using a fixed-period permutation. For example, suppose that the length of period is 3 and the permutation function f is given by

i: 1   2   3
$f(i)$: 3   1   2

Then the plaintext string CRYPTOGRAPHY is enciphered as

plaintext = CRY PTO GRA PHY
ciphertext = RYC TOP RAG HYP.

It is relatively easy to recognize the use of a transposition cipher because the relative frequencies of the letters in the ciphertext will match the expected frequencies in plaintext. Given sufficient ciphertext, breaking a transposition cipher is a straightforward task. A result from information theory states that the expected number of characters required to break a transposition cipher with period d is given by $(\log_2 d!)/D$, where D is a redundancy factor of the language [Denning, 1982].

A substitution cipher replaces each unit of plaintext with a corresponding unit of ciphertext. Typically, the ciphertext alphabet is a rearrangement of the plaintext alphabet. A simple example is a *Caesar cipher,* which performs a right circular shift of the letters of the alphabet by a fixed number of positions. For instance, if the shift is three places, the plaintext CRYPTOGRAPHY is enciphered to FUBSWRJUDSKB. With sufficient ciphertext, a substitution cipher is also relatively easy to break. The expected number of characters required to break a substitution cipher with an alphabet of n letters is given by $(\log_2 n!)/D$ [Denning, 1982]. In order to effectively increase n in this formula, one-to-many mappings, such as homophonic substitution ciphers, and multiple mappings, such as polyalphabetic substitution ciphers, can be used [Diffie and Hellman, 1979].

Two approaches are used to deal with the encryption of variable-length strings. If plaintext is encrypted bit by bit, it is called a *stream cipher.* If the plaintext is broken into fixed-length blocks, with encryption performed on each block, it is called a *block cipher.* In pure block ciphers, two identical plaintext blocks will be transformed into two identical ciphertext blocks, thereby providing the cryptanalyst with the opportunity to analyze repeated patterns. A preventive measure with this approach is to use *block chaining* or *cipher feedback.* By this technique, each cipherblock becomes a function of previously enciphered blocks; for example, if B_i and C_i denote the ith plaintext and ciphertext blocks, respectively, then one feedback scheme is

$$C_1 = E(B_1, K)$$
$$C_i = E(B_{i-1}, K) \oplus C_{i-1}$$

Cryptosystems based on pure transposition or pure substitution are not sufficiently strong. Shannon proposed that the strength of cryptosystems be increased through the composition of weaker functions to create a *product cipher* [Shannon, 1949]. For example, if plaintext is first encrypted by a function T and then reencrypted by some function S, the final ciphertext is the result of encryption by the product cipher ST.

8.7.4   The Data Encryption Standard (DES)

The Data Encryption Standard (DES) is the official National Bureau of Standards (NBS) encryption scheme (adopted in January 1977) to be used by federal departments and agencies, as well as others, for the cryptographic protection of nonclassified computer data. The DES is a block cipher that uses a product cipher on each individual block (feedback cipher variations are also possible). Formally, encryption may be described as a product cipher

$$\text{DES} = (IP^{-1}) J_{16} \cdots J_1(IP)$$

performed on each 64-bit block P of plaintext. *IP* is a bit-wise permutation with inverse IP^{-1}. The 64-bit result of the permutation is expressed as the concatenation of two 32-bit halves:

$$IP(\text{P}) = L_0 R_0$$

$J_i(L_{i-1}R_{i-1})$ for $1 \le i \le 16$ is defined as

$$L_i = R_{i-1}$$
$$R_i = L_{i-1} \oplus f(R_{i-1}, K_i)$$

where K_i is derived from the secret 56-bit *K*. The ciphertext is given by

$$\text{C} = IP^{-1}(R_{16}L_{16}) = \text{DES}(\text{P})$$

Decryption consists of computing $\text{DES}^{-1}(\text{C})$, where DES^{-1} differs from DES only in that the keys are used in reverse order (that is, J_i uses key K_{16-i+1}).

The overall DES process is shown in Figure 8.21 [NBS, 1977]. The source of security is in the nonlinear many-to-one function *f*, which is applied to the R_i half blocks. Transposition and substitution are the main internal components of *f*. A detailed description of the DES algorithm is given in the appendix at the end of this chapter.

Knowledge concerning the actual security of the DES is not in the public domain. Controversies over its security center on the possible brute force exhaustive search for the 56-bit key and over the security of the *f* function [Diffie and Hellman, 1977; Morris, et al., 1977; Davida, 1979; Hellman, 1979]. Critics argue that the 56-bit key length is too short and that an exhaustive search will soon be possible using commercially available general-purpose computers. The counterargument is that the concepts of DES are important and useful and that a longer key can be used if necessary.

8.7.5 Public-Key Cryptosystems

In public-key cryptosystems, each subscriber *A* must place a procedure *E* in a public directory. User *B* may send secret messages to *A* by first encrypting the message using *E*. Decryption by *D* can be performed only by *A* since *D* is known only to *A*. More commonly, *E* and *D* are known, but a subscriber must make public the encryption key K_E while keeping secret the decryption key K_D. To be effective, such a system must satisfy the following conditions [Simmons, 1979]:

1. Given plaintext and ciphertext, the problem of determining the keys is computationally complex.

2. It is easy to generate matched pairs of keys (K_E, K_D) that satisfy the property

   $$D(E(M, K_E), K_D) = M$$

3. The encryption and decryption functions *E* and *D* are efficient and easy to use.

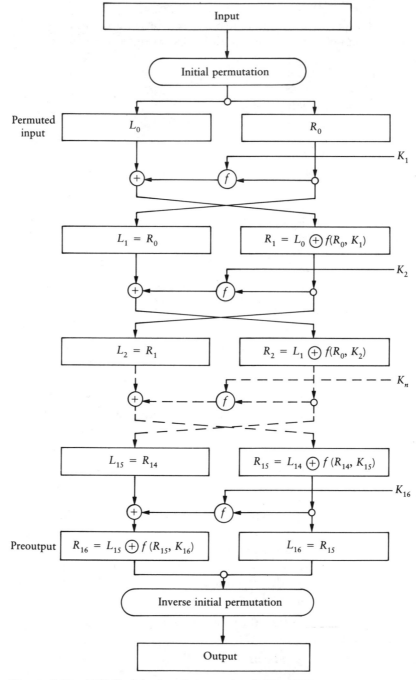

Figure 8.21 DES Enciphering Computation [NBS, 1977. Reprinted by permission of National Bureau of Standards].

4. Given K_E, the problem of determining K_D is computationally complex.

5. For almost all messages it must be computationally infeasible to find ciphertext-key pairs that will produce the message. (In other words, an attacker is forced to discover the true (M, K_E) pair that was used to create the ciphertext C)

An additional commutative property

6. $E(D(M, K_D), K_E) = D(E(M, K_E), K_D) = M$

suggested by Diffie and Hellman [1977], provides a convenient signature (authentication) facility (see Section 8.7.6).

Current approaches to satisfying condition (4) take a computationally hard problem and make the difficulty of finding the key equivalent to solving this problem. Examples of such problems are factoring the product of two very large prime numbers, the general knapsack problem, and finding the logarithm of an element in a large field with respect to a primitive element of the field. These examples provide attractive cryptosystems since they cannot be solved in polynomial time by any "known" techniques, yet encryption and decryption can be done in polynomial time. The latter problems fall into the category of *NP(nondeterministic polynomial)-complete* problems. The fastest "known" algorithms for systematically solving *NP*-complete problems have worst-case time complexities that are exponential in the size n of the problem. Condition (2) is typically satisfied by use of a *trapdoor one-way function f*, which is easy to compute; but for almost all x in the domain of f, it is computationally infeasible to solve $y = f(x)$. Furthermore, the inverse of f is easy to compute once certain secret *trapdoor* information is known. Any trapdoor one-way function f and its inverse f^{-1} can serve as an (E,D) pair for a public-key cryptosystem.

As an example, we give a brief description of the Rivest–Shamir–Adleman (RSA) scheme [Rivest, et al., 1978]. The security is based on the difficulty of factoring the product of two large prime numbers. The selection of keys is performed as follows:

1. Two large prime numbers p and q are selected, using some efficient test for primality [Rabin, 1976; Solovay and Strassen, 1977]. These numbers are secret.

2. The product $n = p * q$ is computed.

3. A number $d > max(p,q)$ is picked at random from the set of integers that are relatively prime to and less than $L(n) = (p-1)(q-1)$.

4. The integer e, $0 < e < L(n)$, is computed from $L(n)$ and d such that

$$e * d = 1 \ (mod \ L(n))$$

(It is known that for every integer X such that $0 \leqslant X \leqslant n - 1$, $(X^e)^d (mod \ n) = (X^d)^e (mod \ n) = X$. This serves as the basis for the encryption and decryption algorithms.)

5. The pair (n, e) is placed in a public directory as the encryption key.

The following variation of Euclid's algorithm is suggested by Rivest, et al. [1978] for computing e. Calculate $gcd(L(n),d)$ by computing the sequence

$$\{X_0 = L(n), X_1 = d, X_{i+1} = X_{i-1} \, mod(X_i) \text{ for } i \geqslant 1\}$$

terminating the sequence when some $X_k = 0$ is generated. For each X_i, determine A_i and B_i such that $X_0 * A_i + X_1 * B_i = X_i$. If $X_{k-1} = 1$, then $e = B_{k-1}$, which is the multiplicative inverse (modulo $L(n)$) of d. To ensure that some reduction modulo n takes place during the encryption process, it is necessary that $e > \log_2 (n)$. If this is not the case, another value of d should be selected.

The following encryption and decryption algorithms are used:

1. The plaintext is first encoded into a sequence of integers in the range 0 to $n - 1$. (See step 4 of the key selection process.)

2. Each integer, M_i, $0 \leqslant M_i \leqslant n - 1$, of the encoded plaintext is encrypted by

$$C_i = E(M_i, K_E) = E(M_i, (n, e)) = M_i^e \, (mod \, n)$$

3. Decryption is performed, using the decryption key (n, d), to obtain

$$M_i = D(C_i, K_D) = D(C_i, (n, d)) = C_i^d \, (mod \, n)$$

Rivest, et al. illustrate their scheme by the following example. Let $p = 47$, $q = 59$, $n = 2773$, and $d = 157$. Then $L(n) = (p - 1)(q - 1) = 2668$, and $e = 17$. Assuming the alphabet for a plaintext message consists of only uppercase letters, the characters are encoded by: *blank = 00, A = 01, B = 02, . . . , Z = 26*. Each successive four digits is taken to be an integer M_i. The plain text message IT IS ALL GREEK TO ME becomes

0920 0009 1900 0112 1200 0718 0505 1100 2015 0013 0500

Each block is encrypted and decrypted separately; for example, the first encrypted block is $920^{17}(mod \, 2773) = 0948$ and decrypted by $948^{157}(mod \, 2773)$. Encryption and decryption is very efficient. For example, an encryption operation requires only five multiplications since $M^{17} = (((M^2)^2)^2)^2 \cdot M$ and a decryption operation requires only 11 multiplications since $C^{157} = (C^2)^2 \cdot (C^4)^2 \cdot (C^8)^2 \cdot (((C^{16})^2)^2)^2 \cdot C$. These schemes are directly derivable from the binary forms of 17 and 157.

A cryptanalyst would attempt to factor n into p and q, compute $L(n)$, and then compute d from $L(n)$ and e. The security of the RSA algorithm rests on the difficulty in factoring n. Rivest, et al. recommend a 200-digit n, whose factorization by known techniques would require more than 10^{23} operations. An 1-μs/operation computer would require over 10^9 years to perform the factorization.

8.7.6   Authentication and Digital Signatures

A *digital signature* is a property, private to a subject, that may be used for authentication purposes (for example, signing a message). The problem is particularly acute in a public-key cryptosystem since the public key is readily available for anyone to use. Suppose A sends a message M to B. B must be sure that the A's identification has not been forged. The problem is readily solved by having A first encrypt the message using its decryption key K_{DA} and then, after attaching its identification, encrypting the result using B's public key:

$$E((A,D(M,K_{DA})),K_{EB})$$

B decrypts the message using its private key K_{DB} to produce

$$A,D(M,K_{DA})$$

Since the proclaimed sender is A, B knows that either decryption will be successful using the public key K_{EA} or the sender is an imposter.

Although the signature on a message establishes the original source of the message, it is possible that a third subject might intercept and later "replay" a message. To guard against such possibilities, a rapidly changing value such as time of day or sequence number may be included as part of the original message. In this way, obsolete or repeated messages may be detected. This technique of guarding against replays can also be used in a conventional cryptosystem.

In a public-key cryptosystem, it is possible for a subject A to later disavow having sent a message and repudiate its signature by making public its decryption key. A preventive technique for this is to use a trusted subject N for notarization. Suppose subject A wishes to send message M to subject B. A dates the message M with timestamp TS_1, signs it to form $X = A,D([M:TS_1],K_{DA})$, and sends $E(X,K_{EN})$ to N. N dates and signs the message, forming $Y = D([X:TS_2],K_{DN})$, and returns $E(Y,K_{EA})$ to A. A sends this notarized message $E(Y,K_{EB})$ to B. B is able to decrypt the message using first its own decryption key, followed by N's public key, and finally A's public key. Any latter disavowal of authenticity by A will be denied by a central authority.

8.7.7 The Use of Encryption for Stored Information

In most operating systems, certain administrators or system programmers can acquire the capability to access any file (for example, superuser capability in UNIX) or it is possible for an appropriately knowledgeable normal user to circumvent existing access controls. In these circumstances, encryption can serve as a final line of defense in protecting stored information. Since we are not dealing with communication between subjects, only the owner of the file needs to know the encryption key, and as a consequence, conventional cryptosystems are highly suitable. Most modern operating systems offer such an encryption facility as a standard service. The user is asked to supply a password that serves as (or is transformed to) the encryption/decryption key. In particular, Konheim, et al. [1980] describe the use of DES for this purpose. Block chaining is introduced to ensure that identical plaintext blocks will not transform to identical ciphertext blocks. Any length of password is possible. Oldehoeft and McDonald [1984] further extended this technique to allow for not only block chaining and a password of any length, but a user designation of the number of internal DES iterations to perform. They illustrate how to automatically generate a key schedule to match any of 16 possible designations. In terms of security, fewer iterations provide a tradeoff of less work and a weaker basic mechanism against a longer key (since the number of iterations is secret, the effect is the same as increasing the length of the key by four bits).

8.8   User Authentication

Internal security assumes a secure interface to the computer system. If perpetrator A can successfully masquerade as user B, then A can access all of B's objects. Even if B's information is encrypted, A can create new objects and delete or change existing objects. As a result, effective user authentication is critical to the overall security of the computer systems.

Part of the authentication process may be to control access to the computer interface device. This generally falls under managerial control and entails such constraints as personnel screening or limiting access to terminals. The assumption in this section is that the would-be perpetrator is able to gain access to the physical interface and the problem is one of user authentication by the operating system.[7] Numerous authentication techniques have been or are under current investigation and several others have been proposed as possible future approaches. These include such things as question-answering systems, magnetically encoded cards, voice prints, fingerprints, and retina scans. By far the most popular authentication scheme is the use of passwords, and this technique is the subject of discussion here.

In the logon process, the user supplies a unique identification (typically publicly known) followed by a secret password (typically selected by and known only to the user). Based on internally stored information (password table), the system checks to see if the (id, password) pair is valid. The security of the system then entirely depends on the secrecy of the password table and the strength of the individual passwords. In other words, the password should be both invisible and difficult to guess.

One approach to maintaining secrecy of passwords is to use access controls to protect the password table; that is, the system should allow access only to the authentication program that executes as a protected subsystem. However, the possibility that the password table might be exposed by accident or that administrator or systems programmers have access to the table make this approach unattractive. A modern approach (such as in UNIX) is to keep the passwords in encrypted form. Under this scheme, the authentication program performs encryption on the plaintext password before checking for (id, encrypted password) validity. The requirement is that, even if both the encryption function and the password table are known, it must be economically infeasible to find the original password (the assumption here is that the password is a randomly selected bit string of sufficient length). Such a requirement is met by a noninvertible function known as a *one-way cipher*.

A function E is noninvertible if given $E(X)$, X must be determined by exhaustive search. In effect, E must serve as a suitable random number generator. A number of such functions are available [see Purdy, 1974]. In fact, any conventional encryption algorithm such as the DES can be used for this purpose. Suppose E is such an encryption algorithm. From the last section, if K is the key and P is the plaintext message, then the ciphertext is given by

$$C = E(P, K)$$

---

[7]The problem of system authentication by the user, although equally important in some environments, is not covered here.

A one-way cipher, for authentication purposes, can be implemented by letting the password play a role in both K and M such that

encrypted password = *E(password, f(userid. password))*

where f is a function that produces a key of appropriate length. Inversion requires knowledge of the password since

password = *D(encrypted password, f(userid.password))*

We now proceed under the assumption that a sufficiently secure authentication method has been selected and concern ourselves with the problem of password selection.

In practice, users do not generally tend to select random character strings, and studies have indicated that trial-and-error methods to guess passwords can be quite successful [Morris and Thompson, 1979]. Many individuals have a tendency to use easy-to-remember passwords such as logon name, first name, last name, nickname, name of close relative, city or street name, license plate number, room number, and social security number. Thus, knowledge about an individual may increase the probability of guessing a password. Further, even if personally related information is not used, many individuals tend to use short passwords. A study has indicated that 80% of all passwords have a length less than or equal to five characters.

A trial-and-error method consists of selecting a trial password, performing encryption, and comparing the result with one (or all) entries in the password table. If the password table is not known, then an actual logon attempt must be made rather than looking at the password table. A systematic attack would be to write a program that will select trial passwords from an on-line dictionary (a large commercial dictionary typically contains 250,000 entries). In a recent study, a dictionary search uncovered about one-third of the passwords used in a UNIX installation [Morris and Thompson, 1979].

Assuming a random sequence of characters in a password and assuming that the encrypted password table is not known, the following formula relates the length of the password to the *expected work (EW)* required to guess a password:

$$EW = \frac{(\text{time to try a password}) * (\text{number of possible passwords})}{2}$$

Denote

R = transmission rate (characters per second) along the logon communication line

C = number of characters transmitted in a logon attempt

N = number of characters in the password

S = size of the alphabet from which characters in the password are selected

D = penalty delay (in seconds) imposed after an incorrect logon attempt

Then

$$EW = \frac{(S^N * ((C/R) + D))}{2}$$

If $S = 26$, $N = 6$, $C = 20$, $R = 10$ and $D = 0$, then EW is approximately one year. If D is changed to 2, then EW becomes approximately two years. By using computers to automate logon attempts and fast communication lines, R can be significantly increased and longer passwords become necessary. Longer passwords can be enforced by providing a password entry program that prohibits the use of short ones.

Some password entry programs, in addition to requiring a minimum length, perform a vowel–consonant pattern analysis and will reject the selection if it bears too much similarity to standard language patterns. A proposed password is analyzed using an inverse "spelling checker" algorithm. If any k-character subsequence does not result in a spelling violation, then the password is rejected. Some systems provide a password generator program that will create pronounceable, although unintelligible passwords (typically six to eight characters). In summary, the recommended practice is to use relatively long passwords, consisting of a random sequence of characters.

8.9   Summary

Security is one of the most important issues in the design of both centralized and distributed computer systems. This chapter is concerned with internal computer security and describes methods for controlling access to stored information and for controlling the flow of information from one storage object to another, as well as methods of securing information as it is transmitted over communication channels. For effective security, a total approach is necessary. A major design problem is the systematic and effective integration of these methods in a distributed system. Since numerous problems remain to be solved, computer security promises to remain an important area of future research.

Appendix: Details of the DES Algorithm

The information presented in this section follows the discussion on the DES given in NBS [1977]. All figures are taken from the same source.

Initial Permutation and Its Inverse

The initial permutation IP is shown in Table 8.3. Reading from left to right and top to bottom, the permuted result has bit 58 of the input as its first bit, bit 50 as its second bit, and so on. The inverse initial permutation IP^{-1} is shown in Table 8.4.

The Cipher Function f

A sketch of the calculation of $f(R_{i-1}, K_i)$ is shown in Figure 8.22. R_{i-1} is first expanded to a 48-bit block $E(R_{i-1})$, using the bit-selection table E shown in Table

Table 8.3 Initial Permutation *IP* [Reprinted by permission of National Bureau of Standards].

				IP			
58	50	42	34	26	18	10	2
60	52	44	36	28	20	12	4
62	54	46	38	30	22	14	6
64	56	48	40	32	24	16	8
57	49	41	33	25	17	9	1
59	51	43	35	27	19	11	3
61	53	45	37	29	21	13	5
63	55	47	39	31	23	15	7

Table 8.4 Inverse Initial Permutation IP^{-1} [Reprinted by permission of National Bureau of Standards].

				IP^{-1}			
40	8	48	16	56	24	64	32
39	7	47	15	55	23	63	31
38	6	46	14	54	22	62	30
37	5	45	13	53	21	61	29
36	4	44	12	52	20	60	28
35	3	43	11	51	19	59	27
34	2	42	10	50	18	58	26
33	1	41	9	49	17	57	25

Table 8.5 Bit-Selection Table *E* [Reprinted by permission of National Bureau of Standards].

		E BIT-SELECTION TABLE			
32	1	2	3	4	5
4	5	6	7	8	9
8	9	10	11	12	13
12	13	14	15	16	17
16	17	18	19	20	21
20	21	22	23	24	25
24	25	26	27	28	29
28	29	30	31	32	1

8.5. For example, the first three bits of $E(R_{i-1})$ are the bits in position 32, 1, and 2 of R_{i-1}, while the last three bits are selected from positions 31, 32, and 1 of R_{i-1}. Some bits of R_{i-1} are represented twice in order to provide for the expansion. K_i is a block of 48 bits extracted from the 64-bit initial key K. K was initially expanded from 56 bits to 64 bits by adding a parity bit for each set of 7 bits. The calculation of K_i will be described later.

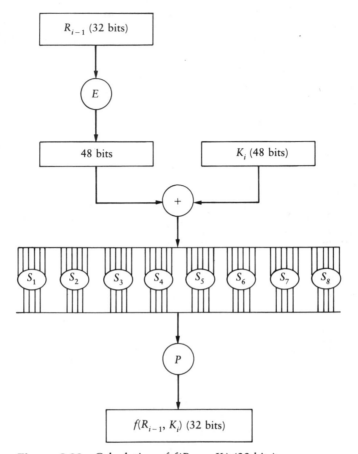

Figure 8.22 Calculation of $f(R_{i-1}, K_i)$ (32 bits)
[Reprinted by permission of National Bureau
of Standards].

After an exclusive-OR of $E(R_{i-1})$ with K_i, the result is broken into eight 6-bit blocks, denoted by $B_1, \ldots, B_8$, and the jth block is sent to the jth selection function (called an S-box) S_j. S_j returns a 4-bit block $S_j(B_j)$ using the jth mapping defined in Table 8.6. $S_j(B_j)$ is the value represented in base 2 of the entry (k, l) of S_j, where k is a number represented in base 2 by the first and last bits of B_j and l is a number represented in base 2 by the middle 4 bits of B_j. For instance, $S_1(011011)$ is 0101. (The first and last bits 01 give a row index decimal value of 1 and the middle four bits 1101 give a column index decimal value of 13. $S_1(1,13)$ is 5, which is equivalent to the 4-bit binary value 0101.)

The permutation function P yields a 32-bit output from a 32-bit input and is defined in Table 8.7.

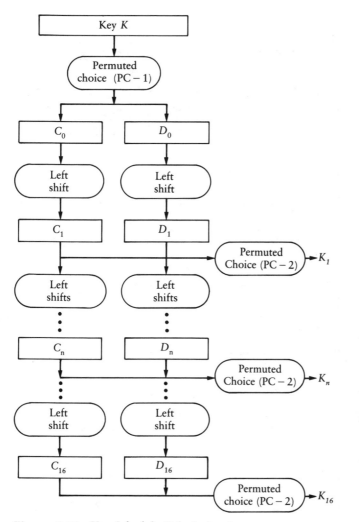

Figure 8.23 Key Schedule Calculation for Encipherment [Reprinted by permission of National Bureau of Standards].

Key Schedule Calculation

Figure 8.23 shows how each 48-bit K_i is selected for the encryption phase from the expanded 64-bit key K. Permuted choice $PC-1$ selects 56 of the 64 initial key bits K by discarding the parity bits and permuting the remaining bits as shown in Table 8.8. The two parts of the table show how to form the two 28-bit halves, C_0 and D_0. For the general step, the blocks C_i and D_i are left circularly shifted one or two positions, according to the shift schedule shown in Table 8.9. The permuted choice

Table 8.6 Selection functions (S-boxes) [Reprinted by permission of National Bureau of Standards]

	Row	Column															
		0	**1**	**2**	**3**	**4**	**5**	**6**	**7**	**8**	**9**	**10**	**11**	**12**	**13**	**14**	**15**
S_1	0	14	4	13	1	2	15	11	8	3	10	6	12	5	9	0	7
	1	0	15	7	4	14	2	13	1	10	6	12	11	9	5	3	8
	2	4	1	14	8	13	6	2	11	15	12	9	7	3	10	5	0
	3	15	12	8	2	4	9	1	7	5	11	3	14	10	0	6	13
S_2	0	15	1	8	14	6	11	3	4	9	7	2	13	12	0	5	10
	1	3	13	4	7	15	2	8	14	12	0	1	10	6	9	11	5
	2	0	14	7	11	10	4	13	1	5	8	12	6	9	3	2	15
	3	13	8	10	1	3	15	4	2	11	6	7	12	0	5	14	9
S_3	0	10	0	9	14	6	3	15	5	1	13	12	7	11	4	2	8
	1	13	7	0	9	3	4	6	10	2	8	5	14	12	11	15	1
	2	13	6	4	9	8	15	3	0	11	1	2	12	5	10	14	7
	3	1	10	13	0	6	9	8	7	4	15	14	3	11	5	2	12
S_4	0	7	13	14	3	0	6	9	10	1	2	8	5	11	12	4	15
	1	13	8	11	5	6	15	0	3	4	7	2	12	1	10	14	9
	2	10	6	9	0	12	11	7	13	15	1	3	14	5	2	8	4
	3	3	15	0	6	10	1	13	8	9	4	5	11	12	7	2	14

S_5

0	2	12	4	1	7	10	11	6	8	5	3	15	13	0	14	9
1	14	11	2	12	4	7	13	1	5	0	15	10	3	9	8	6
2	4	2	1	11	10	13	7	8	15	9	12	5	6	3	0	14
3	11	8	12	7	1	14	2	13	6	15	0	9	10	4	5	3

S_6

0	12	1	10	15	9	2	6	8	0	13	3	4	14	7	5	11
1	10	15	4	2	7	12	9	5	6	1	13	14	0	11	3	8
2	9	14	15	5	2	8	12	3	7	0	4	10	1	13	11	6
3	4	3	2	12	9	5	15	10	11	14	1	7	6	0	8	13

S_7

0	4	11	2	14	15	0	8	13	3	12	9	7	5	10	6	1
1	13	0	11	7	4	9	1	10	14	3	5	12	2	15	8	6
2	1	4	11	13	12	3	7	14	10	15	6	8	0	5	9	2
3	6	11	13	8	1	4	10	7	9	5	0	15	14	2	3	12

S_8

0	13	2	8	4	6	15	11	1	10	9	3	14	5	0	12	7
1	1	15	13	8	10	3	7	4	12	5	6	11	0	14	9	2
2	7	11	4	1	9	12	14	2	0	6	10	13	15	3	5	8
3	2	1	14	7	4	10	8	13	15	12	9	0	3	5	6	11

Table 8.7 Permutation Function P [Reprinted by permission of National Bureau of Standards].

	P		
16	7	20	21
29	12	28	17
1	15	23	26
5	18	31	10
2	8	24	14
32	27	3	9
19	13	30	6
22	11	4	25

Table 8.8 Permuted Choice $PC-1$ [Reprinted by permission of National Bureau of Standards].

57	49	41	33	25	17	9
1	58	50	42	34	26	18
10	2	59	51	43	35	27
19	11	3	60	52	44	36
63	55	47	39	31	23	15
7	62	54	46	38	30	22
14	6	61	53	45	37	29
21	13	5	28	20	12	4

$PC-2$ selects 48 of the 56 bits and permutes the remaining bits, as shown in Table 8.10, to derive each key K_i. The shift schedule is designed such that $C_{16} = C_0$ and $D_{16} = D_0$. The same algorithm is used for decryption, but the left shifts become right shifts and the shift schedule is used in reverse order.

Key Words

$*$ – property	asymmetric encryption	ciphertext
access attributes	block cipher	clearance
access control list	capability	cleartext
access matrix model	capability list	communication security
access rights	chosen plaintext attack	confinement problem
active wiretapping	chosen ciphertext attack	copy flag

Table 8.9 Shift Schedule for Encipherment [Reprinted by permission of National Bureau of Standards].

Iteration Number	Number of Left Shifts
1	1
2	1
3	2
4	2
5	2
6	2
7	2
8	2
9	1
10	2
11	2
12	2
13	2
14	2
15	2
16	1

Table 8.10 Permuted Choice $PC-2$ [Reprinted by permission of National Bureau of Standards].

14	17	11	24	1	5
3	28	15	6	21	10
23	19	12	4	26	8
16	7	27	20	13	2
41	52	31	37	47	55
30	40	51	45	33	48
44	49	39	56	34	53
46	42	50	36	29	32

covert channels
cryptanalysis
cryptography
decipherment
decryption
decryption key
digital signature
domain
encipherment
encryption
encryption key
external security
file security
greatest lower bound operator
interface security
internal security
lattice

least privilege	protection rings	storage channels
least upper bound	protection state	stream cipher
operator	public key	symmetric encryption
legitimate channel	reference monitor	timing channels
object monitor	security	trapdoor one-way
one-way cipher	security kernel	function
ownership	security level	Trojan horse
passive wiretapping	selective confinement	trusted subjects
plaintext	problem	user authentication
product cipher	simple security property	verifiability
protection	star-property	

Questions

1. List as many preventive measures as you can that should be taken to protect information and programs from browsing. Take into consideration all sorts of memory, I/O devices, and computer printouts.

2. What principles should be followed to thoroughly protect operating systems from asynchronous operating system attacks?

3. In the access matrix model, are there any access attributes whose correctness is guaranteed regardless of the trustworthiness of subjects?

4. In Figure 8.8 it is possible for S_1 and S_2 to be trapped in permanent loops in such a way that one process is trying to open a file while the other is trying to test whether the file is open or not. How can this problem be avoided?

5. Give two examples of an object monitor used to protect resources and show how they are represented in the access matrix.

6. Explain Figures 8.14 and 8.15.

7. Encipher "SECURITY" using each of the following algorithms:

   a. Permutation with the period of length 3 given by

   $$\begin{array}{cccc} i: & 1 & 2 & 3 \\ f(i): & 3 & 1 & 2 \end{array}$$

   b. Caesar cipher

   c. Caesar cipher followed by the permutation (a)

   d. DES algorithm using the ASCII bit representation for characters and a key 00 $\cdots$ 0 (Confirm that deciphering produces the original text.)

   e. RSA algorithm with $p = 47$, $q = 59$, $d = 157$, and an encodment scheme $blank = 00$, $A = 01$, $B = 02$, $\ldots$, $Z = 26$ (Confirm that deciphering produces the original text.)

8. What are the differences and similarities between conventional signatures made on paper and digital signatures? Can a digital signature replace a conventional signature?

9. Discuss the advantages and disadvantages of the following three methods for protecting passwords:

   a. An encrypted password table with its possible exposure

   b. A physically separated and secure password table under constant surveillance

   c. A double-encrypted password table with password and a password table key; the password table key is physically separated, secure, and under constant surveillance; furthermore, the password table can be frequently reencrypted

   In all cases, it is assumed that the password entry program is confined.

10. Where should an encryption or decryption program be included? Can it be a part of user programs or a part of operating systems? Justify your answer.

11. How are surveillance programs used in threat monitoring?

12. Can an audit log be used to detect security violations?

13. A computer security expert claims that one of the measures necessary to obtain computer security is the separation of programmers and operators. Why does this improve security?

Problems

1. Information security requires a total approach. How would you choose a set of measures to achieve security of a system? State the criteria.

2. State the criteria used in defining granularity of protected objects. How does the principle of least privilege affect this decision? Does performance consideration affect the decision?

3. Devise a digital signature system based on conventional encryption.

4. Suppose that all information in computer systems is encrypted—even within main memory and during all processing. How can this improve security? What are the difficulties in applying this method to real systems?

5. Examine how information flows in concurrent programs. Consider semaphores, sequencers, message-passing mechanisms, and monitors. What additional constraints, if any, does this place on the flow control mechanisms described in this chapter?

6. Extend the access control matrix model to allow for the explicit existence of "protected subsystems" that

   a. are entered by using the primitive "enter(*params*)" and exited by using the primitive "exit(*params*)," and that

   b. operate on caller-supplied objects as well as local objects (the parameters are capabilities of the form (O,α), where O is the name of the caller's object and α is the capability that may be exercised by the subsystem).

The subsystem must be constrained to access the caller's objects only in the manner intended.

7. Assume the following primitive operations as the only means for effecting changes to the protection state (as represented by an access matrix A):

enter r **into** $A[S, O]$	**delete** r **from** $A[S, O]$
create_sub S	**create_obj** O
destroy_sub S	**destroy_obj** O
read_contents from $A[S, O]$	

Higher level calls for protection services are implemented in terms of these primitive commands; for example, **create object** O as described in the text would be implemented by the sequence of primitive commands {**create_obj** O; **enter** owner **into** $A[S,O]$}. In general, the following format is used to implement a higher level command:

$c(R_1, \ldots, R_m, p_1, \ldots, p_k)$

begin
    if r_1 in $A[ps_1, po_1]$ **and/or** ... **and/or** r_m in $A[ps_m, po_m]$
    then begin op_1; ... op_n **end**
end

where parameters R_i are access rights, parameters p_i are process or object identifiers, r_k are access rights, and op_i are primitive commands.

Using this format and specifying all necessary conditions, show how to implement the following higher level system commands (described in the text), as executed by subject S_0:

a. **transfer** α **to** S, O

b. **grant** α **to** S, O

c. $w := $ **read** S, O

d. **create subject** S

e. **destroy object** O

8. Assume a capability system in which process P_1 wishes to dynamically share an object with process P_2. To accomplish this, P_1 wishes to *transfer* (or *grant*) a capability C to P_2. Outline a complete protocol for dynamically authorizing the sharing of the object. Be specific in outlining the function performed by P_1, P_2, and the security kernel. What, if any, information must be acquired external to the computer system? How would the protocol change for an access control system?

9. A logon procedure requires the typing of an account name and a password. If an incorrect name is entered, a message is printed after two seconds and the user is allowed to retry. If an incorrect password is entered, a message is printed

after two seconds whereupon the user is allowed to retry the password. After three successive incorrect passwords, the user is required to reenter the account name. The password alphabet consists of 100 characters, and the minimum password length is three characters. A would-be perpetrator requires, on the average, two seconds to type an account name and one-quarter of a second to type each password character. Which of the following strategies would result in a higher security for users who are presently using a minimum password length?

a. Changing the minimum password length to four characters

b. Adding a delay of 10 seconds after three successive incorrect passwords

10. Suppose information is classified on the basis of (i) content level—(C for confidential, S for secret), and (ii) department—($D_1, \ldots, D_4$), where the set relationship among departments is given by:

$$D_1 \subset D_3 \subset D_4$$
$$D_2 \subset D_4$$
$$D_2 \cap D_1 = \phi$$
$$D_2 \cap D_3 \neq \phi$$

In case of proper containment, $D_i \subset D_j$, two distinct departments are assumed, D_i and $D_j - D_i$. In the event that $D_i \cap D_j \neq \phi$ and there is no containment of one in the other, it is useful to define an additional department for the intersection. Singularly, the natural permissible information flows are dictated by the partial orders (i) $C \leqslant S$, and (ii) $D_i \leqslant D_j$ if and only if $D_i \subseteq D_j$.

Assume the set of security classes

$$K = \{(x,y): x \in \{C,S\} \text{ and } y = \text{some department}\}$$

Construct a lattice of secure information flow such that

a. K contains a minimum number of classes

b. $(x_1,y_1) \leqslant (x_2,y_2)$ if and only if $x_1 \leqslant x_2$ and $y_1 \subseteq y_2$

11. A plaintext message is constructed from the 27-character alphabet { blank, a, ..., z} and encrypted by (i) numerically encoding the characters: blank $\rightarrow$ 00, a $\rightarrow$ 01, ..., z $\rightarrow$ 26, and (ii) using the RSA algorithm with n = 2773 and e = 17 on each successive block of four digits. The resulting ciphertext is

```
0931 1643 0175 1964 1698 0989 2624 0522 2342 1908 0170 0381
1134 0317 0813 1472 2287 1655 1331 2049 1904 2624 1278 1444
1684 1662 2641 0508 0562 1655 0931 0505 2072 0317 2244
```

Find the decryption key d and write a program to decode the ciphertext.

12. The DES algorithm exhibits a symmetry under complementation that allows for an expected 50% reduction in cryptanalytic work under a chosen plaintext attack. This symmetry is given by

$$C = DES(P, D) \text{ implies } \overline{C} = DES(\overline{P}, \overline{K})$$

where $\overline{X}$ denotes the complement of X. (*Hints:* For any two binary values A and B, $\overline{A} \oplus \overline{B} = A \oplus B$. If $L(P)$ is a permutation of P, then $L(\overline{P}) = \overline{L(P)}$.)

a. Formally prove the symmetry property.

b. Assuming the existence of a procedure to compute DES, write an algorithm that will exhaustively search for the key, exploiting the symmetry property. Verify that the expected time to discover a key is half the expected time required for the DES algorithm.

13. Suppose $C = $ DES(M,K). Using the description of the DES algorithm, given in Section 8.6.4, along with properties of the f function, given in the appendix to this chapter, formally prove that $M = $ DES(C,K).

14. One method proposed to strengthen the DES is to perform double encryption with two keys, that is

$$\text{ciphertext} = \text{DES}((\text{DES}(\text{plaintext},K_1),K_2).$$

a. Convincingly show that double encryption does not imply twice the work for decryption.

b. Can a similar statement be made for triple encryption?

15. Professor P and student S are two independent subjects in a computer system. As an assignment, S creates a program A that reads a file α and writes another file β with the statement **exec** A(α,β).

P has created a checking program B that performs the statement **exec** A(D,O), where D and O are owned by P. After execution of A, B looks in O to see if the answers are correct. P does not trust S or any of its programs and S has private files that P should not access. Each is, therefore, suspicious of the other.

a. Using the concept of subjects and objects, illustrate without the use of protected subsystems how one would attempt to solve the problem. In particular, show the initial access control matrix and the sequence of relevant operations performed by P and S. What are the weaknesses of your solution?

b. Suppose S creates A as a protected subsystem. Repeat part (a) and show how the solution is strengthened.

16. Assume the existence of a secure and trusted key generator process KG, which knows all the secret keys for each user in a conventional cryptosystem. If user A wishes to communicate with KG (or vice versa), then A's secret key K_A is used. The protocol for a simple exchange of messages between A and KG would be

$$\text{A} \rightarrow \text{KG: (A, } S_{K_A} \text{ (message))}$$
$$\text{KG} \rightarrow \text{A: (KG, } S_{K_A} \text{ (reply)).}$$

If user A wishes to communicate with user B, then A must first request a *session key* K_{AB} from KG:

$$\text{A} \rightarrow \text{KG: (A, } S_{K_A} \text{ (request key for session with B))}$$

K_{AB} will be used for encryption and decryption of all messages transmitted between A and B during the session. Since A is initiating the session, KG will have no direct communication with B, and it is the responsibility of A to actually send K_{AB} to B. (KG is, of course, aware of the identity of both of the communicating parties A and B because of A's request for a session key.)

Describe a secure communication protocol between A and KG and between A and B. During the session, A sends n messages to B and B sends a reply for each of the messages. Be sure to illustrate how each participant uses keys for encryption and decryption.

17. A conventional cryptosystem S_K with block chaining is used to encrypt user files. More specifically, let $(X_1, \ldots, X_N)$ denote the N blocks of plaintext and let $(Y_1, \ldots, Y_N)$ denote the corresponding blocks of ciphertext, where encryption is performed by

$$Y_0 = \text{ICV (initial chaining value)}$$
$$Y_i = S_K(X_i \oplus Y_{i-1})$$

and decryption is performed by

$$Y_0 = \text{ICV (initial chaining value)}$$
$$X_i = S_K^{-1}(Y_i) \oplus Y_{i-1}.$$

Suppose a computer error is made in encrypting the jth block so that the actual encrypted text is $(Y_1, \ldots, Y'_j, \ldots, Y_N)$. Formally show how much, if any, of the original plaintext can be recovered at decryption time (assuming no computer errors during decryption).

18. Assume objects are statically bound to security classes. Show the compile-time checks on the information flow to certify the security of the following program:

```
1.    program p(f,g);
2.    type ar: array [1..10] of integer;
3.    var f: file of char class F;
4.       g: file of char class G;
5.       i: integer class I;
6.       x: integer class X;
7.       a: ar class A;
8.       m: integer class M;
9.    procedure max(b: ar class B; var n: integer class N);
10.   var j: integer class J;
11.   begin
12.      j := 2;
13.      n := b[1];
14.      while j ≤ 10 do
15.         begin
16.            if b[j] > n
17.               then n := b[j];
18.            j := j + 1;
19.         end;
20.   end;
21.   begin (* main *)
```

```
22.      reset (f);
23.      i := 1;
24.      while i ≤ 10 do
25.         begin
26.            read(f,x);
27.            if x < 100
28.               then a[i] := x
29.               else a[i] := (−2) ∗ x;
30.            i := i + 1;
31.         end;
32.      max(a,m);
33.      write(g,n);
34.   end. (∗ main ∗)
```

19. Assume objects are statically bound to security classes.

   a. For the following program, illustrate the compile-time certification checks:

```
1.    program p1(k,m,f,g,h);
2.    var k: file class K;
3.         m: file class M;
4.         f: file class F;
5.         g: file class G;
6.         h: file class H;
7.         a: integer class A;
8.         b: integer class B;
9.    begin
10.      input a from f;
11.      input b from g;
12.      while b ≠ 0 do
13.         begin
14.            if a > 0 then output b to h;
15.            if a > b then output a − b + 1 to k;
16.            output b to m;
17.            input a from f;
18.            input b from g;
19.         end
20.      end
21.   end.
```

   b. The following partial orders define two lattices:

   > L1: $C \leq S$
   > L2: $D_0 \subseteq D_1 \subseteq D_3, D_0 \subseteq D_2 \subseteq D_3$

   Assume a lattice of security classes constructed from the cross-product of L1 and L2 and determine the security of the program in part (a) if $A = (S,D_3)$, $B = (C,D_1)$, $F = (S,D_2)$, $G = (C,D_1)$, $H = K = (S,D_3)$, and $M = (C,D_3)$.

20. Consider the following program:

```
1.    program outer (f, g, h);
2.    var a,c: integer class HIGH;
3.         b,d: integer class LOW;
4.         h: file of char class HIGH;
5.         g,f: file of char class LOW;
6.    procedure inner (in(x,y: integer); out(w:integer); inout(z:integer));
7.      begin
8.        w := x;
9.        z := y + z;
10.     end;
11.   begin (* outer *)
12.     reset(f);
13.     reset(g);
14.     rewrite(h);
15.     d: = 1;
16.     read(f,a);
17.     read(g,b);
18.     inner(a,b,c,d);
19.     write(h,c,d)
20.   end.
```

a. Perform a compile-time certification analysis of program outer. Since the classes of the formal parameters of procedure inner are left unspecified, assume that the information flow must be checked for every call.

b. Same as part (a) but assume that inner is an external procedure so that the compiler has to perform an analysis based on the interface specification of line 6. The parameters carry directionality attributes to aid the analysis.

21. Assume the following program:

```
1.    program test(f,g,h,k);
2.    var i,j: integer class LOW;
3.         x: array [1..100] of integer class LOW;
4.         n: integer class LOW;
5.         s: real class HIGH;
6.         h,f: file class HIGH;
7.         k,g: file class LOW;
8.    begin
9.      i := 1;
10.     j := 1;
11.     input n from g;
12.     input s from h;
13.     while i < n do
14.       begin
15.         input x[i] from g;
16.         i := i + x[i];
```

```
17.        output i to k;
18.        s : = s * x[j];
19.        output s to f;
20.        j : = i
21.     end
22.  end.
```

a. Show the compile-time certification for this program.

b. What, if any, uncertifiable flows exist in this program? It is assumed that changes to files survive program terminations due to program exception.

22. The *cipher block-chaining method (CBC)* mode of DES is used to mask block-aligned replication of data patterns by specifically ensuring that each ciphertext block is a function of *all* previous ciphertext blocks. The CBC scheme is shown in Figure 8.24 [Voydock and Kent, 1983], where *IV* denotes some 64-bit initial value, B_i denotes the ith 64-bit block of plaintext, and C_i denotes the ith 64-bit block of ciphertext.

Unfortunately, many application programs are unable to determine (from the encrypted bit stream of information) whether or not the ciphertext has been tampered with by an intruder. As a countermeasure, an *error checkcode* may be attached to the ciphertext message. Let $P = B_1 B \ldots B_n$ denote the plaintext message and $C = C_1 \ldots C_n X$ denote the ciphertext message, where the checksum $X = B_1 \oplus \cdots \oplus B_n$. Formally show that an interchange of ciphertext blocks C_i and C_j will escape detection.

23. Assume static binding of security classes and compile-time certification.

a. Specify certification rules for Pascal-like **repeat, for,** and **case** statements.

b. Extend the certification technique to include **goto** statements.

24. Define a descriptor-based tagged architecture to enforce at run time a statically bound information flow protection model.

25. Consider a segmented system in which a process accesses its segments only through its own segment descriptor table. The descriptor contains access control bits for read, write, and execute. Is this segmentation hardware sufficient to construct an operating system under which mutually suspicious processes can cooperate?

26. Main memory of a computer is divided into blocks, each of which has two access control registers (ACR). An ACR consists of two fields:

   Key   Access attributes

The CPU has a key register (KR), and each time access to a cell in a block is requested, the contents of the KR are compared to the contents of the Key field for the ACR of the block. If they match, the Access attributes are examined. If there is no violation, the access is permitted. Is it possible, based on this hardware, to construct an operating system under which mutually suspicious processes can cooperate?

If so, define and describe the operations or commands that will most likely

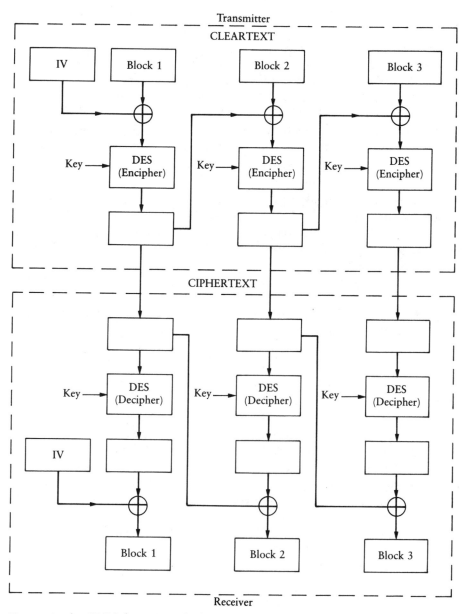

Figure 8.24   CBC Scheme [Voydock and Kent, 1983].

need to be implemented (as operating system routines) and called by a process via supervisor calls or system calls. Give an example of how the operations are used.

   If not, propose some hardware modifications that will allow for a solution.

27. The public key for an RSA algorithm is given by $(n, K_E) = (242917, 101)$. Find K_D.

References

Andler, S., and J. P. Anderson. (October 1972). "Computer security technology planning study." *ESD-TR-73-51,* 1, ESD/AFSC, Hanscom AFB, Bedford, MA.

Bell, D. E., and L. J. LaPadula. (November 1973). "Secure computer systems: mathematical foundations." *ESD-TR-278,* 1, ESD/AFSC, Hanscom AFB, Bedford, MA.

Berson, T. A., and G. L. Barksdale. (1979). "KSOS—development methodology for a secure operating system." *Proceedings of the AFIPS National Computer Conference,* pp. 365–371.

Biba, K. J. (April 1977). "Integrity considerations for secure computer systems." *ESD-TR-76-372, ESD/AFSC,* Hanscom AFB, Bedford, MA.

Broadbridge, R., and J. Mekota. (June 1976). "Secure communications processor specification." *ESD-TR-76-351, AD-A055164,* Honeywell Information Systems, McLean, VA.

Conway, R. W.; W. L. Maxwell; and H. L. Morgan. (April 1972). "On the implementation of security measures in information systems." *Communications of the ACM,* 15, 4, pp. 211–220.

Davida, G. I. (July 1979). "Hellman's scheme breaks DES in its basic form." *IEEE Spectrum,* 16, 7, p. 39.

Denning, D. E. (1975). "Secure information flow in computer systems." Ph.D. thesis, Purdue University, West Lafayette, Ind.

———. (May 1976). "A lattice model of secure information flow." *Communications of the ACM,* 19, 5, p. 236.

———. (July 1977). "Certification of programs for secure information flow." *Communications of the ACM,* 20, 7, pp. 504–512.

———. 1982. *Cryptography and Data Security,* Addison-Wesley, Reading, Mass.

Dennis, J. B., and E. C. Van Horn. (March 1966). "Programming semantics for multiprogrammed computations." *Communications of the ACM,* 9, 3, pp. 143–155.

Diffie, W., and M. E. Hellman. (November 1976). "New directions in cryptography." *IEEE Transactions on Information Theory,* IT-22, 6, pp. 644–654.

———. (June 1977). "Exhaustive cryptanalysis of the NBS data encryption standard." *Computer,* 10, 6, pp. 74–84.

———. (March 1979). "Privacy and authentication: an introduction to cryptography." *Proceedings of the IEEE,* pp. 397–427.

Fabry, R. S. (1974). "Capability-based addressing." *Communications of the ACM,* 17, 7, pp. 403–411.

Fenton, J. S. (1974). "Memory less subsystems." *The Computer Journal,* 17, pp. 143–147.

Filipski, A., and J. Hanko. (April 1986). "Making Unix Secure." *Byte,* pp. 113–128.

Gifford, D. K. (April 1982). "Cryptographic sealing for information security and authentication." *Communications of the ACM,* 25, 4, pp. 274–286.

Gold, B. D.; R. R. Linde; R. J. Peeler; M. Schaefer; J. F. Scheid; and P. D. Ward. (1979). "A security retrofit of VM/370." *Proceedings of the AFIPS National Computer Conference,* 48, pp. 335–344.

Graham, G. S., and P. J. Denning. (1972). "Protection: principles and practices." *Proceedings of the AFIPS Spring Joint Computer Conference,* 40, pp. 417–429.

Grohn, M. J. (June 1976). "A model of a protected data management system." *ESD-TR-76-289*, SD/AFSC, Hanscom AFB, Bedford, MA.

Harrison, M. A.; W. L. Ruzzo; and J. D. Ullman. (1976). "Protection in operating systems." *Communications of the ACM,* 19, 8, pp. 461–471.

Hebbard, B., et al. (January 1980). "A penetration analysis of the Michigan terminal system,"*ACM Operating Systems Reviews,* 14, 1, pp. 7–20.

Hellman, M. E. (July 1979). "DES will be totally insecure within ten years." *IEEE Spectrum,* 16, 7, pp. 32–39.

Hinke, T. H., and M. Schaefer. (November 1975). "Secure data management system." *RADC-TR-75-266,* Rome Air Development Center, AFSC, Griffiss AFB, N.Y.

Illife, J. K., and J. G. Jodeit. (October, 1962). "A dynamic storage allocation scheme." *Computer Journal,* 5, 3, pp. 200–209.

Jones, A. K., and B. H. Liskov. (December 1976). "A language extension mechanism for controlling access to shared data." *IEEE Transactions on Software Engineering,* SE-2, 4, pp. 277–285.

Kahn, K. C., et al. (December 1981). "iMAX: A multi-processor operating system for an object-based computer." *Proceedings of the 8th Symposium on Operating System Principles,* pp. 127–136.

Konheim, A. G.; M. H. Mack; et al. (1980). "The IPS cryptographic programs." *IBM Systems Journal,* 19, 2, pp. 253–283.

Lampson, B. W. (March 1971). "Protection." *Fifth Princeton Conference on Information and Systems Sciences,* pp. 437–443.

———. (October 1973). "A note on the confinement problem." *Communications of the ACM,* 16, 10, pp. 613–615.

Landwehr, C. E. (September 1981). "Formal models for computer security." *ACM Computing Surveys,* 13, 3, pp. 247–275.

Lempel, A. (December 1979). "Cryptology in transition: a survey." *ACM Computing Surveys,* 11, 4, pp. 285–304.

Linde, R. R. (1975). "Operating system penetration." *Proceedings of the AFIPS National Computer Conference,* 44, pp. 361–368.

Liskov, B. H.; A. Atkinson; and C. Schaffert. (August 1977). "Abstract mechanisms in CLU." *Communications of the ACM,* 20, 8, pp. 564–576.

McCauley, E. J., and P. J. Drongowski. (1979). "KSOS—the development of a secure operating system." *Proceedings of the AFIPS National Computer Conference,* 48, pp. 345–353.

Meyer, C. H., and S. M. Matyas. (1982). *Cryptography: A New Dimension in Computer Data Security,* John Wiley, New York.

Millen, J. K. (May 1976). "Security kernel validation in practice." *Communications of the ACM,* 19, 5, pp. 243–250.

Morris, M., and K. Thompson. (November 1979). "Password security: a case history." *Communications of the ACM,* 22, 11, pp. 594–597.

Morris, R.; N. J. A. Sloane; and A. D. Wyner. (July 1977). "Assessment of the National Bureau of Standards proposed federal data encryption standard." *Cryptologia,* 1, 3, pp. 281–291.

Myers, G., and B. R. S. Buckingham. (October 1980). "A hardware implementation of capability-based addressing." *Operating Systems Review,* 14, 4, pp. 13–25.

National Bureau of Standards. (January 1977). *Data Encryption Standard,* Federal Information Processing Standards, Publication 46.

Oldehoeft, A. E., and R. McDonald. (1984). "A software scheme for user-controlled file encryption." *Computers and Security,* 3, pp. 35–41.

Organick, E. I. (1972). *The Multics System: An Examination of Its Structure.* MIT Press, Cambridge, MA.

Peterson, J. L., and A. Silberschatz. (1985). *Operating System Concepts.* Addison-Wesley, Reading, Mass.

Popek, G. J.; and C. S. Kline. (December 1979). "Encryption and secure computer networks." *ACM Computing Surveys,* 11, 4, pp. 331–356.

Popek, G. J.; M. Kampe; et al. (1979). "UCLA secure Unix." *Proceedings of the AFIPS National Computer Conference,* 48, pp. 355–364.

Purdy, G. B. (August 1974). "A high security log-in procedure." *Communications of the ACM,* 17, 8, pp. 442–445.

Rabin, M. O. (1976). "Probabilistic algorithms." In *Algorithms and Complexity* (Ed. J. F. Traub), Academic Press, N.Y. pp. 21–40.

Redell, D. D., and R. S. Fabry. (August 1974). "Selective revocation of capabilities." *Proceedings of IRIA Conference, Protection in Operating Systems,* Rocquencourt, France.

Ritchie D. M., and K. Thompson. (July 1974). "The Unix time-sharing system." *Communications of the ACM,* 17, 7, pp. 365–376.

Rivest, R. L.; A. Shamir; and L. Adleman. (February 1978). "A method for obtaining digital signatures and public key cryptosystems." *Communications of the ACM,* 21, 2, pp. 120–126.

Saltzer, J. H., and M. N. Schroder. (1975). "The protection of information in computer systems." *Proceedings of the IEEE,* 63, pp. 1278–1308.

Schiller, W. L. (March 1975). "The design and specification of a security kernel for the PDP 11/45." *ESD-TR-75-69,* The Mitre Corporation, Bedford, Mass.

Schroeder, M. D.; D. D. Clark; and J. H. Saltzer. (November 1977). "The MULTICS kernel design project." *Proceedings of the Sixth Symposium on Operating System Principles,* pp. 43–56.

Shannon, C. E. (October 1949). "Communication theory of secrecy systems." *The Bell System Technical Journal,* 28, pp. 656–715.

Simmons, G. J. (December 1979). "Symmetric and asymmetric encryption." *ACM Computing Surveys,* 11, 4, pp. 305–330.

Snyder, L. (March 1981). "Formal models of capability-based protection systems." *IEEE Transactions on Computers,* C-30, 3, pp. 172–181.

Solovay, R., and V. Strassen. (March 1977). "A fast Monte-Carlo test for primality." *SIAM Journal on Computing,* 6, pp. 84–85.

Stonebraker, M., and E. Wong. (November 1974). "Access control in a relational database management system by query modification." *Proceedings of the 1974 ACM Annual Conference,* pp. 180–186.

Thompson, K. (August 1984). "Reflections on trusting trust." *Communications of the ACM,* 27, 8, pp. 761–776.

Voydock, V. L., and S. T. Kent. (June 1983). "Security mechanisms in high-level network protocols." *Computing Surveys,* 15, 2, pp. 135–171.

Walter, K. G.; W. F. Ogden; et al. (June 1975). "Structured specification of a security kernel." *Proceedings of the International Conference on Reliable Software,* pp. 285–293.

Wulf, W.; E. Cohen; et al. (June 1974). "HYDRA: the kernel of a multiprocess operating system." *Communications of the ACM,* 17, 6, pp. 337–345.

Wulf, W. A.; R. L. London; and M. Shaw. (December 1976). "An introduction to the construction and verification of Alphard Programs." *IEEE Transactions on Software Engineering,* SE-2, 4, pp. 253–265.

Suggested Readings

Adleman, L. M., and R. L. Rivest. (November 1978). "The use of public-key cryptography in communication system design." *IEEE Transactions on Computers,* C-16, 6, pp. 20–23.

Akl, S. G. (February 1983). "Digital signatures: a tutorial survey." *Computer,* 16, 2, pp. 15–24.

Bright. H. S. (October 1977). "Cryptanalytic attack and defense: ciphertext-only, known-plaintext, chosen-plaintext." *Cryptologia,* 1, 4, pp. 366–370.

Bright, H. S., and R. L. Enison. (1976). "Cryptography using modular software elements." *Proceedings of the AFIPS National Computer Conference,* 45, pp. 113–123.

Davies, D. W. (February 1983). "Applying the RSA digital signature to electronic mail." *Computer,* 16, 2, pp. 55–62.

DeMillo, R. A., ed. 1978. *Foundations of Secure Computation,* Academic Press, New York.

DeMillo, R., and M. Merritt. (February 1983). "Protocols for data security." *Computer,* 16, 2, pp. 39–50.

Denning, D. E. (February 1983). "Protecting public keys and signature keys." *Computer,* 16, 2, pp. 27–35.

Diffie, W., and M. Hellman. (1976). "Multiuser cryptographic techniques." *Proceedings of the AFIPS National Computer Conference,* 45, pp. 109–112.

Ehanadham, K., and A. J. Bernstein. (1979). "Conditional capabilities." *IEEE Transactions on Software Engineering,* SE-5, 5, pp. 458–464.

Ehrsam, W. F.; S. M. Matyas; et al. (1978). "A cryptographic key management scheme for implementing the data encryption standard." *IBM Systems Journal,* 17, 2, pp. 106–125.

Evans, A., Jr., and W. Kantrowitz. (August 1974). "A user authentication scheme not requiring secrecy in the computer." *Communications of the ACM,* 17, 8, pp. 437–442.

Fak V. A., ed. (May 1983). *SECURITY, IFIP/Sec'83: Proceedings of the First Security Conference.* North-Holland Publishing, Stockholm, Sweden.

Feistel, H.; W. A. Norz; and J. L. Smith. (November 1975). "Some cryptographic techniques for machine to machine data communications." *Proceedings of the IEEE,* 63, 11, pp. 1545–1554.

Gait, J. (September 1977). "A new nonlinear pseudorandom number generator." *IEEE Transactions on Software Engineering,* SE-3, 5, pp. 359–363.

Gardner, M. (August 1977). "Mathematical Games" (section), *Scientific American,* 237, 2, pp. 120–124.

Good, D. I. (October 1977). "Constructing verified and reliable communications processing Systems." *ACM Software Engineering Notes,* pp. 2–5.

Hellman, M. E. (November 1978). "An overview of public-key cryptography." *IEEE Transactions on Computers,* C-16, 6, pp. 24–32.

———. (1978). "Security in communications networks." *Proceedings of the AFIPS National Computer Conference,* 47, pp. 1131–1134.

———. (August 1979). "The mathematics of public-key cryptography." *Scientific American,* 241, 3, pp. 146–157.

Herlestam, T. (1978). "Critical remarks on some public-key cryptosystems." *BIT,* 18, pp. 493–496.

Hoffman, L. J. 1977. *Modern Methods for Computer Security and Privacy,* Prentice-Hall, Englewood Cliffs, N. J.

Horowitz, E., and S. Sahni. (April 1974). "Computing partitions with applications to the knapsack problem." *Journal of the ACM,* 21, 2, pp. 277–292.

Hsiao, D. K.; D. S. Kerr; and S. E. Madnick. 1979. *Computer Security.* Academic Press, New York.

IBM Corporation. 1977. *IBM Cryptographic Subsystem Concepts and Facilities.* IBM Systems Library Order Number GC22-9063, IBM Corporation, Data Processing Division, White Plains, N.Y.

Kak, S. C. (February 1983). "Data security in computer networks." *Computer,* 16, 2, pp. 8–10.

Kieburtz, R. B., and A. Silberschatz. (1978). "Capability managers." *IEEE Transactions on Software Engineering,* SE-4, 6, pp. 467–477.

Kline, C. S., and G. J. Popek. (1979). "Public key vs. conventional key encryption." *Proceedings of the AFIPS National Computer Conference,* 48, pp. 831–837.

Lennon, R. E. (1978). "Cryptography architecture for information security." *IBM Systems Journal,* 17, 2, pp. 138–150.

Lipton, S. M., and S. M. Matyas. (February 1978). "Making the digital signature legal—and safeguarded." *Data Communications,* 7, 2, pp. 41–52.

Matyas, S. M., and C. H. Meyer. (1978). "Generation, distribution, and installation of cryptographic keys." *IBM Systems Journal,* 17, 2, pp. 126–137.

McGraw, J. R., and G. R. Andrews. (1979). "Access control in parallel programs." *IEEE Transactions on Software Engineering,* SE-5, 1, pp. 1–9.

Merkle, R. (April 1978). "Secure communication over insecure channels." *Communications of the ACM,* 21, 4, pp. 294–299.

Merkle, R., and M. E. Hellman. (September 1978). "Hiding information and receipts in trapdoor knapsacks." *IEEE Transactions on Information Theory,* IT-24, pp. 525–530.

Merkle, R. C. (July 1981). "On the security of multiple encryption." *Communication of the ACM,* 24, 7, pp. 465–467.

Meyer, C. H. (1973). "Design considerations for cryptography." *Proceedings of the AFIPS National Computer Conference,* 42, pp. 603–606.

National Bureau of Standards. 1978a. *Design Alternatives for Computer Network Security.* Special Publication, Vol. 1, NBS, Washington, D. C.

————. 1978b. *"The Network Security Center: A System Level Approach to Computer Security."* Special Publication, Vol. 1, NBS. Washington, D. C.

Needham, R. M., and M. D. Schroeder. (December 1978). "Using encryption for authentication in large networks of computers." *Communications of the ACM,* 21, 12, pp. 993–999.

Pless, V. (November 1977). "Encryption schemes for computer confidentiality." *IEEE Transactions on Computers,* C-26, 11, pp. 1133–1136.

Pohlig, S., and M. E. Hellman. (January 1978). "An improved algorithm for computing logarithms in GF(p) and its cryptographic significance." *IEEE Transactions on Information Theory,* IT-24, 1, pp. 106–110.

Popek, G. J. (June 1974). "Protection structures." *IEEE Computer,* pp. 22–33.

————. (1974). "A principle of kernel design." *Proceedings of the AFIPS National Computer Conference,* 43, pp. 977–978.

Popek, G. J., and C. S. Kline. (1978). "Design issues for secure computer networks." In *Operating Systems, An Advanced Course, Lecture Notes in Computer Science* (Eds. R. Bayer, R. M. Graham, and G. Seegmuller), Springer-Verlag, N.Y.

Rabin, M. 1978. "Digitalized signatures." In *Foundations of Secure Computing* (Eds. R. Demillo et al.), Academic Press, N.Y.

Rabin, M. O. (September 1977). "Complexity of computations." *Communications of the ACM,* 20, 9, pp. 625–633.

Saltzer, J. (April 1978). "On digital signatures." *ACM Operating Systems Review,* 12, 2, pp. 12–14.

Sendrow, M. (1978). "Key management in EFT environments." *Proceedings of COMPCON 1978,* pp. 351–354. [Available from IEEE, New York.]

Shannon, C. E. (July and October 1948). "The mathematical theory of communication." *The Bell System Technical Journal,* 27, pp. 379–423, 623–656.

Smith, J. L. *The Design of Lucifer, a Cryptographic Device for Data Communications.* 1971. Rep. RC 3326, IBM, White Plains, N.Y.

Sugarman, R. (July 1979). "On foiling computer crime." *IEEE Spectrum,* 16, 7, pp. 31–32.

Tuchman, W. (July 1979). "Hellman presents no shortcut solutions to the DES." *IEEE Spectrum,* 16, 7, pp. 40–41.

U. S. Department of Defense. 1984. *Reference Manual for Ada.* ANSI/MIL-STD-1815A-1983, American National Standard Institute, Inc.

Walker, B. J.; R. A. Kemmerer; and G. Popek. (February 1980). "Specification and verification of the UCLA Unix security kernel." *Communications of the ACM,* 23, 2, pp. 118–131.

Westin, A. F. 1970. *Privacy and Freedom,* Atheneum Press, N.Y.

Wilkes, M. V. 1968. *Time-Sharing Computer Systems.* American Elsevier, N.Y.

Queuing Models of   9
Computer Systems

9.1 Introduction

The performance of a computer system can be evaluated in a variety of ways. Foremost, we can evaluate a a system based on our experience in its use; from this we can gather empirical evidence about system parameters and their effects on performance. In addition, we can measure current performance by benchmarking a system with a known set of jobs. These same jobs can be run on alternative systems or configurations to determine how performance is improved.

Both of these approaches require a great deal of effort. Further, they require that the system be installed and operating before any performance information can be obtained. An alternative approach, system modeling, involves the construction of abstract models that accept system and workload parameters and exhibit performance measures that have predictive value. Except for the simplest, these models have internal structures that resemble the actual systems being evaluated. A simulation model is a program that behaves like an actual computer system: Modules represent parts of the system and interact in authentic ways, and there is a simulated notion of time elapsing as the program executes. These models can be accurate reflections of systems and hence give valuable predictive information about them. Their construction can, however, be expensive, and their execution times may be significant.

In this chapter we introduce *analytic models* of computer systems based on classical queuing theory. These techniques have been generalized to model complex systems and their workloads. Analytic modeling is popular because of its low cost and flexibility. Its principal drawback is the existence of real systems with characteristics that cannot be adequately reflected in analytic models. In this case, simulation is the only useful modeling technique.

The goal in this chapter is to introduce the reader to the major approaches currently in use in analytic modeling. We will present the simplest case, the single queue, and explain its behavior in some detail. Some useful generalizations on the single queue will be included. Networks of queues are generally used to model complex systems. If jobs arrive from and depart to a universe outside the model, this *open system* is amenable to simple analysis; we present the classic results. If a constant number of jobs exist in a system, this *closed system* must be analyzed in different ways. We will introduce the two approaches to closed systems. Finally, an analysis technique based on measurements of real systems that is less dependent on queuing theory is included. Throughout we will refer the reader to generalizations that increase the power of analytic models in characterizing complex computer systems.

The reader may want to investigate some of the topics in this chapter further or may seek background information. In addition to the specific references cited, Ferrari, et al. [1983] is a good performance evaluation text. An applied probability and statistics volume of interest is Trivedi [1982]; specific applications to areas of interest to computer scientists are included.

9.2 Dynamic Behavior of a Single Queue

The single queue is the simplest analytic model we can consider. Figure 9.1 shows a queue with the parameters of interest.

> *Arrival process:* Jobs arrive intermittently from elsewhere at times that are not known in advance. This process continues indefinitely. The external population might be finite or infinite in size.

> *Queue capacity:* The queue may be able to accommodate any number of jobs, or have a finite capacity. In this chapter the former is always assumed.

> *Queue discipline:* The queue may be organized as a first-come, first-served (FCFS) structure, or may have other interesting forms to be discussed as needed.

> *Service process:* There may be just one or more than one processor serving jobs in the queue. If there are several, they are assumed to be identical. A *service time distribution* is a probability distribution function that describes the time required to serve a job. These are usually *exponential,* although others are valuable.

A concise abbreviation for the parameters of a queue is *Kendall notation* [Kendall, 1951]. We can characterize a queue with:

A/B/c/k/m/Z

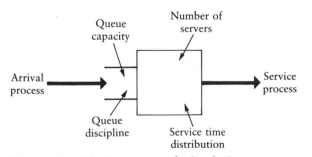

Figure 9.1 The Parameters of a Single Queue.

where

A = arrival process ("M" is the most common and means that arrivals follow a Poisson distribution)

B = service process ("M" here means an exponential service distribution)

c = the number of identical servers

k = the maximum queue size, assumed to be infinite

m = the customer population, assumed to be infinite

Z = the name of the queueing discipline assumed FCFS

Often the last three parameters of Kendall notation are assumed and not included. The queue we consider in Section 9.2.3 is the "M/M/1" system.

9.2.1 Performance Measures

Several performance measures will be valuable to us, including:

1. Mean queue length
2. Mean waiting time before service begins
3. Mean time that a job spends in the system
4. Utilization of processor capacity
5. Relation between arrival and service distributions

The last is not a performance measure, but we must know it to determine that the system is stable and that the other measures have some meaning.

9.2.2 The Poisson Distribution

The *Poisson distribution* is a commonly used description of how arrivals from an external population occur. Here we develop the information we need about this distribution.

Poisson Postulates

Specifically the distribution is based on the following *Poisson postulates*. Let $N(t)$ be the number of arrivals that occur in a time interval of length t.

1. In a "small" time interval of length Δt, the probability of exactly one arrival is proportional to the size of the interval:

   Prob[1 arrival] = $\lambda \Delta t$

2. In this interval Δt, the probability of more than one arrival is negligible:

   Prob[>1 arrival] = $o(\Delta t)$

A function (or expression) f is "o(Δt)" if it has the following property:

$$\lim_{\Delta t \to 0} \frac{f(\Delta t)}{\Delta t} = 0$$

That is, $f(\Delta t) \to 0$ "faster than" $\Delta t \to 0$.

3. The occurrence of an arrival in a small time interval is independent of other arrivals and also independent of the time since the last arrival.

These postulates may seem to describe an arcane process, but the assumptions are valid in a wide variety of circumstances.

Development of the Poisson Distribution

Define the probability of n arrivals in a time interval $(0,t)$ as follows:

$$P_n(t) = \text{Prob}[N(t) = n]$$

with properties

$$P_n(t) \geq 0, P_0(0) = 1, \quad P_n(0) = 0 \text{ for } n > 0, \quad \sum_{n=0}^{\infty} P_n(t) = 1$$

From the Poisson postulates, we see that

$$\text{Prob}[\geq 1 \text{ arrivals in interval } \Delta t] = \lambda \Delta t + o(\Delta t)$$

Consider two successive intervals $(0,t)$ and $(t, t + \Delta t)$, with Δt "small." First consider the case of no arrivals at all:

$$P_0(t + \Delta t) = P_0(t)P_0(\Delta t) = P_0(t)(1 - \lambda \Delta t - o(\Delta t))$$

No jobs arrive in the first interval of length t, and no jobs arrive in the small interval Δt that follows. Forming the difference quotient,

$$\frac{P_0(t + \Delta t) - P_0(t)}{\Delta t} = -\lambda P_0(t) - \frac{o(\Delta t)}{\Delta t}$$

Taking the limit as $\Delta t \to 0$ results in the differential equation (with initial condition)

$$P'_0(t) = -\lambda P_0(t), \quad P_0(0) = 1$$

This has the solution

$$P_0(t) = e^{-\lambda t}$$

For the case when one or more arrivals occur $(n > 0)$,

$$P_n(t + \Delta t) = P_n(t)P_0(\Delta t) + P_{n-1}(t)P_1(\Delta t) + \sum_{k=2}^{n} P_{n-k}(t)P_k(\Delta t)$$

$$= P_n(t)(1 - \lambda \Delta t - o(\Delta t)) + P_{n-1}(t)\lambda \Delta t + o(\Delta t)$$

This expresses all possible ways of attaining n arrivals at the end of the two successive intervals. Any that involve more than one arrival in the time interval Δt are o(Δt).

Forming the difference quotient and letting $\Delta t \to 0$ as before, we obtain the differential equation with initial conditions:

$$P'_n(t) = -\lambda P_n(t) + \lambda P_{n-1}(t), \quad P_0(0) = 1, P_n(0) = 0 \text{ for } n > 0$$

The solution is the Poisson probability distribution function with parameter λ. It subsumes the $n = 0$ case as well:

$$P_n(t) = \frac{e^{-\lambda t}(\lambda t)^n}{n!}$$

This has mean and variance both given by λt.

Distribution of Interarrival Times

It is useful to consider the *distribution* of *interarrival times*. Suppose an arrival has just occurred at time 0. The time of the next arrival is less than or equal to t if and only if at least one arrival occurs in the interval $(0,t)$. The probability distribution of interarrival times T is given by:

$$F(t) = \text{prob}[T \leq t] = \sum_{n=1}^{\infty} P_n(t)$$
$$= \sum_{n=0}^{\infty} P_n(t) - P_0(t)$$
$$= 1 - e^{-\lambda t}$$

an exponential distribution with mean $1/\lambda$ and variance $1/\lambda^2$. A Poisson arrival process always has an exponential interarrival time distribution.

Aggregation and Branching of Poisson Streams

Suppose that k Poisson input streams with respective parameters λ_i aggregate into a single input stream. For each input stream,

$$\text{Prob}[N_i(t) = n_i] = \frac{e^{-\lambda_i t}(\lambda t)^{n_i}}{n_i!}$$

The resulting aggregate input stream is also Poisson:

$$\text{Prob}[N(t) = n] = \frac{e^{-\lambda t}(\lambda t)^n}{n!}$$

where

$$\lambda = \sum_{i=1}^{k} \lambda_i, \quad n = \sum_{i=1}^{k} n_i$$

In addition, when a Poisson input stream with parameter λ splits into k paths, each selected with probability r_i, the resulting streams are each Poisson with parameter λ_i:

$$\text{Prob}[N_i(t) = n_i] = \frac{e^{-\lambda_i t}(\lambda_i t)^{n_i}}{n_i!}$$

where

$$\lambda_i = r_i\lambda, \quad n = \sum_{i=1}^{k} n_i$$

These results will help us to understand how systems of queues operate.

9.2.3   Analysis of a Single M/M/1 Queue

In this simplest case, the *M/M/1 queue,* jobs arrive according to a Poisson process with parameter λ and are serviced in times drawn from an exponential distribution with mean service rate μ. That is, the mean service time is $1 / \mu$. In order to obtain needed performance measures, we must express the probability that the queue is of each possible size.

Steady-State Queue-Length Probabilities

Let $S_n(t) = \text{Prob}[n$ items are in the queue at time $t]$, *including the job being served.* In this chapter we always include the jobs receiving service when we speak of queue lengths. By "steady state" we mean a time-independent pattern of behavior. That is, if the limit exists, then

$$S_n = \lim_{t \to \infty} S_n(t)$$

describes the probability of n jobs in the queue.

The queue size is determined by both the Poisson arrival process, discussed above, and the exponential service process. If Z is the random variable denoting service time, the cumulative probability distribution is

$$\text{Prob}[Z \leq t] = 1 - e^{-\mu t}$$

Let $Q_j(t) = \text{Prob}[j$ departures in interval of size $t]$. One can show that

$$Q_1(\Delta t) = \mu\Delta t + \text{o}(\Delta t)$$

if there is at least one job in the queue. For $j > 1$,

$$Q_j(\Delta t) = \text{o}(\Delta t)$$

if more than one job exists in the queue, and

$$Q_0(\Delta t) = 1 - \mu\Delta t - \text{o}(\Delta t)$$

if there is at least one job present.

The *queue-length probabilities* will be developed in two cases along the same lines as the Poisson arrival process. Consider the probability that the queue is empty after two successive intervals $(0,t)$ and $(t,t + \Delta t)$:

$$S_0(t + \Delta t) = S_0(t)P_0(\Delta t)$$
$$+ S_1(t)P_0(\Delta t)Q_1(\Delta t)$$
$$+ o(\Delta t)$$

The terms correspond to the case in which there are no jobs at time t and no arrivals occur in the interval Δt, the case in which one job exists at time t with no arrivals and one departure in the interval Δt, and all other cases involving at least one arrival and one departure. Substituting known quantities,

$$S_0(t + \Delta t) = S_0(t) - \lambda \Delta t S_0(t) + \mu \Delta t S_1(t) + o(\Delta t)$$

Forming the difference quotient and letting $\Delta t \rightarrow 0$,

$$S_0'(t) = -\lambda S_0(t) + \mu S_1(t), \quad S_0(0) = 1$$

A similar development is shown for $n \geq 1$:

$$S_n(t + \Delta t) = S_n(t)P_0(\Delta t)Q_0(\Delta t)$$
$$+ S_{n-1}(t)P_1(\Delta t)Q_0(\Delta t)$$
$$+ S_{n+1}(t)P_0(\Delta t)Q_1(\Delta t)$$
$$+ o(\Delta t)$$
$$= -(\lambda + \mu)\Delta t S_n(t) + S_{n-1}(t)\lambda \Delta t + S_{n+1}(t)\mu \Delta t + o(\Delta t)$$

Obtaining the differential equation as usual,

$$S_n'(t) = -(\lambda + \mu)S_n(t) + \lambda S_{n-1}(t) + \mu S_{n+1}(t), \quad S_n(0) = 0$$

These equations are not as simple as those in the development of the Poisson distribution. However, recall that we want steady-state probabilities, meaning that $S_0'(t) = S_n'(t) = 0$. If the steady state exists, substitute 0 for the left-hand sides of the two differential equations to obtain

$$S_1 = \left(\frac{\lambda}{\mu}\right)S_0$$

$$S_{n+1} = \left(1 + \frac{\lambda}{\mu}\right)S_n - \left(\frac{\lambda}{\mu}\right)S_{n-1}$$

Define $\rho = \lambda/\mu$. Assuming

$$\rho < 1 \quad \text{and} \quad \sum_{n=0}^{\infty} S_n = 1$$

we obtain the queue-length probability formulas

$$S_n = \rho^n(1 - \rho), \quad S_0 = 1 - \rho$$

Note that ρ is processor utilization, and that $S_0 = 1 - \rho$ intuitively. The condition $\rho < 1$ is necessary for steady state to exist.

Performance Measures

Throughout most of the rest of the chapter we state results without accompanying derivation. The performance measures of interest for a single queue include the *mean queue length:*

$$\bar{n} = \frac{\rho}{1 - \rho}$$

The *mean waiting-line length* (jobs not getting service) is:

$$\bar{w} = \frac{\rho^2}{1 - \rho}$$

The next two performance measures are called *Little's laws* [Little, 1961] and are applicable in all situations that we will consider in this chapter. The *mean time in system* is given by:

$$\bar{t} = \frac{\bar{n}}{\lambda}$$

The *mean waiting time before service* is

$$\bar{t}_w = \frac{\bar{w}}{\lambda}$$

Little's laws mean that $\bar{t}$ is proportional to $\bar{n}$ and that $\bar{t}_w$ is proportional to $\bar{w}$.

9.2.4   Generalizations on the Single Queue

There are several useful versions of the single queue beyond the simple M/M/1 system. We consider three of them here.

M/M/c Queue

The first generalization, the *M/M/c queue,* allows c identical processors to serve the first c members of the queue, if they are present. In this case steady state depends on $\lambda / (c\mu) < 1$. The probability that the queue is empty is given by:

$$S_0 = \cfrac{1}{\displaystyle\sum_{n=0}^{c-1} \frac{(\lambda/\mu)^n}{n!} + \frac{1}{c!}\frac{(\lambda/\mu)^c}{1 - \lambda/(c\mu)}}$$

The mean time prior to service is:

$$\bar{t}_w = \frac{(\lambda/\mu)^c S_0}{c!c\mu(1 - \lambda/(c\mu))^2}$$

and it is intuitively clear that

$$\bar{t} = \bar{t}_w + \frac{1}{\mu}$$

Little's laws apply, so $\bar{n}$ and $\bar{w}$ are easily computed.

M/M/∞ Queue

The second generalization, the *M/M/∞ queue,* supposes an infinite number of identical servers operating on a single queue. This is useful for modeling a subsystem with an arbitrary number of terminals with only one queue whose mean service time is the mean think time of users. In this case steady state is assured regardless of the relation between λ and μ. Clearly,

$$\bar{w} = \bar{t}_w = 0$$

Intuition and Little's law give us

$$\bar{t} = \frac{1}{\mu}, \quad \bar{n} = \lambda \bar{t}$$

M/G/1 Queue

With the third generalization, the *M/G/1 queue,* we relax the assumption that service time is described by an exponential probability distribution. The distribution is general with cumulative probability distribution

$G(x) = $ Prob[service time $\leqslant x$]

Depending on the nature of G, we have two cases. In each we need to obtain the *expected value* (mean service time) $E[x]$ and the *second moment* $E[x^2]$ for G.

DISCRETE CASE In the first case G is defined on a finite set $\{x\}$. $P[x] = $ Prob$[X = x]$. The expected value and second moment of the distribution are given by:

$$E[x] = \sum_{\{x\}} x P[x], \quad E[x^2] = \sum_{\{x\}} x^2 P[x]$$

CONTINUOUS CASE In the second case G is a differentiable function. The density function is $g(x) = G'(x)$. The expected value and second moment are:

$$E[x] = \int_0^\infty x g(x)\, dx, \quad E[x^2] = \int_0^\infty x^2 g(x)\, dx$$

PERFORMANCE MEASURES In either case, we have the following general performance measures. For steady state to exist, we must have $\lambda < 1 / E[x]$. The processor utilization is:

$$\rho = \lambda E[x]$$

The mean queue length is:

$$\overline{n} = \rho + \frac{\lambda^2 E[x^2]}{2(1 - \rho)}$$

and the mean waiting-line length is:

$$\overline{w} = \frac{\rho^2 E[x^2]}{2(E[x])^2(1 - \rho)}$$

Little's laws apply for this case as well.

By using different general distributions, we can obtain many specific M/G/1 queuing results. Here are three examples:

1. Suppose

   $$G(x) = 1 - e^{-\mu x}, \quad g(x) = \mu e^{-\mu x}$$

   That is, G is simply the *exponential distribution*. Using the continuous case, the reader is encouraged to verify that M/M/1 performance results are obtained.

2. Consider a disk with a head for each track that reads and writes single sectors of fixed size. Let

   N = the number of sectors in each track

   R = time required for a single disk rotation

   S = random variable for service time

   = rotational delay + transmission time

   = rotational delay + R / N

   The general cumulative distribution is

   $$G(x) = \begin{cases} 0 & \text{if } x < \dfrac{R}{N} \\ x/R - 1/N & \text{if } \dfrac{R}{N} \le x \le R + \dfrac{R}{N} \\ 1 & \text{if } x > R + \dfrac{R}{N} \end{cases}$$

   and the density function is

   $$g(x) = \begin{cases} 1/R & \text{if } \dfrac{R}{N} \le x \le R + \dfrac{R}{N} \\ 0 & \text{otherwise} \end{cases}$$

   We obtain the mean service time

   $$E[x] = \int_0^\infty x g(x) \, dx = \frac{R}{2} + \frac{R}{N}$$

which is not a surprising result. The second moment is

$$E[x^2] = \frac{R^2(N^2 + 3N + 3)}{3N^2}$$

These expressions can be used in the general performance formulas to obtain the characteristics of this device.

3. As a third example, consider an electronic replacement for a disk that requires exactly $1/\mu$ time to handle each request. The general distribution function is:

$$G(x) = \text{Prob}[S \leqslant x] = \begin{cases} 0 & \text{if } x < \dfrac{1}{\mu} \\[2mm] 1 & \text{if } x \geqslant \dfrac{1}{\mu} \end{cases}$$

The expected value and second moment are

$$E[x] = \frac{1}{\mu}, \quad E[x^2] = \frac{1}{\mu^2}$$

Then

$$\overline{w} = \frac{\rho^2}{2(1 - \rho)}, \quad \overline{n} = \overline{w} + \rho$$

and Little's laws can be used to obtain $\overline{t}$ and $\overline{t}_w$. This *deterministic service time* case is sometimes referred to in Kendall notation as an M/D/1 queue.

9.3   Open Networks of Queues

We now consider a network of queues among which jobs move after arriving at a queue from outside the network. Eventually all jobs exit the network after leaving some queue. This kind of network has a remarkable and simple solution method first presented by Jackson [1957].

There are K queues in the network, each operating under an FCFS ordering. Jobs arrive from outside to queue m as a Poisson process with parameter λ_m. To enforce the existence of an external arrival stream, not all the λ_m can be allowed to be zero. Each queue m has c_m identical servers, each with exponentially distributed service rate with mean μ_m. When a job leaves queue m, it arrives (immediately) at queue n with probability p_{mn}. This $K \times K$ matrix $[p_{mn}]$ describes static routing probabilities among the queues. A job leaves the system after leaving queue m with probability

$$1 - \sum_{k=1}^{K} p_{mk}$$

To ensure that a system departure is possible, not all rows of the routing matrix are allowed to sum to 1. The network must be connected; that is, there are no isolated subnetworks.

At each queue m, jobs arrive in general from up to $K + 1$ sources: possibly from outside the network and possibly after leaving each queue in the network (including queue m itself). Let e_m denote the aggregate arrival rate of jobs from all sources to queue m. Note that if the system has a steady state, e_m must also be the departure rate from queue m. The aggregate arrival rates can be found as the solutions to the K linear equations:

$$e_m = \lambda_m + \sum_{k=1}^{K} p_{km} e_k \quad m = 1, \ldots, K$$

Let $P_{k_m}^m$ be the probability of k_m jobs at queue m, and let $P_{k_1, k_2, \ldots, k_K}$ be the probability that k_1 jobs are at queue 1, k_2 are at queue 2, and so forth. Jackson's remarkable result is that each of these queues operates as an M/M/n_m queue in isolation, with arrival rate e_m. Specifically,

$$P_{k_1, k_2, \ldots, k_K} = \prod_{m=1}^{K} P_{k_m}^m$$

$$P_k^m = \begin{cases} P_0^m (e_m / \mu_m)^k / k! & \text{if } k \leq c_m \\ P_0^m (e_m / \mu_m)^k / (c_m! c_m^{k-c_m}) & \text{if } k > c_m \end{cases} \quad m = 1, \ldots, K$$

as long as $e_m < c_m \mu_m$ for each queue. This means that the performance measures for each queue in the network can be obtained by applying M/M/1 or M/M/c single-queue results from earlier in this chapter. System output from each queue m where such is possible is just the arrival (and hence departure) rate e_m multiplied by the probability that jobs exit from queue m.

Jackson's solution depends on the observation that at each queue jobs are processed by servers with exponential service distributions. The departing job stream, when viewed as an arrival stream from its other side, is a Poisson process (exponential interarrival times). The routing matrix splits this into multiple Poisson streams. The internal arrivals at each queue are hence Poisson streams, and their aggregate (along with external arrivals) results in a Poisson arrival process at each queue. We will mention more recent work later in which open networks can be analyzed without restricting servers to an exponential distribution.

As an example, consider the network in Figure 9.2. Jobs arrive from outside the network to queue 1 at rate $\lambda_1 = 4.5$; no other external arrivals occur. Jobs leave queue 1 and arrive at queues 2, 3, and 4 with respective probabilities 0.5, 0.25, and 0.125. Jobs leave the system from queue 1 with probability 0.125. All jobs exiting queues 2, 3, and 4 return to queue 1. The servers at the queues operate at rates $\mu_1 = 40$, $\mu_2 = 10$, $\mu_3 = 10$, and $\mu_4 = 5$; in addition, queue 2 has $c_2 = 2$ such servers ($c_1 = c_3 = c_4 = 1$). This exemplifies a common configuration of queues: the *central server system*. Queue 1 represents the CPU with other queues modeling devices of the system. One could include the possibility of $p_{11} \neq 0$ to model time-sliced CPU scheduling.

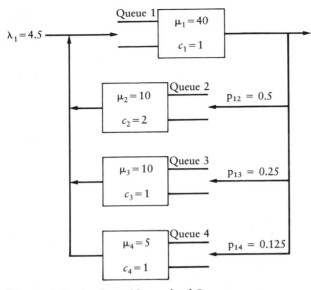

Figure 9.2 An Open Network of Queues.

We first determine the aggregate arrival rates at each queue:

$$e_1 = 4.5 + e_2 + e_3 + e_4$$

$$e_2 = 0.5e_1$$

$$e_3 = 0.25e_1$$

$$e_4 = 0.125e_1$$

These yield the solution $e_1 = 36$, $e_2 = 18$, $e_3 = 9$, and $e_4 = 4.5$. In each case the aggregate arrival rate is less than the service capacity, so we have a steady state.

The expressions for the probability that k_m jobs reside at each queue m are (after simplification):

$$P^1_{k_1} = (0.1)(0.9)^{k_1}$$

$$P^2_{k_2} = \frac{(1/19)(1.8)^{k_2}}{2^{k_2-1}}$$

$$P^3_{k_3} = (0.1)(0.9)^{k_3}$$

$$P^4_{k_4} = (0.1)(0.9)^{k_4}$$

The probabilities that each queue is empty are obtained from M/M/1 results for queues 1, 3, and 4, and from M/M/2 single-queue results for queue 2. These expressions allow us to answer questions about system-idle probability, job distribution probabilities, and so on. Performance results for single queues of the appropriate type are directly applicable.

9.4 Closed Networks—Normalization Constant Method

Consider now networks without exogenous arrivals or departures; the number of jobs in the system is constant and denoted N. Models of this kind are useful in determining the characteristics of pure interactive systems that have a fixed number of users at terminals entering commands that require processing by a CPU and a variety of devices. Jackson generalized his open system results to open and closed systems with service rates that depend on queue sizes [Jackson, 1963]. Gordon and Newell [1967] reorganized the notation for closed systems. Finally, in Buzen [1972] we find computational algorithms that make these techniques practical to apply to nontrivial networks. This section is based on the work of these authors.

We again assume a FCFS queuing discipline and exponential distributions for describing service times. In a closed system the matrix $[P_{mk}]$ describes the static routing probabilities among queues, but each row sums to 1 since system departures are impossible. Service rates may be dependent on the queue size at each queue m: $\mu_m(k)$ = mean service rate at queue m when k jobs reside there. Although this is a generalization of multiple servers, we usually use it for just that purpose. Note that $\mu_m(k) = k\mu$ when $k \le c_m$ and is $c_m\mu$ when the queue is larger. Another example of load-dependent service might arise when modeling the seek phase of a moving-head disk scheduled in a "shortest seek time first (SSTF)" fashion. The mean time required to move to the cylinder of the next request decreases as the queue size increases. Queues with load-dependent service rates will be referred to as LD queues; the simpler queues are LI queues.

Let n_m = the number of jobs at queue m. A *state* of the system (a distribution of N jobs across K queues) is a vector of K integers $\underline{n} = (n_1, n_2, \ldots, n_K)$ that satisfies the conditions

$$\sum_{m=1}^{K} n_m = N, \quad n_m \ge 0$$

The steady-state probability of each state is

$$P(\underline{n}) = \frac{1}{G(N)} \prod_{m=1}^{K} f_m(n_m)$$

where

$$f_m(n_m) = \begin{cases} v_m^{n_m} / \prod_{k=1}^{n_m} \mu_m(k) & \text{if queue } m \text{ is LD} \\[2ex] (v_m / \mu_m)^{n_m} & \text{if queue } m \text{ is LI} \end{cases} \qquad m = 1, \ldots, K$$

and $G(N)$ is a *normalization constant* that ensures that all the probabilities $P(\underline{n})$ sum to 1.

But why is $G(N)$ necessary? In a closed system the aggregate arrival rates at queues, denoted v_m here, are the solutions to the linear system

$$v_m = \sum_{k=1}^{K} p_{km} v_k, \quad m = 1, \ldots, K$$

Unlike the similar system encountered with open networks, this system has no unique solution: It is *underdetermined*. This means that if the vector $\underline{v}$ is a solution to the system, then so is $x\underline{v}$ for any value $x \neq 0$. We may obtain any useful solution by arbitrarily choosing one of the v_m values—for example, set $v_1 = 1$. This means that the values obtained from the "probability" formulas $f_m(n_m)$ are not unique, but are in fact unnormalized probability expressions, and $G(N)$ is needed to convert them to properly behaving probabilities. We write $G(N)$ with the system population as parameter, but recognize that it depends on many system parameters. We might refer to the solutions $\underline{v}$ as *visit ratios* instead of aggregate arrivals to emphasize that they are correct only in their ratios to each other.

Let $S(N,K) = \{states\}$, the set of all feasible system states. Then

$$1 = \sum_{\underline{n} \text{ in } S(N,K)} P(\underline{n}) = \frac{1}{G(N)} \sum_{\underline{n} \text{ in } S(N,K)} \left(\prod_{m=1}^{K} f_m(n_m) \right)$$

implying that

$$G(N) = \sum_{\underline{n} \text{ in } S(N,K)} \left(\prod_{m=1}^{K} f_m(n_m) \right)$$

Unfortunately, this is not a computationally feasible way to find the needed normalization constant. The number of states across which we must sum is

$$\frac{(N + K - 1)!}{(K - 1)!N!}$$

9.4.1   Efficient Computation of the Normalization Constant

In Buzen [1972] we find an answer to our problem. There, a recurrence is presented that computes the needed $G(N)$ in polynominal time, unlike the exponential time algorithm that the definitions of the preceding section suggested. Define an auxiliary function

$$g_m(n) = \sum_{\underline{n} \text{ in } S(n,m)} \left(\prod_{m=1}^{K} f_m(n_m) \right)$$

so that $g_K(N) = G(N)$ and $g_K(n) = G(n)$, $n = 0, \ldots, N$. That is, $g_K(n)$ is the normalization constant for the network with n jobs. Note that the grounding values for the recurrence are

$$g_1(n) = f_1(n) \qquad n = 0, \ldots, N$$

and

$$g_m(0) = 1 \qquad m = 1, \ldots, K$$

Buzen's algorithm gives us two versions of the recurrence, depending on whether the queue under consideration is LI or LD:

$$
g_m(n) = \begin{cases} g_{m-1}(n) + (v_m / \mu_m)g_m(n-1) & \text{if queue } m \text{ is LI} \\ \displaystyle\sum_{k=0}^{n} f_m(k)g_{m-1}(n-k) & \text{if queue } m \text{ is LD} \end{cases}
$$

for $n = 1, \ldots, N$; $m = 2, \ldots, K$

The recurrence is two-dimensional, with the left column and top row of a matrix initialized by the grounding values of the recurrence. Desired values (including the normalization constant) are found in the last column of the array:

$$
G(n) = g_K(n), \quad n = 1, \ldots, N
$$

Figures 9.3(a) and 9.3(b) show how the computation proceeds. In the LI case, each value in the array depends on values to the left and above. For LD queues, elements are computed using values in the preceding column from the top through the current row.

Of course, space conservation is possible when this is coded as a computer program. It is easy to see that two columns of space suffice by alternating between them as the target of the current computation. In fact, one can do better. In the LI case, the value being computed can overwrite the value that is (conceptually) to the left in the "preceding" column; for LD queues, values can be overwritten by performing computations from the last row upward. In this way the space requirements for Buzen's algorithm can be reduced to a single vector of $N + 1$ elements. This single-vector version was suggested in Bruell and Balbo [1980].

9.4.2   Queue-Length Probabilities for LD Queues

In order to compute the desired performance measures, it is necessary to have mechanisms for computing the probabilities of various queue lengths for LD queues. The computations described here work for LI queues as well, but are superfluous for LI queues unless these probabilities are desired in themselves. Let $p(m, n) =$ Prob[n of the N jobs are at queue m]. From the definitions, its computation requires summing across all system states that have n in position m of the state vectors. This is nearly as infeasible as computing $G(N)$ from its definition. To efficiently find these probabilities, therefore, we must define another recurrence grounded by:

$$
h_m(0) = 1, \quad m = 1, \ldots, K - 1
$$

with the general form

$$
h_m(n) = G(n) - \sum_{k=1}^{n} f_m(k)h_m(n-k), \quad n = 1, \ldots, N; \; m = 1, \ldots, K - 1
$$

Figure 9.3(a) Buzen's Algorithm—LI Case.

	1		$m-1$	m		K
0	1	...	1	1	...	1
1	$f_1(1)$					$g_K(1)$
	.					.
	.					.
	.					.
$n-1$	$f_1(n-1)$	...		$g_m(n-1)$	...	$g_K(n-1)$
				$\downarrow$		
n	$f_1(n)$		$g_{m-1}(n) \rightarrow$	$g_m(n)$		$g_K(n)$
	.					.
	.					.
	.					.
N	$f_1(N)$					$g_K(N)$

Figure 9.3(b) Buzen's Algorithm—LD Case.

	1		$m-1$	m		K
0	1	...	1	1	...	1
1	$f_1(1)$		$g_{m-1}(1)$			$g_K(1)$
	.		.			.
	.		.			.
	.		.			.
$n-1$	$f_1(n-1)$		$g_{m-1}(n-1)$			$g_K(n-1)$
n	$f_1(n)$	...	$g_{m-1}(n) \rightarrow$	$g_m(n)$	...	$g_K(n)$
	.		.			.
	.		.			.
	.		.			.
N	$f_1(N)$					$g_K(N)$

and, for the final queue K,

$$h_K(n) = g_{K-1}(n), \quad n = 1, \ldots, N$$

If the two-column implementation of Buzen's algorithm is used, the second-to-last column supplies the needed values for the preceding formula. With $h_m(n)$ defined, the queue-length probabilities can be expressed by:

$$p(m,n) = \frac{f_m(n)h_m(N-n)}{G(N)}, \quad n = 0, \ldots, N; \; m = 1, \ldots, K$$

These computations need to be performed only for LD queues m.

9.4.3   Performance Measures

The performance measures of interest here are, for each queue, throughput, processor utilization, mean queue length, and mean time that a job spends at a queue. *Throughput* is given by

$$X_m(N) = v_m \frac{G(N-1)}{G(N)}, \quad m = 1, \ldots, K$$

regardless of whether queue m is LI or LD. *Processor utilization* is

$$U_m(N) = \begin{cases} X_m(N)/\mu_m & \text{if queue } m \text{ is LI} \\ 1 - h_m(N)/G(N) & \text{if queue } m \text{ is LD} \end{cases} \quad m = 1, \ldots, K$$

Mean queue length is computed via

$$\bar{n}_m(N) = \begin{cases} \displaystyle\sum_{k=1}^{N} ((v_m/\mu_m)^k G(N-k))/G(N) & \text{if queue } m \text{ is LI} \\ \displaystyle\sum_{k=1}^{N} K p_m(k,N) & \text{if queue } m \text{ is LD} \end{cases} \quad m = 1, \ldots, K$$

Mean time in queue comes directly from Little's law:

$$\bar{w}_m(N) = \frac{\bar{n}_m(N)}{X_m(N)}, \quad m = 1, \ldots, K$$

Now consider a small example. Alter the example in Section 9.3, on open networks, by defining $p_{11} = 0.125$, eliminating the external arrival process, and considering the system with $N = 2$ jobs in the system. First, we need to find the visit ratios; we set $v_1 = 1$ and see immediately that $v_2 = 0.5$, $v_3 = 0.25$, and $v_4 = 0.125$. The visit ratios are always the branching probabilities in a central server system when the value 1 is assigned to the central server queue.

We will need the values $f_m(n_m)$, so we record them here:

$f_1(0) = 1$	$f_2(0) = 1$	$f_3(0) = 1$	$f_4(0) = 1$
$f_1(1) = 1/40$	$f_2(1) = 1/20$	$f_3(1) = 1/40$	$f_4(1) = 1/40$
$f_1(2) = 1/1600$	$f_2(2) = 1/800$	$f_3(2) = 1/1600$	$f_4(2) = 1/1600$

Next we compute the normalization constants we need using Buzen's algorithm:

	$g_1(n)$	$g_2(n)$	$g_3(n)$	$g_4(n)$
0	1	1	1	1
1	1/40	3/40	1/10	1/8
2	1/1600	5/1600	9/1600	7/800

So the system's normalization constant $G(N) = 7/800 = 0.00875$.

For queue 2 we need the probabilities p(2,n) that n jobs reside there. Using the recurrence relation for h$_2$(n), we obtain (after some arithmetic):

$$p(2,0) = \tfrac{3}{7}, \quad p(2,1) = \tfrac{3}{7}, \quad p(2,2) = \tfrac{1}{7}$$

Finally, the performance measures for each queue are as follows:

Throughput: $X_1(2) = \tfrac{100}{7}$
$X_2(2) = \tfrac{50}{7}$
$X_3(2) = \tfrac{25}{7}$
$X_4(2) = \tfrac{25}{14}$
Utilization: $U_1(2) = \tfrac{5}{14}$
$U_2(2) = \tfrac{4}{7}$
$U_3(2) = \tfrac{5}{14}$
$U_4(2) = \tfrac{5}{14}$
Mean Queue Length: $\overline{n}_1(2) = \tfrac{3}{7}$
$\overline{n}_2(2) = \tfrac{5}{7}$
$\overline{n}_3(2) = \tfrac{3}{7}$
$\overline{n}_4(2) = \tfrac{3}{7}$
Mean Time in Queue: $\overline{w}_1(2) = \tfrac{3}{100}$
$\overline{w}_2(2) = \tfrac{1}{10}$
$\overline{w}_3(2) = \tfrac{3}{25}$
$\overline{w}_4(2) = \tfrac{6}{25}$

9.4.4 Generalizations

The analysis of closed networks of queues has been generalized so that the properties of actual computer system components and of real workloads can be more exactly modeled. We will only mention the generalizations here; the reader is referred to the original sources.

Multiple job classes: It is possible to have R classes of jobs, each with different service rates. That is, $\mu_{m,r}(k)$ is the service rate at queue m for jobs of class r when k jobs are in the queue. Further, the routing probabilities among queues can be different for different job classes, and jobs may be able to change classes while moving among queues. The notation $p_{i,r;j,s}$ denotes the probability that a job in class r leaving queue i arrives at queue j as a class s job. This extension allows system workloads to be more closely modeled, as compute-bound or I/O-bound jobs, or as interactive or background processes, for example.

Open and closed classes: Some classes of jobs may arrive from and depart to a population outside the network, and other classes have jobs that only circulate. Of course, if *class switching* is allowed, jobs that have arrived from outside must remain in open classes, and jobs in closed classes must remain in those classes.

Different queuing disciplines: In addition to FCFS, other disciplines are possible. In an *infinite-servers* (IS) *queue,* the number of processors is always enough to handle any queue size, as in the M/M/∞ single queue. In a *processor-sharing* (PS) *queue,* a finite number of processors is shared by the entire queue; the larger the queue, the slower the processing rate seen by each job. This models a time-slicing dispatching algorithm with arbitrarily small quantum and no switching overhead. Finally, the *preemptive-resume last-come, first-served* (LCFS) *queue* models the case in which an arriving job preempts the running job until it completes or is itself preempted.

General service distributions are possible. However, at FCFS queues, the restriction to exponential service time distributions remains.

All these generalizations require computations that are similar to those seen here (although usually more complex), and all involve computation of the *normalization constant* of the network. When all four of the generalizations listed apply, the networks are sometimes called *BCMP networks* after the four authors of the paper in which they were handled [Baskett, et al., 1975]. Unfortunately, analysis as characterized there requires space that is exponential in *R*, the number of job classes. In Lam and Lien [1983] the reader will find a method called "tree convolution" that eliminates a great deal of computation and also saves storage when most classes visit only a small subset of the queues.

9.5   Closed Networks—Mean Value Analysis

Mean value analysis [Reiser and Lavenberg, 1980] is a technique for computing the same performance measures as in the preceding section without actually computing the normalization constant at all. This is important because numerical difficulties can arise in that computation. Mean value analysis is based on the following:

1. The distribution of queue length probabilities "seen" by a job upon arrival at a queue is the same as the distribution observed from outside the network when the population is reduced by one. This means that performance measures can be reformulated in recursive form based on measures for the system with one fewer job (as will be given below). The formulas make no reference to *G(N)*.

2. Little's law can be applied to the *entire network* to obtain an expression for throughput that does not involve the normalization constant.

For the purposes of discussion, envision a closed central server network with the CPU as queue 1. Let s_m be the mean service time for each job at queue *m*. Since the system is closed, we need a concept for system throughput. Imagine that when a job leaves the CPU it leaves the system and is immediately replaced with another job—this flow represents system throughput. The average number of jobs in the system is actually constant, and denoted *n*. The mean time a job spends in the system (before one of these transitions occurs) is the sum of times spent at each queue. The amount of time spent at queue m is the product of the mean number of visits and the mean time spent per visit. The visit ratios v_m may be interpreted as the mean number of visits to queue m. Then the ratio of mean number of jobs in the system to the time a job spends in the system is system throughput (because the system departure rate must equal the system arrival rate in steady state):

$$X_1(n) = \frac{n}{\displaystyle\sum_{m=1}^{K} v_m \overline{W}_m(n)}$$

For other queues, the throughput is

$$X_m(n) = X_1(n) v_m, \quad m = 2, \ldots, K$$

The entire algorithm for analyzing a network of queues begins by initializing some performance measures for a queue with no jobs:

$$\overline{n}_m(0) = 0, \quad m = 1, \ldots, K; \quad p(m,0) = 1 \text{ for LD queues } m$$

Then performance measures for successively larger system populations are computed. These formulas include the possibility of load-dependent service. At these queues it will be necessary to compute the probability distribution for queue lengths; we present this computation at the point where it can be computed in each iteration.

The computations performed at each iteration (as n increases) are as follows:

1. *Mean time in queue:*

$$\overline{w}_m(n) = \begin{cases} s_m & \text{if queue } m \text{ is IS} \\ S_m (1 + \overline{n}_m(n-1)) & \text{if queue } m \text{ is LI} \\ \displaystyle\sum_{k=1}^{n} k\, s_m(k)\, p(m, k-1) & \text{if queue } m \text{ is LD} \end{cases} \quad m = 1, \ldots, K$$

2. *Throughput:*

$$X_1(n) = \frac{n}{\displaystyle\sum_{m=1}^{K} v_m \overline{W}_m(n)}$$

$$X_m(n) = X_1(n)\, v_m, \quad m = 2, \ldots, K$$

3. *Queue-length probabilities for LD queues:*

$$p(m,k) = s_m(k)\, X_m(n)\, p(m, k-1), \quad k = n, \ldots, 1$$

$$p(m,0) = 1 - \sum_{k=1}^{n} p(m,k)$$

4. *Utilization:*

$$U_m(n) = \begin{cases} s_m X_m(n) & \text{if queue } m \text{ is LI} \\ 1 - p(m,0) & \text{if queue } m \text{ is LD} \end{cases} \quad m = 1, \ldots, K$$

5. *Mean queue length:*

$$\overline{n}_m(n) = X_m(n)\,\overline{w}_m(n), \quad m = 1, \ldots, K$$

The iteration may continue up to some system loan N, or until performance measures indicate system saturation.

Reworking the same closed-system example from the previous section, we begin with

$$s_1 = \tfrac{1}{40}; \quad s_2(1) = \tfrac{1}{10}, \quad s_2(n) = \tfrac{1}{20} \text{ for } n > 1; \quad s_3 = \tfrac{1}{10}; \quad s_4 = \tfrac{1}{5}$$

and

$$v_1 = 1, \quad v_2 = \tfrac{1}{2}, \quad v_3 = \tfrac{1}{4}, \quad v_4 = \tfrac{1}{8}$$

Initially,

$$\overline{n}_1(0) = 0, \quad \overline{n}_2(0) = 0, \quad \overline{n}_3(0) = 0, \quad \overline{n}_4(0) = 0; \quad p(2,0) = 1$$

ITERATION 1

$\overline{w}_1(1) = \tfrac{1}{40}$

$\overline{w}_2(1) = \tfrac{1}{10}$

$\overline{w}_3(1) = \tfrac{1}{10}$

$\overline{w}_4(1) = \tfrac{1}{5}$

$\overline{X}_1(1) = 8$

$\overline{X}_2(1) = 4$

$\overline{X}_3(1) = 2$

$\overline{X}_4(1) = 1$

$p(2,1) = \tfrac{2}{5}$

$p(2,0) = \tfrac{3}{5}$

$U_1(1) = \tfrac{1}{5}$

$U_2(1) = \tfrac{2}{5}$

$U_3(1) = \tfrac{1}{5}$

$U_4(1) = \tfrac{1}{5}$

$\overline{n}_1(1) = \tfrac{1}{5}$

$\overline{n}_2(1) = \tfrac{2}{5}$

$\overline{n}_3(1) = \tfrac{1}{5}$

$\overline{n}_4(1) = \tfrac{1}{5}$

ITERATION 2

$\overline{w}_1(2) = \tfrac{3}{100}$

$\overline{w}_2(2) = \tfrac{1}{10}$

$\overline{w}_3(2) = \tfrac{3}{25}$

$\overline{w}_4(2) = \tfrac{6}{25}$

$$\overline{X}_1(2) = \frac{100}{7}$$

$$\overline{X}_2(2) = \frac{50}{7}$$

$$\overline{X}_3(2) = \frac{25}{7}$$

$$\overline{X}_4(2) = \frac{25}{14}$$

$$p(2,2) = \frac{1}{7}$$

$$p(2,1) = \frac{3}{7}$$

$$p(2,0) = \frac{3}{7}$$

$$U_1(2) = \frac{5}{14}$$

$$U_2(2) = \frac{4}{7}$$

$$U_3(2) = \frac{5}{14}$$

$$U_4(2) = \frac{5}{14}$$

$$\overline{n}_1(2) = \frac{3}{7}$$

$$\overline{n}_2(2) = \frac{5}{7}$$

$$\overline{n}_3(2) = \frac{3}{7}$$

$$\overline{n}_4(2) = \frac{3}{7}$$

Mean value analysis has been extended to cover all the generalizations present in BCMP networks [Bruell and Balbo, 1980; Zahorjan and Wong, 1981]. The Zahorjan and Wong reference also presents an amelioration of a disadvantage of the mean value analysis approach, which is that it requires more data space than the normalization constant algorithms. In addition, the tree convolution scheme of Lam and Lein [1983] has been adapted for mean value analysis in Hoyme, et al. [1986]. Finally, mean value analysis seems to be the more intuitive method.

9.6   Operational Analysis of Queuing Networks

The preceding methods for analyzing queuing network models of queuing systems rely on a number of stochastic assumptions:

1. The system can be modeled by a *stationary stochastic process*. That is, distributions and probabilities do not change over time.

2. Jobs are *statistically independent* of each other.

3. Jobs follow a *Markov process* as they move from queue to queue. This means that the choice of next destination is independent of visit history.

4. The system is in *equilibrium*.

5. Service time distributions can be described by *exponential distributions*.

6. In the long run, averages observed in the system converge to those computed for a steady-state system: the system is *ergodic*.

System analysts have been surprised at the accuracy of the methods based on classical queuing theory in spite of systems not behaving like these assumptions. In this section we present another method called *operational analysis,* whose first developments can be found in Denning and Kahn [1975] and Buzen [1976]. The discussion here follows that in Denning and Buzen [1978]. Operational analysis differs from the preceding methods in that all results rest on these principles:

1. All quantities are measurable and all assumptions are testable.
2. Systems are *flow balanced:* The number of arrivals at a queue equals the number of departures from that queue over the observation period.
3. Queues are *homogeneous:* Job routing is independent of queue lengths, and the mean service time at a queue is independent of the lengths of other queues.

Although no explicit statistical assumptions are made, many of the requirements of operational analysis are very similar to those we needed in the classical approaches.

9.6.1   Operational Quantities

We observe a computer system with K devices, at which queuing may occur for a time period T, measuring these basic variables:

$$
\begin{aligned}
A_m &= \text{the number of arrivals to device } m \\
B_m &= \text{the amount of time that queue m had size } n_i > 0 \\
C_{mn} &= \text{the number of times a job leaves queue } m \text{ and goes to queue } n \\
A_{0n} &= \text{the number of jobs that arrive from outside the system to queue } n \\
C_{m0} &= \text{the number of jobs that leave the system from queue } m \\
W_m &= \text{job-time product accumulated at queue } m
\end{aligned}
$$

Note that the number of completions at queue m is

$$
C_m = \sum_{n=0}^{K} C_{mn}
$$

The number of system arrivals and departures is

$$
A_0 = \sum_{n=1}^{K} A_{0n}, \quad C_0 = \sum_{m=1}^{K} C_{m0}
$$

both zero for closed systems.

From these a number of performance measures are easily computed:

$$
U_m = \frac{B_m}{T} = \text{utilization at queue } m
$$

$$
S_m = \frac{B_m}{C_m} = \text{mean service time at queue } m
$$

$$X_m = \frac{C_m}{T} = \text{output rate at queue } m$$

$$q_{mn} = \frac{C_{mn}}{C_m}, \quad m = 1, \ldots, K = \text{operational routing frequencies among queues}$$

$$= \frac{A_{0n}}{A_0}, \quad m = 0$$

$$X_0 = \sum_{m=1}^{K} X_m q_{m0} = \text{system output rate}$$

$$\bar{n}_m = \frac{W_m}{T} = \text{mean queue length at } m$$

$$R_m = \frac{W_m}{C_m} = \text{mean response time at } m$$

The expression for system output rate is called the *Output Flow Law*; the *Utilization Law* is $U_m = X_m S_m$. Little's law gives us $\bar{n}_m = X_m R_m$.

9.6.2 Job Flow Analysis

The principle of job flow balance tells us that $A_m = C_m$. It is reasonable to assume that their difference is small relative to the actual quantities measured when T is long enough. The *job flow balance equations* analogous to those seen in the classical approaches are:

$$X_n = \sum_{m=0}^{K} X_m q_{mn}, \quad n = 0, \ldots, K$$

As usual, when the network is open, system output rate X_0 is known and the output rates at queues can be computed by solving this system. In a closed system, we again rely on visit ratios:

$$V_m = \frac{X_m}{X_0}$$

This gives us the *Forced Flow Law*:

$$X_m = V_m X_0$$

which says that the flow in any part of the system determines the flow everywhere in the system. Replace each X_m with $V_m X_0$ in the balance equations to get *visit ratio equations*:

$$V_0 = 1$$

$$V_n = q_{0n} + \sum_{m=1}^{K} V_m q_{mn}, \quad n = 1, \ldots, K$$

A unique solution is available if the network is connected; all performance quantities can be computed based on V_m and S_m.

9.6.3   System Response Time

Let

$$\overline{N} = \sum_{m=1}^{K} \overline{n}_m$$

As in mean value analysis, one can apply Little's law to the entire network to obtain the system response time:

$$R = \frac{\overline{N}}{X_0}$$

However, if $\overline{N}$ is not known, we must take another approach, called the *general Response Time Law:*

$$R = \sum_{m=1}^{K} V_m R_m$$

Consider an interactive system like that pictured in Figure 9.4. There are M terminals connected to the system; Z is the mean time that a user thinks after a response has occurred and another command is entered. The computational sub-system with K devices has N active jobs. N corresponds to the number of commands currently being processed, and so $N \leq M$. Here X_0 is the rate at which transactions are being processed by the computational subsystem. The mean time for each user to complete a cycle of thinking and waiting is $Z + R$. Then $(Z + R)X_0$ is the mean number of users in the cycle. Since this is M by definition, we obtain the *interactive Response Time Law:*

$$R = \frac{M}{X_0} - Z$$

9.6.4   Bottleneck Analysis

Consider a closed system with N jobs. We have

$$\frac{X_m}{X_n} = \frac{V_m}{V_n}$$

and

$$\frac{U_m}{U_n} = \frac{V_m S_m}{V_n S_m}$$

As N increases, one or more devices may achieve $U_m = 1$. These are *bottlenecks* that limit system performance; every system has at least one such device. If device b is a bottleneck,

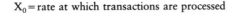

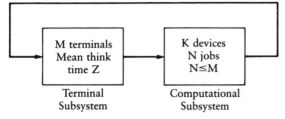

Figure 9.4 A Closed Interactive System.

$$V_b S_b = \max\{V_1 S_1, \ldots, V_M S_K\}$$

As N grows, $U_b = 1$ and $X_b = 1 / S_b$. Since $X_0 / X_b = 1 / V_b$, $X_0 = 1 / V_b S_b$ is the maximum possible system throughout. See Figure 9.5.

The smallest possible value of mean system response time (when no queuing delays occur) is just the sum of the mean times spent at all queues:

$$R_0 = \sum_{m=1}^{K} V_m S_m$$

When $N = 1$, $R_0 = R$. This means that $X_0 = 1 / R_0$ when $N = 1$. If k jobs traversing among the queues luckily manage to avoid each other and incur no queuing delays, then system throughput increases with k: k / R_0. The upper bound applies ($k / R_0 \leq 1 / V_b S_b$), so

$$k \leq N^* = R_0 / V_b S_b = \left(\sum_{m=1}^{K} V_m S_M \right) / V_b S_b \leq K$$

where N^* is the system load at which queuing is a certainty. In Figure 9.5, we see these asymptotes. Observe that the actual curve for system throughput does not achieve asymptotic rates because queuing generally occurs before the system load reaches N^*.

We now examine asymptotic response times. In a closed interactive system with M terminals,

$$R = \frac{M}{X_0} - Z$$

When $M = 1$, $R = R_0$. Since $X_0 \leq 1 / V_b S_b$,

$$R \geq MV_b S_b - Z \geq MV_m S_m, \quad m = 1, \ldots, K$$

As M grows, R approaches $MV_b S_b - Z$. See the response time curve in Figure 9.6. The mean number of terminals whose users are thinking when queuing is certain to occur is

$$M_b = \frac{Z}{V_b S_b}$$

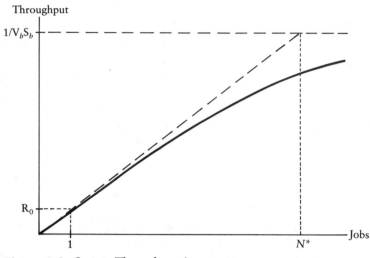

Figure 9.5   System Throughput Asymptotes.

and

$$M_b^* = \frac{R_0 + Z}{V_b S_b} = N^* + M_b$$

is the total number of terminals connected to the system at that point.

Figures 9.5 and 9.6 tell us that reducing $V_m S_m$ at a device other than the bottleneck makes no change in the limiting asymptote for heavy system loads; only a minor effect will be observed on R_0. On the other hand, too much improvement at

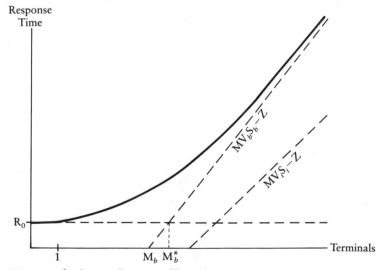

Figure 9.6   System Response Time Asymptotes.

the bottleneck device may be wasteful, because another device will then limit system performance. It is easy to tell just how much improvement is cost effective.

We now present an example [Ferrari, et al., 1983] that applies these techniques to a closed system. Consider a multiprogrammed interactive system modeled by the diagram in Figure 9.7. There is a computational subsystem with the following characteristics:

1. The CPU speed is 1 million instructions per second (1 MIPS), on the average.
2. A drum holds nonresident system programs and files, along with swapping areas. It rotates at 3000 revolutions per minute and transfer time for each word is 3 μs.
3. A movable-head disk holds user files. Its revolution speed is 1500 rpm, mean seek time is 70 ms, and transfer time is 15 μs per word.
4. Main storage is sufficiently large to hold processes executing on behalf of any number of simultaneous users at M terminals.

The interactive workload on the system has these properties:

1. The mean number of CPU instructions per command is 240,000.
2. Each command takes, on the average, 20 intervals of CPU time before completion. This means that 19 intervals of disk or drum service are needed.
3. The mean number of drum accesses is 15, and the mean number of disk accesses is 4 per command.
4. The mean number of words transferred per drum or disk access is 2000.
5. The mean user think time is 5 s.

We are to investigate current performance, and then evaluate two alternatives for improving system throughput.

First, we use operational analysis to obtain performance measures for the system and workload as described. From the data about hardware capabilities and workload demands, we can compute the mean service times at the CPU, drum, and disk:

$$S_1 = 0.012 \text{ s}, \quad S_2 = 0.016 \text{ s}, \quad S_3 = 0.12 \text{ s}$$

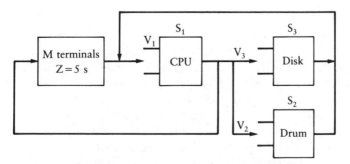

Figure 9.7 Example System for Bottleneck Analysis.

We are given the visit ratios

$$V_1 = 20, \quad V_2 = 15, \quad V_2 = 4$$

Then their respective products are 0.24, 0.24, and 0.48 s. We know immediately that the disk is the bottleneck device, and the optimal response time with one terminal on the system is

$$R_0 = 0.96 \text{ s}$$

The interactive response time depends on the number of terminals M:

$$R = V_3 S_3 M - 5 = 0.48M - 5$$

The number of terminals that will saturate the system is

$$M_3^* = \frac{5.96 \text{ s}}{0.48 \text{ s}} = 12.4 \text{ terminals}$$

At that point, system throughput is 2.08 commands per second.

Suppose we replace the disk with one that is twice as fast. This changes S_3 to 0.06 s, and $V_3 S_3$ is now 0.24 s. The system is now completely balanced (all $V_m S_m$ are equal). Now optimal response is $R_0 = 0.72$ s, and interactive response is $R = 0.24M - 5$. The number of terminals that saturate this system is $M_b^* = 23.83$. Maximum system throughput is $X_0 = 4.16$ commands per second.

Instead of replacing the disk, suppose that we relocate files between the drum and disk so that, on the average, 18 drum accesses and 1 disk access are required per command. Then the products of visit ratios and mean service times is

$$V_1 S_1 = 0.24 \text{ s}, \quad V_2 S_2 = 0.288 \text{ s}, \quad V_3 S_3 = 0.12 \text{ s}$$

Now the drum is the bottleneck device. Under these conditions, the response time for one terminal is $R_0 = 0.648$ s, and general response time is $R = 0.288M - 5$. The maximum terminal load that can be usefully handled is $M_2^* = 19.61$, at which time the system throughput is $X_0 = 3.47$ commands per second. This change results in faster response for a lightly loaded system, but not as many terminals can be handled as with the first alternative under heavy load. Of course, this change (if it is possible) is less expensive than replacing the disk.

9.6.5 Generalizations

As usual, we mention the generalizations to the method we have described; see Denning and Buzen [1978] for more details. Like other methods, operational analysis is generalized to handle load-dependent service behavior by servers at queues. One measures basic variables by *stratified sampling;* that is, time is measured or numbers are recorded at each queue for each of the queue sizes that occur there. Then familiar ideas including queue size distributions and service time distributions can be developed from this data. In order to satisfactorily compute performance measures under these conditions, the probability distributions of system states must be computed. Further, for the same reasons as before, a normalization constant must be computed using Buzen's algorithm.

Operational analysis also leads to some approximate solutions for queuing networks. Even though we know that the system being modeled differs from the model, the effect of the inaccuracies is known, and the expected difference between a real system and the model can be controlled.

9.7 Summary

In this chapter we have surveyed a number of analytic methods for modeling computer systems. The discussions of the single-queue system introduces the nomenclature and helps the reader understand the nature of arrival and service processes. The M/M/1 queue and its generalizations can be used to model computer systems grossly or components in isolation. Jackson's results about open systems gives us a tool for modeling systems more accurately and allows the single-queue results to be directly applicable. For closed systems, we have a choice of methods. The normalization constant approach was made practical by Buzen's algorithm and is most closely tied to classical approaches. Mean value analysis has intuitive value and avoids the necessity for computing the normalization constant. Operational analysis provides a variety of simply applied tools, and has the virtue of being grounded in the observation of real systems. Its generalizations reintroduce ideas about distributions and a normalization constant. The reader should be able to apply the appropriate method for a given situation.

Key Words

analytic models	Kendall notation	$o(\Delta t)$
arrival process	Little's laws	open systems
BCMP networks	M/G/1 queue	operational analysis method
bottleneck	M/M/1 queue	
Buzen's algorithm	M/M/c queue	output flow law
class switching	M/M/∞ queue	Poisson distribution
closed systems	mean queue length	Poisson postulates
exponential distribution	mean time in system	queue capacity
forced flow law	mean value analysis method	queue discipline
general response time law		queue-length probability distribution
interactive response time law	mean waiting-line length	service process
interarrival distribution	mean waiting time before service	throughput
job flow balance equations	multiple job classes	utilization
	normalization constant method	utilization law
		visit ratio equations

Questions

1. Pursue the derivation for M/M/1 queuing results from the more general M/G/1 formulas given in Section 9.2.4.

2. Investigate the performance of head-per-track disks of the current technology. Using the example of M/G/1 queues in Section 9.2.4, determine what service loads they can handle. Be sure to state any assumptions.

3. Consider the open network of four queues characterized by these values:

$$\lambda_1 = 2, \ \lambda_2 = \lambda_3 = \lambda_4 = 0$$

$$\mu_1 = 45, \ \mu_2 = 11, \ \mu_3 = 18, \ \mu_4 = 2$$

$$c_1 = 1, \ c_2 = 2, \ c_3 = 1, \ c_4 = 2$$

$$[p_{ij}] = \begin{bmatrix} 0 & 0.5 & 0.4 & 0.05 \\ 1 & 0 & 0 & 0 \\ 1 & 0 & 0 & 0 \\ 1 & 0 & 0 & 0 \end{bmatrix}$$

   a. Find the steady-state aggregate arrival rates.
   b. Find the steady-state probability that queue m is empty ($m = 1, 2, 3, 4$); find the probability that the system is idle.
   c. Obtain expressions involving k that there are k jobs at queue m ($m = 1, 2, 3, 4$).
   d. Compute the performance measures of interest for each queue.

4. Convert the open system of Question 3 to a closed system by setting λ_1 to zero, and adding a feedback path for queue 1 with the appropriate probability. Assume there are three jobs in the system.

   a. Find the visit ratios by setting $v_1 = 1$.
   b. Calculate $G(N)$. Check your work by summing the "unnormalized" probabilities of all possible system states.
   c. Compute the probability that all jobs are in the same queue.
   d. Compute the performance measures of interest for each queue.

5. Using mean value analysis, compute the performance measures of interest for the queues of Question 4.

6. Consider the closed interactive system shown on the next page, consisting of a terminal subsystem and a computational subsystem:

   a. Determine V_i, the average number of times a job visits each device.
   b. Determine the bottleneck device.
   c. Calculate the saturation point of the computational subsystem and sketch the throughput curve for the computational subsystem.

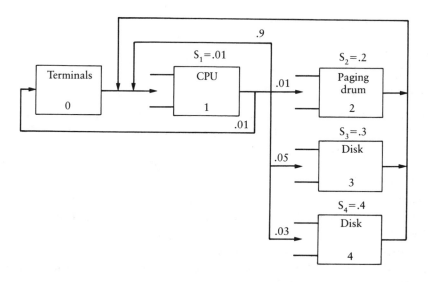

d. Determine the interactive response time formula and the asymptotes provided by the devices. Sketch the curve and the asymptotes.

e. Determine the amount of improvement at the bottleneck device that would be useful.

Problems

1. Derive the relationship

$$\bar{n} = \frac{\rho}{1 - \rho}$$

beginning with the definition of $\bar{n}$:

$$\bar{n} = \sum_{n=0}^{\infty} n S_n$$

(*Hint:* A convergent infinite series can be differentiated in its interval of convergence. This will help you to form an infinite geometric series and substitute a closed form for it.)

2. We now consider general load-dependent arrival and service rates at an M/M/1 queue. When n jobs are in the queue, the arrival rate is λ_n and the service rate is μ_n. Following the development of queue-length probabilities in this chapter, derive

$$S_n = \frac{\lambda_0 \lambda_1 \cdots \lambda_{n-1}}{\mu_1 \mu_2 \cdots \mu_n} S_0$$

For the M/M/c queue, $\lambda_n = \lambda$, and

$$\mu_n = n\mu \quad \text{for } n < c$$
$$\quad = c\mu \quad \text{for } n \geq c$$

Derive the formula given for S_0 in the M/M/c case.

3. Consider a finite queue with capacity L. Arrivals occur according to a Poisson process with parameter λ, except when the queue has L jobs; then they do not arrive at all. Service is exponential with parameter μ. Determine S_n from the generalization in Problem 2. From the definition of $\bar{n}$ derive an expression for the mean queue length.

4. Write a program for analyzing networks of queues that can be classified as BCMP networks [Baskett, et al., 1975] using the normalization constant method. Test the correctness of your model using many examples.

5. Write a program for analyzing networks of queues as generalized in Bruell and Balbo [1980] or Zahorjan and Wong [1981] according to the mean value analysis approach. Check the correctness using the same data as the preceding question.

6. Write a program for analyzing a system using the operational analysis method. Include the generalizations discussed in Denning and Buzen [1978].

7. Design a user-interface scheme so that an analyst can use one of the packages in Problems 4, 5, or 6 with ease. Further, your code should be robust: it should check for input errors and complain in an intelligent fashion.

References

Baskett, F.; K. Chandy; et al. (April 1975). "Open, closed, and mixed networks of queues with different classes of customers." *Journal of the ACM* 22, 2, pp. 248–260.

Bruell, S., and G. Balbo. 1980. *Computational Algorithms for Closed Queueing Networks*. North-Holland, N.Y.

Buzen, J. (September 1972). "Computational algorithms for closed queueing networks with exponential servers." *Communications of the ACM* 16, 9, pp. 527–531.

———. (1976). "Fundamental operational laws of computer system performance." *Acta Informatica* 7, 2, pp. 167–182.

Denning, P., and J. Buzen. (September 1978). "The operational analysis of queueing network models." *ACM Computing Surveys* 10, 3, pp. 225–261.

Denning, P., and K. Kahn. (May 1975). "Some distribution-free properties of throughput and response time." Technical Report CSD-TR-159, Computer Science Department, Purdue University, W. Lafayett, Ind.

Ferrari, D.; G. Serazzi; and A. Zeigner. 1983. *Measurement and Tuning of Computer Systems*. Prentice-Hall, Englewood Cliffs, N.J.

Gordon, W., and G. Newell. (April 1967). "Closed queueing systems with exponential servers." *Operations Research* 15, pp. 252–265.

Hoyme, K.; S. Bruell; et al. (May 1968). "A tree-structured mean value analysis algorithm." *ACM Transactions on Computer Systems* 4, 2, pp. 178–185.

Jackson, J. (1957). "Networks of waiting lines." *Operations Research 5*, pp. 518–521.

———. (1963). "Jobshop like queueing systems." *Management Science* 10, pp. 131–142.

Kendall, D. (1951). "Some problems in the theory of queues." *Journal of the Royal Statistical Society, Series B* 13, pp. 151–185.

Lam, S., and Y. Lein. (March 1983). "A tree convolution algorithm for the solution of queueing networks." *Communications of the ACM 26*, 3, pp. 203–215.

Little, J. (1961). "A proof of the queueing formula $L = \lambda W$." *Operations Research 9*, pp. 383–387.

Reiser, M., and S. Lavenberg. (April 1980). "Mean value analysis of closed multichain queueing networks." *Journal of the ACM 27*, 2, pp. 313–322.

Trivedi, K. 1982. *Probability and Statistics with Reliability, Queueing, and Computer Science Applications*. Prentice-Hall, Englewood Cliffs, N.J.

Zahorjan, J., and E. Wong. (Fall 1981). "The solution of separable queueing network models using mean value analysis." *ACM SIGMETRICS Performance Evaluation Review* 10, 3, pp. 80–85.

Suggested Readings

Adiri, I. (October 1971). "A dynamic time-sharing priority queue." *Journal of the ACM* 18, 4, pp. 603–610.

———. (October 1971). "A note on some mathematical models of time-sharing systems." *Journal of the ACM* 18, 4, pp. 611–615.

Allen, A. O. 1978. *Probability, Statistics, and Queueing Theory*. Academic Press, N.Y.

Baskett, F. (October 1971). "The dependence of computer system queues upon processing time distribution and central processor scheduling." *Proceedings of the ACM SIGOPS Third Symposium on Operating System Principles*, Stanford University, Palo Alto, CA., pp. 109–113.

Buzen, J. P. (October 1971). "Analysis of system bottlenecks using a queueing network model." *Proceedings of ACM SIGOPS Workshop System Performance Evaluation*, pp. 82–103.

———. (1975). "Cost effective analytic tools for computer performance evaluation." *Proceedings of IEEE COMPCON*, pp. 293–296.

———. (1976). "Operational analysis: the key to the new generation of performance prediction tools." *Proceedings of IEEE COMPCON*.

———. (1978). "Operational analysis: an alternative to stochastic modeling." *Proceedings of the International Conference on Performance of Computer Installations*, North-Holland, Amsterdam, pp. 175–194.

———. (1978). "BEST/1—design of a tool for computer system capacity planning." *Proceedings of AFIPS National Computer Conference* 47, pp. 447–455.

Chang, A., and S. Lavenberg. (1974). "Workrates in closed queueing networks with general independent servers." *Operations Research* 22, 4, pp. 838–874.

Giammo, T. (1976). "Validation of a computer performance model of the exponential queueing network family." *Acta Informatica* 7, 2, pp. 137–152.

Hughes, P. H., and G. Moe. (1973). "A structural approach to computer performance analysis." *Proceedings of 1973 AFIPS National Computer Conference* 42, pp. 109–119.

Kameda, H. (April 1982). "A finite-source queue with different customers." *Journal of the ACM* 29, 2, pp. 478–491.

Kleinrock, L. 1976. *Queueing Systems. Volume 1: Theory*. John Wiley, N.Y.

———. 1976. *Queueing Systems. Volume 2: Computer Applications*. John Wiley, N.Y.

Kobayashi, H. 1978. *Modeling and Analysis: An Introduction to System Performance Evaluation Methodology*. Addison-Wesley, New York.

Lavenberg, S. S. 1983. *Computer Performance Modeling Handbook*. Academic Press. N.Y.

Lazowska, E. D.; J. Zahorjan; et al. (1984). *Quantitative System Performance*. Prentice-Hall, Englewood Cliffs, N.J.

———. (August 1986). "File Access Performance of Diskless Workstations." *ACM Transactions on Computer Systems* 4, 3, pp. 238–268.

Lipsky, L., and J. D. Church. (September 1977). "Applications of a queueing network model for a computer system." *ACM Computing Surveys* 9, 3, pp. 205–221.

Muntz, R. R. (June 1975). "Analytic modeling of interactive systems." *Proceedings of IEEE* 63, 6, pp. 946–953.

Muntz, R. R., and J. W. Wong. (1974). "Asymptotic properties of closed queueing network models." *Proceedings of Eighth Princeton Conference Information Sciences and Systems*, pp. 348–352.

Rose, C. A. (September 1978). "Measurement procedure for queueing network models of computer systems." *ACM Computing Surveys* 10, 3, pp. 263–280.

Sakata, M.; S. Noguchi; and J. Oizumi. (1971). "An analysis of the $M/G/1$ queue under round-robin scheduling." *Operations Research* 19, pp. 371–385.

Sauer, C. H., and K. M. Chandy. (January 1979). "The impact of distributions and disciplines on multiple processor systems." *Communications of the ACM* 22, 1, pp. 25–34.

Index

As Benjamin/Cummings accelerates its exciting publishing venture in the Computer Science and Information Systems, we'd like to offer you the opportunity to learn about our new titles in advance. **If you'd like to be placed on our mailing list** to receive pre-publication notices about our expanding Computer Science and Information Systems list, just fill out this card **completely** and return it to us, postage paid. Thank you.

NAME_____

STREET ADDRESS_____

CITY_____STATE_____ZIP_____

BUSINESS_____

ASSOCIATION AFFILIATION:_____

_____

TELEPHONE (_____) _____

AREAS OF INTEREST:

41 ☐ Operating Systems (Please specify)_____

_____

42 ☐ Programming Languages (Please specify)_____

_____

43 ☐ Systems Languages (Please specify)_____

_____

44 ☐ Artificial Intelligence
45 ☐ Computer Graphics
46 ☐ Software Documentation
47 ☐ Systems Analysis and Design
48 ☐ Systems Architecture
49 ☐ Data Communications
50 ☐ Software Engineering
51 ☐ Microcomputer Literacy

52 ☐ Other (Please specify)_____

_____

☐ I am writing.
Area:_____

cut along dotted line

Mae

||.|...|.|||....|.|.|.|.|.|.|.|.|.|.|.|||...|.||

BUSINESS REPLY CARD

FIRST CLASS   PERMIT NO. 450   MENLO PARK, CA 94025

Postage will be paid by Addressee:

Product Manager

**The Benjamin/Cummings
Publishing Company, Inc.®**

2727 Sand Hill Road
Menlo Park, California 94025-9980